Praise for Robert Borofsky's *Yanomami*

If there is one book that redefines anthropology for the twenty-first century, this is it. It is a ground-breaking study that takes us to the ethical heart of the social sciences. Using the Yanomami controversy as a lens for examining anthropology itself, Borofsky asks anthropologists—from introductory students to advanced scholars—how we should craft the values that define our work and ourselves. This is an essential book for our times.   **Carolyn Nordstrom,** *University of Notre Dame*

Finally, a text that truly illuminates the issues of anthropological ethics and helps anthropologists to think and act effectively. In the form of an inquest on the Yanomami controversy, Borofsky lets all sides and the AAA be heard in their own words, creating a context where no reader is left to be carried away by any one set of arguments. The debates reveal deep perplexities that lie at the heart of our discipline. Marvelous for undergraduate and graduate teaching and for professionals and equally suited for reflective reading and class discussion, this book will forever change my teaching of anthropology as well as my own thinking.
Fredrik Barth, *Boston University*

What better way to learn anthropology than through one of its great controversies? Written in a lucid and concise manner, *Yanomami* is really two books in one: first, it is a riveting, issues-oriented text that is ideal for sparking interest and provoking discussion among introductory students; second, it is an invaluable analysis of critical disciplinary questions that every anthropologist and anthropologist-in-the-making need ponder.   **Alex Hinton,** *Rutgers University*

The discipline of anthropology has a great debt to Rob Borofsky, who has given us a careful, deliberate reflection that is both specific and general: specific, because the book takes up a fierce debate that has riven the community of anthropologists, scientists, and health personnel working with the indigenous people of the Amazon Basin; general, because, as Borofsky reminds us, this debate is at heart about the imbalances of power that characterize our world. *Yanomami* is not only a great teaching tool, one shaped by the input of students, but also a cautionary lesson that should be read by all scholars and journalists who work across gradients of class, culture, and language.   **Paul Farmer,** *Partners in Health*

This is a terrific book for teaching students about the possibilities and practices of anthropology. As ethical individuals and as engaged scholars, we have to confront the deep and ongoing contradictions of anthropology's relationship to the vulnerable peoples it studies. Borofsky shows the potential for revitalizing anthropology in the twenty-first century and challenges students and teachers to work for change right now.   **Philippe Bourgois,** *University of California, San Francisco*

Yanomami

CALIFORNIA SERIES IN PUBLIC ANTHROPOLOGY

The California Series in Public Anthropology emphasizes the anthropologist's role as an engaged intellectual. It continues anthropology's commitment to being an ethnographic witness, to describing, in human terms, how life is lived beyond the borders of many readers' experiences. But it also adds a commitment, through ethnography, to reframing the terms of public debate—transforming received, accepted understandings of social issues with new insights, new framings.

Series Editor: Robert Borofsky (Hawaii Pacific University)

Contributing Editors: Philippe Bourgois (UC San Francisco), Paul Farmer (Partners in Health), Rayna Rapp (New York University), and Nancy Scheper-Hughes (UC Berkeley)

University of California Press Editor: Naomi Schneider

Yanomami

THE FIERCE CONTROVERSY AND WHAT WE CAN LEARN FROM IT

Robert Borofsky

Hawaii Pacific University

WITH

Bruce Albert, Raymond Hames, Kim Hill,
Lêda Leitão Martins, John Peters,
and Terence Turner

UNIVERSITY OF CALIFORNIA PRESS

BERKELEY   LOS ANGELES   LONDON

University of California Press
Berkeley and Los Angeles, California

University of California Press, Ltd.
London, England

© 2005 by the Regents of the University of California

Library of Congress Cataloging-in-Publication Data

Borofsky, Robert, 1944–
Yanomami : the fierce controversy and what we can learn from
    it / Robert Borofsky ; with Bruce Albert . . . [et al.].
        p.   cm. — (California series in public anthropology ; 12)
    Includes bibliographic references and index.
    ISBN 0-520-24403-6 (cloth : alk. paper)
—ISBN 0-520-24404-4 (pbk. : alk. paper)
    1. Yanomamo Indians — Study and teaching (Higher)
2. Yanomamo Indians — Public opinion.   3. Yanomamo
Indians — Social conditions.   4. Anthropological ethics —
Study and teaching (Higher)   5. Anthropology — Authorship.
6. Anthropology — Field work.   7. Anthropologists —
Professional relationships.   I. Albert, Bruce.   II. Title.
III. Series.

F2520.1.Y3B67 2005   2004049781

Manufactured in the United States of America
13   12   11   10   09   08   07   06   05
10   9   8   7   6   5   4   3

DEDICATION

This book is dedicated to the 119 students who, at a critical time in the Yanomami controversy, heeded the call for involvement and through their thoughtful comments ultimately made a difference in shaping the final El Dorado Task Force Report. (The students' names and college affiliations, where available, are listed below.) We, as a discipline, are in these students' debt. Thank you.

Lisa Andreae, Lauren Austin (Middlebury), Robyn Berg (Montana), Keith Bishop (Denison), Josh Brown (Idaho), Kelley Buhles (San Diego State), Jarred Butto (Bucknell), Wes Cadman (Gettysburg), Jennie Campana (Bucknell), Sze-Ming Cheng (CSU Hayward), Parke Cogswell (Middlebury), Stephanie Corkran (San Diego State), Mark Corrao, Mike Cretella (Middlebury), Kenneth Crockett, Alissa Cropper (CSU Hayward), Matthew Dalstrom, Elizabeth Danforth (Iowa State), Ian Davis, Jaclyn Diamond (Gettysburg), Alex Alan Dumlao (Hawaii Pacific), Amelia Dunlap (Denison), Jason Durbin (San Diego State), Gabriel Epperson (Middlebury), Gabriel Espiritu (Bucknell), Duke Feldmeier, Harverst Ficker (Middlebury), Tommy Fisher (Gettysburg), LaTasha Fisher (CSU Hayward), Patrick Foiles (Idaho), Crystal Foster (Montana), Sami Freitas (Hawaii Pacific), Oren Frey (Middlebury), James Fryrear (San Diego State), Domonic Gaccetta (Hawaii Pacific), Lillie Green (Gettysburg), Jeanette Guiral (Hawaii Pacific), Janelle Guzman (CSU Hayward), Vuong Ha, Fritz Hanselman (Brigham Young), Joanna Harbaugh (Iowa State), Kerry Harris, Cora Hinton, Liz Holland (Gettysburg), Alexis Hollinger (Middlebury), Elizabeth Hopkins (CSU Hayward), Katrina Huber, Deanna Hughes (Case Western Reserve), Lorna Illingworth (Middlebury), Issues in Anthropology Class (York), Erin Jensen (Middlebury), Laura Jones (Gettysburg), Rachel Judge (CSU Hayward), Sarah Keiser, Chad Klein, Justin Knox (Middlebury), Sarah Kretzmer (Gettysburg), Joseph Lewis (Middlebury), Maribeth Long (Middlebury), Laurie Lynch (Case Western Reserve), Diana Mabalot (Hawaii Pacific), Tiana Massey (CSU Hayward), Craig McCallum (Idaho), Hillary McDonald (Middlebury), Kelly McDonald (Montana), Kristine Meier (Gettysburg), Bryan Miller, Sarah Mitchell, Richard Montgomery (Idaho), Bridget Mooney

(CSU Hayward), Christopher Moreno (San Diego State), Mathew Morrow (Bucknell), Mushoba Njalamimba, Amy Norman (Missouri, St. Louis), Mary Katherine O'Brien (Middlebury), Emily Okikawa (Hawaii Pacific), Michael Okikawa (Hawaii Pacific), Keisha Oxendine, Karisa Peer (Middlebury), Sara Pryor (Bucknell), Beata Przybylo (San Diego State), Keani Rawlins (Hawaii Pacific), Casey Reid (Southwest Missouri State), Cynthia Reyes (CSU Hayward), Adam Richardson, Brandy Richardson (Gettysburg), Shanti Rieber (San Diego State), Jennifer Rustad (San Diego State), Todd Ruttenberg (San Diego State), Peter Santos (Bucknell), Elizabeth Schmerr (Iowa State), Nirvi Shah (San Diego State), Kristy Shroeder, Ellen Simon, Estrella Slater (Hawaii Pacific), Jocelyn Small (Gettysburg), Eric Stadler, Molly Stevenson (San Diego State), Whitney Strohmeyer (Middlebury), Lawrence Stutler (Iowa State), Jennifer Tavegia (Montana), Max Theis (Middlebury), Christina Thompson (CSU Hayward), Corinna Tiumalu (CSU Hayward), Holly Traynor, Eleanor Tutwiler (Middlebury), Tomoka Uchida (Middlebury), Andrew Ulrich, Adrian Valadez (CSU Hayward), Amy Vance (Gettysburg), Gregory Waters (Gettysburg), Amy Wegner (Middlebury), James Werbe, Tara Weyen, Kristin Wilkinson (CSU Hayward), Matthew Wilson (Middlebury), Jeremy Wilson-Simerman (Hawaii Pacific), Casey Wixson, and Siobhan Young (Gettysburg)

CONTENTS

ACKNOWLEDGMENTS

One might wonder why an anthropologist who has spent the past thirty years residing in Hawaii and three and one-half years conducting fieldwork in the Cook Islands would be writing about the Yanomami controversy. Literally and figuratively, I am far from "home" in working on this book and, as a result, have a number of people to thank for guiding me through the nuances and complications surrounding the controversy. I particularly appreciate the help of two people: Ray Hames and Les Sponsel. Both provided what I view as honest, thoughtful commentary that reached beyond the "boxed" positions of the two opposing camps. The book is much richer for their assistance. I am also deeply grateful to the six participants in part 2's roundtable discussion: Bruce Albert, Ray Hames, Kim Hill, Lêda Martins, John Peters, and Terry Turner.

I want to thank Naomi Schneider at the University of California Press, my compadre in the Public Anthropology Series. William Rodarmor, Carolyn Nordstrom, David Napier, Jonathan Hill, Alex Hinton, Amelia Borofsky, Jeanne Rellahan, and Sandra Heinz provided thoughtful comments that improved the book enormously. The book is better—far better—for their suggestions. I want to offer a particularly large "mahalo" to William and Carolyn. In addition I want to express appreciation to Janet Chernela for allowing me to use her taped interviews in chapter 5. And I want note my appreciation to and respect for a person I have never met, Douglas Hume. His Web site (http://members.aol.com/archaeodog/darkness_in_el_dorado/), especially with its upgrade and new search engine, constitutes the central source for documents regarding the controversy. Without his efforts to preserve the controversy's key documents, many would have been irretrievably lost.

Regarding the Photographic Interlude, I appreciate the generosity of Claudia Andujar, Victor Englebert, Ken Good, and John Peters in letting me use their photographs. The photographs add a visual, aesthetic sense to the book's many words. Claudia Andujar's phottgraph graces the cover. In terms of the book's production, it has been a delight working with Dave Peattie of BookMatters. I would also thank Marilyn Schwartz, Nicole Hayward, and Sandy Drooker of UC Press and Mike Mollett, the copyeditor.

At Hawaii Pacific I would single out Chatt Wright for providing a stimulating, exciting place to work, learn, and write. John Fleckles, once more, has done much to facilitate this book with his ideas, encouragement, and support. Let me also thank others at Hawaii Pacific who have made a difference in the development of this book: Lynette Cruz, Chris Fung, Jeanne Rellahan, Gordon Furuto, Debbie Bohol, Jamie Hatch, Tom Thomas, Joe Esser, Leslie Rodrigues, Janice Uyeda, Darlene Young, Lorrin King, Debbie Laffoon, Holly Yamachika, Mishalla Spearing, Jackson Bauer, Charlie Issacs, Ian Masterson, Nithin Jawali, Surasak Chaudonpassan, and Colin Umebayashi.

Within the larger Hawaii setting, I would like to thank Stan Bowers, Andy Stuber, Mac Shannon, Frank Moniz, Jim Thompson, Brad Bliss, Jeff Grad, Gary Yamashiro, Russell Yoshida, Eric Freitas, Howard Matushima, Janice Shiroma, Tim Cavanaugh, and Brandon Hee. I also want to express my appreciation to my immediate family for being who they are: Amelia, Robyn, and especially Nancy. I would also add my appreciation to the larger Borofsky family: Ruth, Jerry, Jeanne, Nate, Anna, Richie, Antra, Nadine, Larrisa, and Nancy B.

A NOTE TO TEACHERS

What better way to learn about anthropology and how anthropologists practice it than to study one of the discipline's great controversies? It is all here: crucial intellectual and professional questions that confront the discipline, the practical politics of being an anthropologist, and where we go from here as a discipline.

The way anthropology and anthropologists are sometimes presented in textbooks brings to mind the Wizard of Oz. We perceive anthropology (like the wizard) as it wishes to present itself—in ways that inspire awe and respect. *Yanomami: The Fierce Controversy and What We Can Learn from It* lets readers step behind the screen the discipline presents to the world. We gain a sense of what anthropologists, in fact, are like: how they conduct fieldwork, grapple with difficult issues, and live professional lives. One sees the discipline's very human side, up close and clear.

The book is directed at two audiences. Introductory students can read part 1 as a way of "getting their feet wet" with the discipline—learning anthropology by being anthropologists in how they evaluate issues. It is slightly more than a hundred pages and can be read in one week. It provides an overview of the controversy as well as a discussion of the central issues at stake in it. Rather than being told what to think, students have an opportunity to think for themselves about a set of critical disciplinary issues.

Advanced students concerned with contemporary issues—from ethics, research methods, and the uses (and misuses) of ethnography to theory and the discipline's present (and future) dynamics—will also find much food for thought. The book is not only about how anthropologists engage with "others" but about how anthropologists act as a discipline, how they engage with one another—the anthropology of anthropology. Part 2 includes an extended discussion by six experts of the issues at stake in the Yanomami controversy. It constitutes the fullest, most open discussion of the controversy to date. Students are encouraged to wend their way through the various arguments and counterarguments and come to their own conclusions. The last chapter draws students into assessing the discipline and deciding where we might go from here.

Yanomami: The Fierce Controversy and What We Can Learn from It is not meant simply to be read. It is meant to foster discussion and, through that discussion, insight into how anthropology reproduces itself as a discipline. For example, students might explore the questions raised in chapter 6 in small groups and then bring their answers back to the larger class for discussion. They might take a particular issue—such as informed consent or just compensation—and develop a class position on it. They might also reenact the part 2 discussion with its arguments and counterarguments.

Embedded in the text are a number of student aids. A personal note to undergraduates suggests how they might effectively read the book, especially the part 2 discussion. A list of movies relating to the Yanomami is provided for teachers to consider showing in class or to have students watch on their own as a supplement to the book. In addition, each section of chapters 8, 9, and 10 presents key points and questions to help clarify that section's arguments. And questions are set out in chapter 6 for students to ponder. Of critical importance is the Public Anthropology Web site (www.publicanthropology.org), where students can gain additional information and, critically, can help foster change.

In using this book, then, students gain insight into

- the practice of modern-day anthropology, not only as an abstraction but as a reality embodied in a controversy with real people;
- the disciplinary dynamics that shape (and reshape) the anthropological enterprise through time;
- ethical and professional dilemmas that lie at the heart of the discipline today; and
- the excitement of anthropology as a field—as something not only to read but also to participate in actively.

A PERSONAL NOTE
TO UNDERGRADUATES

Yanomami: The Fierce Controversy and What We Can Learn from It deals with one of the most explosive controversies in the history of anthropology. It has all sorts of ideas that will intrigue you, that will challenge you, that will make you think—just what you want from your college education. But it is important to see the forest through the trees in this controversy, to grasp the bigger picture rather than getting lost in a mass of details. What follows are some reading techniques that you can apply not only to this book but to scores of books in other classes. These techniques will be especially useful in reading part 2.

Deciding on a Reading Strategy

Selecting an effective reading strategy is probably the most important decision you make when you begin a book. Different reading materials require different strategies. (One does not read newspapers, for example, the same way one reads Shakespeare.) Choosing an effective strategy depends not only on the book's subject matter but also on how you are to be tested on it. Multiple-choice exams require a different reading strategy than essay exams.

Focusing on Broad Themes When Reading for Essay Exams

Details are important in relation to the book's overall thesis but less important in and of themselves. To do well on an essay exam, you should know a book's argument and how it is constructed. I refer to this reading strategy as "searching for meaning."

Searching for Meaning

Doing well on an essay exam requires more than passively reading words on a page. You must think about what you are reading and, like a detective, actively put together various pieces of information to grasp the author's meaning. Boiled down to its basics, "searching for meaning" involves four steps:

Using chapter headings and subheadings to gain an overview. Before reading a chapter, skim through it, focusing on the headings and subheadings to get an overview of what the chapter is about. The section titles of this volume, especially in chapters 8, 9, and 10, are written with this in mind. Thus, for example, a section in Ray Hames's contribution in chapter 8 is entitled "Is the Critique of Chagnon Justified?" You know, just by looking at the heading, what Hames is going to discuss.

Reading by paragraphs. One of the most effective ways to read chapters in a book such as this is to read "by paragraphs." This technique allows you to concentrate on a chapter's main ideas. Reading by paragraphs means focusing on the key sentence in each paragraph, that is, the sentence that enhances the author's overall argument in the chapter.

The key sentence tends to be either the first, second, or last sentence in a paragraph. On first reading, you will usually discover it is best to put a paragraph's details to one side—not to ignore them but to focus on the central issue raised by the chapter as a whole. Later on, after you understand the chapter's overall argument, you have the option of going back through the chapter and noting these details.

Move quickly from paragraph to paragraph, focusing on the key sentence in each paragraph. When you reach the end of a section (that is, a new heading), pause to see if you have grasped the main idea of the section. You might summarize it in a sentence or two.

The object of reading by paragraphs is not simply to get through a chapter quickly. Rather, it is to distinguish details from main themes. It allows you to comprehend the main points of an author's argument.

Reading slowly does not necessarily improve comprehension. It may, in fact, decrease comprehension. The slower you read, the more details you become mired in and the less likely you are to comprehend the chapter as a whole. Also you do not need to know the meaning of each and every word in a paragraph or to recognize each and every citation to grasp the idea of a chapter. Many terms and citations can be understood in a general way from the context. Key terms may be looked up in a dictionary later. Terms or citations that relate to minor points may be set aside during a first reading.

Reconstructing an author's argument. After finishing a chapter, review the chapter's headings and subheadings again. Having read the chapter, you can now reflect on the author's argument: (1) why the chapter moves in a certain direction; (2) what points are central (and which are tangential) to the chapter's themes; and (3) why one point follows another.

Assessing the author's argument. After reading a book, assess the author's argument. Understanding what the author intends to say, you are now in a position to decide to what degree the argument makes sense, to what degree it is supported by the author's data. Does the author convincingly develop his or her position? Or does the author leave you with unanswered questions?

Instead of conceiving of reading as a passive process—taking in information presented to you—think of reading as an active thinking process. You are searching for meaning from various clues presented in the text. Discovering the clues, making sense of them, is an intellectually stimulating process.

SUGGESTED YANOMAMI / YANOMAMÖ FILMS

The Feast (1970, 29 minutes) Yanomamö feasts are more than ceremonial events. They also have important economic and political implications. In this film one village (Patanowä-teri) invites another (Mahekoto-teri) to a feast to renew an old alliance in the hope of then attacking a third village. *The Feast* won first prize in every film competition in which it was entered. Patrick Tierney asserts the film was staged.

Magical Death (1973, 28 minutes) A study of a Yanomamö shaman in action. Dedeheiwä and a fellow shaman from Mishimishimaböwei-teri conduct two days of rituals in which, through speaking with *hekura,* or spirits, they seek to kill a man from another village. The film's depiction of Yanomamö shamans under the influence of hallucinogenic drugs, with green mucus dripping from their nostrils is graphic. Tierney writes of the film that Timothy Asch (who coproduced many of the Yanomamö films with Chagnon) "begged Chagnon to remove it [the film] from circulation because he had found that his students at USC [University of Southern California] were horrified by the Yanomami's symbolic cannibalism. . . . Chagnon attributed this to jealousy on Asch's part; . . . Chagnon had made the film all by himself, and it won a blue ribbon at the American Film Festival" (2000:112–13).

A Man Called Bee: Studying the Yanomamö (1974, 40 minutes) Provides a sense of an anthropologist (Napoleon Chagnon) at work in the field: his entering a village adorned with feathers, sharing coffee with Dedeheiwä, offering medical help to a baby, and collecting genealogies. The commentary helps viewers understand the problems faced in working in this setting (including the problem Chagnon faced in collecting genealogies).

The Ax Fight (1975, 30 minutes) Discusses an escalating conflict between members of Mishimishimaböwei-teri and guests from another village (who had once belonged to Mishimishimaböwei-teri). The film is divided into four parts: an unedited version that shows what was observed by the camera, an explanation by Chagnon of what transpired, a discussion of the kin relations among the individuals involved, and, finally, a coherent, edited version of the conflict. The film conveys how ethnographic filmmaking, like ethnography, strives to bring coherence out of confusion in making sense of such events. Napoleon Chagnon discusses the contexts surrounding the filming, as well as his strained relationship with Tim Asch, at the Web page "Ethnographic and Personal Aspects of Filming and Producing *The Ax Fight*" (http://www .anth.ucsb.edu/projects/axfight/updates/filming.html) and in the CD-ROM "Yanomamö Interactive: *The Ax Fight.*"

Warriors of the Amazon (1996, 56 minutes) Produced by Andy Jillings (for NOVA/BBC), the film portrays a feast that seeks to bring together two formerly opposed villages to form a new alliance. Most of the film was apparently staged, but it presents in vivid terms an event that was not: the death and cremation of a young mother and her child. Most problematic is why the film crew allowed the young mother to die without offering medical assistance. In the preliminary report of the El Dorado Task Force, Jane Hill writes: "It would have been easy to take the woman, who is quite young, perhaps even still a teenager, to the hospital" (AAA 2001b:18). She continues "There is a grim lesson here for us all: decent ordinary people, in the grip of a racializing representation that the film reproduces in almost every dimension, can behave in ways that deeply shocked members of the Task Force . . . and that must have been a dehumanizing experience for the Yanomami" (19).

HELPING THE YANOMAMI

Purchasing this book *new* has important implications: all royalties from the book go to assisting the Yanomami. There are no royalties for the Yanomami if you purchase the book used. (How the royalties are allocated—to which parties in which amounts—is publicly available on the Public Anthropology Web site [www.publicanthropology.org].)

Here is a small but significant way to help the Yanomami that extends beyond good intentions. Your commitment to provide the Yanomami with royalties, combined with similar commitments from others, means that the Yanomami will to some degree benefit from the controversy that has swirled around them and disrupted their lives.

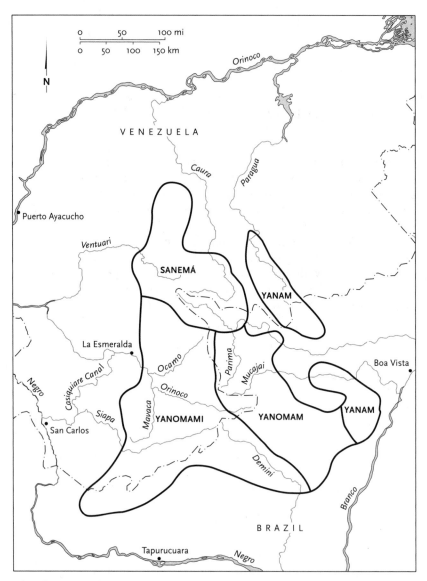

The area where the Yanomami live in southern Venezuela and northern Brazil with the names and locations of the most prominent Yanomami subgroups. (This map is drawn from Roberto Lizarralde's *Grupos Lingüísticos Yanomami*, prepared for the Venezuelan government's census.)

I

1

···

THE CONTROVERSY
AND THE BROADER ISSUES AT STAKE

At first glance, the Yanomami controversy might be perceived as being focused on a narrow subject. It centers on the accusations made by the investigative journalist Patrick Tierney against James Neel, a world-famous geneticist, and Napoleon Chagnon, a prominent anthropologist, regarding their fieldwork among the Yanomami, a group of Amazonian Indians. But it would be a mistake to see the Yanomami controversy as limited to these three individuals and this one tribe.

First, the accusations Tierney made against Neel and Chagnon in his book *Darkness in El Dorado* (2000) generated a media storm that spread around the world. People knew about the accusations in New York, New Zealand, and New Guinea. Tierney accused Neel and Chagnon of unethical behavior among the Yanomami that at times bordered on the criminal. Many perceived the problem as being larger than the mistakes of two famous scientists. They wondered if anthropology and perhaps science itself had gone astray in allowing such behavior to take place.

Second, and critical for the themes of this book, the way the controversy played out offers an important lens through which to examine the entire discipline of anthropology. We see not only how anthropologists idealize themselves in describing their work to others. We also see the actual practice of anthropology—up close and clear. We are led to explore questions central to the discipline.

Readers should keep this point in mind as they read *Yanomami: The Fierce Controversy and What We Can Learn from It*. The controversy goes beyond what Neel and Chagnon stand accused of. It extends beyond the media storm generated by Tierney's accusations and the accusations that others, in turn, made against him. The controversy draws us into examining issues at the heart of modern anthropology. As we will see, there are lessons for the learning here for everyone, whatever their specialty, whatever their status within the discipline. Let me begin by providing certain background information. For clarity's sake, I order the material as a set of commonly asked questions.

WHO ARE THE YANOMAMI AND WHY
ARE THEY IMPORTANT IN ANTHROPOLOGY?

Through the work of Chagnon and others, the Yanomami have become one of the best-known, if not the best-known, Amazonian Indian groups in the world. People in diverse locales on diverse continents know of them. They have become a symbol in the West of what life is like beyond the pale of "civilization." They are portrayed in books and films, not necessarily correctly, as one of the world's last remaining prototypically primitive groups.

The Yanomami are also one of the foundational societies of the anthropological corpus. They are referred to in most introductory textbooks. Anthropology has become increasingly fragmented over the past several decades, with anthropologists studying a wide array of societies. The Yanomami—along with the Trobriand Islanders, the Navajo, and the Nuer—constitute shared points of reference for the discipline in these fragmented times. The Yanomami are one of the groups almost every anthropology student learns about during his or her course of study.

The Yanomami tend to be called by three names in the literature: Yanomami, Yanomamö, and Yanomama. The names all refer to the same group of people. Different subgroups are labeled (and label themselves) with different terms; there is no broadly accepted indigenous term for the whole group. There is a politics of presentation regarding which of these three terms one uses. *Yanomamö* is the term Chagnon gave the collective group, and those who refer to the group as *Yanomamö* generally tend to be supporters of Chagnon's work. Those who prefer *Yanomami* or *Yanomama* tend to take a more neutral or anti-Chagnon stance. I use *Yanomami* in this book because of its wide usage and greater neutrality. (When citing Chagnon in describing the group, I use *Yanomamö* to remain consistent with his usage.) Readers can substitute whichever term they wish.

Chagnon wrote *Yanomamö: The Fierce People* (1968) at a critical time in the discipline's development. American universities expanded significantly in the 1960s and 1970s, and, related to this, so did the discipline of anthropology. Prior to the 1950s, American anthropology had focused on the native peoples of North America and was only seriously turning, in the 1950s and 1960s, to other areas of the world. The Holt, Rinehart and Winston series in which Chagnon published *Yanomamö* emphasized a broadening of the anthropological corpus. The series offered new works for new times. The foreword to *Yanomamö* states that the case studies in the series "are designed to bring students, in beginning and intermediate courses . . . insights into the richness and complexity of human life as it is lived in different ways and in different places" (1968:vii).

I presume, though I have no way of knowing for certain, that at one time or another the majority of anthropologists have read Chagnon's book. At least one, and perhaps several, generations of American anthropologists have been raised on it.

The Yanomami are a tribe of roughly twenty thousand Amazonian Indians living in 200 to 250 villages along the border between Venezuela and Brazil. "The fact that the Yanomamö live in a state of chronic warfare," Chagnon writes, "is reflected in their mythology, values, settlement pattern, political behavior and marriage practices" (1968:3). He continues: "Although their technology is primitive, it permits them to exploit their jungle habitat sufficiently well to provide them with the wherewithal of physical comfort. The nature of their economy—slash-and-burn agriculture—coupled with the fact that they have chronic warfare, results in a distinctive settlement pattern and system of alliances that permits groups of people to exploit a given area over a relatively long period of time. . . . The Yanomamö explain the nature of man's ferocity . . . in myth and legend, articulating themselves intellectually with the observable, real world" (1968:52–53). Chagnon notes that members of one patrilineage tend to intermarry with members of another, building ties of solidarity between the lineages through time. The local descent group—the patrilineal segment residing in a particular village—does not collectively share corporate rights over land. Rather it shares corporate rights over the exchange of women (1968:69), whose marriages are used to build alliances. Chagnon observes, "The fact that the Yanomamö rely heavily on cultivated food has led to specific obligations between members of allied villages: . . . The essence of political life . . . is to develop stable alliances with neighboring villages so as to create a social network that potentially allows a local group to rely for long periods of time on the gardens of neighboring villages" when they are driven from their own by enemy raids (1968:44). While stressing the violent nature of Yanomamö life, Chagnon indicates that there are graduated levels of violence with only the final one—raiding other villages—equivalent to what we would call "war."

It is Chagnon's description of the Yanomami as "in a state of chronic warfare" that is most in dispute. The French anthropologist Jacques Lizot, in *Tales of the Yanomami*, writes: "I would like my book to help revise the exaggerated representation that has been given of Yanomami violence. The Yanomami are warriors; they can be brutal and cruel, but they can also be delicate, sensitive, and loving. Violence is only sporadic; it never dominates social life for any length of time, and long peaceful moments can separate two explosions. When one is acquainted with the societies of the North American plains or the societies of the Chaco in South America, one cannot say that Yanomami culture is organized around warfare as Chagnon does" (1985:xiv–xv).

Chagnon depicts the Yanomami as "the last major primitive tribe left in the Amazon Basin, and the last such people *anywhere on earth*" (1992b:xiii). We need to note, however, that the Yanomami have been in direct or indirect contact with westerners for centuries (see Ferguson 1995:77–98). They are not a primitive isolate lost in time. Ferguson writes: "The Yanomami have long depended on iron and steel tools. All ethnographically described Yanomami had begun using metal tools long before any anthropologist arrived" (1995:23).

In providing this brief overview, I have focused on Chagnon's *Yanomamö* because it is the most widely known account. But there are other recognized

ethnographers who have written about the Yanomami who might be cited as
well: notably, Bruce Albert, Marcus Colchester, Ken Good, Ray Hames, Jacques
Lizot, Alcida Ramos, Les Sponsel, and Ken Taylor.

WHO ARE THE CONTROVERSY'S
MAIN CHARACTERS?

The three individuals who have played the most important roles in the controversy and whose names are repeatedly referred to in discussions of it are James
Neel, Napoleon Chagnon, and Patrick Tierney.

The late **James Neel** has been called by many the father of modern human
genetics. He served on the University of Michigan's faculty for more than forty
years, becoming one of its most distinguished members. He was elected to the
National Academy of Sciences as well as to the American Academy of Arts and
Sciences and was awarded the National Medal of Science and the Smithsonian
Institution Medal. Neel is perceived as the first scientist to recognize the genetic
basis for sickle cell anemia. He conducted research on the aftereffects of atomic
radiation with survivors of the Hiroshima and Nagasaki bombings of World War
II in Japan. He also suggested not only that there was a genetic basis for several
modern diseases such as diabetes and hypertension but that such propensities
resulted from an evolutionary adaptation to environments where salt and calo-
ries were less than abundant. He died in 2000, some months before the publication of Tierney's *Darkness in El Dorado*.

Neel became interested in Amazonian Indians because of his research relating population genetics to principles of natural selection—whether certain
genetic structures contained particular evolutionary adaptive advantages.
Realizing that detailed studies of "civilized populations" would prove less
instructive for examining early human genetic adaptations than "tribal populations," having the Amazon region fairly accessible, and knowing that
Amerindians had entered the Americas fairly recently (he believed between fifteen and forty thousand years ago), Neel sought out relatively undisrupted
groups in the Amazon for study. He wrote in his autobiography: "I realized we
would probably never assemble from studies of existing tribal populations the
numbers of observations necessary to relate specific genes to specific selective
advantages, but at least we could take steps to define the range of population
structures within which the evolutionary forces shaping humans had to operate"
(1994:119). And in the journal *Science* Neel indicates that his studies were based
on the assumption that Amazonian Indians were "much closer in their breeding structure to [early] hunter-gatherers than to modern man; thus they permit
cautious inferences about human breeding structure prior to large-scale and
complex agriculture" (1970:815). Initially, Neel studied the Shavante, another
Amazonian Indian group. But in 1966 he turned to the Yanomami and worked
with them until roughly 1976.

Two additional points need to be noted. First, Neel worked closely with Napoleon Chagnon during this period and, in the early years, helped fund Chagnon's research through his own research grants (which came partly from the Atomic Energy Commission). He viewed Chagnon as "indispensable" to his program: Napoleon Chagnon "had sought me out in Ann Arbor . . . having heard of our developing program. By virtue of the contacts I had already made, I could facilitate his entry into the field; he, for his part, in addition to pursuing his own interests, could put together the village pedigrees so basic to our work" (1994:134). Neel indicates in his autobiography that he encouraged Chagnon to work among the Yanomami.

Second, a devastating measles epidemic broke out "coincident with," to use Neel's phrasing, his arrival in the field in 1968. Neel indicated he had brought two thousand doses of measles vaccine and had planned to hand these over to missionaries in the region. But faced with the epidemic, Neel and his team vaccinated many Yanomami as well. Here is how Neel described his actions: "Much of our carefully designed protocol for that expedition was quickly scrapped as we dashed from village to village, organizing the missionaries, ourselves doing our share of immunizations but also treatment when we reached villages to which measles had preceded us. We always carried a gross, almost ridiculous excess of antibiotics—now we needed everything we had, and radioed for more" (1994:162). To what degree this description accurately reflects Neel's actions during the epidemic is one of the critical questions in the controversy. Tierney accused Neel of worsening the measles epidemic through his actions; others have suggested Neel could have done more than he did to save Yanomami lives during the epidemic.

Napoleon Chagnon, a retired professor of anthropology at the University of California, Santa Barbara, is one of the best-known members of the discipline. His writings, particularly his introductory ethnography *Yanomamö: The Fierce People* and the films associated with it have made his name familiar to millions upon millions of college students since the 1960s. It is not too far-fetched to suggest that Chagnon helped make the Yanomami famous as a tribe around the world and the Yanomami, in turn, have been the basis for Chagnon's own fame.

As is perhaps fitting given the evolutionary orientation of the University of Michigan's Anthropology Department at the time he received his doctorate (1966), Chagnon has emphasized an adaptive/evolutionary perspective in his writings. In the first edition of *Yanomamö*, for example, he stressed that one needed to see Yanomamö social life as an adaptation not only to the physical environment but also to the social and political environment—including chronic warfare.

Readers should keep in mind several points regarding Napoleon Chagnon as they proceed further into the politics surrounding the controversy.

First, Chagnon is a good writer. His chapter "Doing Fieldwork among the Yanomamö" has become a classic in the social sciences. It portrays in vivid terms his early fieldwork experiences in a way that captures the imagination of readers within and beyond anthropology. His basic ethnography of the Yanomami,

Yanomamö, has sold perhaps three million copies—far more than any other ethnographic work in recent times.

Second, Chagnon is a dedicated field-worker. Unlike most anthropologists of his or the present generation, Chagnon has—admirably in my view—striven to go back to the Yanomami year after year to study them through time. He has made at least twenty-five visits since beginning his fieldwork among them in 1964, has resided among the Yanomami for over sixty-three months, and has visited more than sixty of their villages. Few anthropologists can make such a claim, especially for a group in a remote region that is far from the creature comforts of their own homes. The problem is that when the Venezuelan and Brazilian governments restricted his field access, Chagnon engaged in various efforts, some of them violations of Venezuelan law, to continue studying the Yanomami.

Third, Chagnon is controversial. His adaptive/evolutionary approach runs counter to the dominant trend in cultural anthropology, which focuses on how cultural contexts shape human behavior. He is more concerned with the biological underpinnings of human behavior. In trying to make sense of Yanomami conflicts over women, Chagnon states (as quoted in an article about him in *Scientific American*): "I basically had to create . . . my own theory of society." The article continues: "Chagnon's Darwinian perspective on culture jibed with Harvard University scientist E. O. Wilson's 1975 treatise on animal behavior, *Sociobiology*. Chagnon—who tends to refer to his detractors as Marxists and left-wingers—thus became identified with that school of thought, which also made him unpopular among social scientists who believe that culture alone shapes human behavior" (Wong, 2001:2). Chagnon writes, "For better or worse, there is a definite bias in cultural anthropology favoring descriptions of tribal peoples that characterize them as hapless, hopeless, harmless, homeless, and helpless. . . . The Yanomamö are definitely not that kind of people, and it seemed reasonable to me to point that out, to try to capture the image of them that they themselves held. They frequently and sincerely told me . . . 'We are really fierce; Yanomamö are fierce people'" (1992b:xv).

As previously noted, this depiction of the Yanomami as the "fierce people" has been challenged by other Yanomami specialists. There is a political context to this. During the debates over whether or not to set aside a large reserve in Brazil for the Yanomami in the 1980s and early 1990s—one was finally established in 1992—various Brazilian politicians used the depiction of the Yanomami as violent to suggest that they needed to be split up into several small reserves to reduce conflict among them. (The plan, not coincidentally, would have allowed for more gold mining in the region.) What upset many Yanomami specialists was that Chagnon spoke out against this misuse of his work by Brazilian politicians only in the English-speaking press, never in the Portuguese-speaking press of Brazil, where it would have done the most good.

Fourth, Chagnon has been far more forthcoming regarding the details of his fieldwork than have most anthropologists. He is quite open, for instance, about the manipulative techniques he adopted to gather information when informants lied to him, as well as about the lies he himself told to keep Yanomami from asking for his food. He openly admits that the Yanomami made death threats against him. Few anthropologists have been as candid about their fieldwork experiences as Chagnon, and fewer still at the time he wrote about them. Most anthropologists depict their fieldwork in fairly rosy terms, whether or not they actually experienced it that way. The problem for Chagnon is that certain of the fieldwork details he is so forthcoming about violate the American Anthropological Association's code of ethics.

Patrick Tierney is a freelance investigative journalist based in Pittsburgh. He obtained an undergraduate degree in Latin American studies from the University of California at Los Angeles. Those who interact with him on a personal level describe him as gentle and soft-spoken.

Tierney's first book, *The Highest Altar: The Story of Human Sacrifice*, was published in 1989. Clarebooks.co.uk Online Used Books describes it thus: "In 1983 Patrick Tierney went to Peru on an assignment to cover the autopsy of a well preserved five-hundred year old mummy. It was discovered that the child had been buried alive, the victim of human sacrifice. . . . [Tierney] went on to discover that this ancient ritual is apparently still being practiced and tells of his attempts to track down these stories in order to discover the motives behind sacrifice, the motives of the shamans and brujos who perform it." The book is now out of print. But according to Tierney's biographical information, it has been the subject of a National Geographic documentary.

Tierney spent eleven years researching and writing *Darkness in El Dorado*. He started out investigating the disruptive impact gold mining and gold miners were having on the Amazonian region, including on the Yanomami. At some point in this research he turned his attention to the scientists and journalists who have worked among the Yanomami. His gives an account of his research in an article in the *Pittsburgh Post-Gazette*:

> I originally went there [to the Amazon] just documenting the mayhem that was going on . . . and trying to understand what was happening and perhaps alert people as to what can be done to help them. But as that evolved, my own participation changed. . . . It just didn't seem to be an adequate response to document people's deaths in the middle of these kinds of circumstances. . . . [The story about Neel and Chagnon] wasn't the story I was looking for initially, but it's what I came up with. . . . And what seemed to me to be the real story is that these people [the Yanomami] have been used to fulfill fantasies, scientific paradigms and preconceptions. And they've been used in ways that have been extremely harmful to them. (Srikameswaran 2000)

Tierney makes a considerable effort to give *Darkness in El Dorado* the trappings of academic scholarship. The book contains more than 1,590 footnotes; the bibliography contains more than 250 books. The question, however, is whether Tierney's years of research and voluminous citations add up to a credible work.

Several anthropologists suggest that his supporting data are stronger for his case against Chagnon than for his case against Neel. Regarding his claim that Neel helped make the 1968 measles epidemic worse through his actions, the overwhelming consensus is that Tierney is wrong.

To understand the media storm surrounding *Darkness in El Dorado*, readers should take note of how Tierney's publisher publicized it. A statement inside the book's dust jacket (in the hardcover edition) reads in all capitals: "One of the most harrowing books about anthropology to appear in decades. *Darkness in El Dorado* is a brilliant work of investigation that chronicles the history of Western exploitation of the Yanomami Indians." And a CNN.com "Book News" report, dated October 2, 2000, notes, the "publisher W. W. Norton . . . is billing the book as 'an explosive account of how ruthless journalists, self-serving anthropologists, and obsessed scientists placed one of the Amazon basin's oldest tribes on the cusp of extinction.'"

In addition to James Neel, Napoleon Chagnon, and Patrick Tierney, there are three minor characters and one religious group that should be noted here because they are sometimes referred to in the controversy.

Marcel Roche is a Venezuelan doctor. As part of his goiter research, he administered to Yanomami small doses of radioactive iodine in 1958, 1962, and 1968 to measure their iodine metabolism. Apparently none of the Yanomami tested suffered from goiter problems, nor have Yanomami in general suffered from the disease. The Yanomami were simply used as a control study to enhance Roche's understanding of the disease. Most people agree that Roche never asked for what is today termed informed consent—permission from subjects to conduct research on them.

Jacques Lizot is a prominent French anthropologist who lived among the Yanomami for more than twenty years. He is highly critical of Chagnon's writings. Two points tend to be repeatedly asserted about Lizot's time in the field: that he was a strong public defender of Yanomami rights and that he had homosexual relations with a number of Yanomami boys. Related to these sexual relations, Tierney writes: "Lizot probably distributed more clothes and shotguns than any other individual among the Yanomami" (2000:141). And: "Whatever homosexual practices the Yanomami had prior to Lizot's arrival, shotgun-driven prostitution is nothing to brag about in their culture" (2000:137). Lizot has written two books on the Yanomami: *The Yanomami in the Face of Ethnocide* (1976) and *Tales of the Yanomami: Daily Life in the Venezuelan Forest* (1985).

Ken Good was a doctoral student of Chagnon's who had a falling-out with him after they spent time together in the field. (He ultimately got his doctorate working with Marvin Harris, a critic of Chagnon.) Good spent twelve years among the Yanomami and married a Yanomami (Yarima), from whom he is now divorced. He has written about his experiences in *Into the Heart: One Man's Pursuit of Love and Knowledge among the Yanomama* (1991). Building on what Lizot wrote, Good observes, "Chagnon made . . . [the Yanomama (or Yanomami)] out to be warring, fighting, belligerent people. . . . That may be his image of the Yanomama; it's certainly not mine" (1991:175).

The Catholic **Salesian missionaries** have had a prominent presence in Yanomami territory for decades. Early in the twentieth century, Venezuela legally granted the Salesian missionaries responsibility for educating the indigenous inhabitants of the Amazonas region (which includes the Yanomami). That responsibility continues today. Both Chagnon and Lizot have come into conflict with the Salesians. While they have had positive things to say about the missionaries, both have been highly critical as well. One outside observer labeled Chagnon's conflict with the Salesians a "turf war" over who would control research among the Yanomami (Salamone 1996:4). (Chagnon views the Salesians as partly to blame for his being officially barred from studying the Yanomami in Venezuela.)

WHAT EXACTLY IS THE YANOMAMI CONTROVERSY?

Answering this question draws us into examining not only the accusations Tierney made against Neel and Chagnon in *Darkness in El Dorado* but a number of other issues as well. Let me start with Tierney's accusations and then move on to the additional issues.

The Accusations

Tierney made a number of accusations against a number of people in *Darkness in El Dorado*. But the central ones—and the ones latched onto by the media—involved Neel and Chagnon.

Tierney makes two basic accusations against Neel: (1) that Neel helped make the measles epidemic worse, rather than better, through the actions he took to fight the epidemic and (2) that Neel could have done more than he did to help the Yanomami at this time. Because the first of these accusations in effect charged a distinguished scientist with facilitating the deaths of Yanomami, it received the most media attention. This accusation has been dismissed by most people; the second is very much with us.

Tierney makes seven basic accusations against Chagnon: (1) He indicates that Chagnon misrepresented key dynamics of Yanomami society, particularly their level of violence. The Yanomami were not "the fierce people" depicted by Chagnon. They were significantly less bellicose, in fact, than many Amazonian groups. (2) What warfare Chagnon noticed during his research, Tierney asserts, Chagnon himself helped cause through his enormous distribution of goods, which stimulated warfare among the Yanomami as perhaps never before. (3) Tierney accuses Chagnon of staging the films he helped produce, films that won many cinematic awards and helped make *Yanomamö: The Fierce People* a best seller. The films were not what they appeared to be—live behavior skillfully caught by the camera—but rather staged productions in which Yanomami followed preestablished scripts. (4) Tierney accuses Chagnon of fabricating the data used in Chagnon's most famous article, which appeared in *Science* in 1988. The article asserted that Yanomami men who murdered tended to have more wives and more children—or, phrased another way, that violence was an evolutionary adaptive principle. (5) Tierney asserts that Chagnon acted unethically in collecting the genealogies needed for Chagnon's and Neel's research. The Yanomami have a taboo against naming deceased relatives. When asked about deceased relatives, Yanomami would invent names, essentially making a shambles of Chagnon's genealogical data. Tierney claims that Chagnon used unethical techniques to get around this difficulty. (6) Tierney asserts that Chagnon's self-depiction as being the first outsider to make contact with several Yanomami villages is untrue. Long before Chagnon arrived, Helena Valero, an outsider who was kidnapped by the Yanomami in 1932 and who lived among them for fifty years, had visited all the villages Chagnon claimed to have contacted. And (7) Tierney accuses Chagnon of violating Venezuelan law while participating in a plan with two prominent Venezuelans to establish a private Yanomami reserve that would have been controlled by the three of them. This is termed the FUNDAFACI (Foundation to Aid Peasant and Indigenous Families) project. For Chagnon, the project represented a way around the restrictions placed on his visiting the Yanomami by the Venezuelan government.

The publicity generated by Tierney's *Darkness in El Dorado* became part of the controversy. Here is a sampling of what the media said. ABCnews.com reported: "Another red-hot scientific scandal. This time anthropologists and geneticists are getting a noisy wake-up call. A book written by journalist Patrick Tierney, titled *Darkness in El Dorado*, . . . raises a stink so high that the space station astronauts will get a whiff of it" (Regush 2000). *Time* asked: "What Have We Done to Them? . . . A new book charges scientists with abusing the famous Yanomami tribe, stirring fierce debate in academia" (Roosevelt 2000). *USA Today* noted that the "face of anthropology stands riddled with charges that its practitioners engaged in genocide, criminality and scientific misconduct" (Vergano 2000). *Business Week* added: "Tierney makes a persuasive argument that anthropologists for several decades engaged in unethical practices" (Smith 2000). The *New Yorker* spread across its cover: "What happened in the jungle? Patrick Tierney reports from South America on the anthropologist who may have gone too far" (October 9, 2000: cover overleaf).

How did anthropologists respond to the media reports? The *New York Times* wrote: A "new book about anthropologists . . . has set off a storm in the profession, reviving scholarly animosities, endangering personal reputations and, some parties say, threatening to undermine confidence in legitimate practices of anthropology" (Wilford and Romero 2000). The *Chronicle of Higher Education* reported: "Some anthropologists fear that their discipline faces a scandal because of the imminent publication of a book charging several prominent researchers with egregious misbehavior in their work with Amazon tribes. . . . Scholars are worried that the allegations will make it hard for all cultural anthropologists who do fieldwork to persuade their subjects and the public that they are responsible, objective, and trustworthy" (Miller 2000b).

As time went on, other accusations were piled on top of the ones listed above.

Regarding Neel, there were two. First, critics suggested that he had never gotten informed consent for his medical research among the Yanomami. (Informed consent, touched on above, involves getting formal permission from subjects to conduct research on them and is required today in all medical research.) Even if standards of informed consent during the 1960s differed from those existing today, several critics asked if Neel couldn't have done more to inform the Yanomami about the details of his research. This constitutes a critical issue because many Yanomami today claim that they had been led to expect additional medical assistance that drew on the results of Neel's research among them. This assistance has not been forthcoming. Second, with the publication of Tierney's book many Yanomami came to realize that the blood collected during Neel's research was still being preserved in American laboratories. They felt they had never been informed that this would occur. While some Yanomami want to be suitably paid for their deceased relatives' blood, others want it destroyed, viewing it as a sacrilege to preserve the blood of dead Yanomami. What the Yanomami concur on is that they want to reopen negotiations regarding the blood and are willing to contest continued use of it until a suitable agreement is reached.

Regarding Chagnon, three accusations came to the fore. First, various anthropologists in Brazil and the United States brought up an old question of why Chagnon had never openly opposed misuse of his work in the Brazilian press. It seemed a violation of the American Anthropological Association's ethical injunction to do no harm. Second, some anthropologists brought up Chagnon's earlier criticism of Davi Kopenawa, a prominent Yanomami activist who played a key role in the effort to establish a Yanomami reserve in Brazil. They asked if it was right that an anthropologist should undermine the work of an indigenous activist seeking to protect his people. And third, there was the question of how Chagnon should distribute the more than $1 million he made in royalties from his best-selling book *Yanomamö*. Chagnon at one time had set up a fund to assist the Yanomami, but there is no record of the fund ever doing anything to help them. Many asked, shouldn't Chagnon share some of this money with the Yanomami who assisted in the research? Clearly, Chagnon could not have written the book without their help.

As the controversy continued, Tierney was subjected to criticism as well. Several supporters of Neel and Chagnon suggested that *Darkness in El Dorado* was full of inaccuracies. They described many of the footnotes used to back up statements in the main text as distortions of the original sources. Some critics suggested Tierney's book was little more than a malicious, irresponsible attack on two prominent scientists.

With all the attention focused on the Yanomami controversy, we might ask whether the Yanomami have benefited in some way from the controversy that has swirled around them. To date, the answer is essentially no. Despite all the publicity and all the good intentions expressed by anthropological organizations and anthropologists, the Yanomami essentially still live under the same tenuous health conditions as before. This is a scandal in itself. It suggests that the Yanomami seem, for many anthropologists, to be primarily tools for intellectual argument and academic advancement.

American Anthropology's Response

One might think these issues quite sufficient to create debate in anthropology departments around the world. But there is more. There are also important questions regarding the way American anthropology has responded to the controversy.

For example, why did no American organization ever investigate the accusations surrounding Chagnon before the publication of Tierney's *Darkness in El Dorado* in 2000, although the accusations had been circulating for years and were supported, in part, by Chagnon's own writings? Rather than investigating these accusations, most members of the discipline seemed content to ignore them. In fact, thousands of anthropologists continued to use Chagnon's ethnography *Yanomamö* in their classes, even though it was clear that the field practices he described in it violated the American Anthropological Association's code of ethics. Whatever Chagnon's ethical lapses, he remained a hero to many in the discipline. We might ask why so many chose to ignore, rather than investigate, the accusations against him.

We might also voice concern over the way the American Anthropological Association (AAA), American anthropology's largest organization, initially responded to the publicity generated by the publication of Tierney's book. The AAA organized an "open forum" with a number of panelists at its 2000 annual meeting. But as readers will see in chapter 3, most of the panelists were biased against Tierney. In criticizing him, they focused on Tierney's accusation against Neel that had already been disproved. Tierney's accusations against Chagnon were not really addressed.

Readers will have a chance to evaluate for themselves where they stand on the controversy's issues. But my impression—if I may inject it at this point—is that the leaders of the American Anthropological Association initially addressed the controversy more as a problem in public relations than as a problem of professional ethics: they were more concerned with protecting the discipline's image than with dealing directly with the issues Tierney had raised.

To its credit, the association set up a task force to inquire further into the matter. But when the El Dorado Task Force's preliminary report was made public, it appeared to be following the same tack as the panelists at the open forum. The preliminary report caused an uproar among those who wanted to call Chagnon to account. In an effort to calm the troubled waters generated by the report, the Task Force requested public comment on it. The more than 170 responses posted at the association's Web site—most of them from students—caused the Task Force to change course. The comments drew the Task Force into seriously assessing, in its final report, Chagnon's various deeds and misdeeds. It was the first time the association had seriously done so.

Whatever one's view of the Task Force's final report—and opinions differ—it is important to acknowledge the role students played in this phase of the controversy. Never before in the discipline's history, I believe, had students participated with such impact in such a prominent disciplinary debate. That participation is the reason I am dedicating this book to these students. At a critical time, they stood up, got involved, and made a difference in the discipline's politics.

To summarize, the controversy is not simply about the accusations Tierney made against Neel and Chagnon or the accusations various other people have made against Neel, Chagnon, and Tierney. It is also about how American anthropology has responded to these accusations. There is room for cynicism regarding how the controversy has played out in the discipline. But there is also room for hope, given how students helped draw the association's Task Force into directly assessing accusations against a former member.

The Larger Questions

At a still higher level, beyond the accusations and counteraccusations and beyond American anthropology's responses to them, there is yet another set of issues anthropologists and anthropologists-in-the-making need to confront regarding the controversy. These are the generally unspoken questions that lie at the heart of the discipline and that help to explain why American anthropology has been hesitant to confront the controversy head-on. These are the big questions we need to ask but often are afraid to because they put into doubt what we have come to accept as foundational and firm in anthropology.

The first is the *inequality of power* between anthropologists and their informants. Since anthropologists tend to come from countries that are more economically developed and militarily powerful than those they study, it is reasonable to ask, what ethical standards should govern how the more powerful use the intellectual and biological resources of the less powerful? Phrased another way, how does anthropology move beyond colonial practices built up when anthropologists mostly studied the subjugated peoples of imperial powers? What today constitutes a fair and just relationship among the parties concerned? Related to the inequality of power are the issues of informed consent, "doing no harm," and just compensation.

Today the first of these, *informed consent,* is required by almost all funding agencies supporting medical and social research. But how do anthropologists acquire permission from the people being studied? How does one explain a project to a group of people (or inform them) and gain their approval (or consent) when the project involves unfamiliar concepts and practices? Also relevant is the question of the duration of such consent. Is it a one-time thing, or do researchers need to gain it again as they find new ways to use and make money from the initial research that was never envisioned in the initial consent agreement?

The second is the anthropological injunction (embodied in the American Anthropological Association's code of ethics) *to do no harm* to those whom anthropologists study. What this means in practice—what specific actions this directive commits an anthropologist to—remains unclear. Remember that Chagnon, who essentially admitted in his own writings to violating this ethic, was lionized by many within the discipline.

We might, moreover, wonder why the focus is on doing no harm rather than on the third issue, offering *just compensation* to those who assisted in one's research. Anthropologists tend to present generous gifts to informants. But are such gifts sufficient compensation, given that anthropologists take the informants' information back to their universities and use it to build financially satisfying careers that often far exceed what their informants can expect in their own lives? Should these informants, who are living in less-privileged circumstances, be given the assistance to create better lives for themselves as well?

There are no easy answers here, and readers should not expect anthropology, by itself, to right the world's inequities. But these issues should be openly addressed. We need to consider how anthropology as a discipline might reach across the political and economic divides that separate researchers from informants and justly compensate those who help anthropologists build professional careers.

Most anthropologists care deeply about the people they work with. But they get caught up in broader power structures that keep the discipline from moving beyond the colonizing practices of times past. The persistence of such practices today is a part of the Yanomami controversy.

This point leads to another, the issue of *professional integrity*. Is the American Anthropological Association's code of ethics simply a set of nice-sounding abstractions—window dressing to impress those beyond the discipline—or are anthropologists held accountable to the code in some way? What responsibilities does the code entail for individual anthropologists? What does it entail for the discipline as an organized profession? Some might prefer to deal with such questions in terms of abstract pronouncements (of *shoulds* and *should nots*), but the fact is that anthropologists cannot simply claim to be moral and expect others in nonacademic settings to trust them on that basis, especially given the discipline's record to date. Again, there are no easy answers. But we all need consider how to move anthropology beyond talking about morality to practicing a morality that embodies the best ideals of the discipline and that ensures a positive reception for us in places where our reputations precede us.

We need to also consider *the way anthropologists tend to argue past one another* in controversies such as this. Is anthropology simply a matter of vexation and debate—a form of entertainment for intellectual aficionados of the obscure— or is something approaching a consensus possible in a heated matter where the discipline's own behaviors are called into question? Are controversies such as this ever resolvable? Or do people simply give up arguing after a while and go on to something new?

For anthropology, Chagnon is the central character. The discipline embraced him and his work for years, making *Yanomamö* the best-selling ethnography in the past half-century. Understandably, partisans of Chagnon—and there are many in the discipline—tend to focus their criticism of Tierney on his account of Neel, reasoning that if Tierney's case is weakened in one area it is weakened in others. That is why the "Referendum on *Darkness in El Dorado*" (sponsored by Chagnon partisans and passed in November 2003 by the American Anthropological Association) focused on Tierney's fallacious claim that Neel helped make the measles epidemic worse. While Chagnon was a participant in Neel's project, he played a minor role in Neel's measles immunization campaign. Chagnon partisans downplay his violations of the association's ethical code and Venezuelan law. Partisans of Tierney, on the other hand, tend to pass over the charges against Neel and focus on Tierney's accusations against Chagnon, where they feel their case is stronger. One can often tell a person's position in the controversy simply by noting the topic he or she wishes to discuss.

As a result of these tactics, there have been few sustained, back-and-forth discussions between opposing partisans regarding the accusations surrounding Neel and Chagnon. Most of the time opposing partisans talk past one another. The only two sustained conversations I know of are in part 2 of this book and the final report of the AAA's El Dorado Task Force, which is summarized in chapter 11.

In summary, beyond the accusations surrounding Neel, Chagnon, and Tierney, there are critical—indeed, from my perspective, far more critical—issues that need to be addressed in the controversy: those involving relations with informants as well as professional integrity and competence. Given how central these issues are to anthropology, readers can understand, perhaps, why many in the discipline have sought to sidestep the controversy. Confronting these issues will be hard. But the discipline needs to address them if it is to outgrow its image as an agent of colonizing powers and be both welcomed and understood outside the halls of academia.

WHAT IS RIGHT ABOUT CONTROVERSIES SUCH AS THIS?

I have referred above to the problems controversies such as this can create. They may generate negative publicity for the discipline, making the broader public less willing to support it. They may also foster disciplinary divides as anthropologists passionately argue past one another without resolution. Let me turn now to what is right about these controversies and why they are important, indeed essential, for the discipline's cumulative development.

First, controversies such as this provide a basis for conversations across the specialized research worlds anthropologists now participate in. They enable people grounded in different regions and absorbed by different problems to talk about issues that interest—and in this case affect—them all. In Victor Turner's phrasing, controversies such as this offer a temporary "communitas," a temporary moment of community that transcends the structural boundaries that traditionally separate anthropologists from one another. Turner suggests that such "antistructural" moments allow people to perceive the problematic nature of the structures that shape their everyday lives. We see that here. The Yanomami controversy allows us to reflect on the discipline's dynamics in a special way.

Second, controversies such as this are essential for building a cumulative discipline. There has been a sea change in the way anthropologists think about their research since Napoleon Chagnon began his Yanomamö fieldwork in 1964. At that time, there was a general disciplinary sense that anthropologists—in seeking to be scientific—were concerned with "just the facts," as Detective Joe Friday famously put it in the 1950s television program *Dragnet*. Anthropologists saw their job as collecting facts and letting the facts speak for themselves.

Today, there is a greater appreciation that gathering "just the facts" is not a simple process. During the past two decades, the discipline has worked its way through what has been termed "a crisis of representation," an "uncertainty about adequate means of describing social reality" (Marcus and Fischer 1986:8). "No longer is it credible," Fischer asserts, "for a single author to pose as an omniscient source on complex cultural settings" (in Barfield 1997:370). While this perspective has been warmly embraced by a substantial portion of the discipline, it has mostly involved—at the case-study level—authors challenging their own authority in ways that, at times, might be perceived as self-serving.

In examining opposing viewpoints as we do in this controversy, readers have a chance to move beyond such accounts to a deeper, fuller sense of how anthropologists, in fact, construct ethnographies. There are, no doubt, self-serving elements in Chagnon's and Tierney's accounts. But we can ferret many of these out by comparing one account with another and comparing both with other accounts written by different anthropologists who have also worked among the Yanomami.

What is now increasingly evident to most members of the profession—and perhaps should have been in the 1960s—is that anthropology needs different accounts of the same subject to gain greater objectivity, to gain a better sense of the social processes described by anthropologists. Multiple accounts allow us to step behind the screen of anthropological authority—something like seeing the Wizard of Oz in person rather than from behind a screen—and perceive the underlying dynamics at work.

In the search for objectivity, we cannot put our faith in a single account, regardless of the status of the person who produced it. There is always the problem of self-serving rhetoric. *Objectivity does not lie in the assertions of authorities. It lies in the open, public analysis of divergent perspectives.*

What is essential to developing cumulative knowledge—rather than continually increasing the amount of uncertain knowledge, as frequently occurs today—is that anthropological results be publicly called into question. The results must be challenged, the researchers involved must respond, and the broader community must work its way toward consensus on the issue. The problem, of course, is that as long as the material remains obscure—known only by this or that expert—there can never be a real collective resolution of differences.

The hope held out, in chapter 6 and part 2 of this book, is that we can collectively listen to the arguments and counterarguments of experts as they debate. And as in a trial where the jury does not know all the relevant details beforehand but learns them as various experts with opposing views present them, we can come to a set of shared conclusions.

ORGANIZING THIS BOOK
FOR DISCIPLINARY CHANGE

The book is organized into two parts. Part 1, chapters 1 through 7, elaborates on themes discussed above. Critically, it offers readers a chance to decide where they themselves stand on the issues raised by the controversy.

Chapter 2 introduces readers to the controversy's specifics by highlighting certain key statements by Chagnon and Tierney. It uses the various editions of Chagnon's famous *Yanomamö* to better understand Chagnon and why he sought to repeatedly return to work among the Yanomami. It also highlights, with direct quotes, Tierney's precise accusations against Neel and Chagnon.

Chapter 3 shows how the controversy unfolded within American anthropology. It elaborates on the concerns regarding Chagnon's behavior before the publication of *Darkness in El Dorado*, the reasons American anthropology so widely embraced Chagnon and his work despite Chagnon's obvious ethical problems, and the ways in which the American Anthropological Association responded to the controversy over time. The chapter lets us see American anthropology in a new way.

Chapter 4 discusses two questions at the heart of the controversy and of the discipline. First, it considers the "do no harm" ethical standard for research and the power relations implicit in it. It goes on to suggest that just compensation is a better standard for negotiating relationships in the field. Second, the chapter examines how anthropologists seek to credentialize statements—how they seek to make their assertions seem true—and the flaws in the methods used.

Chapter 5 presents a sampling of Yanomami views regarding the controversy. Understandably, the concerns of the Yanomami interviewed are not necessarily the concerns of Western readers. The two perspectives are entwined in interesting ways.

Chapter 6 sets out key questions regarding the controversy that readers need to consider, need to answer for themselves. Extensive quotations from part 2 of the book illustrate opposing perspectives and provide the background readers require to reach their own conclusions. It is the central chapter in the book.

Chapter 7 draws key themes of the controversy together, asking readers to help foster the ethical discipline most anthropologists assert they want. It builds on the model of "student power" discussed in chapter 3.

Part 2, chapters 8 through 11, presents a detailed debate among six leading experts. Rather than having the experts present their opinions and leave it at that, the experts engage with each other through three rounds of argument and counterargument. Part 2 constitutes the fullest, most open discussion of the controversy's central concerns to date.

In chapter 8 the six experts offer their positions on the central ethical issues raised by Patrick Tierney's *Darkness in El Dorado* and the best manner for dealing with them. In chapter 9 the experts comment on one another's positions (as set out in chapter 8). Chapter 10 concludes the discussion by having each expert comment one final time on the other participants' perspectives. The arguments and counterarguments of the six experts, as they unfold through the three rounds, allow readers to make sense of the issues more effectively than if there were only one expert enunciating his or her views. Readers are better able to weigh one position against another.

Chapter 11 concludes part 2 with two assessments of the controversy. The first involves a joint letter written by the six experts in the part 2 discussion plus myself. It offers our points of agreement regarding issues central to the controversy. The chapter also includes a summary of the final report of the American Anthropological Association's task force on the controversy as well as a description of the task force's preliminary report and a sampling of comments made about it. The chapter concludes by asking you, the reader, for your personal assessment of the controversy.

An appendix summarizes who affirms what about which topics in chapters 8, 9, and 10. Readers can use the summary as a guide for exploring a particular participant's position or a particular issue in the controversy.

Behind this formal organization is another organization that is meant to draw readers into not only reflecting on key disciplinary issues but addressing them in a way that fosters change. Archibald MacLeish wrote, in "Ars Poetica," that "a poem should not mean but be." That is what this latter organization strives for. The book is conceptualized and structured to draw readers into a disciplinary activism that can help shape anthropology's development over the coming decade.

First, the book seeks to enlarge the public sphere of discussion. As noted, experts frequently argue past one another, leaving the rest of the discipline as passive observers, trying to make sense as best they can of what is going on. Chapter 6 sets out the information readers need to draw their own conclusions. If readers wish to explore particular subjects further, they need only turn to part 2, where experts on both sides present their arguments and counterarguments vis à vis one another. The model, as noted, is of a jury trial where ordinary citizens listen to conflicting arguments and gain enough information to reach a consensus with their peers on an issue. The goal is to draw more people—both students and professors—into discussing the controversy's central questions. The issues raised by the controversy are too important to leave to a few experts. They involve us all. We should, therefore, all participate in the deliberations regarding them.

Second, the book seeks, in empowering readers, to develop a new political constituency for transforming the discipline. It is understandable that many anthropologists have had trouble addressing the controversy's central issues because they are invested in the present system. These anthropologists worked their way through the discipline's existing structures as they progressed from being graduate students to employed professionals. While they may acknowledge the limitations of the discipline, these structures represent the world they know, the world they feel comfortable with. One would not expect most of them to lead the charge for change. But introductory and advanced students are less invested in this system. If anything, they have a stake in changing it so as to create new spaces for themselves. Chapter 7 gives them the tools to foster this change.

Readers might wonder how this suggested activism will ultimately affect the people anthropologists study. In terms of specific changes in the discipline as a whole, that remains to be seen. But *all* the royalties from this book will go to helping the Yanomami. Neither the political projects presented in chapter 7 nor the royalties from this book are the final word on helping those who help us in our research. But they do represent a start in nourishing the change many want and hope for in the discipline. There is possibility in the air.

2

....

CHAGNON AND TIERNEY
IN THEIR OWN WORDS

In moving deeper into the controversy, we will start with the key figures' own words to learn what they did (and did not) say before we turn to what others suggest they said. Since the material on Neel is limited—we have covered most of it already and will discuss the rest in chapter 6—this chapter focuses on Chagnon's and Tierney's work. I start with Chagnon.

NAPOLEON CHAGNON

Chagnon's description of his first day of fieldwork has captivated millions of students over the past thirty-five years. Here are selected passages from his chapter "Doing Fieldwork among the Yanomamö":

> My first day in the field illustrated to me what my teachers meant when they spoke of "culture shock." I had traveled in a small, aluminum rowboat propelled by a large outboard motor for two and a half days. This took me from the Territorial capital, a small town on the Orinoco River, deep into Yanomamö country. . . .
>
> We arrived at the village, Bisaasi-teri, about 2:00 PM and docked the boat along the muddy bank. . . . It was hot and muggy, and my clothing was soaked with perspiration. It clung uncomfortably to my body, as it did thereafter for the remainder of the work. The small, biting gnats were out in astronomical numbers, for it was the beginning of the dry season. My face and hands were swollen from the venom of their numerous stings. . . .
>
> The entrance to the village was covered over with bush and dry palm leaves. We pushed them aside to expose the low opening to the village. The excitement of meeting my first Indians was almost unbearable as I duck-waddled through the low passage into the village clearing.
>
> I looked up and gasped when I saw a dozen burly, naked, filthy, hideous men staring at us down the shafts of their drawn arrows! Immense wads of green tobacco were stuck between their lower teeth and lips making them look even more hideous, and strands of dark-green slime dripped or hung from their noses. We arrived at the village while the men were blowing a hallucinogenic drug up their noses. One of the side effects of the drug is a runny nose. The mucus is always saturated with the green powder and the Indians usually let it run freely from their nostrils. My next discovery was that there were a dozen or so vicious dogs snapping

at my legs, circling me as if I were going to be their next meal. I just stood there holding my notebook, helpless and pathetic. Then the stench of the decaying vegetation and filth struck me and I almost got sick. I was horrified. What sort of a welcome was this for the person who came here to live with you and learn your way of life, to become friends with you? . . .

We arrived just after a serious fight. Seven women had been abducted the day before by a neighboring group, and the local men and their guests had just that morning recovered five of them in a brutal club fight that nearly ended in a shooting war. The abductors, angry because they lost five of the seven captives, vowed to raid the Bisaasi-teri. When we arrived and entered the village unexpectedly, the Indians feared that we were the raiders. On several occasions during the next two hours the men in the village jumped to their feet, armed themselves, and waited nervously for the noise outside the village to be identified. . . .

I pondered the wisdom of having decided to spend a year and a half with this tribe before I had even seen what they were like. I am not ashamed to admit, either, that had there been a diplomatic way out, I would have ended my fieldwork then and there. I did not look forward to the next day when I would be left alone with the Indians; I did not speak a word of their language and they were decidedly different from what I had imagined them to be. The whole situation was depressing, and I wondered why I ever decided to switch from civil engineering to anthropology. (1968:4–6)

As previously noted, Chagnon is very forthcoming about his experiences in the field. It is something I admire in his writing. There is less of the rosy glow common to most ethnographies and more of the real problems anthropologists face in struggling to do research in a difficult situation.

Chagnon's description of how he handled his food supply has become a classic within the discipline: "Food sharing is important to the Yanomamö in the display of friendship. 'I am hungry,' is almost a form of greeting with them. I could not possibly have brought enough food with me to feed the entire village, yet they seemed not to understand this." "I found peanut butter and crackers a very nourishing food, and a simple one to prepare on trips. . . . More importantly, it was one of the few foods the Indians would let me eat in relative peace. It looked too much like animal feces to excite their appetites. I once referred to the peanut butter as the dung of cattle. They found this quite repugnant." Chagnon goes on to describe another occasion: "I was eating a can of frankfurters and growing very weary of the demands of one of my guests for a share in my meal. When he asked me what I was eating, I replied: 'Beef.' He then asked, 'What part of the animal are you eating?' to which I replied, 'Guess!' He stopped asking for a share" (1968:7).

Chagnon also openly discusses how he gathered genealogical information for his and Neel's research, despite Yanomamö's sometimes strenuous opposition to the project:

There was a very frustrating problem. . . . I could not have deliberately picked a more difficult group to work with in this regard: They have very stringent name taboos. They attempt to name people in such a way that when the person dies and they can no longer use his name, the loss of the word in the language is not inconvenient. . . . The taboo is maintained even for the living: One mark of prestige is the courtesy others show you by not using your name. The sanctions behind the taboo seem to be an unusual combination of fear and respect. . . . As I became more proficient in the language and more skilled at detecting lies, my informants became better at lying. One of them in particular was so cunning and persuasive that I was shocked to discover that he had been inventing his information. . . . He would look around to make sure nobody was listening outside my hut, enjoin me to never mention the name again, act very nervous and spooky, and then grab me by the head to whisper the name very softly into my ear." (1968:10–12)

To find out the needed genealogical information against Yanomamö wishes, Chagnon says that "I began taking advantage of local arguments and animosities in selecting my informants. . . . I began traveling to other villages to check the genealogies, picking villages that were on strained terms with the people about whom I wanted information. I would then return to base camp and check with local informants the accuracy of the new information. . . . Despite . . . precautions, I occasionally hit a name that put the informant into a rage, such as that of a dead brother or sister that other informants had not reported. . . . These were always unpleasant experiences, and occasionally dangerous ones, depending on the temperament of the informant" (1968:12).

A positive result of Yanomamö: The Fierce People selling so many copies and staying in print for so many years is that Chagnon has had an opportunity to update and revise his book four times; the second edition was published in 1977, the third in 1983, the fourth in 1992, and the fifth in 1997. By studying the changes Chagnon made as he progressed from one edition to another we can gain important insights into Chagnon's motivations as an anthropologist and as an author. Let me highlight some of the themes that come through in examining these changes.

First, Chagnon is concerned with presenting an ever-deeper understanding of the Yanomamö as he learns more about them. He went from nineteen months of fieldwork among the Yanomamö in 1968 (the first edition) to sixty-three months in 1997 (the fifth edition). He is able to infuse the chapters on social organization and political organization with increasingly sophisticated analyses of village dynamics, alliance making, and village movements through time. He writes, in the third, fourth, and fifth editions, that his fieldwork includes an important lesson for anthropologists: "It is in some cases impossible to understand a society's 'social organization' by studying only one . . . community . . . for each community is bound up in and responds to the political ties of neighboring groups" (1997:1). In his first forty-two months of fieldwork, Chagnon was able to visit more villages (sixty) than any other anthropologist who worked among the Yanomamö has been able to do in a comparable period of time. The implication here is that Chagnon, because of his peripatetic fieldwork style, is able to analyze the Yanomamö in a way few others can.

This focus on visiting so many Yanomamö villages—anthropologists tend to stay put in one village rather than moving around—relates to what we might perceive, in Chagnon's research, as a sense of haste. Implicit in this style of fieldwork is a concern for studying the Yanomamö before they are overwhelmed and transformed by outside forces (see 1977:xi): "The 'first contact' with a primitive society is a phenomenon that is less and less likely to happen, for the world is shrinking and 'unknown' tribes or villages are now very rare. In fact, our generation is probably the last that will have the opportunity to know what it is like to make contact" (1992a:31). In a dramatic fashion that adds excitement to the book, Chagnon describes certain of his "first-contact" experiences with Yanomamö.

Second, Chagnon is intent on addressing criticisms of his work, especially what others view as his overstatement of Yanomamö violence. In the second edition, he emphasizes that most waking hours of Yanomamö are taken up with something besides warfare and that warfare varies from region to region. Still, he asserts, "a meaningful description of Yanomamö . . . warfare necessarily requires the presentation of facts . . . many of us would prefer not to consider. Infanticide, personal ferocity, club fights, and raids . . . have to be described and explained, no matter how unpleasant they might appear to us" (1977:163). The fourth edition discusses reasons other anthropologists working with the Yanomamö report less violence than Chagnon does. He suggests that lowland Yanomamö, particularly in the Shanishani drainage area, are more belligerent as an ecological strategy for safeguarding their large, desirable garden plots. In the highlands, where there is less competition for land, there is less conflict. Chagnon drops the subtitle of the book, "The Fierce People," in the fourth edition in response to criticism of it. As he explains: (a) "Fierce" often comes across in Spanish and Portuguese translations as conveying negative, animal-like overtones. (b) Some colleagues objected to the subtitle and, as a result, refused to assign his book in their classes. And (c) certain colleagues suggested the Brazilian government was using the "fierce" description to justify oppressive policies against the Yanomamö (see 1992a:xii).

A third theme is Chagnon's concern with maintaining the *Yanomamö*'s popularity with student audiences. As he noted in the second edition, "I decided [in writing the book] that I would let my own experiences as a student be my guide as an author, for I wanted to communicate with students of anthropology as with my professional colleagues. I remember . . . how much I enjoyed reading monographs that were sprinkled with real people, that described real events, and that had some sweat and tears, some smells and sentiments mingled with the words" (1977:xi). True to his word, in the third edition he added a case study entitled "The Killing of Ruwähiwä." The fifth edition added another case study, "Alliance with the Mishimishimaböwei-teri." (Chagnon notes that he added the latter case study partly to fit with a new interactive CD-

ROM he helped produce on the topic. By 1997 such interactive materials were becoming increasingly popular in classes and a major selling point for texts.) Clearly critical to the publishing success of Chagnon's *Yanomamö* are a number of vivid ethnographic films relating to his fieldwork. One, *The Feast*, won first prize in every film competition in which it was entered. The films convey a realistic sense of Yanomamö life, building upon and, in turn, enhancing points Chagnon develops in his text. (The second and later editions list these films in case readers wish to view them.)

A fourth theme is Chagnon's increasing concern for the Yanomamö themselves. In the second edition, he includes a chapter entitled "The Beginning of Western Acculturation" that discusses the outside changes that were beginning to engulf the Yanomamö. The chapter gives his account of the 1968 epidemic that devastated the Yanomamö (note that this account differs slightly from Neel's account, which I presented in chapter 1).

> In 1967, while participating with my medical colleagues in a biomedical study of selected Yanomamö villages, we collected blood samples that clearly showed how vulnerable and isolated the Yanomamö were: They had not yet been exposed to measles. Thus, in 1968, when we returned again to extend this study, we brought 3,000 measles vaccines with us to initiate an inoculation program in the areas we visited. Unfortunately, the very week we arrived an epidemic of measles broke out at a number of mission posts and began spreading to the more remote villages as the frightened Yanomamö tried to flee from the dreaded epidemic. We worked frantically for the next month trying to vaccinate a barrier around the epidemic, ultimately succeeding after visiting many villages. . . . Still, a large number of Yanomamö died in the epidemic in some regions—villages that were remote and difficult to reach." (1977:146)

In the fourth edition, Chagnon affirms his stance as a "committed advocate of not only Yanomamö cultural survival and human rights but also native rights and conservation issues all over the globe" (1992a:ix). "It was very difficult for me to write the final chapter," Chagnon notes in the preface. This was partly because of the destructive effects of the Brazilian gold rush and partly "having to do with the negative effects of being too frank about describing some of the politics that interfere with doing anthropological field research, effects that might compromise my effectiveness as an advocate of the Yanomamö, their rights, and their cultural survival at a time when these issues hang in the balance. There is much opposition in both Venezuela and Brazil to anthropologists who want to work among the Yanomamö, and my efforts will be most effective if I am able to return and learn about their new problems and try to develop ways to solve them" (1992a:xii–xiii).

In saying this, Chagnon nonetheless takes a position that upsets many activists working in the Amazon. He criticizes Davi Kopenawa, the most prominent Yanomamö activist in Brazil, calling him a spokesperson "for his [non-Yanomamö] mentors." "Everything I know about Davi Kopenawa is positive and

I am convinced he is a sincere and honest man," Chagnon writes in the fourth edition, but

> my concern is that he is being put into a difficult position. . . . For one thing, . . . he cannot possibly speak for Venezuelan Yanomamö. . . . There is also the danger that if Yanomamö "leaders" can be easily created by interested outside parties, every interested group will create and promote their own leader in order to advance their own special interests. In 1990 the Brazilian mining interests paraded their own Yanomamö leader . . . who advocated *their* rights just as strongly as Davi Kopenawä advocates the policies of his mentors. . . . I am astonished at how manipulative the various "outsiders" are in establishing and grooming the candidates whose political positions seem to reflect those of their mentors as much as anything else." (1992a:233–34)

Chagnon concludes the chapter with a position statement:

> My anthropological career has now come full gamut. I started out as just another anthropologist, a scientist, attempting to document and explain a different culture as best I could. By repetitively returning and becoming more and more intimately associated with people like Kaobawä and Rerebawä [two of his informants], I became "involved" in their culture and now want to make sure that they and their children are given a fair shake in the inevitable changes that are occurring. I can do so only by becoming, as they say, involved—by becoming more active and becoming an advocate of their rights and their chances to have a decent future, one that does not condemn them to becoming inferior members of the lowest possible rung of the socioeconomic ladder—bums and beggars in Puerto Ayacucho, alcoholics and prostitutes in the ghettos of Caracas. The rest of my useful career will be dedicated to this. (1992a:244–46)

A final theme that comes through in the five editions is that despite some hard times, Chagnon enjoyed fieldwork among the Yanomamö, and they, in turn, came to appreciate him. In the second edition he writes, "Suffice it to say that the danger [he faced] contrasted with and intensified the pleasure of my happier experiences . . . and the enormous amount of valuable new information I collected" (1977:154). In the fifth edition he observes, "Most of the yet-living Yanomamö men who threatened to or tried to kill me in the past are now friends of mine—and we even joke, albeit gingerly, about those long-ago situations. . . . The Yanomamö have come to know, accept, respect, and consider me as a welcome friend because I have treated them fairly, have not taken sides in their quarrels or wars, provided them with medicines, treated their sick, and regularly brought them the material things I knew they desired and needed" (1997:257).

Even with the changes Chagnon makes as he writes and rewrites *Yanomamö* through time, he continues his basic adaptive theme of Yanomami cultural adjustments not only to their physical environment but to their social and political environments. In the fifth edition, for example, he talks about how new technologies are allowing him to develop a "more sophisticated interpretation of Yanomamö cultural and economic adaptation to their political and geographical environment" (1997:xii)—the same theme espoused in the first edition.

An extension of this adaptive theme can be seen in the famous (and controversial) article "Life Histories, Blood Revenge, and Warfare in a Tribal Population," published in *Science* in February 1988. He writes, "In this article I show how several forms of violence in a tribal society are interrelated and describe my theory of violent conflict among primitive peoples in which homicide, blood revenge, and warfare are manifestations of individual conflicts of interest over material and reproductive resources [i.e., women]" (1988:985).

The article's abstract reads: "A theory of tribal violence is presented showing how homicide, revenge, kinship obligations, and warfare are linked and why reproductive variables must be included in explanations of tribal violence and warfare. Studies of the Yanomamö Indians of Amazonas during the past 23 years show that 44 percent of males estimated to be 25 or older have participated in the killing of someone, that approximately 30 percent of adult male deaths are due to violence, and that nearly 70 percent of all adults over an estimated 40 years of age have lost a close genetic relative due to violence" (1988:985). Chagnon is reiterating what he perceives as the violent nature of Yanomamö society. It was the next point that stirred up a hornets' nest: "Demographic data indicate that men who have killed have more wives and offspring than men who have not killed." Killers are more successful biological reproducers than nonkillers. Violence, he is saying, trumps nonviolence in evolutionary terms. As readers will see, others challenge Chagnon's claims. But there is no doubting the provocativeness of his article. It stirred up much debate.

In concluding this section, I would note a contrast in Chagnon's treatment of two topics that are repeatedly referred to in the controversy. As we have seen, Chagnon openly discusses the Yanomami taboo against naming deceased relatives as well as the problems he encountered and how he sought to circumvent them. But he does not discuss the Yanomamö concern with the blood of deceased relatives. He notes that Yanomamö feel the deceased's body should be cremated at death. (Relatives may eat some of the deceased's ashes.) But he does not discuss how the Yanomamö feel about having body fluids, such as blood, preserved after an individual's death, especially in a faraway country.

PATRICK TIERNEY

Tierney makes a number of accusations in *Darkness in El Dorado* against a number of people, but the ones that have most been taken note of—perhaps because they have received the most publicity—are the ones against Neel and Chagnon. Because Tierney organizes his book chronologically, the accusations, especially against Chagnon, are woven into a number of chapters and do not unfold systematically. Still, as one chapter builds on another, Tierney's case against both individuals become clear. If we cut and paste a little to bring related points in different chapters together, we might highlight two accusations against Neel and the seven accusations against Chagnon.

Tierney's accusations against Neel are far more serious and—in my reading of the media reports—sparked the most attention. They are also the most controversial.

First, Tierney accuses Neel of making the deadly 1968 measles epidemic worse, rather than better, through his actions. Essentially, Tierney accuses Neel of aiding and abetting the deaths of Yanomami as part of a larger, vaguely defined project to explore Yanomami susceptibility to measles. "It is difficult to imagine a group at higher risk to a live measles virus [vaccine] than the Yanomami," Tierney states in discussing the vaccine Neel used to inoculate Yanomami against measles in 1968 (2000:60).

> Yanomami at the Ocamo mission received the Edmonston B [vaccine] without the recommended gamma globulin coverage [meant to lessen adverse reaction to the shot], which doubled the risk of reaction [to the vaccine]. . . .
> There was no doubt . . . that a full measles rash and fevers first appeared among the Ocamo Yanomami within a week of the Indians' vaccination. Prior to the Yanomami's severe vaccine reactions . . . no one had seen the disease's telltale lesions. (2000:60, 67)
> Chagnon and Neel described an effort to "get ahead" of the measles epidemic by vaccinating a ring around it. As I have reconstructed it, the 1968 outbreak had a single trunk, starting at the Ocamo mission and moving up the Orinoco with the vaccinators. (69)
> Clearly he [Neel] and his doctors distributed medicine and cared for some of the sick they encountered. But his choice of vaccine [the Edmonston B] suggested he wanted new data [on genetic questions of selective adaptation] and his impatience with Venezuelan authorities meant that he had no backup from government doctors when crisis occurred.
> Moreover, Neel barely slowed his pace of blood-collecting or filming, both of which required massive payments of trade goods, a reckless policy during an epidemic [because the infected people would, in trading goods to other villages, spread the disease]. . . . The scientists kept moving on and the epidemic moved on with them. (82)

In the prepublication galleys, Tierney suggested that Neel's use of the Edmonston B vaccine itself might have caused some cases of measles. In the version that was published, Tierney backs away from explicitly asserting that: "It is unclear whether the Edmonston B became transmissible or not. That was the question that perplexed the expedition." (Apparently the possibility that the vaccine might cause measles was raised in one of the expedition's radio transmissions that Tierney examined.) He adds: "The chaos and deaths that followed vaccination . . . can be explained in terms of the extraordinary high vaccine reactions, coupled with simultaneous exposure to malaria and bronchopneumonia" (2000:81).

Tierney then goes on to suggest that Neel's excitement at the measles epidemic "was understandable. Witnessing measles as it infected an aboriginal group was a once-in-a-lifetime event. It seems to have been the only time in recent history when scientists were present at such an outbreak. And Neel was on hand with a documentary filmmaker to capture the scenes. . . . It was as if the sound and video had been suddenly added to the sixteenth-century Spanish chronicles" (2000:72). Of all of the accusations presented here, this first one—regarding Neel's role in the epidemic—is the one most often rejected by those familiar with the controversy.

Tierney's second accusation is that Neel could have done more than he did to help the Yanomami during the epidemic. When push came to shove—in terms of making choices between treating Yanomami and pursuing personal research goals—Neel, while trying to act humanely, emphasized his research.

> Neel's expedition, with its two doctors and a nurse and 250 doses of vaccine, passed through Platanal, invited all of the Mahekoto-teri to a filming even, but failed to vaccinate them, as it promised Venezuelan authorities. It is difficult to understand that decision today, knowing that 25 percent of the Mahekoto-teri, about thirty individuals, died of measles. . . . [Neel's] expedition had been in the field for almost a month and . . . the scientists were exhausted, sick, and increasingly disgruntled. Most of them were in the jungle for the first time, and each had a demanding research agenda. Their scientific hopes were all pinned on reaching the remote village of Patanowä-teri. It was hard to turn back to care for sick Indians, especially when the scientists, like the missionaries, were still not sure what was going on (Tierney 2000:78).

Some scholars who have examined the evidence, especially those critical of Chagnon, tend to accept this second accusation against Neel.

Tierney offers an intriguing perspective on the need for Yanomami genealogies and the collection of blood samples by Neel. "Students of [Chagnon's] *The Fierce People*, have gotten only the vaguest inkling about why the agency that manufactured atomic bombs spent large sums studying the Yanomami" (2000:37). The reason was "the AEC [the Atomic Energy Commission] wanted thousands of Yanomami blood samples, together with their corresponding genealogies, to determine mutation rates in a completely 'uncontaminated' population" (2000:43). This meant that Chagnon, in collecting data for Neel, had to travel far more than the anthropological norm, moving from village to village both to collect the necessary genealogical data and to prepare villagers for the collection of their blood by Neel's team.

This brings us to Tierney's accusations against Chagnon. First, Tierney accuses Chagnon of misrepresenting key dynamics of Yanomami society, especially its level of violence. He points out that "the Yanomami have a low level of homicide by world standards of tribal culture and a very low level by Amazonian standards. Compared to other tribes, they are fearful of outsiders" (2000:13). He quotes a former student of Chagnon, Ken Good: " 'In my opinion, the Fierce People is the biggest misnomer in the history of anthropology'" (2000:131). Tierney adds, "Chagnon's other students would also report much lower levels of violence than their mentor found" (2000:131). Tierney goes on to suggest that Chagnon's focus on violence played into the hands of Brazilian gold miners intent on disrupting plans for a large Yanomami land reserve in Brazil. (Mining would be illegal within such a reserve.) According to Tierney, the Brazilian military chief of staff, General Bayna Denis, justified drastically reducing the size of this reserve "by explaining that the Yanomami were too violent and had to be separated [into several small reserves] in order to be civilized" (2000:160). "María Manuela Carneiro da Cunha [a past president of the Brazilian Anthropological Association] accused Chagnon of doing violence to the Yanomami's chances of survival through his theories of violence" (2000:160).

Second, Tierney accuses Chagnon of stimulating, through his gift giving, the very warfare Chagnon suggests was prominent among the Yanomami. Tierney writes: "Within three months of Chagnon's sole arrival on the scene three different wars had broken out, all between groups who had been at peace for some time and all of whom wanted a claim on Chagnon's steel goods." He quotes Brian Ferguson, who has written a book on Yanomami warfare: " 'Chagnon becomes an active political agent in the Yanomami area. . . . He's very much involved in the fighting and the wars. Chagnon becomes a central figure in determining battles over trade goods and machetes'" (2000:30). "Whatever else can be said about Yanomami warfare," Tierney continues, "it is not 'chronic.' . . . All the violence among Chagnon's subjects can be spelled out in two stark spikes, both corresponding to outside intrusion" (2000:34). Tierney adds that the "deadliest war ever recorded among the Yanomami" occurred between villages allied with SUYAO (United Yanomami Communities of the Upper Orinoco, a Yanomami trade cooperative) and villages allied with Chagnon and Brewer-Carías as part of their FUNDAFACI (Foundation to Aid Peasant and Indigenous Families) project (the incident is described later in this section). "The outbreak of the wars occurred at around the same time as Chagnon's entry into Yanomami territory, in the early summer of 1990" (2000:227–28).

Third, Tierney accuses Chagnon and others of staging films on the Yanomami and portraying them as real events. Regarding the award-winning film *The Feast*, he asserts that Chagnon and the filmmaker Timothy Asch drew two Yanomami groups together—when they were not necessarily inclined to meet—and plied them with trade goods so as to act out the film's scenes. "Chagnon saw himself as recording 'specific events,'" Tierney writes. "The Yanomami recall his staging them" (2000:84). "The Yanomami understood that Chagnon wanted scenes of violence" (102). The Yanomami were afraid of cameras, Tierney notes: "The Yanomami believe cameras kill. . . . Cameras are like sci-fi ray guns, whose energy envelops and steals its target's spiritual essence" (83–84). The problem wasn't the staging but the fact that the staging was never revealed in the film. The whole context suggested the films were live footage of real events when, in fact, this was not the case. Left undisclosed is how the Yanomami felt about images of themselves being caught on film.*

Fourth, Tierney accuses Chagnon of falsifying data in Chagnon's famous *Science* article: "In the *American Ethnologist*, Jacques Lizot accused Chagnon of having created villages whose demographics were unlike any known communities and whose exact location was 'impossible to determine.'" He observes that while Chagnon's "charts on fertile killers looked good on paper, there was no way to confirm or refute them. Not only were the 'killers' anonymous, so were the twelve villages they came from" (2000:164). Through independent research, Tierney claims to have rechecked Chagnon's analysis and finds the data far more ambiguous than Chagnon acknowledges: "Minute manipulations in each age category could easily skewer all the results. . . . The spectacular superiority of killers for the entire study depended on a big bachelor herd under age 25 whose members were both peaceful and infertile" (176). He also notes that Chagnon's thesis differs from the recollections of Helena Valero, who lived among the Yanomami for fifty years: "This divergence began with motives and dates, but, most crucially, it included the actual number of victims and their specified killers" (247).

Fifth, Tierney asserts that Chagnon acted unethically in collecting Yanomami genealogies. Not only did Chagnon go against the Yanomami name taboo in collecting people's names but he used techniques that antagonized Yanomami informants. He gathered data by relying on children and marginal individuals as well as by playing individuals and villages off against one another. "His divide-and-conquer information gathering exacerbated individual animosities, sparking mutual accusations of betrayal." Tierney makes reference to "the ugly scenes" Chagnon "witnessed and created" (2000:33). Tierney writes: "Although it might appear that these were simply the antics of an ego out of control, there was a logic to Chagnon's anthropological methods. He had . . . to get the Yanomami to divulge their tribal secrets" (48).

---

*Tierney also discusses the staging of the well-known NOVA/BBC special on the Yanomami, *Warriors of the Amazon*. Andy Jillings, the director of the documentary, noted in a telephone interview with Tierney: "I was looking for a group that was fairly unacculturated and that was at war and suing for peace. So Jacques [Lizot] and I went out to another group that was at war, but they were not home much of the time. I wanted an unacculturated group because you can't make a film about the Yanomami if they're wearing Black Sabbath T-Shirts. We spoke to the more remote group but, basically, we were hijacked because the Karohi people said, 'Why don't you have the feast here?' They saw all our trade goods and they didn't want them going to the other group. The feast of reconciliation [between two warring groups] was a set-up. We might have facilitated it. But they wanted it" (2000:220). The film's highlight was the cremation ritual of a recently deceased woman. Rather than nursing the woman back to health, the film crew recorded her dying. Mike Dawson, who had lived among the Yanomami for more than twenty-five years, told Tierney, "With a little bit of help, they [the mother and her newborn infant] could have pulled through. The film crew interfered in every aspect of their [Yanomami] lives. Let's be real. They're giving them machetes, cooking pots, but they can't give a dying woman aspirin to bring her fever down?" (2000:217)

Sixth, Tierney indicates that Chagnon misrepresented his first-contact experiences: "It is a remarkable fact and a remarkable theft. Every single place . . . and every single village . . . that Chagnon has touted as his discovery, was intimately known and visited by Helena Valero [before him]" (2000:246).

Finally, Tierney asserts that Chagnon violated Venezuelan law in what came to be known as "the FUNDAFACI affair." Chagnon allied himself with Charles Brewer-Carías, an entrepreneur with a reputation for mining remote regions of Venezuela, as well as with Cecilia Matos, the mistress of the then president Pérez. The three hatched a plan to set up, under their control, a vast Yanomami "nature reserve" roughly the size of Maine (2000:9; on page 188 Tierney states the area involved was the size of Connecticut). Tierney notes that the reserve "would have given him [Chagnon] unprecedented power, but it required overthrowing the legal structure already established in Yanomami territory" (10). Tierney suggests that by 1990, opposition to Chagnon's research among both Venezuelan academics and the Yanomami had increased, and, as a result, Chagnon was finding it ever harder to continue his periodic trips to the field. "With Matos and Brewer . . . for allies, Chagnon devised a . . . bold . . . plan to permanently circumvent all the institutions that controlled the Yanomami Reserve. The three . . . would simply create their own, private reserve, a Yanomami park. At the same time, . . . they began a fierce press campaign against the Salesian" missionaries who opposed the plan (186). "According to . . . Venezuela's assistant attorney general for indigenous affairs, the various trips by Brewer and Chagnon, which cost millions of dollars in government transportation costs, 'were illegal because there is no evidence they even submitted their plans to the DAI [Indian Agency] for approval'" (191).

Concluding this section, I would add two points regarding *Darkness in El Dorado*. The first concerns Tierney's view of Neel's role in the measles epidemic. I talked to Tierney two times about it when he visited Hawaii. (He was invited by a group of Hawaiian activists.) Both conversations progressed in much the same way. I would indicate that I viewed the measles accusation regarding Neel as without empirical support. He would respond by expressing regret about including this accusation because it was the part of the book reviewers had most vociferously attacked. He perceived, correctly I believe, that it distracted from other more extensively discussed issues—especially his accusations against Chagnon. When I suggested that he delete the accusation regarding Neel from later editions of his book or admit that he might have been mistaken in his analysis, he always backtracked. Perhaps there might be a grain of truth, he would suggest, in what he had written. I take this to mean that Tierney, in his heart of hearts, wants to believe the controversial accusation against Neel is true, although few others do. He realizes the assertion has created serious problems and has cast a shadow of doubt over his whole work. This he regrets. Still, there is something inside him, I believe, that resists his letting go of the accusation.

Second, Tierney never accuses Neel or Chagnon of committing genocide. As we have seen, Tierney makes a number of serious accusations against each of them, but he never refers to genocide. My research suggests that it was Chagnon who first brought up the accusation of genocide. In 1989 Chagnon responded to a published letter from the Brazilian anthopologist Carneiro da Cunha (which, while critical of Chagnon's behavior, never refers to genocide): "The suggestion . . . that I am encouraging or promoting genocide is gratuitous and insulting. It is also libelous" (1989b:24). I perceive in Chagnon's response a way of discrediting his attackers by overstating their case. ("See what they accuse me of? What type of people would make such a patently false statement?")

We need not get drawn into the theatrics involved on either side of the argument. It is far better to stick with Chagnon's and Tierney's positions as they themselves represent them. These are provocative enough.

3

·····························

HOW THE CONTROVERSY HAS PLAYED OUT
WITHIN AMERICAN ANTHROPOLOGY

EARLY RUMBLINGS

The Yanomami controversy had been brewing for years before the publication of Tierney's *Darkness in El Dorado* in 2000. Most anthropologists did not take much notice. Still, elements of the controversy were there if one cared to look.

Elements of the controversy could be seen in 1988 when Maria Manuela Carneiro da Cunha, the past president of the Brazilian Anthropological Association (ABA), wrote to the American Anthropological Association's (AAA's) Committee on Ethics regarding Napoleon Chagnon. The committee never addressed her concerns, but her letter was eventually published in the *Anthropology Newsletter*. Carneiro da Cunha wrote: "The recent appearance in the Brazilian press of two articles on the Yanomami Indians based on Napoleon Chagnon's latest paper on Yanomami 'violence' [the article in *Science*] . . . has prompted us to call your attention to the extremely serious consequences that such publicity can have for the land rights and survival of the Yanomami in Brazil." (She is referring to the ways in which Chagnon's work had gotten entangled in the politics surrounding the establishment of a Yanomami reserve.) After challenging Chagnon's claims regarding the high rate of Yanomami violence in detail, she concludes: "The Brazilian Anthropological Association (ABA) feels that it is fundamental *to insist* on the need to bring to the awareness of North American anthropologists the political consequences of the academic images they build about the peoples they study. The case of the Yanomami in Brazil, who have been suffering a brutal process of land expropriation which is justified in discriminatory images based on dubious scientific conclusions, are in this respect a particularly grave and revealing case. . . . We urge the AAA to take the necessary steps to call to the attention of the North American anthropological community the ethical and moral repercussions of their writings for critical situations such as this" (Carneiro da Cunha 1989:3).

Chagnon was invited by the editor to reply to Carneiro da Cunha's letter. Chagnon responded by concurring with Carneiro da Cunha regarding the "senseless, inaccurate and irresponsible portrayal of the Yanomamö" by members of the press. But he went on to offer a detailed rebuttal of her accusations against him, concluding that "despite the disclaimer by the AAA that it does not 'endorse' the position of either the ABA or me, this exchange has some serious implications for ethnographic reporting by U.S. researchers working in other countries. The AAA's policy of 'reciprocity' (guaranteed publication) to sister AA organizations might be opening the door to an avalanche of complaints that, like this one, are rather more political, not to mention libelous, than they are professional, scientific or ethical. I am astonished that the AAA has accepted for publication in the *AN* an accusation against one of its members, without considering its possible accuracy, that he is (1) falsifying and manipulating data, (2) doing so with a 'fidelity' that fosters genocidal practices and (3) implies he is describing the people among whom he has worked in racist terms" (1989b:24).

There was more to the exchange, though this only came out later. The *Anthropology Newsletter* subsequently published a letter by a Chagnon supporter (Machalek) but refused to publish a letter by a supporter of Carneiro da Cunha (Albert). The reason was never made clear.

Elements of the controversy could also be seen in 1994 in the aftermath of the massacre at Haximu of sixteen Brazilian Yanomami by gold miners. (Initial accounts in the *New York Times* placed the count at twenty, then seventy-three, before it was revised down to the now accepted figure of sixteen.) On the Venezuelan side of the border, a controversy erupted regarding who was authorized to investigate the actions of gold miners against the Yanomami. Two investigative teams were formed. The initial investigative team included Chagnon and Charles Brewer-Carías. When various Venezuelans protested this team's membership, a second investigative team was formed. By chance, the two teams met near the massacre site. According to Tierney, Judge Aguilera (the head of the second team) ordered Chagnon (from the first team) "to cease and desist [in his investigation] or face arrest. . . . Chagnon was escorted to Caracas by Colonel Márquez, who took his notes and urged him to leave the country immediately, which, in fact, Chagnon did" (Tierney 2000:200). Behind this conflict lay a broader one. According to Salamone: "Principal among [the] . . . concerns [involved] is control of research in the Orinoco region of Venezuela. The issue, in many people's views, is whether Chagnon or the Salesian [missionaries] should control research in the sector" (1996:4; cf. Chagnon 1977:150).

Chagnon made his criticisms of the Salesians public following his expulsion. In a *New York Times* op-ed piece, he wrote, "The Salesian policies include attracting remote Indian groups to their missions, where they die of disease at four times the rate found in remote villages. While the Salesians claim they no longer attract converts by offering shotguns, that was their policy until 1991. Over the past five years there has been a rash of shotgun killings. Yanomami from the missions raid distant, defenseless villages, often traveling in power boats borrowed from the Salesians. They kill the men with guns, abduct the women and gang-rape them. . . . The Salesians have done little to stop this practice. It is likely that many more Yanomamö die from mission policies than at the hands of *garimpeiros* [gold miners]" (1993a:12).

Chagnon elaborated on these accusations in the *Times Literary Supplement*:

"So far the Brazilians have sponsored and conducted a far more effective, professional investigation than the Venezuelans. And for this embarrassment the Venezuelan government must thank the Salesian missionaries, as well as their own reluctance to defend their nation's secular legal right to pursue justice in the face of the opposition and intimidation of the Catholic Church. Clearly, the Salesians are attempting to preserve their virtual monopoly of political authority in Venezuela's Amazonas" (1993b:11).

The Salesians responded with an attack of their own. The *Chronicle of Higher Education* observed:

> This year and last [1993–94], documents attacking Mr. Chagnon's scholarship have been sent, some anonymously, to many anthropology departments in the United States, as well as to the National Science Foundation. The documents included newspaper articles critical of him and Mr. Brewer Carías. Some of the anonymous mailings were postmarked in New Rochelle, N.Y., where the Salesians have their U.S. headquarters. Mr. Chagnon says the Salesians are orchestrating a smear campaign against him. Father Cappelletti acknowledges sending some of the materials, but not anonymously. One item Father Cappelletti did send was an English translation of a posting to a computer bulletin board in which Mr. Lizot [the French anthropologist referred to in chapter 1] derides Mr. Chagnon personally and professionally. 'Everyone is sick and tired of the maniac,' Mr. Lizot wrote. (Monaghan 1994)

Seeking resolution of the conflict, Salamone organized a session at the American Anthropological Association Annual Meeting, which he describes: "On December 2, 1994 an extraordinary event took place. . . . Napoleon Chagnon . . . met with Father Jose Bortoli, a Salesian missionary to the Yanomami on the Orinoco River for 20 years" (1997:1). The transcript of the session (published in Salamone 1996) makes evident that the two parties were trying their best to set aside their differences. It all seemed to be working—that is until Terry Turner, a critic of Chagnon, made the following statement during the question period:

> "Professor Chagnon has recently said in print in the American Anthropological Association newsletter that I [Terry Turner] have forfeited all credibility as an anthropologist because I have referred to Davi Kopinawa [*sic*] as a genuine Yanomami leader, where he is only a mouthpiece for NGO's. It's not only a matter of this being false, it's a matter of this undermining the most effective spokesman for Yanomami interests. . . . To undermine him in such an untruthful way, without knowing him and obviously without taking the trouble to analyze the text of his speeches . . . directly damages the interest of the Yanomami. And I submit that this is in apparent contradiction to the ethical dictates of this association" (Salamone 1996:49–50).

When asked if he wanted to reply, Chagnon responded: "You're goddamn right I'd like to. I came here in a spirit of conciliation with an interest in advocating the rights for the Yanomami and I'm going to ignore all of Professor Turner's comments, which I think are out of place in the spirit of what we're attempting to accomplish in this meeting today" (Salamone 1996:50). The transcript stops at this point, but people who were at the session indicated that the confrontation between the two pretty much ended at this point as well. Other people then asked other questions and the ensuing discussion moved off in another direction. No one took up Turner's point regarding whether Chagnon had possibly violated the American Anthropological Association's code of ethics.

The following year, Brian Ferguson published a book entitled *Yanomami Warfare: A Political History.* In the book Ferguson develops a general theory of warfare focusing on the Yanomami as a case study. He asserts that "the existence and variation of actual Yanomami warfare in historical context is explainable largely by reference to changing circumstances of Western contact, which, contrary to established opinion, has been important to the Yanomami for centuries" (1995:xii). He continues: the events of conflict discussed in his book "display a pattern . . . [of] actors . . . [employing] force instrumentally [i.e., using violence] in order to enhance their access to and control over Western goods" (306). Ferguson concludes that "the wars and other conflicts of the middle 1960s—those made famous in *Yanomamö: The Fierce People*—are directly connected to changes in Western presence . . . including the arrival of Chagnon himself" (278).

warfare is because of post-contact

Reviewing Ferguson's book for the *American Anthropologist,* Chagnon writes: "Ferguson comes uncomfortably close to claiming that my presence among the Yanomamö, especially between 1964 and 1970, 'caused' the wars I described, a politically correct and increasingly popular theme in some of the anonymous hate mail denouncing me that has been put into circulation since 1993 and is occasionally claimed in print by some writers" (1996:670). "It is difficult to avoid the conclusion," Chagnon continues, "that much of contemporary cultural anthropology, even the kind of 'scientific' anthropology that Ferguson claims he is doing, is an enterprise that promotes politically correct fairy tales intended to repudiate and denigrate colleagues while solemnly claiming that it is good academic behavior. These activities are now preventing anthropologists from doing fieldwork in many places, including the Yanomamö region" (672).

A PAINFUL CONTRADICTION

Many anthropologists might have missed the 1989 exchange between Carneiro da Cunha and Chagnon. After all, there were thirty-two pages in that issue of the *Anthropology Newsletter.* And many might have missed the session organized at the 1994 AAA Annual Meeting by Salamone. There were over five hundred sessions, workshops, and meetings that year at the gathering. Likewise, there were hundreds of anthropology books published in 1995 along with Ferguson's, and Chagnon's review was one of over fifty in the issue in which it appeared.

But one would find it hard to explain how most anthropologists missed the critical contradiction regarding Chagnon's work that faced the discipline for more than three decades. Without doubt, Chagnon's ethnography has been fantastically successful in terms of sales. No one knows exactly how many copies have been sold. George Spindler, coeditor of the Case Studies in Cultural Anthropology series that published *Yanomamö*, indicated that original sales (sales directly from the publisher) probably numbered around one million. But the book has been sold and resold on the used book market as well. That total is impossible to ascertain, but Spindler suspected that one might well add another one to two million in sales. Sales of the book thus total perhaps three million. (Tierney, citing a quote attributed to Chagnon that appeared in a Brazilian magazine, puts the number between three and four million (2000:8, 331n4). These are phenomenal figures, unmatched by any other anthropological account in the past forty years. "Best-selling" ethnographies sell around forty thousand copies, and most ethnographies usually sell between one and three thousand copies.

Part of the book's success clearly can be attributed to the films, produced in collaboration with Timothy Asch, that complement the book. In their introduction to *Yanomamö*'s third edition, George and Louise Spindler point to the films: "In our extended experience as instructors of introductory anthropology . . . the combination of a challenging, exciting case study and well-executed ethnographic films is unbeatable" (1983:vii). Chagnon's writing style has been important as well. Leslie Sponsel observes: "It is very well written, sprinkled with personal anecdotes and candid reflections, dangerous and heroic adventures, cultural surprise and shock, tragedy and humor, and sex and violence" (1998:101). "We recommend *Yanomamö: the Fierce People*," the Spindlers state, "as one of the most instructive and compelling writings available in anthropology" (1983:viii).

There is only one problem. Chagnon writes against the grain of accepted ethical practice in the discipline. What he describes in detail to millions of readers are just the sorts of practices anthropologists claim they do *not* practice. Let me quote from two introductory textbooks as a way of conveying how anthropologists generally describe their discipline to students. Here is Haviland's popular *Cultural Anthropology* describing an anthropologist's obligations to the people he or she studies: "Because fieldwork requires a relationship of trust between fieldworker and informants, the anthropologist's first responsibility clearly is to his or her informants and their people. Everything possible must be done to protect their physical, social, and psychological welfare and to honor their dignity and privacy. In other words, *do no harm*" (2002:26). In Nanda and Warms's *Cultural Anthropology*, it is described this way: "Anthropologists are always required to reflect on the possible effects of their research on those they study. Three main ethical principles that must guide the field-worker are obtaining the informed consent of the people to be studied, protecting them from risk, and respecting their privacy and dignity" (2002:63).

The American Anthropological Association's "Statement of Ethics" (adopted in 1971 and amended in 1986) reads, under "Relations with those studied": "In research, anthropologists' paramount responsibility is to those they study. When there is a conflict of interest, these individuals must come first. Anthropologists must do everything in their power to protect the physical, social, and psychological welfare and to honor the dignity and privacy of those studied" (AAA 1971/1986). The 1998 "Code of Ethics of the American Anthropological Association" reaffirms this position: "Anthropological researchers must do everything in their power to ensure that their research does not harm the safety, dignity, or privacy of the people with whom they work, conduct research, or perform other professional activities" (AAA 1998:III, A.2).

Note the contrast between these statements and the way Chagnon described his efforts to circumvent the Yanomami name taboo in his genealogical research: "If the informants became angry when I mentioned the new names I acquired from the unfriendly group, I was almost certain that the information was accurate. . . . When I finally spoke the name of the dead woman, [the informant] flew out of his chair, raised his arm to strike me, and shouted: 'You son-of-a-bitch! If you ever say that name again, I'll kill you'" (1968:12–13). In *Studying the Yanomamö*, Chagnon elaborated further: "[Because] I could not expect to easily get the true names of the residents from the residents themselves . . . I had to resort to . . . tactics such as 'bribing' children when their elders were not around, or capitalizing on animosities between individuals, or photographing the people and taking the photos to other villages for identification. . . . There is . . . no better way to get an accurate, reliable start on a genealogy than to collect it from the [person's] enemies" (1974:91, 95).

Chagnon also discussed Yanomamö's reactions to his presence in various villages: "There was great danger, for as my personal relationship with Möawä developed, it grew more tense, and in the end he almost killed me with his ax. . . . I recall vividly the long trek through the gloomy forest to contact Börösöwä's village, and how Börösöwä and his brothers tried to do me in while I slept. . . . And beyond this village lay Tananowä's. . . . I turned back from that trip when Rerebawä told that Tananowä, whom I had never met, vowed to kill me if I ever came to his village, for he concluded that I was practicing harmful magic against him. He, along with some of my Patanowä-teri friends, had made an effigy of me . . . and ceremoniously shot it full of arrows" (1977:153–54). In *Studying the Yanomamö*, Chagnon writes: "My study of the Shamatari groups began with threats to my life and ended that way" (1974:166).

Chagnon's relationships with several informants, in other words, tended at times toward the confrontational—especially in his early years of research. He dedicated himself to collecting data many Yanomami did not want him to have.

James Clifford, in discussing the fieldwork of French anthropologist Marcel Griaule, points out that there are alternative fieldwork styles to the standard Anglo-American model of sympathetic rapport characterized by close relationships and respect. Marcel Griaule emphasized "a recurring conflict of interests [in fieldwork], an agonistic drama, resulting in mutual respect, complicity in a productive balance of power" (Clifford 1983:140). This was Chagnon's style.

Readers need to realize that invading people's privacy and violating their taboos also falls within the bounds of earlier American fieldwork practices. Here is how Eliza McFeely describes the fieldwork of Matilda Stevenson and Frank Cushing among the Zuni of the American Southwest in the 1880s: "In any number of . . . instances, Stevenson bullied her way into ceremonial chambers where she was not welcome; by her own account, she rode roughshod over Zuni guides to make them take her to shrines they wished to keep secret from her. . . . [Cushing characterized his uninvited move into the house of the Pueblo's civil leader] as impetuous and aggressive, casting himself as a hero who was willing to defy common courtesy and potentially hostile hosts in the pursuit of science" (2001:57, 89). But in terms of current American and British standards—as expressed in introductory texts *and* the American Anthropological Association's code of ethics—Chagnon's style of research is anomalous.

It is useful in this context to contrast Chagnon's behavior with that of E. E. Evans-Pritchard under very trying circumstances. During his initial fieldwork among the Nuer of Sudan, Evans-Pritchard found that "the local Nuer would not lend a hand to assist me in anything and they only visited me to ask for tobacco, expressing displeasure when it was denied them. When I shot game to feed myself . . . they took the animals and ate them in the bush, answering my remonstrances with the rejoinder that since the beasts had been killed on their land they had a right to them. . . . When I entered a cattle camp it was not only as a stranger but as an enemy, and they [the Nuer] seldom tried to conceal their disgust at my presence, refusing to answer my greetings and even turning away when I addressed them" (1940:10–11). As for data collection, "After a while the people were prepared to visit me in my tent, to smoke my tobacco, and even to joke and make small talk, but they were unwilling either to receive me in their windscreens [homes] or to discuss serious matters. Questions about customs were blocked." After offering an example of how informants circumvented his questions, he continues, "I defy the most patient ethnologist to make headway against this kind of opposition. One is just driven crazy by it" (1940:12–13).

Yet Evans-Pritchard did not turn to Chagnon's confrontational style. Instead he focused on a few select locales where he could directly observe the Nuer. "As I could not use the easier and shorter method of working through regular informants I had to fall back on direct observation of, and participation in, the everyday life of the people. From the door of my tent I could see what was happening in the camp or village and every moment was spent in Nuer company" (1940:15). Chagnon writes in the preface to the third edition of *Yanomamö* that he visited some sixty villages during his first forty-two months in the field (1983:ix). Given the difficulties he faced in traveling to and dealing with informants in a host of diverse locales, it is—in my opinion—an impressive effort. But why do it? Especially when he notes that "it takes months to establish rapport with individuals in a new group and to discover who the good informants are" (1974:94).

In reading through Chagnon's field exploits, one is led to repeatedly ask, why rush from place to place, generating antagonism here, having people threaten you there, and often being uncertain who is exactly telling you accurate information? Evans-Pritchard was able to get around the problem of recalcitrant informants by staying put in one place for a period and observing everyday life. Chagnon tended to keep moving.

Chagnon explains his mobility in the following terms: "It became increasingly clear that each Yanomamö village was a 'recent' colony or splinter group of some larger village, and a fascinating set of patterns—and problems—began to emerge. . . . The simple discovery of the pattern had a marked influence on my fieldwork: it meant that I would have to travel to many villages in order to document the genealogical aspects of the pattern" (1983:30).

But that is not the only explanation. Through mentions here and there one can piece together another story: Chagnon had to collect the genealogical data needed by Neel to make sense of Neel's massive blood sampling. Chagnon was forced by the terms of his funding through Neel to keep on the go—handing out goods (e.g., 1974:183, 186), collecting genealogies, and then, rather than making a particular village his home, moving on to another village. Rarely does Chagnon provide details of Neel's project. The main reference occurs in a footnote that appears in the second and later editions. The primary description of Chagnon's relation to Neel's blood sampling project by Chagnon comes from *Studying the Yanomamö*. "One of my tasks is to provide my colleagues with minimal genealogies for use in family studies of inherited genes. Since the genealogies are necessary, I am often in the position of having to select my informants from among total strangers and accept what they say" (1974:92). Occasionally in reading Chagnon one detects a frustration with his having to follow a schedule not his own: "I had advised my medical colleagues that to complete *my* [Chagnon's italics] study, I had to have four months of additional research among the Shamatari unencumbered by rigorous airplane schedules and the urgency to get perishable blood samples to point X at time Y" (1974:180).

I have spent some space trying to provide a sense of Chagnon's fieldwork as it comes through from his various accounts. A question that faces us as a discipline is why so few anthropology teachers of introductory classes objected to a fieldwork style that runs counter to what most of them espouse in principle.

In addressing this question, I would note that a sympathetic reading of Chagnon's texts suggest that he himself realized something was amiss in this style of fieldwork. He is at pains in several places to downplay his conflicts with the Yanomamö. In the second edition, for example, he notes: "The reciprocal and generally good-natured mischief with which the Yanomamö and I treated each other during my first 15-month stay among them gradually evolved into a much warmer and more intimate relationship as I returned to live among them nearly every year since I wrote the first edition of *Yanomamö: the Fierce People*" (1977:xii). And resonating with the more general style of American anthropology today, he writes: "The great privilege I have had in my life was to have met people like Kaobawä, Rerebawä, and Dedeheiwä and to learn from them something about the quality of their way of life" (1977:196).

The book has proved so popular in part because of the way Chagnon portrayed himself. He was Indiana Jones before Indiana Jones. Susan Sontag writes of "The Anthropologist as Hero," in which she refers to the way anthropologists use difference to challenge, to cast doubt on our accepted assumptions and habits (1966). But Chagnon represented a different anthropologist as hero. He was the adventurer who overcame a host of physical and social obstacles to return home with "the goods." He domesticated the exotic, the dangerous, in the name of Western science. Observe how he describes his work: "I have nearly been killed by the Yanomamö several times. . . . I knew, in those cases, that it was risky to go to some of the places where this was a possibility, but I was willing to take those known risks" (1992a:238). After mentioning various people who sought to kill him during his fieldwork, he continues: "Suffice it to say that the danger contrasted with and intensified the pleasure of my happier experiences . . . and the enormous amount of valuable new information I collected, . . . information that will contribute to a greater understanding of population dynamics and political processes . . . [and] the role of warfare in the history of our species" (1977:153–54).

Chagnon was able to beat the Yanomamö at their own game: "I soon learned that I had to become very much like the Yanomamö to get along with them on their terms: sly, aggressive, and intimidating" (1968:9). "I developed a very effective means for recovering almost all [of my] . . . stolen items. I would simply ask a child who took the item and then take that person's hammock when he was not around, giving a spirited lecture to the others as I marched away in a faked rage with the thief's hammock" (1968:10).

For American audiences attuned to violence on television and in newspapers, there was more than enough to excite the most jaded of readers. Here was pure adventure. George and Louise Spindler note in their editorial remarks to the first edition that the Yanomamö have "a high capacity for rage, a quick flash point, and a willingness to use violence to obtain one's ends. . . . To the ethnographer it is frightening, frustrating, disgusting, exciting, and rewarding" (1968:vii-viii). "The thing that impressed me most," Chagnon states in the first edition and repeats in later editions, "was the importance of aggression in their culture. I had the opportunity to witness a good many incidents that expressed individual vindictiveness on the one hand and collective bellicosity on the other" (1968:2–3).

And if violence were not enough, there were also provocative statements regarding male-female relations like the following: "Most fighting within the village stems from sexual affairs or failure to deliver a promised woman—or out-and-out seizure of a married woman by some other man" (1983:7). And: "Once raiding has begun between two villages . . . the raiders all hope to acquire women if the circumstances are such that they can flee without being discovered" (1968:123). Of his 1988 *Science* article regarding the relation of violence to reproductive success, Chagnon writes in the fourth edition, " *Unokais* (men who have killed) are more successful at obtaining wives and, as a consequence, have more offspring than men their own age who are not *unokais*" (1992a:205).

It was all there—adventure, violence, and sex à la American—recorded in the name of science. Chagnon's work resonated with large audiences of students in ways that most ethnographies never come close to managing.

Chagnon might well perceive his accounts as simply "telling it like it is." But without additional information that adds greater humanity to the Yanomamö, readers are left with a sense of what is termed orientalism—a playing up of Yanomamö differences in ways that enhance our own power and status at their expense. This is an attitude almost all anthropologists criticize. Remember his first meeting with Yanomami (quoted in chapter 2): "I looked up and gasped when I saw a dozen burly, naked, filthy, hideous men staring at us down the shafts of their drawn arrows!" (1968:5). The description appears in all five editions of his book and is widely anthologized. It reinforces Western images of Amazonian Indians as "primitive" and "savage" compared to us.

To summarize, there is a puzzling contradiction between the espoused aims of anthropology and the overwhelming success of Chagnon's book. I can only conclude that many anthropology teachers and students, caught up in the excitement of Chagnon's work, forgot anthropology's abstract pronouncements regarding appropriate styles of fieldwork and writing. They went for adventure, violence, sex, and, of course, the films.

What Tierney's *Darkness in El Dorado* did was to expose this contradiction to the whole world. No wonder Tierney's book made a lot of anthropologists mad. Whatever Tierney's mistakes—and there clearly are mistakes—he pointed out a contradiction anthropologists had grown comfortable with. There was something almost inevitable about Tierney's exposé. The contradiction was too obvious not to be commented upon eventually. But it took an outsider—a journalist— aided and abetted by the media to make anthropologists take note. Many anthropologists seemed willing to ignore the whole problem.

THE AMERICAN ANTHROPOLOGICAL ASSOCIATION'S AMBIVALENT RESPONSE

As discussed in the previous section, the discipline—viewing it as a collective group for the moment—knew about the problems surrounding Chagnon's fieldwork years before the publication of Tierney's book. But the American Anthropological Association resisted investigating them. It responded mostly with a cascade of nice-sounding abstractions followed by little concrete action. The leaders of the association took steps in the wake of the media storm generated by *Darkness in El Dorado* that at first continued this pattern.

While Tierney's book was still in prepublication galleys, Terry Turner and Les Sponsel wrote a confidential e-mail memo to the president (Louise Lamphere) and president-elect (Don Brenneis) of the AAA as well as to the chair of the Committee for Human Rights (Barbara Johnston). At the behest of Johnston, Turner writes, "we agreed to send a second version to the Chair of the Ethics Committee and the Presidents of the . . . Societies of Latin American Anthropology and Latino and Latina Anthropology" (Turner 2000b:2). Somehow, one of these e-mails was passed on to someone else who, in turn, forwarded it on to others. The process snowballed and within perhaps forty-eight hours the memo had circled the world. Within another forty-eight hours, most of the discipline knew about it.

Turner states in a September 28, 2000, letter to Dr. Samuel Katz that "the sole purpose of the memo was to describe . . . [Tierney's] allegations, in order to warn the leaders of the association of the nature of the allegations that were about to be published" (Turner 2000b). The Turner-Sponsel memo begins: "We write to inform you [i.e., the leaders of the AAA] of an impending scandal that will affect the American Anthropological profession as a whole in the eyes of the public and arouse intense indignation and calls for action among members of the Association." In elaborating on these accusations, the gap between Tierney's assertions and what Turner and Sponsel accepted of them got lost. Turner and Sponsel referred to Tierney's "convincing evidence" and to his "well-documented account." They also sought to catch the AAA's attention with a few provocative turns of phrase. For example, they refer to Tierney's account as a "nightmarish story—a real anthropological heart of darkness beyond the imagining of even Josef Conrad." (One might suspect that they felt frustrated, given the years the issue had been ignored, and wanted to ensure that the AAA leadership understood the importance of Tierney's accusations.) Turner and Sponsel were certainly right about one thing: as they suggested, Tierney's accusations became seen "by the public, as well as most anthropologists, as putting the whole discipline on trial" (Turner and Sponsel 2000).

Turner and Sponsel were both well versed in the controversy surrounding Chagnon's fieldwork. Both had talked to Tierney about it. It is understandable, then, that Turner would write that "Tierney's accounts of . . . [Chagnon's] activities checked out with what we knew, although Tierney provided much new data." According to Turner, Tierney kept the accusations about Neel "under authorial wraps for as long as possible" (Turner 2000b). Turner and Sponsel found out about them only when they read the final galleys of Tierney's book in August 2000, just before the book's publication. Turner and Sponsel assumed that if the accusations they knew about were correct, then the new ones about Neel—which they were not familiar with—probably should be taken seriously.

It turns out they were too hasty in making that assumption. As Turner explains, once the "confidential" memo had been sent to the AAA leadership, he and Sponsel turned to investigating Tierney's specific accusations against Neel.

> After sending the memo, we set out to check for ourselves on the most sensational (and to us, the most unfamiliar) of Tierney's allegations (that the vaccination campaign, through the vaccine it used, had actually started the measles epidemic). Experts we consulted confirmed that the consensus of medical opinion was that a vaccine could not cause contagious cases of the disease against which it immunizes. This appeared to contradict the possibility that Dr. Neel could have caused

the epidemic through the vaccinations, either deliberately or accidentally. . . . Both Sponsel and I have made a point, in our contacts with journalists and the media, of repudiating irresponsible media reports of "genocide," or any intention to cause death as part of an experimental plan, by Dr. Neel or anyone else connected with the expedition. (Turner 2000b)

But it was too late. Given the discipline's past resistance to addressing the controversy surrounding Chagnon, one might have predicted what transpired next. Rather than engaging with the substance of Turner and Sponsel's message—that negative publicity was about to hit the discipline—some sought to shoot the messengers. For them, Turner and Sponsel's memo became the scandal.

Instead of confronting the breadth of issues raised by Tierney and the media, many anthropologists focused on Tierney's accusations regarding Neel and on the Turner-Sponsel memo. As previously noted, focusing on Neel had a particular advantage for those who wanted to continue sidestepping the role of anthropologists in all this. Neel was a geneticist, and soon after the book's publication most experts realized that the accusation that Neel helped facilitate the spread measles was false. Focusing on Neel allowed anthropologists to downplay the role of the discipline in the whole affair.

Still, the American Anthropological Association clearly heard Turner and Sponsel's message regarding the approaching whirlwind of negative publicity. The first recorded AAA response, entitled "Statement on Allegations Made in the Book *Darkness in El Dorado*" reads in part: "The American Anthropological Association is aware of the publication of the book *Darkness in El Dorado* by Patrick Tierney. The book makes serious allegations. . . . If proven true they would constitute a serious violation of Yanomami human rights and our Code of Ethics. . . . The Association is anticipating conducting an open forum during our Annual Meeting to provide an opportunity for our members to review and discuss the issues and allegations raised in the book" (AAA n.d.).

The issue of having an open forum is discussed further in another statement from the American Anthropological Association dated October 19, 2000, and entitled "Questions and Answers."

Q: Why is the AAA holding an open forum regarding the allegations?
A: . . . As a scientific and professional organization we are committed to a fair and impartial discussion of the issues raised by the book. . . .
Q: How does the AAA respond to the accusations that the forum is one-sided?
A: These charges are absolutely false. We are holding an open forum at our Annual Meeting in November designed to include both sides of this controversy, as well as impartial experts in the field, so that the allegations and issues which they raise can be fairly debated and discussed among our members. (AAA 2000a)

Before the open forum, the Executive Board decided to "establish a Special Ad Hoc Task Force of seven members, six of which will be appointed by the AAA President from among the members of the Committee on Ethics and the

Committee for Human Rights, chaired by AAA Past President James Peacock, and charged . . . to examine assertions and allegations contained in Darkness in El Dorado as well as others related to the controversy" (AAA 2000c). The basic conclusion of the Ad Hoc Task Force, as reported by the Executive Board, was that "it finds many of the allegations made in the Tierney book to have such serious implications for anthropologists and for the Yanomami that they are deserving of further attention from the AAA" (AAA 2000c). The Ad Hoc Task Force, in other words, reiterated the basic point of the Turner-Sponsel memo. But there was a critical difference. The AAA labeled this report confidential. And when the AAA said confidential, it meant confidential. No copy of the report has ever been made public. Nor, for that matter, has the full membership of the Ad Hoc Task Force been made public.

An open forum was held on November 16 at the annual meeting. Was the open forum balanced? Did it, as claimed, "include both sides of this controversy, as well as impartial experts in the field?" If this occurred, then the majority of the members present missed it. This is how the forum was perceived by one person there:

> I thought at first that so many panelists meant that Tierney and Chagnon's sides were each to be heard. Not. Tierney was isolated and visibly distanced at one end of the elongated panel table. . . . [Napoleon Chagnon] was represented by Dr. Irons, seated to the left. That led me to expect that the three women sitting to the right of the podium must be taking Tierney's perspective. Wrong. One after another, each panelist rose to excoriate Tierney over mistakes they claimed he had made, over his determination to "prevent" scientific medical research to aid remote indigenous people, and all kinds of other positions I had never heard or read that he had taken. . . . They . . . seemed to merge rumor and published text together into an intertextual morass which amounted more to diatribe than to critique (Curran and Takata 2000).

The writer wasn't alone in feeling that the session was slanted against Tierney. Reporters at the open forum had a similar impression. Geri Smith wrote in *Business Week*: "Tierney underwent a four-hour grilling at the November AAA . . . special symposium called to discuss his book" (2000:24). John Noble Wilford of the *New York Times* reported "Mr. Tierney bore the brunt of attack when appearing on a panel on Thursday and at a news conference afterward" (2000:24).

What happened? Not only were the panelists stacked against Tierney but they mostly focused on the accusations surrounding Neel—accusations that no one involved in the controversy besides Tierney still clung to. Only Irons— Chagnon's chosen defender at the session—spoke at any length regarding Chagnon. If there were significant critiques of Chagnon or Neel at the session by speakers other than Tierney, then the press, and many at the meeting, including myself, missed them.

One might well have assumed from the Thursday night open forum that Tierney's key arguments had been thoroughly refuted. In fact, of course, only the

argument regarding Neel helping to facilitate the spread of measles had really
been criticized, and that had been refuted weeks before. To those versed in the
controversy, it looked like beating a dead horse. From the open forum, one would
have thought that Chagnon had played only a minor role in the book, that almost
all of Tierney's accusations centered on Neel.

The next night, the AAA allowed an open mike session on the controversy.
Instead of a stage-managed panel with presentations slanted in a particular direction, individuals were free to line up and offer three-minute statements. Miller,
in the *Chronicle of Higher Education*, summarizes what happened: "Although no
one offered a four-square endorsement of Mr. Tierney's facts or conclusions,
many of the 20 or so speakers took the microphone to fault Mr. Chagnon in particular and anthropologists in general for questionable conduct in the field"
(2000a).

The AAA Executive Board, at its meeting on February 3 and 4, 2001, established an El Dorado Task Force based on the recommendations of the private Ad
Hoc Task Force report. Louise Lamphere, the AAA president, described the purpose of the task force in the *Anthropology Newsletter*: "The Board designated the
work of the task force as an inquiry, not an investigation. We are not the American Bar Association; we do not license our members, nor do we have a process
in place by which we can impose sanctions. Our concern is with the book Patrick
Tierney has written and the allegations he makes. The Task Force will gather evidence from a broad variety of sources: AAA members, the book's author and key
anthropologists mentioned in the book. . . . The Task Force . . . will gather information in a fair and open manner and will carefully consider evidence that either
substantiates Tierney's allegations or casts doubt on them" (2001:59).

The Executive Board's report for February 3 and 4, 2001, states:

> Members of the Task Force were appointed by the AAA President. The Chair, Jane
> H. Hill (Arizona) is a linguistic anthropologist specializing in American Indian
> languages, and former President of AAA. Fernando Coronil (Michigan) is a cultural
> anthropologist specializing in the Venezuelan state. Janet Chernela (Florida
> International University) is a cultural anthropologist specializing in Amazonian
> indigenous societies. Trudy Turner (Wisconsin-Milwaukee) is a biological anthro-
> pologist specializing in genetics of non-human primates and in ethics. Joe Watkins
> (Bureau of Indian Affairs) is an archaeologist specializing in relations between
> Indians and archaeologists and in the involvement of Indian people in archaeol-
> ogy and anthropology. Watkins is Chair of the AAA Ethics Committee. (2001c)

I want to deal with the question of why President Lamphere chose these five
people, since a major critique of the Task Force is that it did not interview at
length many of the key anthropologists mentioned in the book (or even Tierney).
There was no open discussion regarding the selection. And only Janet Chernela
had, in any real sense, experience with the Amazon region; she had some interaction with a Brazilian NGO working with the Yanomami and had studied an

unrelated Tukanoan group some distance from the Yanomami. Fernando Coronil, a citizen of Venezuela, had extensive expertise on Venezuelan politics but little on the Yanomami. Joe Watkins, a Choctaw Indian, works on the archaeology of the southern Great Plains and relations between Native Americans and archaeologists. Trudy Turner specializes in the life history of vervet Monkeys in Africa as well as genetic diversity and ethics. Jane Hill works on Native American languages of the Uto-Aztecan family (spoken in Mexico and the United States).

In other words, no one on the original Task Force had extensive field experience with the Yanomami. In the summer of 2000, under what she refers to as pressure from the Chagnon camp for a more balanced Task Force, Lamphere added a sixth member, Ray Hames. A student of Chagnon, Hames has conducted extensive fieldwork among the Ye'kwana and Yanomami Indians of Venezuela.

One might recognize that the membership of the Task Force represents all four of anthropology's subfields. Affirming the value of subfield integration has been a continuing theme of the AAA in recent years as specialization has pushed different subfields in different directions and threatened the unity of the AAA (see Borofsky 2002). Viewed in structural-functionalist terms, in this time of stress the AAA leadership sought to reaffirm disciplinary solidarity. However, it is not readily apparent that either archaeological or linguistic issues were central to the controversy.

There is another, more political, way to look at the Task Force's composition. One needs to be careful, though: students do not necessarily follow the opinions of their teachers in lockstep. But readers should be aware of the relationships that exist. Coronil was a student of Terry Turner, who has been a critic of Chagnon. Trudy Turner held a postdoctoral fellowship in 1981–82 in the Department of Human Genetics, University of Michigan. Though she claims never to have had close contact with Neel, who headed the department the year Turner began her fellowship, she has proved to be a strong defender of Neel. Hames, as previously noted, was a student of Chagnon. Chernela was chair-elect of the AAA's Committee for Human Rights at the time, and Joe Watkins was chair of the AAA's Committee on Ethics. (Only in the final report do we learn that both Watkins and Chernela were members of the Ad Hoc Task Force Committee.) Hill, an honored past president who was not seen as affiliated with any particular camp, wrote the first piece on the controversy published in the *Anthropology News*: "Is it possible to turn this public-relations disaster not only into a 'teachable moment' inside the profession but into an unforeseen opportunity to get out the good word about anthropology and anthropologists?" (2000:5).

Aside from trying to respond to the concerns of Chagnon's supporters with the selection of Hames (to balance the selection of Coronil, perceived by supporters of Chagnon to be in the opposite camp), Lamphere downplays the politics of her selections. She conveys in personal conversations a sense of wanting to get on with the task with a reasonable set of people who would represent a fair sampling of the constituencies involved. Still, many involved in the controversy found the selections problematic. Why were more experts on the Yanomami not brought in, for example? Hames's selection upset many. In fairness to Hames, it should be noted that he did not want to be on the Task Force. Lamphere had asked two other behavioral ecologists (with little experience with the Yanomami), and both had turned her down. Hames had recommended John Peters (a participant in this book's part 2 discussion) because of his in-depth experience with the Yanomami. But Lamphere rejected Peters. Given this context, Hames felt, despite his reservations, that he should help, since the Task Force obviously needed someone with knowledge of the Yanomami.

By mid-2001, the Task Force had begun seriously going about the business of collecting information and framing a preliminary report. An understanding of how it proceeded in this process is critical. Following established academic style, different Task Force members took on different assignments. They specialized in areas of particular interest. Trudy Turner, for example, was assigned the accusations surrounding Neel; Fernando Coronil, the accusations surrounding Chagnon's work with FUNDAFACI (the Foundation to Aid Peasant and Indigenous Families, which sought to set up a private Yanomami reserve in Venezuela). Ray Hames examined Chagnon's involvement in Yanomami warfare.

We need to note four problems with the process. First, the report indicates that each of these people took positions that might have been expected of them given their backgrounds. The side taking was not blatant. Much detailed data and many citations were mustered to support the varying perspectives. But there were few surprises. No one collected piles of information and then took a totally new position based on that material. At best, there was a slight softening of positions, an offering of subtleties and complexities to go with the perspectives that outsiders to the Task Force assumed specific individuals would take.

Second, there was little systematic investigation of topics from divergent perspectives. Coronil and Hames, for example, did not both study FUNDAFACI but turned their attention to different topics. As a result, members had to rely mostly on the information a particular person collected if they wished to challenge that person's conclusions. They had no independent, confirming source to assess another member's analysis.

To make matters worse, there were no public hearings where scholars more familiar with the data than those on the Task Force could challenge the position statements being drawn up. It was all done hush-hush, mostly in private with only the occasional leak.

Third, we come back to the Task Force's composition. In my opinion, having Ray Hames on the Task Force was a sound idea. He was thoroughly familiar with the controversy. But why not have other experts similarly versed in these matters on the Task Force as well? Why, for example, was John Peters rejected? The critical weakness of the Task Force, I would suggest, is that there was no engagement between experts deeply versed in the subject—as occurs in part 2 of this book. It was mostly well-intentioned people holding to positions that, some would suggest, were formulated well before the members ever met as a Task Force.

4) Fourth, the Task Force's preliminary report obscured who wrote what. It was presented as a consensus of the collective Task Force, though it was later discovered that two Task Force members had not even read it. The *Chronicle of Higher Education* provides the best account of what unfolded when the preliminary report was publicly presented at the AAA Annual Meeting in November 2001: "Two of the six members of the panel that is studying the controversy said they have not endorsed the report, and one asked that it be withdrawn. . . . [Mr. Coronil] urged his colleagues to refashion the report as a series of working papers credited to the individuals who had done research on each issue. 'As far as I'm concerned, the report was not discussed,' he concluded, to . . . [a] round of sustained applause" (Miller 2001). As for the preliminary report itself, it "essentially exonerated the late James V. Neel . . . of Mr. Tierney's charges that he had exacerbated a deadly measles epidemic in 1968 and withheld treatment from sick Yanomami in order to further a research experiment. . . . But Mr. Tierney had spent several chapters describing the alleged transgressions of Mr. Chagnon. In its investigation of these charges, the committee has so far cleared Mr. Chagnon of a few of the most serious charges, criticized him for a few relatively minor lapses in judgment, and left other allegations unaddressed" (Miller 2001). Critics of the Task Force cried whitewash.

The uproar that followed the preliminary report brought about two positive outcomes: First, at its next meeting, in February 2002, the Task Force decided to openly acknowledge who wrote which sections of the report. An author's positioning was no longer obscured by the Task Force supposedly speaking with a collective voice. (At this point, they clearly did not.) Second, and, more critically, the Task Force decided to open up the preliminary report for public comment by way of the Web. People were encouraged to voice their opinions—in a place where all could see them—regarding the strengths and weaknesses of the preliminary report.

This decision transformed the debate. The chief antagonists on both sides had, in many ways, stopped listening—that is, honestly listening—to one another. In their rebuttals they would acknowledge some detail in the other's position and then reframe the issues in terms advantageous to themselves. Most of the time they talked past one another when they talked to each other at all.

To the surprise of many, over 170 comments were put up on the Web site between March 1 and April 19. One hundred nineteen students weighed in with one or more assessments of the report (compared with 36 professors). These students' statements helped transform the debate. The responses made clear that a lot of people were discussing the Task Force's report in very public ways. Because the student comments could not be precisely pigeonholed into this or that camp, they drew Task Force members into focusing on the common public good rather than on placating this or that constituency.

The involvement of a large number of students clearly shook things up. To my knowledge, nothing like this had ever occurred in the history of the discipline. A long dormant and often de-emphasized part of the association was making its opinions felt. It was "student power" in action. No one on the Task Force that I talked to felt that such an outpouring from students could be dismissed— in sharp contrast to members' reactions to positions taken by key figures on one or the other side of the debate. More was involved here than just principle. Anthropologists and journalists from around the world were also reading these comments, which were a matter of public record. Who wanted to be caught ignoring such a massive public outpouring?

While the students' positions varied widely, they tended to be more critical of Chagnon than the Task Force was. Several astutely critiqued the Task Force itself. (One suggested there should be a new task force to write a report on the errors of the current one.)

As a result of the Web postings, Ray Hames, who had always been ambivalent about being on the Task Force, resigned. In his resignation letter he says, "My association with Chagnon presents the appearance of bias. Consequently, I feel it is in the best interest of the American Anthropological Association that I resign from the Task Force. . . . The goal of the Task Force is to produce an accurate and unbiased appraisal of ethical research practices by anthropologists among the Yanomamö. Any false perception that this goal was not met can only harm our association and vitiate the findings of the Task Force" (2002). It was an honest assessment—especially given the lack of effort to balance his perspectives with those of other Yanomami experts holding different views.

Another result of the student outpouring was that members of the Task Force at their next meeting (in April 2002) started to reach across their differences and explore the possibility of developing a real consensus on certain issues—particularly relating to Chagnon, who all along, with a strong set of supporters, was the most problematic figure to investigate. People began to carefully listen to one another and seek out shared points of agreement. Ideally they would have brought Yanomami experts as well as a host of Yanomami into their discussion (or at least used a speakerphone to collectively ask the Yanomami questions in Roraima, Brazil, for example). Still, as a result of the student outpouring, Task Force members turned toward more seriously addressing the problems Tierney had raised regarding Chagnon than many critics thought possible.

Chagnon deserves better than death by a thousand small cuts. He should not have to contend with unsubstantiated innuendo. He deserves a fair chance to address the accusations against him in open court where others, too, can see what he is being accused of and why. Because Chagnon has refused to participate in such discussions, part 2 of this book constitutes the most open, balanced discussion we are likely to have on this matter in the foreseeable future. It is not perfect. But, more so than in the Task Force's final report (see chapter 11), it gives readers the information to draw their own conclusions regarding the controversy's central issues. It is *not* done for them by a special task force meeting in private.

4

....

BROADER ISSUES AT STAKE
IN THE CONTROVERSY

Different anthropologists define cultural anthropology in slightly different ways. Kroeber, in his classic 1948 introductory text, *Anthropology*, observes that cultural anthropology "sometimes . . . seems preoccupied with ancient and savage and exotic and extinct peoples. The cause is a desire to understand better all civilizations" (1948:4). Felix Keesing in 1958, writes that "the cultural anthropologist looks at human behavior comparatively" (1958:v). His son Roger, almost twenty years later, suggests that cultural anthropology is "concerned with the study of human customs: that is, the comparative study of cultures and societies . . . especially what used to be called 'primitive' peoples" (1976:3). Kottak says that "cultural anthropologists study society and culture, describing, analyzing, and explaining social and cultural similarities and differences" (1997:5–6). If one does a little bit of editing here and there, adjusting this phrasing, adapting that, the definitions clearly overlap.

But more interesting than the fact that the definitions overlap is what they all leave out. Since its disciplinary beginnings, cultural anthropology has tended to be the study of less powerful groups by scholars from more powerful groups. Whether you phrase it as the First World studying the Third, "us" studying "them," or the richer studying the poorer, there is almost always a power differential involved. Those with more power are usually studying those with less.

Anthropologists do not return empty-handed from their research. They return with knowledge that they then systematically circulate to others in the form of publications and lectures. In most cases, this knowledge circulation enhances their careers. Few anthropologists make thousands of dollars from their publications and lectures. (Chagnon is a rare exception in this regard.) But most anthropologists make hundreds of thousands of dollars over their careers, and those careers are enhanced by their publications. The publications constitute critical stepping-stones for professional advancement.

The less powerful give something of value to the more powerful who are studying them. Anthropologists—out of respect, kindness, guilt, or a combination of all three—tend to provide a host of compensating gifts. But rarely, if ever, do these gifts add up to the monetary value anthropologists earn as they advance through their academic careers based on visiting and writing about the less powerful.

This is not to say the power differential goes unnoticed. It is widely perceived by all the parties involved. This dynamic gets expressed in the writings of indigenous activists. One such activist, Hereniko, asks: "'Do outsiders have the right to speak for and about Pacific Islanders? . . . Westerners seem to think they have the right to express opinions (sometimes labeled truths) about cultures that are not their own in such a way that they appear to know it from the inside out. . . . The least that outsiders can do . . . is to invite indigenous Pacific Islanders, whenever possible, to share the space with them, either as copresenters or as discussants or respondents. Not to do so is to perpetuate unequal power relations between colonizer and colonized'" (quoted in Borofsky 2000:86). Prins notes that "'the image made in Accra to commemorate the achievement of political independence by Ghana shows the fleeing agents of colonialism. Along with the [administrative] District Officer is the anthropologist, clutching under his arm a copy of Fortes and Evans-Pritchard's *African Political Systems'*" (quoted in Kuper and Kuper 1985:870).

Some anthropologists acknowledge the problem in their writings. Lévi-Strauss observes, "It is an historical fact that anthropology was born and developed in the shadow of colonialism" (1994:425). Asad says, "It is not a matter of dispute that social anthropology emerged as a distinctive discipline at the beginning of the colonial era, that it became a flourishing academic profession towards its close, or that throughout this period its efforts were devoted to a description and analysis—carried out by Europeans, for a European audience—of non-European societies dominated by European power" (1973:14–15). Anthropology is, he continues "rooted in an unequal power encounter . . . that gives the West access to cultural and historical information about the societies it has progressively dominated" (16–17).

We should be cautious here. The broad outline is clear, but there are shades of gray that also need to be taken into account. Clifford notes that while colonial domination framed most anthropological accounts of times past, anthropologists "adopted a range of liberal positions within it. Seldom 'colonists' in any direct instrumental sense, ethnographers accepted certain constraints while, in varying degrees, questioning them" (1983:142).

What concerns me here is how anthropologists, once they acknowledge this power differential, tend to respond to it. Many offer various forms of appreciation to informants: gifts, money, and/or help. A decent percentage of anthropologists, moreover, continue contact with informants long after they, the anthropologists, have left the field. Interestingly, pre–World War II *American Anthropologists* published obituaries of key informants. This suggests that many informants held honorable, publicly acknowledged places within the discipline during this period.

But at a broader level, the abstract formulations anthropologists offer for

addressing this power differential, while frequently sounding nice, tend to perpetuate the power structures. Let me illustrate my point with the anthropological injunction to "do no harm." The injunction draws power from the
Hippocratic dictum "As to disease make a habit of two things—to help, or at
least, to do no harm" (*Epidemics* I. II). The 1998 Anthropological Association
statement on ethics asserts that "anthropological researchers must do everything
in their power to ensure that their research does not harm the safety, dignity, or
privacy of the people with whom they work, conduct research, or perform other
professional activities (AAA 1998).

But when things are falling apart politically and economically in a society, is
doing no harm a reasonable standard to follow? There is self-absorption in the
"do no harm" framing: the injunction implies that we—the outsiders, the westerners, the powerful—are the major source of other people's troubles. If we
leave others alone, everything should be fine. In the case discussed below, the
troubles of the Ik people in Uganda did not stem from actions by the West but
from specific actions by the Ugandan government.

What does "do no harm" mean when informants have been suffering—perhaps for decades—before you arrive? Do you help lessen the pain, the problems?
Or do you simply sidestep the pains, believing that since you did not cause them,
they are not your problem?

The Ik offer a good illustration of the issues involved. Bordering on starvation, the Ik were falling apart as a society when Colin Turnbull studied them. The
back cover of the 1987 paperback edition of Turnbull's book explains: "In *The
Mountain People*, Colin M. Turnbull . . . describes the dehumanization of the Ik,
African tribesmen who in less than three generations have deteriorated from
being once-prosperous hunters to scattered bands of hostile, starving people
whose only goal is individual survival. . . . Drought and starvation have made
them a strange, heartless people, . . . their days occupied with constant competition and the search for food."

How does one respond to a situation such as this? Appiah ponders the question why "the former general secretary of Racial Unity [i.e., Turnbull] had done
so little to intervene? Why had he not handed over more of his own rations?
Taken more children to the clinic in his Land Rover? Gone to the government
authorities and told them that they needed to allow the Ik back into their hunting grounds or give them more food?" (2000:58).

Turnbull took a group-dictated letter to government authorities at Moroto
regarding the Ik's plight. "I delivered the letter and a report of my own, without
much conviction that either would carry any weight" (1987:109). And when they
apparently did not, he went off to the capital, Kampala, to stock up with fresh
supplies for himself. That was it: no insistence, no pleading, no seeking to bring
pressure on local authorities from those higher up, no public exposé with the
hope of helping the Ik (see also Grinker 2000:166). What Turnbull did in his
book, instead, is offer a general reflection on the state of humanity: "Most of us
are unlikely to admit readily that we can sink as low as the Ik, but many of us

do, and with far less cause. . . . Although the experience was far from pleasant, and involved both physical and mental suffering, I am grateful for it. In spite of it all, . . . the Ik teach us that our much vaunted human values are not inherent in humanity at all, but are associated only with a particular form of survival called society, and that all, even society itself, are luxuries that can be dispensed with" (1987:12, 294; see also Grinker 2000:156, 163).

Keeping the issue at an abstract level—doing no harm, reflecting on what the Ik teach us about ourselves—means the power differential is never addressed. The anthropologist remains an observer of other people's suffering and, in Turnbull's case, deaths. This standard allows anthropologists to claim the high road of morality—they have not caused ill by their presence—while letting the sufferings of the status quo prevail.

I want to emphasize that there is no simple answer to resolving the power differentials embedded in the ethnographic endeavor. It is not from want of caring that the problem remains the uninvited guest in most anthropological publications and most anthropological meetings. Most anthropologists care about helping those who so caringly helped them.

But what constitutes help? One might share one's income with one's informants. But would they do the same if the positions were reversed? And is money the answer—a framing of the field relationship in terms of capitalistic exchange? Or is some kind of continued caring more sensible: a partaking of each other's proffered gifts through time?

In his *Theory of Justice* and *Justice as Fairness*, the late political philosopher John Rawls offers a framework for finding our way through the complexities. Rawls asserts: "The fair terms of social cooperation are to be given by an agreement entered into by those engaged with it." Given people may not "agree on any moral authority, say a sacred text or a religious institution or tradition. . . . What better alternative is there than an agreement between . . . [people] themselves reached under conditions that are [perceived as] fair to all?" (2001:15). Rawls is saying that concerns over compensation need to be resolved by the parties themselves. Given that the two parties often come from different backgrounds and likely possess differing values, they need to find points of common reference if they are to build a mutually satisfying relationship.

Rawls emphasizes that these discussions need to be more than negotiated exchanges. They need to involve a concern for a shared sense of justice. He assumes that the parties—with their different perspectives—are positioned behind "a veil of ignorance" where "they do not know how the various alternatives [they are discussing] will affect their own particular case and they are obliged to evaluate [the] principles of who will get what solely on the basis of general considerations" (1971:136–37). In other words, both sides must establish the terms of their relationship with each other not knowing which side they ultimately will be on—the one they bargained for, or the other. "No one knows his place in society, his class position or social status . . . and the like" (137).

Rawls's point, adapted to the ethnographic endeavor, means establishing a just sense of engagement based on shared discussions. True, the anthropologist, having a clearer sense of the value gained from his fieldwork in relation to the rewards returned to informants, is likely to be at an advantage in such discussions. But following Rawls we might ask what would be a fair agreement for the anthropologist if he found himself on the other side of the relationship, if he were the informant? Start with the possibility that the tables could be reversed, Rawls is suggesting, and seek a just solution based on that.

There is the question of continued ties. Is it reasonable to simply grab what one can, strew gifts here and there, and then vanish? Or is the ethnographic endeavor—perhaps started in the field-worker's youth—something that endures through the years, even when the anthropologist does not necessarily visit informants or they him? Might one view the issue also as a matter of knowledge exchange? Informants provide anthropologists with the data (or tools) they need to write thoughtful publications. Might anthropologists, in turn, provide informants with the tools to effectively engage with the injustices, inequities, and diseases they face on an ongoing basis?

What is critical here is that the terms of the negotiation be public: that they be included in the publications themselves. It is important that others who live in the society, who read the publication, or who later visit the locale studied have an opportunity to understand on what terms the anthropologist gathered the information being presented in his or her publications. The power differentials do not disappear here. They are embedded in structures both parties to the ethnographic relationship will likely not change—short of a revolution that neither will likely lead. But the differentials are acknowledged, softened through a negotiated, fair exchange, and made public so others can understand and assess the exchange.

THE PROBLEMATIC WAYS IN WHICH ANTHROPOLOGISTS SEEK TO RESOLVE CONTROVERSIES

When accusations fly back and forth—as they do in this controversy—how do anthropologists make their way through the torrent of words, the thicket of argumentation? Anthropologists generally rely on certain signs of credibility. They assess credibility in the work of others in a number of ways.

First and foremost, anthropologists pay attention to whether the researcher "was there." A researcher is more credible if he or she has lived in a particular locale and interacted with people there. Chagnon uses this technique to make his work more credible. In the first edition of *Yanomamö: The Fierce People*, he writes "I spent a total of twenty-three months in South America of which nineteen were spent among the Yanomamö" (1968:1). And in the fifth edition, he writes: "To date I have spent 63 months among the Yanomamö" (1997:viii). To make sure readers understand that he was seriously at work during this time—because he could conceivably have spent much of his time lounging around taking in the sights—he reinforces his expertise with personal anecdotes, statistics, and photos. In *Studying the*

Yanomamö, Chagnon presents interviews (1974:80–82), detailed genealogies (100, 134), computer printouts (109), photographs (114), and tables (131, 136). All these data convey an important message: Chagnon knows what he is talking about.

Tierney uses the same technique. He includes a host of personal, first-hand experiences with Yanomami to reinforce his critique of Chagnon. He writes, for example, "The real shock came when I visited a village on the Mucajaí River in Brazil, where Chagnon claimed to have discovered a Yanomami group that embodied the tribe's ultimate form of 'treachery.' In reality, these Indians had lived in relative harmony for more than a century. I was amazed to find that Chagnon had even created his own topography—moving a mountain where one did not exist and landing cargo planes where they had never touched down—while quoting people he could never have spoken to in this part of the jungle" (2000:8). Tierney also offers tables full of data (2000:165, 321). Tierney's point is that he too has first-hand knowledge of the Yanomami.

Second, anthropologists give credence to work that presents new research material. For example, Chagnon writes that his field research involved traveling "further and further into uncontacted regions attempting to document political histories of specific villages " (1983:ix). Chagnon, in studying what appear to be previously uncontacted people, gathers new information—information that should allow us to gain further insight into the Yanomami. Tierney claims to have uncovered new information as well: data relating to the specific villages and individuals referred to in Chagnon's famous *Science* article. He suggests that Chagnon overstates the Yanomami's murder and marriage patterns in the article. The dust jacket on Tierney's book asserts: "Tierney, who gained access to dozens of unedited audio tapes of documentaries, provides an astonishing link between the Atomic Energy Commission and . . . [Chagnon's] anthropological forays." In offering new material, anthropologists seem more credible than if they simply restate what others have asserted.

Third, anthropologists look for references to the work of other scholars: generally, the greater the number of sources cited, the more credible the work. By this standard, no one comes close to Tierney. He has more than 1,590 footnotes. He cites more than 250 books, dissertations, and magazine articles; 8 government documents; 13 films and documentaries; 36 unpublished sources; and more than 90 interviews.

A fourth technique for establishing credibility is to build one's new material on accepted knowledge (cf. Shapin 1994). If a new account overlaps with already accepted material, then it tends to be seen as credible to others. This is what occurred when Turner and Sponsel wrote their memo. Turner and Sponsel were familiar with many of Tierney's accusations against Chagnon; they had made similar charges themselves. So why not take Tierney's accusations regarding Neel equally seriously? Tierney seemed a credible researcher—based in the material of his they had read.

A fifth way to establish credibility is to speak from a position of status. People with high status tend to be seen as more credible than those with lower status.

A good example is Clifford Geertz. Because he seems to have limited knowledge of the Yanomami or the whole controversy, one might wonder why he should review Tierney's *Darkness in El Dorado* for the *New York Review of Books* and offer his assessment of the controversy. The answer is that he is one of the best-recognized anthropologists in the United States. His aura of credibility extends beyond his areas of expertise.

"Hard charges," Geertz suggests, "demand hard evidence, or, failing that, at least an enormous mass of it." Tierney's effort in this direction, he continues, "is uneven, in many places vague or insubstantial, and in some, it is, as the critics have charged, simply unfair—ideologized second-guessing. But, as the instances accumulate and their implications come home, it all, in some strange way, begins to add up. Whatever caused the measles epidemic . . . a case gets made, however clumsily, that something was seriously amiss in the relation between these confident and determined *soi-disant* 'scientists' with their cameras, their vials, their syringes, and their notebooks and the beset and puzzled, put-upon 'natives' to whom they looked for facts to fill them with" (2001:20).

About placing blame on anthropologists, Geertz writes: "Given all that has happened to the Yanomami over the past half-century, encountering anthropologists . . . surely ranks as historical small change, a very small blip on a very large curve. . . . They have been plagued by a good deal more than measles which, however grave, are a one-time thing" (2001:21). It all sounds, well, authoritative. He seems to be speaking with the confidence of competence.

But should we trust such techniques? They make sense to most anthropologists, but there are flaws and fallacies in each of the techniques that need to be noted.

① Let us start with "being there" as a way of establishing credibility. Certainly Chagnon gained expertise through extensive fieldwork. But as will become clear in part 2 of this book, other researchers who have lived longer among the Yanomami—Albert, Good, Lizot, Peters—disagree with Chagnon on certain points. "Being there" works only when no one else comes forward to challenge your account. Tierney has spent less time living among the Yanomami than Chagnon has. But Tierney supplements his observations with the work of the above noted anthropologists. Whom should we then believe?

② The second technique is to present new information. But how new is Chagnon's new material? It appears his uncontacted villages had been previously contacted. Citing a host of references, Sponsel suggests that Yanomami communities "have been influenced by Western contact, directly and/or indirectly, for some 250 years. At various times these influences have included slave raiders, rubber tappers, loggers, miners, missionaries, explorers, scientists, the military, border commissions, government censuses, malaria patrols, and so on" (1998:113). And how do we know that Tierney's identifications of the villages Chagnon used in his *Science* article are accurate? Just because Tierney lists certain villages Chagnon visited does not mean these are the villages Chagnon used in his analysis. It may be new information, but is it correct?

(3) The third technique is to gain credibility through extensive citations of others' work. Tierney's effort to do this has come in for extensive criticism. One expert on the Yanomami, Alcida Ramos, says: "*Darkness in El Dorado* has been commended . . . for its solid documentation. Indeed, there is a profusion of end notes, but these require close examination. For instance, to challenge Chagnon's data on polygyny, Tierney chooses a sentence from a Waorani ethnography. . . . To support his description of 'the sad history of the Marash-teri and their struggle with the gold rush,' he cites an article by Bruce Albert written about a Yanomami community well before the gold rush" (2001:275). Tierney has interviewed all the participants in the discussion in part 2 of this book: Albert, Hames, Hill, Martins, Peters, and Turner. At least two of them—Hames and Hill—strongly object to Tierney's summary of their conversations. What then should we infer about Tierney's massive documentation?

(4) Fourth, we noted above that Turner and Sponsel were slow to challenge Tierney's accusations regarding Neel because Tierney's criticisms of Chagnon fit with what they themselves already knew. In the rush to warn leaders of the American Anthropological Association regarding the gathering storm, they perceived time to be of the essence. Once they had a chance to investigate the accusation that Neel played a key role in the spread of the measles epidemic, they found it to be wrong.

Finally, we should be cautious in accepting the proclamations of high-status anthropologists outside their areas of competence. We might wonder why high-status anthropologists should understand the controversy better than others—especially when they make no claims to have steeped themselves in the ethnographic material. I am uncertain what Geertz knows about the Yanomami. But I do know that in a *New York Review of Books* analysis of another controversy—between Obeyesekere and Sahlins regarding Captain Cook—he also positioned himself as the arbiter between squabbling intellectuals. In that controversy, Geertz missed important facts basic to the case (cf. Borofsky 1997). We need to be cautious in assuming that others—whatever their status—know things that reach beyond their areas of expertise.

In seeking to make sense of the Yanomami controversy, I am suggesting that we need to reflect on the ways in which we assess controversies within the discipline. We need to cast a critical eye on how we evaluate credibility because in the very ways we strive to resolve disputes we sometimes perpetuate them.

To summarize, the Yanomami controversy extends beyond the specific accusations made against one or another individual. It also involves issues of power—between anthropologists and those who help them—as well as intellectual competence regarding how anthropologists resolve controversies such as this. We will return to these issues in chapter 6.

5

....

KEEPING YANOMAMI PERSPECTIVES
IN MIND

In dealing with the Yanomami controversy, we must not lose sight of the Yanomami themselves. Throughout the controversy, claims of concern for the Yanomami's welfare have produced a lot of political posturing. But as noted in chapter 1, the Yanomami do not seem to have substantially benefited from the piles of paper this posturing has produced. In talking about the Yanomami, we often seem to be talking about our hopes for ourselves as ethical professionals.

Hearing Yanomami voices and experiencing Yanomami perspectives on the controversy, however, is not easy to do because (1) the Yanomami speak with many voices, not one; (2) some of the events of interest happened decades ago; and (3) the material drawn from interviews is not easily presented to readers.

First, the Yanomami do not necessarily speak with a collective voice but with many voices, many perspectives. Yanomami are well aware of this. When the Yanomami Piri Xiriana visited the AAA's annual meeting in 2002, for example, he refused to act as a spokesperson for Yanomami views with the AAA, even on a matter where there appears to be broad Yanomami concern: the storage of Yanomami blood in the United States. He indicated that the matter was something Yanomami needed to discuss among themselves in their own gatherings. (He suggested the AAA send individuals to the Yanomami who could discuss the problem with them; together, they could decide how to proceed.) He pointedly rejected the association's proposal that the Yanomami send a few representatives to the United States to discuss the problem with AAA representatives. Piri Xiriana's subsequent attempt to foster discussion on the topic has focused on five villages along the upper Mucajaí River. But there are certainly other Yanomami, in both Brazil and Venezuela, who might be consulted. The problem is there is no collective body of Yanomami to represent their views to outsiders. Yanomami organize themselves in a range of groups but never as a whole tribe. It is one of their traits as Yanomami.

A second problem with these interviews is that the Yanomami interviewed are at times discussing experiences that occurred over thirty years ago. Some recall what they experienced as small children, others what they heard particular individuals say. These views have been shaped and reshaped with the passage of time.

One aspect of this, for example, is the perception by some Yanomami of themselves as "fierce." I can well imagine, as we read in chapter 1, certain Yanomami conveying in encounters with Chagnon that they were fierce. This would be a way of affirming their competence as warriors—especially if they are not as violent as non-Yanomami groups (as Tierney suggests) or if there is regional variation in Yanomami violence (as Chagnon suggests). It would be a politically useful ideology for intimidating others and protecting themselves no matter what the actual degree of violence was.

But such an assertion (particularly to outsiders) takes on a different tone during the political struggles to establish a Yanomami land reserve in Brazil in the 1980s. Asserting Yanomami fierceness became a political ploy by certain Brazilian politicians to subvert Yanomami demands for a large reserve. They depicted the Yanomami as too violent for a large reserve; they needed to be broken up into several smaller reserves. Despite considerable opposition, a single large reserve was eventually established in 1992.

Today for Yanomami to publicly affirm their fierceness to outsiders is basically to undermine their political cause. Periodically, one or another prominent individual in Brazil calls for reducing the size of the present reserve.

In searching for a sense of objectivity in this politically charged matter, readers need to remember that most Yanomami specialists view the Yanomami as less violent and warlike than Chagnon suggests. Still, we might wonder to what degree Yanomami self-representations to outsiders have changed with changing political times.

The third problem is that it is difficult to present the interview material to readers. My initial inclination was to offer verbatim transcripts so readers could see how the interviews unfolded word by word. Readers of these interviews indicated that they found the unedited format confusing. Some interviewees seemed to ramble, and the connection between particular points was not always clear. As a result, I have organized the interview material around certain themes. This format lacks the *in situ* sense of how Yanomami express themselves, but it allows readers to readily grasp how Yanomami perspectives on the controversy's central concerns differ from those expressed by anthropologists, the critical point of this chapter. (Readers interested in examining the unedited interviews can turn to the first page of the bibliography to find their locations on the internet.)

What comes through in the interviews is that the Yanomami are concerned about different things than we are. We are primarily concerned about the validity of Tierney's accusations; the Yanomami are more concerned about the blood collected by Neel that is still being preserved in American laboratories.

The excerpted interviews in this chapter come from six different sources. For the discussion in part 2, I asked both Bruce Albert and Lêda Martins—who were in Brazil during part of 2001—to interview several Yanomami in order to gain their perspectives on the issues raised by the controversy and what anthropologists might do to help them. Bruce Albert interviewed Yanomami activist Davi

Kopenawa; the interview took place, in the Yanomami language, on April 8 at Boa Vista, the capital of the Brazilian state of Roraima, which is where most Brazilian Yanomami live. Lêda Martins conducted two sets of interviews: The first, on April 19, occurred during a conference on the health of indigenous people near the Brazilian capital of Brasília with five Yanomami (Carlos Krokonautheri, Ivanildo Wawanawetery, Roberto Pirisitheri, Geraldo Parawautheri, and Alexandre Hawarixapopitheri); Davi Kopenawa acted as a translator from Yanomami to Portuguese and, in the process, voiced some of his own opinions. The second interview occurred on May 18 in Boa Vista. This interview, in Portuguese, was with Geraldo Kuesitheri Yanomami and Peri Porapitheri.

Janet Chernela, a member of the AAA's El Dorado Task Force, interviewed Davi Kopenawa twice, once in Boa Vista on June 10, 2000, and once in a Yanomami village in Roraima on June 7, 2001. (Because the first of these interviews occurred before the publication of Tierney's book and is less relevant to the controversy's central concerns, it is not excerpted below.) Chernela also interviewed Julio Wichato on November 24, 2001, at Shakita, a small village by the Mavaca River in the upper Rio Orinoco region of Venezuela, during the first National Conference of Venezuelan Yanomami (called in part because of the controversy). Chernela indicates that she was interested in talking to a Yanomami "who was unbiased and familiar with the professional aspects of blood collection." (Wichato has worked as a nurse for the Venezuelan health ministry for the past eighteen years.) The interview was conducted in Spanish.

Janet Chernela also recorded two formal presentations in the United States by Yanomami relating to the controversy. One was by José Seripino, a Venezuelan Yanomami, at George Washington University on September 7, 2001. The other was by Toto Yanomami, a Brazilian Yanomami, on April 6, 2002, at a conference on the controversy held at Cornell University.

This chapter, then, includes a certain range of opinions. Brazilian and Venezuelan Yanomami are represented. And although Davi Kopenawa dominates the discussions—understandably, perhaps, because he is the Yanomami activist best known by non-Yanomami—other Yanomami have also been interviewed. To my knowledge, these interviews represent the major corpus of material presently available in English on Yanomami reactions to the controversy's central issues. The fact that more interviews are not readily available suggests listening to Yanomami perspectives remains a work in progress.

YANOMAMI BLOOD

Davi Kopenawa makes his concern clear. "My mother gave blood. Now my mother is dead. Her blood is over there [in the United States]. Whatever is of the dead must be destroyed. Our custom is that when the Yanomami die, we destroy everything. To keep it, in a freezer, is not a good thing." Toto Yanomami states: The doctors "collected these things: blood, urine [inaudible], saliva, and feces. I want it to come back to the Yanomami. . . . I want all of it returned. . . . Blood is important in shamanism. . . . All the blood of the Yanomami belongs to [the deity] Omami. . . . Those people have died! . . . Yanomami never take blood to keep. Yanomami don't . . . take blood to study and later keep [it] in the refrigerator. . . . The doctors have already examined this blood; they've already researched this blood. Doctors already took from this blood that which is good—for their children, for the future. . . . So we want to take all of this Yanomami blood that's left over." Ivanildo Wawanawetery makes the same point: "That person who donated blood and who . . . does not live anymore . . . that is an injustice. . . . Who knows . . . how many people have died and even today they have their blood. . . . [It] is in the other country. . . . Someone . . . who gave blood and no longer lives . . . and his blood is still in another country" (2001b).

The Yanomami remember receiving trade goods in exchange for their blood. Wawanawetery reports that the Americans "gave knives, beads, fishing line, and so they convinced the people" to give their blood. Kopenawa states: "The whites said things like this: 'I'm going to give you a machete . . . when you come give blood. . . . I'll give you fishing hooks!' That's why people went to them to give their blood" (2001a).

But there does not appear to be anything approaching informed consent from the Yanomami perspective regarding two critical issues. First, Yanomami claim they were never informed that the blood would be stored past its initial examination in American laboratories. Kopenawa notes (interspersing his views with those of Carlos Krokonautheri in the Martins interview): "The American didn't help to explain . . . 'Look, this blood is going to stay many years.' He didn't say that. . . . The Yanomami were thinking that he would take the blood and then read it and then throw it away. That's what the Yanomami thought. That's why they gave the blood. . . . They thought it was to see some disease, malaria, tuberculosis, flu, or some other disease" (2001c). Kopenawa repeats this point in his interview with Albert: "The white man didn't tell us . . . 'We're going to store your blood in the cold, and even if a long time goes by, even if you die, this blood is going to remain here'—he didn't tell us that! Nothing was said" (2001a). Second, the Yanomami say they were never apprised of the blood test results—what was learned about Yanomami blood. As Kopenawa suggests, Yanomami presumed the blood samples were being taken not just for the benefit of the outsiders but for the benefit of Yanomami as well. He states: "We want to know the findings. What did they find in the blood—information regarding disease?" (2001b). José Seripino (in his presentation at George Washington University) makes the same point: "I was only ten years old. I thought 'Okay. This will help us.' But what happened? We haven't seen the outcome'" (2001). Julio Wichato observes, "The problem is that they studied it [the blood] and didn't send us the results. If they help us it's different. . . . It's important that they send the results" (2001). Wawanawetery asserts that the researcher "created fear . . .

when he [the Yanomami] didn't give up his blood, the guy was going to get sick, right? If he didn't give blood the guy was going to get sick, he was going to die. Those who were donating blood would live" (2001). The implication I draw from this statement is that the Yanomami were told by a researcher that analysis of their blood would help them learn who had which diseases, thus facilitating treatment.

Yanomami appear to be of two minds regarding what should now be done with their deceased relatives' blood. On the one hand, some would like to be justly compensated for the blood used by Americans. This is Davi Kopenawa's point: "You should give something in return for what it [the blood] is worth. . . . The fact is, they already took away that blood. Go ahead. But give something in return for what it's worth. If you go ahead [with your research] without compensating us, we will feel injured" (2001a). Kopenawa says in another interview, "If . . . our blood is good for their bodies [i.e., helps them cure diseases]—then they'll have to pay. If it helped cure a disease over there, then they should compensate us" (2001b). This is the implication, too, in Toto Yanomami's statement quoted previously: "Doctors already took from this blood that which is good— for their children, for the future" (2002). Kopenawa suggests, "If they don't want to pay, then they should consider returning our blood. . . . If he [the American researcher] doesn't want to return anything, then lawyers will have to resolve the issue. I am trying to think of a word that whites do . . . sue. If he doesn't want to pay, then we should sue" (2001b). Kopenawa says (in the Martins interview, translating for Geraldo Parawautheri), "I'm going to translate. . . . He's the son of a chief, but his father passed away. . . . the blood can't be kept as if the Yanomami were alive. Since he's not alive [Geraldo's father], they can't [keep his blood]. . . . The napë [non-Yanomami] prohibit [things] as well. . . . If they want to [do] research, they have to pay the Yanomami. Then they can use it" (2001c). On the other hand, some Yanomami want their blood destroyed or returned, period—even if it is valuable to American researchers. They feel that the researchers have had enough time to gain what they want from the blood. Wichato says, "We don't want them to continue studying our blood. . . . Whether they send the [collective] results or not—they cannot study it anymore. They have to return it or destroy it. That's all! If they send the results we won't know whose blood belongs to whom anyway. . . . We don't want them to continue working with this blood" (2001). In translating the Alexandre Hawarixapopitheri interview, Kopenawa states that Hawarixapopitheri's "father died. . . . This blood that's there is already dead, already died, and we don't want this blood kept as if the owner were alive. But the owner's dead, so they have to get rid of the blood. That's what he wants" (2001c). Toto Yanomami says, "This blood belonging to the Yanomami is here in this country [the United States]. We met in our communal longhouse to talk about this. We thought that it had been thrown out. But it still exists. So I came here to find this blood and take it back. . . . We hope that you whites can help us resolve this situation to get this blood and take it back. . . . I want all that the whites took. I want all of it returned" (2002).

THE YANOMAMI AS FIERCE

Another topic that comes up in the interviews, particularly for Davi Kopenawa, is how anthropologists depict the Yanomami—especially as fierce. Kopenawa is aware of Chagnon's criticisms of him, and he in turn has strong criticisms of Chagnon. We must remember that Yanomami fierceness is a politically charged issue and Kopenawa is dealing not only with the explicit question of whether Yanomami are fierce but with the implicit concern that the Yanomami way of life be valued by outsiders (to protect the Yanomami and their reserve from opposing political forces in Brazil). Following is an excerpt from Chernela's interview with Kopenawa:

> KOPENAWA: So this Chagnon, . . . he said that the Yanomami are no good, that the Yanomami are ferocious. So this story, he made this story [up]. He took it to the United States. He had a friend who published it. It was liked. His students thought that he was a courageous man, an honest man, with important experience.
>
> CHERNELA: What is the word for courageous?
>
> KOPENAWA: *Waiteri*. He is *waiteri* because he was there. He is *waiteri* because he was giving orders. . . . He ordered the Yanomami to fight among themselves. He paid with pans, machetes, knives, fishhooks. . . . The life of the Indian that dies is very expensive. But he paid little. He made them fight more to improve his work.
>
> CHERNELA: But why did he want to make the Yanomami fight?
>
> KOPENAWA: To make his book. To make a story about fighting among the Yanomami. He shouldn't show the fights of the others. The Yanomami did not authorize this. He did it in the United States. He thought it would be important for him. He became famous. He is speaking badly about us. He is saying that the Yanomami are fierce, that they fight a lot, that they are no good. . . . The Yanomami should not authorize every and all anthropologist who appears. . . . When he [Chagnon] arrived [at a village], and called everyone together, he said, [Yanomami] . . . "That *shabono* [village], three or four *shabonos*," as if it were a ball game [with Yanomami fighting each other]. "Whoever is the most courageous will earn more pans. If you kill ten more people I will pay more. If you kill only two, I will pay less." . . . Our relatives came from Wayupteri and said, "This Chagnon is very good. He gives us a lot of utensils. He is giving us pans because we fight a lot."
>
> CHERNELA: They killed them and they died [i.e., Yanomami killed other Yanomami]?
>
> KOPENAWA: Yes. Because they used poison on the point of the arrow. This isn't good. This kill[ing] . . . Children cried; fathers, mothers, cried. Only Chagnon was happy. Because in his book he says we are fierce. We are garbage. The book says this; I saw it. I have the book. He earned a name . . . *Watupari*. It means king vulture—that eats decaying meat. We use this name for people who give a lot of orders. . . . He ordered the Yanomami to fight. (2001b)

José Seripino too, perceives Yanomami fierceness not as a trait embedded in Yanomami society but as something stimulated by Chagnon. "It's not all the

[handwritten margin notes: "instigating violence"; "Yanomami are not as 'fierce' as others think."]

time that the Yanomami are angry. . . . Sometimes not. It's not all the time. This is a lie that he [Chagnon] invented in his book. If he treats the Indian badly then the Yanomami could get angry" (2001).

PERCEPTIONS OF CHAGNON

This brings us to the question of how Yanomami perceive Napoleon Chagnon and his fieldwork. While some have mixed reactions, most Yanomami interviewed perceive Chagnon's fieldwork in negative terms. Kopenawa is the most vocal but also is perhaps the most interesting. One might read Kopenawa's remarks about Chagnon's losing his fear as the Yanomami version of Chagnon's description in chapter 2 of how he learned to hold his own against repeated Yanomami demands. The following is from Chernela's interview with Kopenawa:

> When he [Chagnon] first arrived he was afraid. Then he developed courage. He wanted to show that he was brave. If the Yanomami could beat him, he could beat them. This is what the people in Toototobi told us. I am here in Watorei, but I am from Toototobi. . . .
>
> So I knew him. He arrived speaking Yanomami. People thought he was Yanomami. He accompanied the Yanomami in their feasts . . . taking [the hallucinogen] *ebena*, and after, at the end of the feast, the Yanomami fought. . . . [he] took photos. And so he saved [the fight], he "kept" the fight. So, after, when the fight was over, and the Yanomami lay down in their hammocks, in pain, the anthropologist recorded it all on paper. He noted it all on paper. He wrote what he saw, he wrote that the Yanomami fought. He thought it was war. This isn't war, no! . . . He should have helped us to stop fighting. But he didn't. He's no good. (2001b)

Regarding the collecting of genealogical information, Kopenawa observes: "He wrote down the day, the time, the name of the *shabono*, the name of the local descent group. He put down these names. But he didn't ask us. So we are angry." Regarding Chagnon's gifts, Kopenawa states: "He had a lot of pans. I remember the pans. Our relatives brought them from there. They were big and they were shallow. He [Chagnon] bought them in Venezuela" (2001b).

Wichato provides a personal account of an event described in Tierney, the destruction of a Yanomami village's *shabono* by a helicopter (2000:4–5). "Yes, I saw [Chagnon] . . . when I was eighteen. . . . He contracted a helicopter. The pilot knew me and I had no way to get there. So he said, let's go. He took me [to the helicopter] and there was Chagnon. We got to Ocamo. . . . He took me to Siapa. . . . There was a VERY large *shabono*. "Let's go down here" [he said]. The helicopter was BIG—it blew out houses [i.e., parts of the *shabono*] within twenty meters! So people came out with bows and arrows to shoot the helicopter. Chagnon said to go back down. The pilot said no and went up again. Then Chagnon wanted to go back. . . . He ruined the *shabono*. . . . This is what he was like, Chagnon. He got fuel and we went again" (2001).

[handwritten note: Chagnon ruined a village but didn't care]

Regarding Chagnon's gift giving, José Seripino suggests that Chagnon did not always keep his promises. In the village of Shakita (a village Tierney claims was named for Chagnon [2000:137]), Seripino asserts that Chagnon "worked with this man closely. Now . . . he [Chagnon] promised this person a motor and he disappeared without giving it. He never [returned and] paid that debt" (2001). In fairness to Chagnon, it is unclear whether this "promise" was part of what Chagnon perceived as yet another Yanomami demand on his limited goods—a subject discussed in chapter 2—or a real commitment made but never fulfilled. Nor is it clear whether Chagnon intended to provide the motor but was unable to because of restrictions on his returning. Still, it is important to recognize what is being conveyed: some Yanomami feel Chagnon should have provided particular informants with more gifts than he did.

[handwritten margin note: they do not feel rightfully compensated]

KOPENAWA'S VIEW OF THE CONTROVERSY

Davi Kopenawa has a definite view on the controversy between Chagnon and Tierney. As part of her interview, Chernela had Kopenawa ask her questions and comment on her answers. Kopenawa asks: "I want to ask you about these American anthropologists. Why are they fighting among themselves? Is it because of this book [by Patrick Tierney]? Is this book bad? Did one anthropologist like it and another one say it's wrong?" About Tierney, Kopenawa says, "I met him in Boa Vista. I went to his house. He didn't say anything to me about what he was doing" (2001b).

Kopenawa continues, "I don't like these anthropologists who use the name of the Yanomami on paper, in books. One doesn't like it. . . . This isn't good. They are using our name as if we were children. The name Yanomami has to be respected. It's not like a ball to throw around, to play with, hitting from one side to another" (2001b).

Kopenawa discusses the money he presumes various people are making from publishing books on the Yanomami.

I think that the head of the anthropologist . . . has [or is focused on] money. . . . Chagnon made money using the name of the Yanomami. He sold his book. Lizot too. . . . I want to know how much they are making each month. How much does any anthropologist earn? And how much is Patrick [Tierney] making? Patrick must be happy. This is a lot of money. They may be fighting but they are happy. They fight and this makes them happy. They make money and fight. . . .

Patrick left the fight to the others! He can let the anthropologists fight with Chagnon, and he, Patrick, he's outside, he's free. He's just bringing in the money—he must be laughing at the rest. It's like starting a fight among dogs. Then they fight, they bark and he's outside. He spoke bad of the anthropologist—others start fighting, and he's gaining money!

The name Yanomami is famous . . . more famous than the name of any anthropologist. So he [Patrick] is earning money without sweating, without hurting his hands, without the heat of the sun. He's not suffering. He just sits and writes, this is great for him. He succeeded in writing a book that is bringing in money. Now he should share some of this money with the Yanomami. We Yanomami are here, suffering from malaria, flu, sick all the time. But he's there in good health—just spending the money that he gained in the name of the Yanomami Indians. . . . This is a fight between men who make money. (2001b)

YANOMAMI VIEWS OF ANTHROPOLOGY AND ANTHROPOLOGISTS

The Yanomami interviewed were familiar with enough anthropologists to realize that not all anthropologists are alike. Toto Yanomami stated (in his presentation to anthropologists at Cornell): "You are anthropologists. You work! Some work well, others badly" (2002). The problem, as Peri Porapitheri indicates, is that Yanomami cannot initially tell the good from the bad:

> If he [the anthropologist] wanted to work clean, without doing things against us, he could work in any region. . . . We do not recognize an exploiter at first, but we are going to find out through his voice: "Look! I came here to help sick people, to [build] a hospital, to give medicine, help to acquire vaccines. I will give you presents."
>
> This type of talk I already know, he wants to negotiate, right? He wants to do research, and there are so many things, right? Research on health, research to deceive the Yanomami, research to exploit. He will take advantage if Yanomami believe in what he says. He is going to say that the Yanomami are agreeing to everything.
>
> I am not going to believe in everything. . . . I am going to ask him a lot of questions. . . . There are . . . many white people whose work we do not know. . . . So, he [the anthropologist] . . . start[s] working, then after[ward] he take[s] away pictures, books, he sells, he produces and sells. He will say, "Look! I did this, I did that. And I will send the government to help you and money will come in your name because you are suffering very much. I have spoken with the Ministry of Health." Then everybody will believe him because the majority of the Yanomami do not know the white people's ways. (2001b)

From the Yanomami perspective, "helping" generally means helping to fight disease. Geraldo Kuesitheri Yanomami explains: "An anthropologist, if he learns to work with health teams, this helps us. This is very important. . . . [The anthropologist] knows how to work with photos, with the writing of the Yanomami [language], translation, translating Yanomami [to] Portuguese. If someone were to do this without an anthropologist, it wouldn't come out right. There would be no way [for outsiders] to explain things to the Yanomami. Without an anthropologist, there's no way [for the Yanomami] to understand" (2001).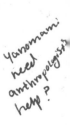

Kopenawa makes the same point: "An anthropologist should really help, as a friend. He shouldn't deceive. He should defend . . . [a Yanomami] when he is sick, and defend the land as well . . . saying [to others] 'You should not come here—the Yanomami are sick' [and could get sicker if you come because the Yanomami are so vulnerable to outside diseases]. If a Yanomami gets a cold, he can die" (2001b).

Kopenawa makes clear that anthropologists can act as intermediaries for the Yanomami, helping outsiders to understand them and vice versa. Anthropologists can give voice to what Yanomami are thinking. Even Chagnon, from Kopenawa's perspective, has an important role to play in this regard. (He is more fluent in the Shamatari dialect than Kopenawa.) "Bruce Albert, Alcida Ramos are not Yanomami. . . . Look, Alcida [Ramos] speaks Sanuma. Chagnon speaks Shamatari. And Bruce [Albert] speaks our language. So there are three anthropologists who can call three Yanomami [groups together] to speak at . . . [a collective] meeting [of these distinct groups]. . . . The Yanomami can speak his own language. These anthropologists can translate [for outsiders what is being said]. They [the outsiders] have to hear our language. They have to hear us in our own language. What does the Yanomami think? What does the Yanomami think is beautiful? You have to ask the Yanomami themselves" (2001b).

Kopenawa is clearly familiar with the ways to woo Western readers as well as with the value of positive publicity. He has to be if he is to be an effective advocate of Yanomami interests in Brazil and in the international community. Kopenawa is able to phrase his points in a way that resonates with Western values. Of all the Yanomami quoted in this chapter, Kopenawa is most able to inspire us about the Yanomami cause. Asked by Chernela if he had a message for the American Anthropological Association, Kopenawa replied:

I would like to speak to the young generation of anthropologists. Not to the old ones who have already studied and think in the old ways. I want to speak to the anthropologists who love nature, who like indigenous people—who favor the planet earth and indigenous peoples. This I would like. . . . To write a new book that anyone would like, instead of speaking badly about indigenous peoples.

There must be born a new anthropologist who is in favor of a new future. And the message I have for him [or her] is to work with great care. If a young anthropologist enters here in Brazil or Venezuela, he should work like a friend. Arrive here in the *shabono*. He should say, "I am an anthropologist; I would like to learn your language. After, I would like to teach you." Tell us something of the world of the whites. The world of the whites is not good. It is good, but it is not all good. There are good people and bad people. So, "I am an anthropologist here in the *shabono*, defending your rights and your land, your culture, your language; don't fight among yourselves, don't kill your own relatives."

We already have an enemy among us—it is disease. This enemy kills indeed. It is disease that kills. We are all enemies of disease. So the anthropologist can bring good messages to the Indian. They can understand what we are doing, we can understand what they are doing. . . . [They can help] the Yanomami understand the ways of the whites [so we can] . . . protect ourselves.

They cannot speak bad of the Yanomami. They can say, "The Yanomami are there in the forest. Let's defend them. Let's not allow invasions [of gold miners]. Let's not let them die of disease." But not to use the name of the Indian to gain money. The name of the Indian is more valuable than paper. The soul of the Indian that you capture in your image is more expensive than the camera with which you shoot it.

You have to work calmly. You have to work the way nature works. You see how nature works. It rains a little. The rain stops. The world clears. This is how you have to work, you anthropologists of the United States. (2001b)

6

....

YOU DECIDE

Specialization seems an obvious way to handle the massive amounts of materials we are confronted with in a controversy such as this. There are so many publications to read and so little time to read them. It seems better to focus on one subset of the material and let someone else focus on another. But such specialization creates problems for developing wider, collective, conversations.

In 1893 Emile Durkheim published *The Division of Labor in Society*, in which he set out two general forms of social solidarity: *mechanical* (in which people possessed solidarity because of their shared experiences) and *organic* (in which solidarity grew from people of different experiences needing to cooperate with one another). The idea of organic solidarity as applied to anthropology is that although scholars specialize, each specialization contributes to an overall shared disciplinary project. The parts come together to make a whole. Such organic solidarity is apparently what the El Dorado Task Force sought. Each member specialized in a topic and brought his or her research to the whole group for discussion. But when Task Force members disagreed, there was no way to assess the validity of a member's analysis that was independent of the data they provided to support it. (Without the public pressure from the many e-mails—a theme I will return to in chapter 7—I suspect the Task Force would not have come to the consensus it did regarding the accusations concerning Chagnon.)

Because of specialization, anthropologists tend to focus on narrowly framed questions without having either a clear path for how these narrow questions come together into broader ones or, equally important, how they can communicate effectively across their different data sets to resolve disagreements. Researchers often find it difficult to converse outside the arenas of their expertise. Readers looking for published points of reference—remembering that this isn't a problem solely within anthropology but within the wider society, too—might look at Putnam's *Making Democracy Work* (1993) and *Bowling Alone* (2000), as well as Habermas's *The Structural Transformation of the Public Sphere* (1989).

As previously noted, controversies within the discipline often act as temporary "antistructural" bridges that unite people across the specializations that divide them. The Yanomami controversy draws us into a common community partly because of the critical media attention it has attracted and partly because there are important discipline-wide issues that need to be collectively discussed.

But this sense of community is weakened by the dominance of experts in controversies such as this. Nonexperts often feel intimidated by those who claim competence over a vast array of specialized details most of us are unfamiliar with. Unless they spend months "getting up to speed"—becoming familiar with all the citations one or another expert cites—many readers wonder how they can competently form opinions that count, how they can discuss the issues involved intelligently. In other words, there is often only an appearance of shared public space in many controversies, a recognition of shared concerns but a limited amount of participation by the discipline's members. Many remain passive onlookers, intrigued by the energy generated from the controversy but not directly participating in the controversy itself.

We can address this problem within the discipline by applying the model of a jury trial. In such a trial, jury members—like many readers—do not know all the ins and outs of a case. But by listening to people who do know these details argue back and forth, they are able to form a reasonable judgment regarding the case.

There are two difficulties we must deal with, however. First, many times in anthropology experts argue past one another. To limit this, the discussion in part 2 of this book involves back-and-forth engagement between participants. A requirement that the experts respond to one another's statements through time allows readers to see the contours of each one's argument—how each responds to criticisms and what those responses suggest about that person's argument. Second, since the participants are academics, the arguments are sometimes phrased in academic ways and can leave readers puzzled as to what an author really means. To address that, this chapter highlights various sides of the key questions involved in the controversy. Part 2, Chapters 8 through 11, constitutes a resource for readers to look through at will. A summary of the main points put forward by each participant is provided in the appendix.

The material readers need to form their opinions about the controversy's central questions is presented below. Readers interested in going into greater detail regarding specific accusations will want to explore part 2. This chapter offers you an opportunity to decide where you stand on a set of key disciplinary concerns. As we saw with the El Dorado Task Force's preliminary report (when 119 students offered their commentaries), some matters are too important to leave to others. It is our discipline; we all need to share in shaping it.

THE PART 2 PARTICIPANTS

The participants in the part 2 discussion are repeatedly referred to throughout this chapter. In this section I give some details about their backgrounds so readers will have a context within which to place their comments.

Bruce Albert, a social anthropologist, is research director at the Research Institute for Development (Paris, São Paulo) and vice-president as well as cofounder (in 1978) of the CCPY (Pro-Yanomami Committee). Born in Morocco, he has worked among the Brazilian Yanomami since 1975, conducting ethnographic research on the social organization and religious practices of the Yanomami of Brazil and on the impact of social change among them. He has also done research on indigenous NGOs and policies of sustainable development in the Brazilian Amazon and has published on the ethics of anthropological fieldwork.

Raymond Hames is professor of anthropology at the University of Nebraska. Between 1975 and 1999, Hames made six field trips to the Yanomamö. His first was as a graduate student, under the direction of Napoleon Chagnon. His trips in the mid-1980s were with Chagnon when they were coprincipal investigators for a project funded by the National Science Foundation (NSF). Hames's initial research dealt with human ecology and time allocation, while more recent research has dealt with food exchange, marriage, child health, and parental investment in offspring from an evolutionary perspective. As previously noted, Hames was for a time a member of the El Dorado Task Force.

Kim Hill is a professor in the program in human evolutionary ecology at the University of New Mexico. He has worked for more than twenty-five years with lowland South American Indians, including groups in Paraguay, Bolivia, Venezuela, and Peru. He was a colleague of James Neel at the University of Michigan and has known Napoleon Chagnon since the 1980s. Hill is married to Venezuelan anthropologist Magdalena Hurtado, who has known some of the individuals referred to in Tierney's book since childhood. He also knows personally or has met many of the other main characters in the Tierney book—including Lizot, Father Bortoli and other Salesian missionaries, New Tribes missionaries, and Alfredo Aherowe, the Yanomamö guide who took Tierney to remote villages—during his travels to the upper Orinoco in 1988 . On that trip, Hill discussed the field behaviors of such anthropologists as Chagnon and Lizot with Yanomamö informants.

Lêda Martins is an assistant professor of anthropology at Pitzer College. Born and raised in Brazil and trained as a journalist, she was involved with a Yanomami health project sponsored by the Brazilian government from 1991 to 1995. This project was then the major vehicle for health care assistance to the Yanomami in Brazil. For the past thirteen years, Martins has been collaborating with human rights organizations in support of indigenous rights, especially relating to land protection and health care. She received her doctorate from Cornell University in 2003.

John F. Peters is professor emeritus of sociology at Wilfrid Laurier University. Two years after the Yanomami of the Mucajaí River made known contact with outsiders, Peters and his wife took up residence among them, sponsored by a Brazilian missionary organization. They lived with Yanomami of the Mucajaí

River from 1958 until 1967. As a nurse, Peters's wife was fully engaged in medical work. Living in "pristine times" with the Yanomami, both of them sought
to help the Yanomami in their ensuing contacts with government officials, gold
miners, and medical personnel. Between 1973 and 1996, Peters made several
research trips back to the Yanomami to augment the cultural and demographic
data he had collected during his initial residence as well as to document patterns
of change. He is the author of *Life among the Yanomami* (1998) and, with coau-
thor John Early, *The Xilixana Yanomami of the Amazon* (2000).

Terence Turner is professor of anthropology at Cornell University. He has been
extensively involved in human rights and indigenous support activities in South
America, having served on the Ethics Committee of the American Anthropo-
logical Association from 1969 to 1972, headed the Special Commission of the
American Anthropological Association to Investigate the Situation of the
Brazilian Yanomami in 1991, and been a member of the AAA Committee for
Human Rights from 1992 until 1997. In 1998 he was the recipient of the Solon
T. Kimball Award of the American Anthropological Association for outstanding
contributions to the application of anthropology to human rights and develop-
ment issues, primarily for his work with the Kayapó, Yanomami, and other
South American indigenous groups.

With this sense of who the part 2 discussants are, let us turn to the central issues
raised by the Yanomami controversy.

QUESTIONS OF POWER

I have noted that anthropology tends to have a colonizing image. Anthropologists from First World countries often work with informants from Third World
countries; those with more power tend to study those with less (n.b. Nader
1969). This political dynamic strikes at the heart of the discipline's hopes: how
can anthropology be truly open to difference and value alternative perspectives
if there are power dynamics just off stage that emphasize Western dominance?
    In terms of the Yanomami controversy, the concern for power might be
phrased a bit differently: how do we establish just relations with those who help
us in our research, especially when, as is frequently the case today, our informants are minorities who live within nation states where real political power is
controlled by others? The informants an anthropologist works with are often at
the bottom rungs of a power hierarchy where—unlike in the anthropologist's
own life—healthy living conditions, a reasonable life span, and social justice
may be more a hope than a reality.
    Within the controversy, four issues touch on this issue of power: getting in-
formed consent, following the ethic of "do no harm," offering informants just compensation, and working in foreign countries. We will discuss each of these in turn.

(1) Transparency on purpose/consequences
(2) Subjects understand
(3) subjects agree

Getting Informed Consent

Informed consent refers to the requirement of funding agencies that (1) the researchers they support have properly informed their subjects regarding the purposes of their research and the possible negative effects of it on them, (2) the subjects involved affirm an understanding of such possible effects, and (3) the subjects have nonetheless offered their consent, without coercion, to participate in the research. The American Anthropological Association's code of ethics specifically affirms the importance of informed consent in anthropological research (AAA 1998:III.A.4).

To help make sense of the concept, let me provide a bit of history. The insistence on informed consent, especially in medical research, grew out of the medical experiments conducted by Nazi scientists during World War II. Subjects were forced to participate in experiments that debilitated or even killed them. As a result, during the Nuremberg War Trials, the War Crimes Tribunal drew up standards for medical research that became formalized as the Nuremberg Code. While this code is widely accepted in principle, it has never attained legal status in either American or German law. The 1947 Nuremberg Code states: "The voluntary consent of the human subject is absolutely essential . . . and [the subject] should have sufficient knowledge and comprehension of the elements of the subject matter involved as to enable him to make an . . . enlightened decision" (see http://www.cirp.org/library/ethics/nuremberg). A statement by the World Medical Association, called the Declaration of Helsinki (because it was adopted in 1964 by the World Medical Assembly meeting in Helsinki, Finland) affirms much the same point (World Medical Association 2000). For American researchers, the 1979 Belmont Report is another critical statement relating to informed consent, because it grew out of the 1974 National Research Act that formed the National Commission for the Protection of Human Subjects in Biomedical and Behavioral Research. It reads, in part: "Respect for persons requires that subjects, to the degree that they are capable, be given the opportunity to choose what shall or shall not happen to them. . . . [This involves] disclosure [of all pertinent information] . . . ascertaining that the subject has comprehended the information . . . Informed consent requires conditions free of coercion" (National Commission for the Protection of Human Subjects of Biomedical and Behavioral Research 1979).

The principle of informed consent seems fine in the abstract. Clearly, people should have the right to decide whether to participate in experiments that might seriously affect them. But operationalizing the concept is tricky, especially in nonmedical, non-Western settings. What does it mean to be properly informed, for example, when research subjects do not understand the explanations offered because they involve a different worldview than the one with which they are familiar? How long does consent last? If subjects allow researchers to collect their blood, for example, does that mean the researchers are free to make money from the blood when, years later, they find special antibodies in it? Or do the researchers need to return to the subjects—who may or may not still be alive—and gain further informed consent since the subjects had not been made aware that the researchers might gain hundreds of thousands of dollars from the donated blood samples?

The best way to approach these abstract questions is through the lens of a specific case study: the collection of blood during Neel's 1968 expedition.

None of the participants in the controversy claim that Neel followed a formal protocol for informed consent, let alone one that conforms to today's standards. Based on an examination of Neel's field notes, Turner says, "There seems to have been no attempt to secure informed consent from the Yanomami . . . for the taking of biological samples."

Supporters of Neel argued that this lack of formal informed consent stems from the lack of a formal protocol in place at the time Neel conducted his research. (The Belmont Report was published only in 1979.) Still, Chagnon made an earnest effort to explain the project to the Yanomami in terms they could understand, at a time when most researchers were not doing this. Hames refers to a conversation he had with Chagnon in 2001 in which Chagnon said he talked to Yanomami about Neel's project:

- Belmont Report was published in 1979, after Neel's expedition.

> For a year before Neel's arrival and during the [blood] collection phase he told the Yanomamö in all the villages to be sampled that Neel's team wanted to examine their blood in order to determine whether there were things that indicated whether or not they had certain kinds of diseases, especially *shawara* (epidemic diseases) and that this knowledge would help treat them more effectively if they became ill.
>
> Clearly Chagnon could not give the Yanomamö a crash course in infectious disease, genetics, and epidemiology to more fully explain the purposes of the research. Nevertheless, it seems to me that he [Chagnon] gave them information consistent with their ability to comprehend the research. I would also add that the participants in biomedical research done in the West often do not have a very sophisticated understanding of the nature of the research in which they are subjects. . . . Most important, . . . no harm was done to the Yanomamö by having them serve . . . [in] Neel's investigation.

Chagnon tried his best to inform them.

Albert counters that the demand for informed consent dates back to the Nuremberg Code of 1947 and the Declaration of Helsinki of 1964. The failure to follow proper guidelines of informed consent, he notes, was more than simply a one-time mistake. It involved a consistent pattern among those working with the Yanomami: "Even if it appears to have been common practice in the United States in the 1950s and 1960s to neglect the norms established by the Nuremberg Code (especially with ethnic minorities and vulnerable persons . . .), the fact remains that such disregard for the principle of informed consent by James Neel's team cannot be discarded today as if it were a secondary or anachronistic issue. This is all the more so as we find out that this type of conduct continued along the same lines the following decade in biomedical research among the Yanomami and various other indigenous groups."

Given that Neel did not follow the protocol used for informed consent that is accepted today, the key question is whether he followed the general spirit of informed consent in his research. Two points make the issue more complicated than it first appears.

First, as we saw in chapter 5, the Yanomami feel they were not informed that the blood samples would be kept in American laboratories well after many of the donors had died. Chagnon's explanation, cited above, makes no reference to this. But then Chagnon also does not refer to this Yanomami concern in his ethnographic material. We are left to wonder if this was something Chagnon failed to learn about in his research and, hence, failed to inform the Yanomami about. Or was it a minor Yanomami concern during the 1960s that, with more researchers studying them, became an increasingly salient issue for the Yanomami?

Second, Hames points out that no physical harm came to Yanomami from their participation in Neel's research. In fact, clearly good came out of Neel's blood sampling. Based on knowledge gleaned from samples collected in 1966 and 1967, Neel brought measles vaccine as a precautionary measure to help the Yanomami in 1968. That vaccine proved critical, saving many Yanomami lives when the 1968 measles epidemic struck.

Hill observes: "The blood samples collected by the first Yanomamö expedition [i.e., the one before the 1968 expedition] clearly were not collected under TODAY'S guidelines of informed consent . . . [but] the blood collection allowed Neel to discover that the Yanomamö had no antibodies to measles and thus motivated him to acquire and deliver the measles vaccine that saved many lives [in the 1968 epidemic]. It is important to note that Neel began plans for vaccination before hearing that an actual epidemic had started, and he did this because of information that he obtained through systematic blood sampling [during the earlier trip]."

The intriguing thing about Neel's help is that the Yanomami interviews in chapter 5 never mention it. I will return to this issue below.

The problem of replacing formal informed consent with the more slippery notion of doing well by one's research subjects—as Neel clearly did—becomes evident in Yanomami frustration at not seeing the results of Neel's research. Everyone agrees that Neel did not send the Yanomami the medical results of his blood sampling. Essentially, Neel defined helping on his terms rather than on Yanomami terms. Based on her interviews (excerpted in chapter 5), Martins states:

> Chagnon and other members of the expeditions did not get close to giving a reasonable explanation to the Yanomami about the purposes of the [blood] sampling [given that he never explained about the storing of their blood]. In consequence, any deal was invalid. Indeed, I think that Chagnon's . . . [explanations to the Yanomami] were deceptive. . . . To say to a group of people with very limited knowledge of Western medical science and suffering from ravaging diseases that giving

their blood will help to determine if they have certain illnesses and in consequence provide some kind of treatment is to lure them with implied clinical assistance for their current situation and not to simplify the explanation of a research project. It seems that it was exactly the implied promise of clinical treatment in the short run that convinced the Yanomami to give away their blood. . . . The Yanomami specimens collected in Neel's project have not resulted in any treatment to alleviate their suffering from any illness to the present day.

[handwritten margin note: worded so it sounded like the cure would be about Current illnesses]

We are left to ponder what constitutes valid informed consent. How does one effectively explain technical details to people unfamiliar with them? Who is to blame, for example, when a critical question—the storage of a dead person's blood in foreign laboratories—is not explained?

This brings us to the question of continuous informed consent. Is informed consent a one-time thing—a compact that lasts for the life of the sample—or is it more of a single-use compact where the person provides consent only for the use stipulated in the initial agreement? Albert writes: "Supposing that . . . [the] facts [of Neel's research] were fully explained, who would be expected to give consent to . . . a blind agreement for his or her blood DNA to be used in unknown ways, now and in the future, by an unknown number of laboratories around the world? It is obvious in this context that guidelines for negotiating agreements for each stage of research are needed, especially if scientists wish to gain the confidence of indigenous peoples."

Neel apparently used the Yanomami blood for his research on genetic diversity, the research funded by the Atomic Energy Commission. Neel kept the blood samples, presumably so he (or perhaps someone else) might use them later in additional ways.

The Yanomami now want to reopen negotiations regarding these blood samples. They infer, correctly, that some researchers may use the blood to advance their careers as well as to possibly make money. As we saw in chapter 5, some Yanomami want a part of this money. Others want to have nothing to do with such research. They want their relatives' blood destroyed. What does one do to resolve this matter, especially when many of the original donors have died? Whom does one consult? Who now owns the blood, especially given that no formal informed consent was obtained from the Yanomami donors?

....

INFORMED CONSENT: QUESTIONS TO PONDER

1. As an anthropologist, how would you explain your research to the people you are working with so that they have a clear understanding of what they are agreeing to when they consent to participate in your project?

2. How would you verify this agreement so that outside funding agencies would be assured that you have indeed complied with their requirement that you have gained informed consent?

3. In lieu of gaining formal informed consent, is doing good—as Neel did—a reasonable way to follow the spirit of informed consent as embodied in the Nuremberg Code? Or does it set up another standard that is easier to follow but more open to a wide range of interpretations and hence abuse?

4. How would you handle the problem of continuous informed consent? Would it be fair for the people involved to concur to a blind agreement? Or do you think researchers should return to the people and get their agreement for each and every additional use of the original data beyond what was initially agreed to? How should researchers handle the cases of people who have died between the time of the original research and a subsequent request?

Following the Ethic to "Do No Harm"

The origin of the phrase "do no harm" in medicine is clear. It comes from ancient Greece, from Hippocrates' *Epidemics*. But exactly how it came to play a central role in the ethics of American anthropology is less certain. While it sounds nice, it is a deeply problematic formulation. Is it enough for anthropologists to leave their informants with a range of problems, confident that because they, the anthropologists, did not cause them, they need not help in easing them? It seems a rather harsh standard to follow, given that informants are not holding to the same standard in interacting with anthropologists. Informants *actively* assist anthropologists in gaining information these anthropologists need to build professional careers.

The "do no harm" ethic raises a number of issues. The first involves what one does when particular representations of a group can bring that group harm. As already noted, media reports about Chagnon's 1988 article in *Science* were used by Brazilian politicians who wanted to cut up the planned large Yanomami reserve into several smaller ones—ostensibly because the Yanomami were too violent to interact with one another but more likely to allow more room for gold mining.

Chagnon spoke out against the abuse of his work by Brazilian politicians. But he did so only in the English-speaking press, not in the Portuguese-speaking press of Brazil. How far must anthropologists go to respond to misuse of their work in supporting a group of people? Must they speak out in any language, anywhere, if their work is having a negative impact on the people they have worked with? For the Yanomami, the negative consequences were fairly clear. But what about cases where the negative consequences of an anthropologist's writings are more open to debate? We might also ask a critical question: given the gold resources in the Yanomami reserve, would the Brazilian politicians have been less vociferous in their opposition to the reserve if Chagnon had never written about the Yanomami?

A different case concerns a 1995 interview Chagnon gave to the widely read

Brazilian magazine *Veja*. Chagnon criticized pro-Indian rights groups, suggesting that they idealized Indians and obscured their violent ways. Brazilian activists viewed the article as an attack on their efforts to protect the Yanomami (given that the Yanomami reserve's size continues to be a subject of controversy). Chagnon has said that he viewed the interview as telling it like it was.

Chagnon clearly supports the Yanomami cause, but he has a different strategy for helping them than that chosen by the Yanomami themselves (and their supporters in Brazil). Rather than portraying the Yanomami in terms Western readers find desirable, he wants to emphasize that they share the same base traits—in terms of violence and ill manners—as ourselves. His sense of shared humanity is less uplifting than that portrayed by Kopenawa.

One cannot help but notice the negative view Kopenawa has toward Chagnon (discussed in chapter 5). He calls him a *watupari*, or king vulture.

But do Kopenawa and other Yanomami have the right to define who they are for their own political ends? The Yanomami define themselves as less violent than Chagnon portrays them, and many anthropologists agree. But what would happen if more anthropologists sided with Chagnon? Would this more negative view of the Yanomami be important to highlight as well, even though, as Kopenawa indicates, Yanomami prefer not to have books that speak badly of them? Does one have to present a politically correct view—highlighting the positive and ignoring the negative—to help the informants who help you? What happens to ethnographic accuracy under the political circumstances encountered in Brazil?

On one side of these issues is Albert:

> Nobody maintains that the Yanomami do not practice warfare or that Yanomami individuals are not occasionally violent (true for most societies, including the United States). . . . But many people do maintain that it is unethical and politically damaging to reduce the richness of Yanomami society and culture to the stereotypical image of "the barbaric violence [that] Chagnon documented" [in the words of a 1995 *Time* magazine article]. . . . It requires only a minimal ethical sensibility and political awareness to understand that such long-term pejorative labeling and its apparent scientific authority can be (and have been) used by anti-Indian agitators to rationalize and encourage violations of Yanomami rights—nobody ever said such labeling caused them. . . . We need to ask why Napoleon Chagnon never publicly came out [in Brazil] to condemn the use of his work by sensationalist journalists and unscrupulous politicians, or to support the international movement in defense of Yanomami survival.

On the other side is Hames:

> No matter what precautions ethnographers take to qualify or even sanitize their ethnographic accounts of indigenous populations, ethnographic accounts can always be used against them. At the same time, I would emphasize that such

accounts are insignificant explanations of why governments and other powerful interests seek to destroy indigenous peoples. . . . Belief that government officials are swayed by ethnographic reports rests on a number of assumptions that I believe are faulty. It . . . assumes that generals and others not only read scientific reports on indigenous peoples but such that such reports affect their decision-making processes. By implication it means that if the Yanomamö were described as peaceful, then military and economic interests would be inhibited from taking indigenous land because they could not rationalize control, partitioning, or seizure of Yanomamö land. . . . What is completely ignored by those who criticize Chagnon's alleged lack of interest in what the press has to say about the Yanomamö is the way in which he has utilized the press to portray the plight of the Yanomamö. . . . Given the enormous readership of his ethnography, my best guess is that his writings have done more to reach the educated public about the serious problems faced by the Yanomamö than those by any other individual or organization.

[margin note: Politicians will do whatever. Goes both ways.]

A second issue raised by "do no harm" involves gathering information that many in a society prefer to keep secret. This is essentially the problem Chagnon faced in collecting Yanomami genealogies. He *needed* to collect genealogical information as part of his research for Neel. (Intriguingly, Chagnon indicates — in his forthright manner — that some of the genealogies collected are not that accurate (1974:93, 101). No one doubts that Chagnon used data-gathering techniques that were offensive to the Yanomami. But what was he to do when the Yanomami persistently and creatively lied to him? To complicate matters, other researchers collected genealogies; Chagnon was not alone in doing that. But they did it by working with people they lived with for a lengthy period. Given the nature of his funding, Chagnon did not have this luxury. Because of his research for Neel, he was forced to collect genealogies from people he was not personally involved with. What should he have done? Should he have given up his research funding from Neel when he found out about the Yanomami name taboo?

[margin note: He had to. Nature of his job and funding.]

Hill observes: "Tierney asserts that Chagnon infuriated the Yanomamö by obtaining the names of adults and dead people. But Peters and Albert also obtained names and genealogies of hundreds of living and dead Yanomamö, and all available evidence suggests that their study populations were quite accepting of these activities. Thus, there is little doubt that there are appropriate ways to obtain such information and that Yanomamö names are not absolutely taboo, as Tierney asserts." Albert, who tends to oppose Hill on a number of issues, in this case takes a position that overlaps with Hill's. Had Chagnon "used the more typical slow pace and low-profile attitude that most anthropologists use during fieldwork," he writes, Chagnon "would never have found himself in situations of having to resort to bribery, trickery, or offensive behaviors to collect names. The chaotic and peripatetic nature of his . . . [research for Neel] probably did force him into such situations."

The intriguing thing about the Yanomami's interviews in chapter 5 is that they do not roundly criticize Chagnon's genealogical research, certainly not in comparison to Chagnon's depiction of the Yanomami as fierce. The techniques

Chagnon used to collect genealogies clearly violate the AAA's code of ethics, but only Kopenawa refers to them, and then only in passing. Wichato is more critical of Chagnon's destruction of a Yanomami *shabono* through the downdraft of a helicopter he was traveling in. Although this incident is discussed by Tierney (2000:4–5), it is not referred to in either the part 2 discussion or the "Introductory Statement of the El Dorado Task Force Final Report." As we saw in chapter 5, what causes anthropologists much concern about Chagnon's actions is not always what causes the Yanomami concern.

A third issue raised by "do no harm" centers on Chagnon's comments regarding the Yanomami activist Davi Kopenawa. As we saw in chapter 2, Chagnon referred to Kopenawa as a spokesperson for certain non-Yanomami "mentors." The statement raises an important question: should anthropologists openly criticize indigenous activists in ways that conceivably weaken these activists' political power?

Participants in the part 2 discussion clearly affirm that anthropologists should support indigenous activists and the NGOs that assist them. Turner states that Chagnon violated the American Anthropological Association's code of ethics by "repeated and untruthful attacks on NGOs, anthropological activists, and Yanomami leaders." Hames writes: "The major fault I find in the *Veja* interview [discussed above] is the overall mean-spirited view that Chagnon presents of missionaries and NGOs. While much of what he says is accurate, it is not sufficiently balanced by the positive activities of those seeking to help the Yanomamö."

We need to be careful here. Without doubt Kopenawa is the best-known Yanomami spokesperson in Brazil. He is adept at phrasing Yanomami concerns in ways that non-Yanomami audiences can grasp. But he is certainly not the only spokesperson, nor is it clear that the Yanomami seek a single spokesperson for their cause. Remember, there is no overarching authority structure that unites all Yanomami. Perhaps that is why Piri Xiriana refused to act as spokesperson for Yanomami concerns when he attended the AAA meeting. He did not want to assume a position of power he did not, in fact, have.

We also need to be careful in using the spokesperson framework as a way of interpreting Yanomami concerns. Chagnon's point can be interpreted as suggesting that there are many Yanomami spokespeople and that they can be, at times, creations of outside political forces. Viewed in this way, he is correct. Outside groups often want a single spokesperson to ease the task of getting to know a group in all its complexity. But these outsiders' convenience does not necessarily reflect indigenous realities.

We see the problem with the AAA. It wants to help the Yanomami address the blood storage issue. But faced with Xiriana's refusal to act as a spokesperson for Yanomami collective interests and too busy to find funding to visit the Yanomami in their own assemblies (Xiriana's alternative solution), it has quietly set the issue temporarily aside. Moving beyond listening to selected individuals is hard work. It involves investigating how a range of Yanomami view a particular issue. What is striking about efforts to gain Yanomami views of the controversy is how few Yanomami have been interviewed to date.

That said, it is important to note that the Yanomami interviewed perceive anthropologists as allies, as helpers in their struggle for survival. This attitude contrasts with one held in many areas of North America and the Pacific, where indigenous activists often view anthropologists in antagonistic terms (see Borofsky 2000:11–20). In writing ethnographies of a group, anthropologists may challenge, as Chagnon has done, the view of a group presented by various indigenous activists. That presumably is why Kopenawa has such harsh words for Chagnon. In defining the Yanomami as fierce, Chagnon is not only making the Yanomami politically vulnerable but, at the same time, taking away from them their ability to define themselves as they wish.

A fourth issue relating to "do no harm" involves what happens when a disaster befalls the group being studied, as occurred for Neel with the 1968 measles epidemic. Should Neel have stopped his research and attended solely to the needs of the Yanomami so he could save more lives? Or did he also have an obligation to his funding agency to complete the work he had been initially funded for—work that allowed Neel to visit the Yanomami and carry out his measles vaccination campaign?

Turner suggests that Neel could have done far more than he did. "Revising . . . the research itinerary that called for spending enough time in each village to collect enough samples to reach the target of 1,000 blood specimens— to permit the most rapid possible vaccination of all the villages within the expedition's reach would . . . have required [Neel's] giving the vaccinations top priority at the expense of the tightly planned research program, in effect abandoning the target sample sizes for blood [i.e., 1,000 specimens] . . . and settling for less significant research results. As a number of entries in his field journal make clear, Neel never entertained this possibility, but single-mindedly pressed on for collecting the maximum possible number of blood samples, while sacrificing collection of some other types of data . . . to allow more time for vaccinations and medical care."

Hill writes: "James Neel's actions saved more Yanomamö lives during this epidemic than any other person on the planet, yet he is roundly criticized for not doing more than he did. James Neel was a researcher, and his job in 1968 was to collect information on human genetic diversity. The Venezuelan government and the missionaries who lived in the area full time had much more responsibility than Neel to avert the measles crises." And, taking issue with Turner, he states, "Because of the urgency and chaos of the field situation, . . . the vaccination of threatened villages . . . [did take] precedence over any research design. He [Neel] gave vaccinations in some villages to which he never returned and gave vaccinations to many people whose names were never recorded."

As noted, it is striking that the Yanomami interviews in chapter 5 do not highlight Neel's efforts to help them. One might explain this as resulting from the interviewers not being interested enough to pursue the topic in their interviews. But I lean toward a different explanation.

While there is no doubt that Neel saved many lives, the vaccination process apparently was ⟨traumatic at times.⟩ We should note two points.

① First, Neel lacked enough measles immune gamma globulin (MIG) to give it with each vaccination to lessen reactions to the vaccine itself. Neel indicates that the Yanomami who did not get MIG "unquestionably reacted more violently to the vaccinations than did the . . . [other Yanomami] who received MIG" (Neel, Centerwall, and Chagnon 1970:423). "The recorded response to vaccination with the Edmonston strain [i.e., the measles vaccine Neel used] without gamma globulin" [involved a] "febrile response [i.e., fever] . . . somewhat greater than that described for children in North America" (1970:424). "The reaction to measles vaccine without gamma globulin had been, in some cases, as severe as the disease itself in Caucasian children" (1970:425). Reading between the lines, one senses that Yanomami had significant reactions to the vaccine when it was given without immune gamma globulin.

without MIG, Yanomami suffered severe reactions

② Second, Neel makes quite clear that the key to reduced Yanomami mortality was not simply vaccination in and of itself. There needed to be comprehensive medical care to reduce mortality, because Yanomami were coping not only with measles but with various medical and social complications aggravated by, or resulting from, the measles. Many Yanomami, for example, were also suffering from respiratory infections. "With large groups or even total villages ill with measles," Neel and colleagues add, "there was a collapse of village life" (1970:427). "A minimum of 36 percent of the Indians with measles developed pneumonia. This was the direct cause of a majority of the deaths thus far known to be associated with the epidemic. Fortunately the pneumonia usually responded to penicillin. . . . . . The average case fatality rate among the Yanomama from the measles epidemic is approximately 8.8 percent. This is a high rate by the current standards of the civilized world, but low in comparison to the usual death rate attributed to Indians, undoubtedly because of the medical care and antibiotics supplied by missionaries, a government team, and our group" (1970:425–26). Neel helped with this more comprehensive health care only to a limited degree. He mostly left that to others. As he and his coauthors state: "Unfortunately, efforts to 'get ahead' of the epidemic with vaccine (plus the research protocol) did not permit the medical members of the team to stay in any one village long enough to observe the full cycle of response to the vaccine" (1970:421). Nor, I might add, did he stay long enough to provide comprehensive medical care.

needed more medical care → need didn't engage enough

What appears to us to be Neel helping, then, may well not have been seen in as rosy terms by Yanomami. Reactions to the vaccine, the complications of the untreated respiratory infections and pneumonia, and the trauma of the disease itself—with villagers escaping to the forest for protection—all might have made Neel's accomplishment less noteworthy to Yanomami than we might want to depict it.

Here the ethic of "do no harm" revolves around who does the defining. We are left to ponder: Might Neel have conducted the vaccination campaign in another way? But if he had stopped to provide the needed comprehensive medical care to the villages visited, he would have vaccinated fewer Yanomami. And if he restricted vaccinations only to cases where he could also provide the immune gamma globulin—so as to make the vaccination less traumatic—he would also have reduced the number of Yanomami he was able to vaccinate. What was he supposed to do? What does "do no harm" mean in this context?

Finally, what should be done regarding the Yanomami blood samples now stored in the United States? The feelings of the Yanomami interviewed range from uneasy to very angry about the continued storage of their relatives' blood after their deaths. Whatever Yanomami did or did not consent to in 1968, there is little doubt that they now want to address this issue of blood storage. (One positive result of Tierney's book is that Yanomami have become aware that their relatives' blood was not destroyed.) What does "do no harm" mean in a case such as this? As we have seen, the AAA sought to assist the Yanomami. But Yanomami disagree on what should be done. The AAA's solution—having a few spokespeople represent Yanomami interests—goes against the wishes of the only Yanomami representative it has formally talked to about the problem. Is doing no harm the same as doing nothing, or does one need to be more proactive to undo the harm already done?

....

"DOING NO HARM": QUESTIONS TO PONDER

1. What do anthropologists do when their ethnographic representations of a group bring the group harm? Is it sufficient to write a letter to the editor of a newspaper protesting the misuse of their work, or do they need to offer a much stronger response? Equally important, should anthropologists emphasize a politically correct view of a group to foster its political cause, or should they be willing to harm that cause in the name of ethnographic accuracy?

2. Should there be restrictions on the information anthropologists are allowed to collect? What should anthropologists do if, after living in the field, it appears morally problematic to collect the data promised their funding agencies?

3. To what degree should anthropologists avoid undermining the political power of an indigenous activist in writing about a group? To what degree should anthropologists avoid undermining the power of a group to represent itself as it wishes?

4. To what degree should anthropologists alter their research plans to help the people they study in a time of need? Should a researcher such as Neel transform his research program into a treatment program during a measles epidemic, setting aside his initially planned research despite a promise to his funding agency to carry out that research?

5. What does it mean to help others in the context in which Neel operated? Who should define the best way to help?

6. How should anthropologists approach righting a perceived wrong such as the continued storage of Yanomami blood in the United States? Does doing no

harm mean doing nothing, or does it mean taking an active role to resolve what, for the Yanomami, constitutes an earlier harm that was never addressed?

....

Offering Just Compensation

The American Anthropological Association's present code of ethics specifically refers to doing no harm but makes no direct mention of just compensation (see AAA 1998:III.A.2). Given the way in which informants help anthropologists build professional careers, one might suspect there would be extensive discussion of the topic. There is none.

As previously noted, just compensation is far more involved and expensive than doing no harm. The latter implies that anthropologists need only to avoid creating problems. The former indicates that anthropologists need to help improve the lives of their informants, just as these informants, by giving information, help improve the lives of the anthropologists.

Readers might wonder why this topic is not covered within the code, especially when the ethic of doing no harm is stressed. My impression is that just compensation involves directly addressing the power politics involved in the anthropological endeavor—First World scholars visiting Third World informants. It concerns the power relations that surround the anthropological enterprise.

There are two cases in the Yanomami controversy that relate to the issue of just compensation. The first concerns Chagnon's failure to share royalties from his best-selling book with them; the second involves the degree to which Neel fairly compensated the Yanomami for their blood donations.

On the first case, I suspect many readers would concur that Chagnon should donate some of his royalties to the Yanomami. The central questions are how much and to whom? Readers are presumably willing to be freer with Chagnon's money than with their own. But if the more than a million dollars involved were *too ambiguous* yours, what percentage would you return to the Yanomami? And to whom would you give it? Since there are no Yanomami-wide organizations, how would you distribute it? Would you share the money with all the Yanomami—even those who threatened to kill you or lied to you? Or would you give the money just to those who really helped advanced your research or whom you liked?

According to Peters, "The income of some anthropologists with faculty positions is more than the income of the entire group originally studied." How much giving is enough under such circumstances?

In defense of Chagnon, Hill writes: "Although Chagnon has been singled out here for criticism, this is an issue that applies to many anthropologists. I have seen dozens of field anthropologists over the years work in precisely the same way as Chagnon is alleged to have done. They provide a few gifts to informants and then never again return to share out any of the economic success that comes from a career that was built on that fieldwork. Very few anthropologists could withstand the scrutiny of careful investigation into their own activities on this front." Hill's point is, why simply blame Chagnon—who has been successful in his writing—when the problem is much broader? Hill agrees with others who think that Chagnon might do more, but he points out a problem: "Chagnon paid the Yanomamö for data when it was collected but apparently did not provide any other assistance to the tribe. Is this a fair distribution of the gains that came from the Chagnon-Yanomamö collaboration, or is it exploitation? I believe that this is an issue Chagnon should discuss directly with the Yanomamö who helped him. . . . Unfortunately, Chagnon's enemies made it impossible for him to return to the Yanomamö for many years, so he couldn't possibly have helped them even if that were his top priority."

From Kopenawa's perspective, anthropologists are concerned with money. As he sees it, the controversy's antagonisms increase book sales and therefore money for the controversy's participants. That is the reason they fight. Why shouldn't the Yanomami get some of the money, he asks, especially since anthropologists are using the fame of the Yanomami to become famous themselves? He wants to know something many would like to know: how much are Chagnon and Tierney making each month from the sales of their books? It turns out that their book profits are a closely guarded secret by both Chagnon and Tierney.

On the second case, Neel's collecting of blood, Albert states: "To this day, I still do not see how his [Neel's] blood sampling or research significantly helped the Yanomami in treating their epidemic diseases, as they were promised if they agreed to let their blood be drawn (a promise that, in their eyes, was reinforced by the delivery of trade goods). The Venezuelan and Brazilian Yanomami have kept on dying in the same way for three decades after Neel's project."

The joint letter from the participants in the part 2 discussion (see chapter 11) suggests the following for just compensation:

> Central to providing both balance and justice . . . [in anthropological research] is a negotiated contract among the parties involved regarding the benefits accruing to each as a result of their relationship. Whether interpreted within the framework of gifts or exchanges, there need to be clearly defined rewards. Yet because of the noted political/economic asymmetry [i.e., the relations of power referred to above], anthropologists often are at an advantage in such negotiations—having a clearer sense of the value gained in relation to the rewards returned. As a rule of thumb, one might follow John Rawls's "veil of ignorance," in which anthropologists consider what constitutes a just balance without presuming to know which side— informant or anthropologist—they are on. As Rawls phrases it, with the veil of ignorance, "the parties are not allowed to know the social positions . . . of the parties they represent." What would anthropologists claim to be fair—under these circumstances—for all parties concerned?
>
> We would offer the following as guidelines for answering this question: (a) A mutually agreed upon equitable division of all royalties that accrue to an anthropologist through the publication of works relating to the people involved. Such remuneration might take a range of forms. In the case of the Yanomami, for example, it

could involve reimbursing individuals and groups or using the funds to support projects directed by Venezuelan and Brazilian Yanomami and non-Yanomami . . . NGOs to improve present medical, economic, educational, and environmental conditions. (b) A mutually agreed upon equitable division of all royalties drawn from biological specimens—either from the indigenous group itself or from flora and fauna in the area where the group resides—in a manner similar to that noted above. (c) Given that most anthropologists gain little in the way of royalties they might share with their communities of study, there are still a variety of ways they might redress the basic asymmetries of research.

The key here is working with informants and their communities to address their collective needs as they stipulate them—not as an anthropologist stipulates them. For example, informants may be eligible for governmental assistance but, for a variety of reasons, are unable to gain access to it. Informants may request that anthropologists, given their skills in dealing with bureaucracies, lobby on behalf of their communities. Likewise, communities may be short of medicines, such as antimalarial drugs, which the anthropologist can purchase. The anthropologist can then offer these medicines to the people themselves and/or restock local dispensaries. The essential point is that anthropologists must provide help in terms that the people themselves directly perceive and directly appreciate.

....

JUST COMPENSATION: QUESTIONS TO PONDER

1. Why do you think that "doing no harm" has taken such a prominent role in anthropological ethics in comparison to just compensation?

2. As an anthropologist negotiating with your informants over just compensation, would you tell them about the hundreds of thousands of dollars you are likely to make over the duration of your professional career as a result of research projects such as the one they are involved in?

3. How would you allocate the compensation you agree to offer? Would it go to everyone or only to those who helped you or whom you liked?

4. Does addressing concerns informants themselves define as important constitute a valid form of compensation that avoids framing compensation solely in terms of money—something most anthropologists, despite their living standard, feel they rarely have enough of? How would you go about discovering and addressing the concerns that are important to your informants?

....

Working in Foreign Countries

Most anthropologists need a foreign government's permission to conduct research within that country. And many are aware that at least some of the difficulties encountered by their informants derive from the bureaucratic limitations of that government in serving these people. Yet governmental ineffectiveness is rarely highlighted in ethnographies. Presumably, anthropologists fear that a too-open declaration of governmental incompetence might cost them their entry visas. (Here one's own self-interest overrides a concern for ethnographic accuracy.)

In the Yanomami controversy, two topics touch on this subject: restrictions placed on Chagnon's research; and the role of researchers, such as Neel, in helping those whom a government fails to help.

There are two accounts of the governments of Venezuela and Brazil restricting Chagnon's research. Hill stresses that Chagnon was concerned with controversial theories such as sociobiology.* Hill asserts that it was inappropriate to restrict Chagnon's research access simply because prominent scholars in Venezuela and Brazil disagreed with his intellectual perspective.

> For years Chagnon's enemies have attempted to keep him from gaining access to the Yanomamö because they are displeased with the questions he asks and the results of his scientific research. . . . The Yanomamö have experienced a massive campaign of propaganda by anti-Chagnon/anti-sociobiology forces. Those same Chagnon enemies later use Yanomamö mouthpieces to insist that Chagnon is not welcome. In 1988 I witnessed a meeting at the Platanal mission in which a Salesian priest and two anthropologists discussed ways to keep Chagnon out of the upper Orinoco. That meeting included statements about Chagnon's alleged evil activities in front of several Yanomamö witnesses. I take seriously the fact that some Yanomamö are unhappy with Chagnon's work. But I also believe that the intentional distortion of an academic competitor's viewpoint in order to manipulate native peoples to oppose further research by that person is a blatant violation of professional ethics.
>
> I believe that there is good evidence that Chagnon was denied research access to the Yanomamö only *because* he espoused sociobiological theories (particularly about warfare) and that some anthropologists were actively engaged in this theoretical persecution because of their own muddled ideas about the implications of Chagnon's research.

Martins disagrees, saying that, at least in Brazil, it was Chagnon's political, not intellectual, views that caused the restrictions. "Chagnon encountered great

---

*The term *sociobiology* is also the title of a famous book by E. O. Wilson, and it has taken on certain connotations as a result of this association that do not accurately reflect its present positions. When Hill and Hames refer to sociobiology in part 2 of this book, they are referring to an updated version of sociobiology that puts more emphasis on the environment than Wilson did and is now widely known as *behavioral ecology*. Behavioral ecology "attempts to develop hypotheses regarding variation in behavior strategies that individuals employ to maximize their inclusive fitness" (Hames 2001b:6947. That is to say, it focuses on behaviors individuals and groups use to maximize the reproductive success of themselves and their close relatives—with whom they share certain genes—through adaptations that prove more effective than others in particular environments. We might cite as an example optimal foraging theory, which stresses the importance of using efficient foraging techniques to ensure a group's biological success in a suboptimal foraging environment. Hames notes in chapter 10 that "Chagnon's work on the relationship between combat killing and reproductive success" can be seen as "part of the larger research by behavioral ecologists on the relationship between cultural success and [reproductive/biological] fitness." Hames discusses the approach further in chapter 10.

opposition from Indian leaders, Brazilian anthropologists, Catholic missionaries and local . . . [government] employees, mainly because of the association of his work with the discourse against Indian rights but also in part because of the tales of Chagnon's research in Venezuela that people in [the neighboring Brazilian province of] Roraima heard from across the border. . . . The opposition to Chagnon was not an opposition to science or to sociobiological research in favor of a sociocultural agenda. The people who took part [in opposing Chagnon were] not aware of such fine divisions within academia."

The other key issue concerns Neel's efforts at stemming the measles epidemic. Why should the burden for controlling the epidemic rest on Neel, Hill asks, rather than on the Venezuelan government when government officials and missionaries living in the area had a greater responsibility for treating the Yanomami during the measles crisis than Neel did: "Why exactly Neel should be obligated to donate his valuable time for free to provide medical care to the Yanomamö but anthropologists who hear today that the Yanomamö are suffering from serious health problems (tuberculosis, malaria, etc.) are not 'obligated' to give up part of their incomes to help the Yanomamö (since they can't provide services like Neel did) is unclear to me. Each anthropology student who bought a music CD this month despite knowing about Yanomamö suffering has essentially made the same decision that Neel is accused of . . . namely prioritizing their own needs over those of the Yanomamö."

....

WORKING IN FOREIGN COUNTRIES: QUESTIONS TO PONDER

1. Is it right that a country restricts a foreign researcher when anthropologists in that country disagree with the researcher's intellectual or political views?

2. Should anthropologists be responsible for compensating for the inadequacies of governmental agencies in regions where they work? Is it enough to help ease certain suffering—which you know will recur—when it is politically inconvenient or dangerous to address its underlying causes?

3. To save their research permits, do anthropologists become tools of foreign governments, helping those governments carry out policies in the fields of health and education? Do the anthropologists sell their intellectual and ethical souls when they fail to speak out about social injustices in the foreign countries in which they work?

....

ENSURING PROFESSIONAL INTEGRITY

One can't help but notice the gap between the American Anthropological Association's strong code of ethics on the one hand and the actions it initially took in response to the Yanomami controversy on the other. Martins discusses this in part 2: "The AAA has an ethical code that is very encompassing and progressive, but the mechanisms by which anthropologists are held accountable for their work are not clear. What happens when an anthropologist breaks the code? What is supposed to be done? What accountability exists? I am afraid that if we do not respond to these questions, the burden of dealing with our ethical problems will be always passed to the people who should have the least to be responsible for: the people we choose to study." And Peters points out that because there is no one to adjudicate ethical claims within anthropology, anthropologists "can go and do research wherever they wish, as long as they have permission from the government in the jurisdiction in which the research is taking place. . . . Anthropologists are on their own. Once legitimately in a country, they pretty much ask the questions they wish, in whatever manner they wish, wherever they are, of whomever they choose. . . . No professional bodies . . . placed . . . controls on any of the anthropologists, medical researchers, or cameramen mentioned in the Tierney book."

Why this gap between the code's high-minded aspirations and the limited enforcement of the code in practice? I would suggest that there are two reasons.

First, the American Anthropological Association perceives itself to be in a vulnerable position. It has financial troubles. The association's expenses exceeded its revenues in 2000 by roughly $300,000, in 2001 by roughly $200,000, and in 2002 by more than $1 million. Although membership steadily climbed in the 1990s, today it is somewhat unstable. (Membership dropped by roughly seven hundred members, or 6 percent, between October 2002 and October 2003.) The association is also marked by fractious divides that make archaeologists and physical anthropologists feel not only outnumbered but marginalized at the association's annual meetings. Many archaeologists and physical anthropologists now perceive the Society for American Archaeology and the American Association of Physical Anthropologists as more supportive of their interests than the American Anthropological Association.* The AAA's guide to anthropology departments indicates that only about 40 percent of the anthropologists teaching in academia belong to the AAA.

Given this situation, the AAA's general policy is to avoid controversies that may further divide members. That is why it got out of the business of adjudicating ethical conflicts in 1995. The final report of the "Commission to Review the AAA Statements on Ethics" states: "The AAA [will] no longer adjudicate claims of unethical behavior and focus its resources on an ethics education pro-

---

*To patch over such fractures, the association has set aside one formal seat for archaeologists and one for biological (or physical) anthropologists on its board. Cultural anthropologists, who make up over two-thirds of the AAA's membership (Evans 1998:6) have only one seat reserved for them.

I would add that there is a sense of the power elite in the AAA Executive Board's membership. Students constitute roughly one-third of the association, yet they are allocated only one reserved seat. There are four undesignated seats on the board, which might be seen as softening the bias toward one or another group, but in 2003–04 and 2004–05, none of these seats were held by students. Students today constitute one-third of the membership, in other words, but hold only one-twelfth of the board seats.

gram" (AAA 1995:1). An ethics code "should draw an increasingly divided discipline together . . . At the very least, the code of the discipline's most inclusive organization should not engender division. The work of the anthropological community is too important and the community too small for such divisions" (11).

With Chagnon's strong support within the discipline—remember how many people have used his book *Yanomamö*—the AAA presumably preferred to sidestep the controversy surrounding him. It was the negative publicity generated by Tierney's *Darkness in El Dorado* that clearly forced the association to inquire into Tierney's accusations. With anthropology's public image at stake, the discipline could not be seen as ignoring the book. But I believe that concern over disciplinary divisions is why the association initially focused on the accusations surrounding Neel and why it seemed more involved—until public pressure was brought to bear through the many e-mails—with protecting its public image than with addressing various accusations against Chagnon.

Second, the gap between rhetoric and reality in the AAA's code derives from the state of American anthropology today. The discipline is fractured, with people going off in different directions and espousing disparate concerns. Divisive self-interests are not subsumed under a broader, common good supported by all.

Different people working in different contexts apply the association's code in rather different ways. As the part 2 discussion indicates, what seem to some to be serious moral infractions on Chagnon's part constitute to others mostly minor mistakes. It is the problem of Durkheim's organic solidarity. It is not clear how to form a shared overarching intellectual and moral cohesiveness to counter specialization's fragmenting effects.

This is not to say that the discipline does not espouse certain overarching concerns. It does. But while these may have helped to hold things together in earlier times, they no longer do today. Let me offer two examples.

At one time, the comparative method—in which anthropologists focused on comparing different groups with one another—constituted a unifying disciplinary approach. The definitions of anthropology cited in chapter 4 imply a comparative perspective. But while comparisons are still done today, relatively speaking they play a less significant role within the discipline, numerically and intellectually, than in times past. "The sheer number of comparative articles and books published," in the early 1950s, Nader writes, reminds us "that energetic debates about the intellectual place of comparison are missing among today's anthropological agendas" (1994:85). And Holy, in a book entitled *Comparative Anthropology*, observes that "these days, a great proportion of empirical research is distinctly non-comparative" and "comparisons aimed specifically at generating cross-culturally valid generalizations seem to be conspicuous by their absence" (1987:8, 13).

Another unifying principle claimed by American anthropology is that it represents a four-field discipline, that is to say that it involves integrating research from the subfields of cultural anthropology, archaeology, physical anthropology, and linguistics. This claim is embraced today by the AAA and various anthropology departments that have historically been organized along these lines.

But the statement that anthropology is an integrated four-field discipline does not reflect reality. In an article entitled "The Four Subfields: Anthropologists as Mythmakers" (Borofsky 2002), I point out that only 9.5 percent of the articles published in the *American Anthropologist*—the association's flagship journal—over the past one hundred years actually integrated the subfields in any significant way. At one time, the discipline did share certain interests that allowed anthropologists to, if not integrate the four subfields in their writing, at least be interested in the work produced by colleagues in other subfields. But that was then. As Hymes observed in 1969, Boas "could maintain that the field anthropologist should know the principles and results of linguistics, biological anthropology, and ethnologic-archaeological work (he joined the two in this context), but the context of problems in which he made the statement (essentially the history of peoples) no longer holds for more than a few students" (1969:44). Cultural anthropology—which constitutes over two-thirds of the AAA (Evans 1998:6)—has moved on from the historical reconstructions that once made people in different subfields interested in one another's work. They now focus on a host of other issues that allow for less overlap among the subfields.

The standard formulations for what anthropologists share in common, in other words, do not hold today. With changing times have come changing interests, which means that the discipline lacks an overall coherence to draw on in formulating a common good, a moral center, that unites rather than divides the discipline's diverse constituencies. People apply the ethical code's abstract pronouncements in different ways based on divergent interests.

I would suggest that the solution to both of these problems—the AAA's avoidance of divisive issues and the discipline's lack of coherence—is one and the same. It is to emphasize the discipline's common concern with ethics, particularly as it is manifested in the discipline's ethical stance toward difference. At first glance, this may appear to be a stretch, since it is the divergent perspectives surrounding Chagnon's actions that have proved so divisive within the discipline. But in seeking to understand other people and how they differ from us, anthropologists tend to focus on these people's perspectives, these people's experiences rather than framing (and valuing) them within the perspectives of our own society.

This stance toward difference is more than an intellectual choice. It is a deeply ethical, deeply moral commitment to appreciating others on their own terms.

Anthropology intends more than that other people's differences should be tolerated. It emphasizes that they should be valued, understood, and appreciated within the contexts in which they are lived. Anthropologists do not seek to reshape them in our own terms. Note that despite their opposing views, neither Chagnon nor Tierney (nor any of the part 2 participants) seeks to erase Yanomami ways of life, to make the Yanomami into American citizens. Anthropologists want to help Yanomami to continue being Yanomami as they cre-atively adapt to changing circumstances. As Sahlins famously suggested: "Local people integrate the World System into something even more inclusive: their system of the world" (1994:384). That is the anthropological hope, that in changing, the Yanomami do not become reduced versions of us but enlarged versions of themselves.

Since its founding, anthropology has sought to illuminate alternative ways of living beyond readers' (usually Western readers') familiar ways. Anthropology widens our sense of human possibility, of how life might be lived. In the process, it illuminates the dynamics that shape our behavior. It lets us see more clearly the hows and whys of our own actions.

Anthropology emphasizes that there is a wider world beyond our everyday experiences, beyond what we are familiar and comfortable with. Anthropology's message is a deeply moral one: we need to engage with this world of differences if we are to grow beyond our provincial perceptions.

This ethical stance brings with it certain ethical obligations. Let me highlight two of the most obvious.

First, it involves honoring others' differences from us in ways that help them, not just ourselves. It means more than simply doing no harm. It means assisting those who assist us, in ways that they stipulate, that they themselves want (as the part 2 participants state in their joint letter). It insists on our not submerging their wants to our convenience—doing only what feels comfort-able to us.

Second, it means educating people beyond the discipline to appreciate the dif-ferent ways people lead their lives. To do this, we must communicate with nonacademic audiences in ways they understand. This does not mean, however, giving in to Western audiences' tendency to exoticize others as a way of affirm-ing themselves but leading them to see the value of alternative ways of life.

Chagnon is not to blame for the way millions of students resonated with the violence he perceived among the Yanomami. But one has to wonder why so many professors over so many years seemed caught up in using a book that clearly challenged their formal code of ethics and their commitment to not exoti-cizing others. What does it say about how anthropologists teach anthropology?

What I am suggesting is a postcolonial vision of anthropology for postcolo-nial times. As the Yanomami controversy demonstrates, anthropology cannot build the trust required for continuing research in foreign locales if it sidesteps the ethical conflicts that engage anthropologists. We cannot focus on our own self-interests, leaving a concern for the broader good to others. Who will trust us—abroad or at home—if we pursue only our self-interest? This is one of the clear messages of the Yanomami controversy. To revitalize the discipline, we need to renew our responsibilities to the world around us, to the people who make the practice of anthropology possible.

The AAA can be the vehicle for leading this revitalization. Instead of focus-ing on holding together a divided community, it can draw the discipline into a new sense of purpose, a new sense of unity centered on a shared ethical stance toward difference and the ethical obligations this stance entails.

....

ENSURING PROFESSIONAL INTEGRITY: QUESTIONS TO PONDER

1. What should be the purpose of the American Anthropological Association? Should it be focused on holding together a divided community? Or should it be something grander, something more inspiring?

2. How would placing ethics at the discipline's center transform the discipline? Could an ethical stance toward difference be the new cement to hold anthropology together, above and beyond the specializations that today fragment it?

3. Is it enough to assume that people at a field site, away from their peers, will act morally? Or is something more effective needed to build trust among those who facilitate our research beyond the halls of academia? If so, what would this be?

....

ESTABLISHING CREDIBILITY

One of the tensions that arises in the Yanomami controversy is between approaches that are labeled as scientific and approaches that are viewed as ideological. (A science/nonscience polarization pervades the social sciences.) Some Chagnon supporters view activist approaches as ideological; some Chagnon critics view sociobiological approaches in the same way.

Thus framed, the argument misses the point.

First, there is more than one scientific approach. To assume that there is only one is to radically oversimplify science. For example, Cetina's *Epistemic Cultures: How the Sciences Make Knowledge* examines scientific practices in experimental high-energy physics (at CERN [Organisation Européenne pour la Recherche Nucléaire] in Geneva, Switzerland) and molecular biology (at the Max Planck Institute in Göttingen and Heidelberg, Germany). Cetina emphasizes "the fragmentation of contemporary science; it displays . . . [a] diversity of epistemic cultures" or ways for creating knowledge (1999:3).

Second, the issue is not whether a particular anthropologist's work is scientific. It is whether that anthropologist's work is *credible*. Calling particular research *scientific* in anthropology is often an attempt to establish credibility by name-dropping. Establishing credibility is more complex than that. Chapter 4 discusses how anthropologists, in seeking to present credible accounts, often use certain credentializing styles, such as presenting plenty of citations, that are flawed. Such methods may not only *not* resolve arguments but may, in fact, perpetuate them, letting both sides in an argument talk past each other. I would make the same point regarding labeling something as scientific.

A key issue concerns what is lost in credibility when one pushes a political agenda. It comes up in Hames's defense of Chagnon's accounts of the Yanomami. "Whatever power anthropologists have is founded on the explicit belief that we provide accurate information. If we stray from this obligation we will be dismissed as ordinary political actors who distort reality to promote our political aims. . . . I believe it fundamentally wrong to paint false pictures of native peoples, even if the goal is noble. The problem is that in the long run you will eventually be found out and you will lose credibility. Consequently, your ability to intervene and help will be compromised." "So long as we attempt to falsely portray native peoples as if they were perfect [i.e., nonviolent], according to our system of cultural values, as a rationale to assist them in their legitimate struggles to achieve protection and control of their land, the more we lose credibility as objective analysts. I believe this to be our greatest strength as ethnographers. We are the expert witnesses, so to speak, for the defense of native peoples in the court of public opinion." Albert, who frequently disagrees with Hames, concurs with him on this point: "I have been quite harsh myself in underlining the dangers of 'the questionable use of stereotypical and exoticizing imagery (the ecological and New Age Noble Savage) to which certain NGOs link the recognition of indigenous peoples' rights in order to guarantee their own legitimacy and boost their fund-raising activities'" (see Albert 1997:60).

The above statements sound reasonable. But how do we know that an anthropological description is unbiased, nonpolitical, scientific, or accurate? Surely, we can't trust the anthropologist to tell us that. One need only reflect on the dispute over whether the Yanomami are indeed "fierce": Chagnon suggests one view, Tierney another.

That is why, in the search for objectivity, we can't put our faith in a single account, no matter the status of the person who produced it. There is always the problem of self-serving rhetoric. As I noted previously: *Objectivity does not lie in the assertions of authorities. It lies in the open, public analysis of divergent perspectives.*

The issue is not whether one does (or does not) have a political agenda but rather whether one's analysis has been challenged by other first-hand knowledge in open, public debate. That is what has happened in the Yanomami controversy. Because so many anthropologists have worked among them, we are able to compare one ethnographic account with another. We have not only Chagnon's and Tierney's discussions of "fierceness" but also accounts by Albert, Hames, Lizot, and Good. With so many different ethnographic accounts, readers have the material to work their way toward some sort of resolution—deciding, for example, whether the Yanomami are fiercer in some regions (Chagnon's position) or whether Chagnon overstated their fierceness (Albert's, Lizot's, and Good's position).

Unfortunately, most anthropologists tend to go to new locales and explore new research topics rather than returning to the sites of earlier research and repeating that research. How do we know, when only one anthropologist describes a group, which parts of his or her data are credible? Being the sole anthropologist reduces one's exposure to criticism. But it also reduces one's ability to make credible claims.

I am not saying that one can replicate each and every detail of a previous ethnography. Human behavior is too contextually oriented and too fluid for such precision. But surely anthropologists can go back to the same site and explore some of the same questions. This is rarely done within the discipline. Where would we be if we simply accepted at face value the Yanomami as "the fierce people"? Where would the Yanomami be?

Often, it is not the replicable data themselves that generate trust—because these may not be fully replicable—as much as the negotiated conversations that ensue that analyze the differing results from different research projects. Galison writes about replicability in the important physics monograph *Image and Logic*: "It is surely true, as authors from Michael Polanyi, to Thomas Kuhn, to Harry Collins have insisted, that there are moments when individuals can't spell out rules for replication. That should be occasion, not to stop the inquiry, but to ask: Why not? What pieces of practice will not fit the public discourse of science, and why? Sometimes the movement of machine knowledge may be impeded because no one knows what portion of a complicated procedure is efficacious and what is superfluous. . . . Engineers from different laboratories meet to share tricks about gaskets and seals, about computer analyses and simulations" (1997:xx–xxi).

That is what has happened in this chapter, and it is what happens in part 2 of this book. An open, public discussion of the controversy takes place that allows readers—through examining different perspectives—to make sense of the divergent accounts.

The opposition is not between science and one or another "ideological" stances. The opposition is between claiming objectivity and substantiating it.

There is another way to establish credibility besides the public analysis of divergent perspectives. It flows from the American pragmatic tradition. It involves judging the value of data by the problems they help solve. In this intellectual tradition, deciding whether something is credible means deciding whether it works, whether it resolves the problems one is faced with.

Defining credibility in pragmatic terms draws anthropologists beyond the academic confines of the discipline. We are encouraged to start with the world's problems—as others bring them to us—rather than focusing on the discipline's traditional formulations regarding who said what when. The acid test of our ideas from this perspective is their effectiveness. Which anthropological analyses make a significant difference in the lives of people beyond the academy? Do they solve (or at least lessen) critical public concerns? Do they help the people we work with? Many anthropologists claim this is so. They need to prove it. Certainly the Yanomami would appreciate something more than being the object of academic discussions. Presumably, most groups anthropologists study would.

Holding anthropologists publicly accountable for their ideas—judging them not on how many works they have produced or how many people have cited them but on whether they have indeed helped resolve practical problems—is a higher standard for credibility than is widely held within academia. But that is what the standard of objectivity, referred to earlier, is supposed to lead to. Given the fluid, contextual dynamics of people's behaviors as they respond to an ever-changing world, objectivity as a "rock" on which to build our hopes for the discipline loses its intellectual power unless it is tied to addressing real problems in the real world. Objectivity is not an intellectual abstraction. As Barth suggests, "The cutting edges of our theories can . . . be [I would suggest must be] . . . tested by their relevance and power in practical matters" (1994:350).

The two ways for establishing credibility discussed here—public analysis of divergent perspectives and the judging of work by its pragmatic value—together move ethics to the forefront of the discipline. We combine accuracy with activism, and research with responsibility in ways that renew and enlarge the public space for conversations regarding issues many people around the world deeply care about.

To conclude this section, we might evaluate the credibility of Tierney's *Darkness in El Dorado* based on what we have discussed in this chapter. Using techniques referred to in chapter 4, Hill states, "If the book contains one hundred allegations and the most important ten are investigated carefully and found to be false, what is the logical reaction of most careful readers? They will conclude that the author has little credibility and discount the remaining allegations as unlikely to be true." Turner writes: "Some of the loudest defenders of Neel and Chagnon have attempted to discredit the book as a whole by reference to its flawed treatment of the epidemic, while avoiding discussion of the many parts of the book for which there is abundant evidence in the public record and the testimony of other anthropologists, missionaries, and Yanomami. Some of the most violent attacks on Tierney's book . . . seem directed as much at distracting attention from the truth of many of its allegations as at exposing its relatively few (but important) errors."

How might we assess the book's credibility? The answer is that its credibility is clearly mixed. Some statements are accurate, some are not. One has to check each and every accusation to be sure of its validity, and to date that has not been done. Chagnon's supporters tend to focus on certain accusations, his critics on others. The book's precise credibility thus remains to be determined.

But overarching the specific accusations is a broader accusation regarding the behavior of anthropologists generally and their failure to address the possibility of ethical infractions among them. A section of the joint letter of the part 2 participants (in chapter 11) reads: "While Tierney's *Darkness in El Dorado* contains clear errors, the public uproar his book caused has proved critical in forcing the AAA to address a set of ethical issues it should have addressed on its own well prior to the book's publication." And "despite our clear disagreements regarding Tierney's *Darkness in El Dorado* . . . we collectively affirm it raises important ethical issues which are central to the current discussion."

As a journalistic exposé, the book, has proved effective in a pragmatic sense. It got people's attention and drew anthropologists into acknowledging that there were ethical concerns they needed to deal with.

....

ESTABLISHING CREDIBILITY: QUESTIONS TO PONDER

1. What is the best way for anthropologists to establish credibility with others— both within and beyond academia—who read their work?

2. Why do anthropologists tend to visit new locales with new questions rather than return to the sites of earlier research to repeat that research? Would anthropology be more credible if more anthropologists visited the sites of other anthropologists?

3. Since the credibility of many anthropological analyses remains in dispute, is it reasonable to insist that the assessment of these analyses be based on their effectiveness in dealing with the problems of the world? Would the people we work with appreciate such a perspective?

....

Having set out the key foundational issues involved in the Yanomami controversy and offered readers enough information to draw their own conclusions regarding them, we now turn to whether something might be done to address these issues within anthropology. Knowing what readers now know, the next chapter turns to what actions they might take to bring about disciplinary change.

7

·····························

A PLATFORM FOR CHANGE

Readers who have followed the controversy this far might feel hopeful about the discipline's ability to address the central issues that have been raised. We have progressed from learning about the Yanomami controversy (chapters 1–5) to reading what the experts have to say about its central issues and deliberating over them (chapter 6). We are now able to wend our way through the controversy and evaluate different positions without being overwhelmed by any one scholar's arguments. Readers wishing further elaboration need only turn to part 2 for a detailed discussion of particular points. Many readers may also feel inspired, as I do, by the 119 students who sent in comments to the association's Web site as the El Dorado Task Force sought to finalize its report. Clearly they helped shape the Task Force's final report.

But we might well ask whether such an upbeat mood is justified. Let me explain what causes me concern and why the degree to which American anthropology will seriously address the controversy's central issues remains an open question.

The first concern is exemplified by the "Preface for the El Dorado Task Force Papers," which appears with the final report on the AAA Web site (see AAA 2002) and in the *Anthropology News* (Brenneis 2002:8). It is written by the 2001–03 AAA president and seeks to summarize the final report. What are labeled "substantive conclusions of the report" in the preface sometimes diverge significantly from the report itself. Take, for example, the statements on Tierney's book (the third of the preface's three "substantive conclusions"). The preface reads: "*Darkness in El Dorado* calls attention to the dire plight of the Yanomami. . . . However, the book contains numerous unfounded, misrepresented, and sensationalistic accusations about the conduct of anthropology among the Yanomami. These misrepresentations fail to live up to the ethics of responsible journalism even as they pretend to question the ethical conduct of anthropology." Contrast this with what the final report actually states about *Darkness in El Dorado*: "We concur with the findings of the AAA Executive Board, based on the report of the Peacock Committee [the Ad Hoc Task Force], that the allegations in *Darkness in El Dorado* must be taken seriously. *Darkness in El Dorado* has served anthropology well in that it has opened a space for reflection about what we do and our relationships with those among whom we are privileged to study" (AAA 2002:I.9). And in place of the detailed evaluations sum-marized in the final report, the preface reads: "The AAA believes that the great-est value of this Report is not to find fault with or to defend the past actions of specific anthropologists, but to provide opportunities for all anthropologists to consider the ethics of several dimensions of the anthropological enterprise." The final report, as the summary of it in chapter 11 makes clear, finds fault with Chagnon's behavior. The report's key section (I:21–47) focuses on the degree to which Neel and Chagnon did indeed do what they stand accused of. It seems that despite the efforts of the Task Force to seriously address accusations against Neel and Chagnon in its final report, the preface prefers to dismiss Tierney's accu-sations and affirm nice-sounding abstractions that obscure the deeper issues that need to be addressed.

The second concern is that despite all the international publicity, despite the time, money, and energy American anthropologists have spent examining the issue, and despite a wave of goodwill toward the Yanomami, little in fact has been done to improve their condition. This point is repeatedly made by NGO health practitioners and anthropologists working with the Yanomami as well as by the Yanomami themselves. The result is that anthropology's colonial past lives on in the present. We talk of helping those who help us, but in fact we continue to treat Yanomami as subjects for the advancement of our professional careers.

This sliding back into the status quo should remind us that the controversy extends beyond the flaws and faults of a few people. Focusing only on what Chagnon, Neel, and Tierney did (and did not) do means that we fail to address the key structural problems that haunt the discipline. If we are to grow as a dis-cipline from the controversy, anthropologists need to address these deeper foundational issues.

The discipline's ethics do not reside in the "shoulds" and "should nots" of the association's formal written code. They reside in all of our actions. If we espouse noble aims but settle for the status quo, more controversies of this sort will almost certainly erupt, with yet more negative publicity for the discipline. The world has changed since anthropology was first founded. The discipline's ethics need to change as well if we are to outgrow the discipline's colonial past.

Most anthropologists are concerned, caring people. But as Kroeber (in Thomas 1956:309) phrased it, anthropologists "are notoriously inner-directed." Judging oneself by one's own ethical standards—as tends to occur when there are no shared standards that we all affirm in fact as well as in principle—leaves those standards fairly loose. In part 2 Hill suggests that various anthropologists share some of Chagnon's failings. I believe that Hill is correct.

Why, we might ask, are collective ethical assessments in anthropology so rare in the discipline? As previously noted, the AAA has not adjudicated a claim of unethical behavior since 1995. (The El Dorado Task Force was at pains to emphasize that it was conducting an inquiry, *not* an investigation.)

What is strikingly clear, in terms of how the Yanomami controversy has played out, is that public pressure makes a difference. That is what brings a sense of collective accountability to the private, personalized ethics of the discipline. Perhaps there is an anthropological axiom in this: *people act better morally in public settings than they do in private ones.*

Let me suggest two ways in which we might enlarge the discipline's public space for accountability and make anthropologists' private behaviors more public. First, we need common sets of data, as noted in chapter 6. We need to have anthropologists researching the same groups in roughly the same locales from different perspectives to separate out the describers' biases from their descriptions.

Second, we need to speak intelligibly across our differences so others, including the millions of people outside the discipline who are intrigued by anthropology, can understand our ideas and our data. Critical to enlarging our public discussions is allowing a broad range of readers to assess the credibility of our claims. If others cannot understand our claims, if they cannot check them against other evidence, they cannot assess them. Our claims—no matter how exciting—are therefore clouded with doubt.

We need to remember that the discipline has not only significant structural problems but, as this book suggests, reasonable solutions for dealing with them. To equalize the power differentials in fieldwork, we can adopt Rawls's "veil of ignorance" approach. For the problematic way in which anthropologists evaluate the work of their peers, the jury trial format of part 2 is useful. To illuminate the private morality fostered by ever-increasing specialization, we can nurture the discipline's public accountability through the steps discussed below and in chapter 6. The problems are solvable. The question is: *do we have the political will to solve them?*

A small, concrete step toward building a moral community—for that is what we are really talking about—is to help the Yanomami by purchasing this book *new.* All royalties from the book go to help the Yanomami; they get no money from the sale of used books.

A larger step involves committing ourselves to the same political activism as the students who helped reshape the El Dorado Task Force's final report. The American Anthropological Association clearly means well. Anthropologists tend to care deeply about the people they work with. But American anthropology operates within structural frameworks that limit such caring. And in seeking ways out of the maze, anthropologists often focus on "solutions" that are reiterations of the familiar. The French expression for it is "plus ça change, plus c'est la même chose"—the more things change the more they remain the same.

What follows is a set of steps you, the reader, can take to help transform the structures that limit the discipline ethically. The key is holding American anthropology, and the American Anthropological Association that represents it, accountable for their publicly stated intentions to help set the controversy right.

You can log on to the Public Anthropology Web site (www.publicanthropology.org) and see what the AAA has (and has not) done in this regard. (You can also put your name on a list and receive monthly e-mail updates.) E-mail addresses for key people in the AAA are prominently posted on the site so you can write to them with questions and concerns.

The e-mail addresses of people in the media as well as heads of anthropology funding agencies are displayed. Presumably, many of them would appreciate learning about the association's progress (or lack of progress) in matters they have previously reported on or funded.

The site has space for you to converse with other students on particular subjects. Departmental e-mail addresses are listed so you can reach out to your fellow students at other universities and colleges to compare notes and build coalitions. The goal is to provide students with the tools that will allow them to be an effective pressure group for disciplinary change.

Let me be specific about what the American Anthropological Association has promised to date.

The "Preface for the El Dorado Task Force Papers" and the AAA Executive Board at its May 18–19, 2002, meeting emphasized that in light of the controversy and Task Force final report, the AAA would take a number of actions. We should hold the AAA to its word in this regard.

1. The preface states that "it is clear that the Yanomami are currently in a position of great danger, with exceptionally high rates of infant mortality, African River Blindness, and malaria. Their land, livelihood, and lives are imperiled. Central to the Task Force's concerns is the future of the Yanomami and the ways through which AAA and other concerned individuals and groups might be able to help ameliorate a desperate situation."

At its May 2002 meeting, the AAA Executive Board "called upon appropriate bodies within the AAA to continue to consider those issues raised in the El Dorado Task Force report relating to the current and future conditions of the Yanomami and other indigenous communities in South America, and to devise appropriate responses in collaboration with appropriate indigenous communities and South American colleagues. We look to the newly named AAA Commission on the Status of Indigenous Peoples in South America to lead these efforts" (*Anthropology News,* September 2002:11).

It is one thing to form a commission, another to devise appropriate, collaborative responses. Let us watch to see what the commission and the AAA do in this regard. Let us urge the commission forward so they will be true to their good intentions. The commission members' e-mail addresses are listed on the Public Anthropology Web site (www.publicanthropology.org).

2. The preface continues: "The AAA believes that the greatest value of this Report is . . . to provide opportunities for all anthropologists to consider the ethics of several dimensions of the anthropological enterprise." To follow up on this statement, the AAA Executive Board "called upon the membership of AAA to explore the implications of the El Dorado Task Force Report for anthropological research, practice, and training in the 21st century. We look to the Committee on Ethics to be central in these efforts" (ibid).

Let us watch to see what the Committee on Ethics does. As chapter II points out, the committee has had limited success to date in this regard. Perhaps the committee will do better this time around. We should encourage them. Ethics Committee members' e-mail addresses are listed at www.publicanthropology .org.

3. The AAA Executive Board also decided at its May 2002 meeting that the "AAA will take the initiative in facilitating discussion between the Yanomami and the scientists who hold their blood or other bodily samples as to the disposition of those materials" (ibid). We await the AAA's efforts on this important matter. With more public awareness of the problem—facilitated by students contacting the media—things can evolve in a positive way.

Research suggests that Yanomami blood samples are presently stored in as many as six locations in the United States. For the latest update on which individuals at what institutions are storing Yanomami blood—in case you wish to write a letter to these individuals and the administrators supervising them—see the Public Anthropology Web site (www.publicanthropology.org). The funding agencies that support these individuals' research, when available, are also listed in case you want to express your views to them as well.

The El Dorado Task Force's final report reads, under "Mending the Damage": "We believe . . . [in laying] the beginnings for new collaborations between the Yanomami and the research community. . . . These agreements should include a commitment by the anthropological community to full collaboration with the Yanomami to see that adequate medical care is provided to Yanomami communities, especially in Venezuela where the need is greatest. This effort should not take the form of vague promises. . . . Instead, it should take the form of working with colleagues internationally toward immediate and material benefit in the form of training, equipment, medical supplies and medicines, clinical access and personnel, and other benefits that will be accessible to Yanomami throughout their homeland" (AAA 2002).

We should watch to see to what degree the AAA follows up on this worthwhile proposal. E-mail addresses for individuals directing this effort are listed on the Public Anthropology Web site. You may want to contact them. In addition, e-mail addresses for departments within the Brazilian and Venezuelan governments that deal with the Yanomami are listed. You might wish to express your views to them, too. E-mail addresses for prominent newspapers in both countries are also listed.

If you are interested in contributing to one or more of the NGOs that are helping the Yanomami, their e-mail addresses and Web sites are on the Public Anthropology Web site. Among the most prominent in Brazil are Comissão Pró-Yanomami (CCPY; Pro-Yanomami Commission), Urihi Saúde Yanomami (URIHI), and the Rainforest Foundation, Norway.

Surely, the Yanomami controversy does not represent the only case of difficulties in the anthropological endeavor. The Public Anthropology Web site, as an experiment, offers the opportunity for indigenous communities, through their duly constituted representatives, to write and express concerns with particular anthropological projects or field-workers. The goal is to address problems before they explode into the media, with negative results all around. It is not the job of the Public Anthropology Web site to assess who is right or wrong regarding such controversies. But the Web site can foster discussions modeled on the jury format of part 2, in which an indigenous community and an anthropologist publicly discuss their differences. The goal is to make fieldwork—which is often a private affair, far from one's academic colleagues—be a more public, more accountable, process. If an indigenous community has a concern, please send an e-mail to mail@publicanthropolog.org or write: Center for a Public Anthropology, 814 Kaipii Street, Kailua, HI 96734, USA.

In conclusion, we have seen that there are reasonable solutions to the structural problems that pervade the Yanomami controversy—for the differentials in power, for the private morality fostered by ever-increasing specialization, and for the ways in which anthropologists argue past one another. To repeat, the key question is whether we have the political will to solve them. That is why this chapter outlines a platform for student activism—for students are the group least committed to the status quo and therefore most likely to spearhead change. Still, this is a project that we all can, indeed all should, participate in. We all need to build a more public, ethical anthropology.

The Yanomami controversy constitutes part of a continuing story within the discipline. Anthropology is a historically unique project. No intellectual effort in recorded history has involved as many scholars striving to understand people living in foreign locales on their own terms. Anthropologists do not come to dominate or trade. They come to understand and appreciate. It is a noble endeavor. But it is a project that does not stand alone. Anthropology exists within the Western societies that have fostered it, and that is the problem. As the Yanomami controversy shows, anthropologists have gotten caught up in the imperial politics of their societies as well as the politics of their own discipline. It is a constant tension: seeking to move beyond our societies, we very much remain part of them. But whatever the failures, it does not mean the vision is dead. The beliefs that inspired the discipline remain very much alive. We must nourish them, however, with our hopes and hearts, if they are to flourish.

The Yanomami controversy, by highlighting what has gone wrong in the discipline, draws us to helping set things right. This chapter offers tools to facilitate that process. What is needed now is the willingness to apply those tools.

PHOTOGRAPHIC INTERLUDE

CLAUDIA ANDUJAR

(Brazilian photographer and activist on behalf of the Yanomami)

*"The Yanomami have a deep sense of spirituality,
and I wanted to convey that. I fear for the Yanomami because of their
relative isolation. Few Yanomami understand the world outside their own.
My apprehension drew me to capture their images with respect,
empathy, and a certain sorrow."*

facing page, top: A Yanomami woman, between twenty-two and twenty-five, from Wakathu village. The stick decoration is worn only by women.

facing page, bottom: The shaman is in a trance with both eyes shut. He is about sixty years old and is the headman of the Hwayau village. During the construction of the Northern Perimeter Highway in 1976, the whole Wakathu River valley was infected with measles. A messenger had walked five days from Hwayau to the health outpost where Claudia Andujar was to request help. She and a health practitioner had to walk back to the village to assist as best they could. Half the people of the village died from the measles epidemic. The shaman, who was himself facing death, told her, "When I die everything will become dark, the night [death] will come like the wind or like the morning sun. I will be without defenses or power." He noted that with the introduction of outside diseases, shamans were losing their power to cure people.

above: The women are bathing in a small river during a hunting trip. In preparation for a feast, the Yanomami go off hunting for a week or two to collect the necessary meat they are required to provide their guests. Everyone goes along—women, children, grandparents, and dogs—and they live in a temporary camp. Usually the men go hunting during the day, leaving the women to take care of the children, collect firewood, and carry out other domestic chores. The hunting trips tend to be rather pleasant times with lots of playfulness and laughter.

facing page: Yanomami women often carry their children when they walk through the forest. The women wear baskets on their backs for transporting items, and a child may sit on top of the basket. The child keeps in close bodily contact with the mother until breast-feeding is over, at around three years of age. This picture was taken at Wakathu village.

KEN GOOD

(American anthropologist)

*"When you live among the Yanomami for a long time,
you forget they are naked. As a result, many photographs I took are not
suitable for American audiences, because they show genitalia. I sought pictures
that were aesthetically pleasing as well as anthropologically illuminating.
My goal was to ethnographically document the events I witnessed
during my years of fieldwork but to do so in a way that others
could appreciate the aesthetics of Yanomami life."*

facing page, top: Normally it is the visitors rather than the hosts who extensively decorate themselves with feathers. But this is a special case. The two men are getting ready for a ceremony to initiate a new shaman. The new shaman has been taking drugs and reciting chants for a week. The man on the right is the village headman. The two men are relaxing, talking, and enjoying themselves.

facing page, bottom: This village had been raided by another village, someone had died in that raid, and now the men are getting ready to go on a revenge raid. At a sign from the headman, all the men going on the raid walk to the center plaza of the *shabono* (or communal village house) and bang their arrows against their bows. The men then get into a line, as they are here, raise their arrows in the air, give a shout, and proceed out of the village. The goal is to leave at a time so that they can reach the other village around dawn the next day. The raiding group hopes to kill some unsuspecting person who has wandered outside of the *shabono* (perhaps to urinate). This is a much safer way of gaining revenge than attacking the *shabono* directly, which might result in injuries to the raiding party.

above: When visitors enter a village for a formal feast, the male visitors move to the center of the *shabono*. The headman then scurries around allocating various guests particular hammocks. The visitor reclines in the selected hammock and looks straight ahead—as in this picture—until the host, whose hammock it is, initiates conversation. The guests do not leave the hammocks to get food; rather it is brought to them by their hosts.

facing page: This is a young girl adorned in typical fashion for a special feast. The bead decoration was gotten in an exchange; the yarn and coin (below it) are relatively new, nontraditional adornments. The down feathers are from a buzzard. She is the younger daughter of the village headman. The girl later died at a fairly young age from a respiratory infection.

VICTOR ENGLEBERT

(A Belgian-born award-winning photographer, who has worked
extensively among indigenous peoples and now lives in the United States)

*"My visit to the Yanomami was commissioned by a Time-Life project, and I
had a list of pictures that needed to be taken for it, so I used that as my guide.
The thing that struck me most about the Yanomami, who supposedly had been
isolated for centuries, was how similar they are to us. They have an incredible sense
of humor and a wonderful love for children. You find among them the same types of
people you find in our own society: leaders, clowns, politicians, storytellers, and
paper pushers. As a child, I wanted to become an explorer to learn about
people different from me. Yet it struck me only small things separated the
Yanomami from me: their lack of clothes, for example, and how
they decorated their bodies. What I sought to preserve in my
photographs was our shared humanity with them."*

facing page, top: A Yanomami *shabono*, in the Toototobi region of Brazil. Families
live in the protected areas, with public events occurring in the open plaza at the
village's center.

facing page, bottom: A woman, accompanied by her young child, is bringing
firewood she has collected near her garden back to the *shabono* for cooking.

In these two pictures, members of Toototobi village are decorating themselves in anticipation of the arrival later in the day of a neighboring village for a feast. Feasts are occasions to reaffirm alliances as well as to bury the ashes of the dead and, in some villages, to eat ashes of the dead. These two pictures, taken in 1981, reflect a period of calm and relaxation before the excitement of the feast.

above: A wife is decorating her husband with a red dye (*urucu*) made from the fruit of the annatto tree.

facing page: A father, already decorated for the feast, is decorating his son with the white down of a hawk.

above: Yanomami conversing and relaxing in the *shabono*. The feast's guests have arrived, and one is sitting in his host's hammock. The village headman is conversing with the guest. The photograph conveys a sense of life in the *shabono* as well as some of the implements Yanomami possess.

facing page: A guest at the feast. He has the traditional pensive, straight-ahead look common for the occasion.

A Yanomami male uses a fire to dry some hunting arrowheads he has smeared with a poison extracted from the bark of the virola tree.

A Yanomami shaman (the man in the middle) is preparing *yokoana*, a potent hallucinogenic that will help him get in touch with the spirit world. The man at left grinds dry scrapings from the inside bark of the viola tree in a nut shell. The man at right burns the bark of an ama tree to ashes. *Yokoana* is made by mixing the pulverized ashes of ama bark with the virola powder.

JOHN PETERS

(Roundtable participant, anthropologist, and missionary)

*"These are pictures I took when I was working at the Mucajaí mission
station in the Yanomami region of Brazil. I sought to make a visual record of
the changes that were occurring as the Yanomami came into increasing contact
with Brazilian (and Western) influences. Kurt Kirsch, a Brazilian
missionary, helped with some of the photographs."*

facing page, top: An older man, with his daughter and son-in-law, paddling back
from a field where they are growing sugar cane. The field is about half an hour
away by canoe on the other side of the river. The canoe fairly closely resembles
canoes used in earlier times. Note they are all wearing clothes.

facing page, bottom: Yanomami traditionally used to fish with a bow and arrow.
They would build some scaffolding at the edge of the river, watch for hours, and
then shoot when a fish appeared close by. These fish here were caught with
hooks. Hooks were highly valued during my early years at the mission station.
Using hooks allowed Yanomami to catch not only more but bigger fish.

above: A family is posing for a picture. The man has the down of buzzards on his head for decoration, and the boy has decoration on his face. Traditionally, families never posed together, which helps explain why the woman looks somewhat ill at ease. Recently, more Yanomami appear to want family portraits.

facing page: Two girls are having their picture taken next to a building. Not only is the wearing of clothes noticeable but, in contrast to a decade earlier, these girls seem positively pleased to have their picture taken. They have seen lots of people pose for pictures in Brazilian magazines. The women are wearing decoration on their faces. Their hair is also longer than was previously customary.

Top Row: Davi Kopenawa, the noted Yanomami activist. Here he is speaking to the Brazilian congress in 1988 shortly after becoming a United Nations Global 500 Laureate—an honor awarded by the United Nations Environmental Program. Davi Kopenawa is also the recipient of the Brazilian Order of Rio Branco. (The picture was taken by Claudia Andujar.) *Middle row (left to right):* Roundtable participants Bruce Albert and Lêda Martins. Robert Borofsky is at the right. *Bottom row (left to right):* Roundtable participants Ray Hames, Kim Hill, John Peters, and Terence Turner.

II

8

ROUND ONE

Having set out in part 1 the key events, issues, and individuals associated with the Yanomami controversy, we turn in part 2 to a deeper analysis of them. Where part 1 involved a single authorial voice, part 2 involves seven. Where part 1 guided readers into the controversy's concerns, part 2 is much more like a jury trial where, faced with a set of arguments and counterarguments, readers guide themselves.

At the heart of part 2 is a Roundtable in which six experts (or participants)— Bruce Albert, Raymond Hames, Kim Hill, Lêda Martins, John Peters, and Terence Turner—discuss the controversy's central concerns. (Since these experts' backgrounds are presented in chapter 6, they are not further elaborated upon here.)*

Part 2 constitutes a resource that readers may repeatedly return to as they consider various issues. Readers can either move through part 2 chapter by chapter or explore particular topics using the summary of participants' positions in the appendix. (If readers wish to see what the six experts' views are on just compensation, the inaccuracies in Tierney's book, or other issues they need only turn to the summary statements on them in the appendix.) Either way, readers will gain a richer, deeper understanding of the controversy's key issues and how these six experts argue about them.

Two points need be made regarding the Roundtable.

First, the participants not only assert particular positions but are required to defend them through two sets of exchanges. In this chapter (Round One) the participants set out their views on the question What are the central ethical issues raised by Patrick Tierney's *Darkness in El Dorado*, and what is the best manner for dealing with them? The question is purposely general to leave room for participants with different perspectives to enunciate them. In chapter 9 (Round Two), the six participants comment on one another's positions. One sees the forming of two opposing camps, with Albert, Martins, and Turner on one side, Hames and Hill on the other, and Peters in the middle. In chapter 10 (Round Three) the participants provide their final comments on the issues discussed.

---

*In choosing the experts, I started by asking Ray Hames and Terry Turner, perceiving—correctly as readers will see—that they hold different positions. Hames suggested Kim Hill, and both Hames and Hill proposed contacting John Peters. Turner suggested Bruce Albert, and both of them encouraged me to ask Lêda Martins.

What is striking is that while sharp differences remain among the participants, the three rounds of engagement also lead to points of agreement.

Second, in the jury trial model followed in part 2, it is not necessary to recognize (or remember) each and every citation, each and every detail, but rather to note how participants reply to one another's criticisms. The six participants, as noted, must respond to critiques of their positions. Readers may not be able to assess— simply by reading certain statements—which assertions are closer to what we might term "the truth." But readers can evaluate how well a particular participant responds to another's criticisms as a way of assessing the credibility of that person's argument. Are questions raised about a participant's position that he or she leaves unanswered? Or does the participant effectively address his or her critics?

Readers will see participants in part 2 agreeing often on abstract points. They have a much harder time concurring on the culpability of Neel, Chagnon, or Tierney. All six participants want to do well by the Yanomami. But the struggle throughout the Roundtable concerns how to apply nice-sounding abstractions to concrete cases and concrete people. All participants, for example, concur that anthropologists should do no harm. But to what degree Chagnon did harm—both during his fieldwork and through his writings—is a matter of dispute. This is a problem in anthropology itself: how to connect abstract formulations with concrete cases.

Part 2 is meant not only to be read but also to be used to foster discussion. This might occur in various ways. For example, students might take the position of a certain participant and reenact the Roundtable's arguments with others. They might take an issue, such as informed consent, and develop a class position on it. Or they might argue for or against a particular participant's position.

To facilitate this discussion process, and to help guide readers, each participant's paper in chapters 8, 9, and 10 contains questions relating to accusations and issues addressed in that paper, along with a brief summary of the participant's answers. It also includes questions that you might consider in reading the paper. Collectively, these guide you into the issues being addressed in the paper, the author's position on them, and, most important, the central concerns that you, yourself, need to consider.

The Roundtable in part 2 is very much an open, public debate. It offers information that you must sort through to draw your own conclusions. That is what makes it exciting.

....

REFLECTIONS ON *DARKNESS IN EL DORADO*: QUESTIONS ON BIOETHICS AND HEALTH CARE AMONG THE YANOMAMI

BRUCE ALBERT

In response to the questions posed for this debate (What are the central ethical issues raised by the book *Darkness in El Dorado* and what would be the best man-

KEY ACCUSATIONS AND ISSUES
(see also pp. 317–41)

Looking at the broad picture, how would you assess the value of Darkness in El
    Dorado? Tierney's accusations against Chagnon were not new, and they
    would never have gotten the notice they did if it were not for the accusations
    Tierney lodged against Neel. (see pages 112–13)

Did Neel facilitate the spread of measles during his 1968 expedition? The Brazilian
    doctors commissioned by Albert to investigate the accusations reported that
    Neel's team did not start the 1968 measles epidemic and that the decision to
    use the Edmonston B vaccine was reasonable at the time. (see page 113)

*Did Neel act ethically during the 1968 expedition in the way he balanced his research
    with the need to treat the measles epidemic?* The Brazilian doctors reported that
    Neel had not adequately prepared for the expedition, especially once he knew
    of the Yanomami measles epidemic; they also indicated that Neel gave a
    greater priority to his research than to helping the Yanomami. (see page 114)

*What should now be done to address Yanomami concerns regarding the Yanomami
    blood samples?* The location and legal status of the Yanomami blood samples
    should be determined, and if lawsuits are appropriate, the resulting income
    should be channeled back to the Yanomami. (see pages 117–18)

QUESTIONS TO CONSIDER

*Did Neel violate the medical ethic of "do no harm" in his research? If not, why not?
If so, in what way?*

How should Neel have sought informed consent for his research?

ner of dealing with them?), I will attempt to offer a contribution derived from
my experience as an anthropologist engaged for twenty-six years in projects for
and with the Yanomami of Brazil (regarding land, human rights, health, education, and the environment). These projects were conducted by two NGOs that
Brazilian colleagues, friends, and I founded: the Comissão Pró-Yanomami
(CCPY; the Pro-Yanomami Commission) in 1978; and Urihi Saúde Yanomami
(Urihi Yanomami Health) in 1999. The following commentary therefore favors
a pragmatic outlook, emphasizing what the debate on Tierney's book brings out
as relevant to the current situation of the Yanomami and as a concrete contribution toward their future.

My main concern here is to avoid getting snarled in a theoretical and retroac-
tive exercise about anthropological ethics, which, interesting as it may be,
would be utterly irrelevant for the Yanomami today and would simply feed a professional self-exorcism, largely rhetorical in nature. Recall that, in the late
1980s, Brazilian anthropologists (see Carneiro da Cunha 1989), by way of the

Brazilian Anthropological Association (ABA), tried to initiate an ethical and political debate with the United States anthropological academic community on the
stereotype of "the Fierce People" and its use by the Brazilian military intent on
expropriating Yanomami lands. That ABA effort was met with widespread
indifference or even disdain on the part of most academics in the United
States. It is gratifying to see that, a decade later, this concern was incorporated
by the American Anthropological Association (AAA 2001a) into its agenda for
investigating various denunciations raised by Patrick Tierney's book.

I therefore hope that our debate will deal with violations of Yanomami
rights, without simply getting bogged down in an exercise of retrospection that
might deter us from analyzing their current situation, in which anthropologists
and their associations can play a very important role. Furthermore, we should
not restrict the discussion to evaluating aspects of individual professional ethics
to the detriment of evaluating the responsibility of the institutions involved in
the research in question, a dimension that should lead to concrete measures that
benefit the Yanomami.

DARKNESS IN YANOMAMI STUDIES, THEN AND NOW

As we know, most of the accusations and criticisms made in *Darkness in El
Dorado* are not new: they have been circulating in anthropological debates for
years and, in some cases, decades. Adding interviews, travel reports, and some
documentary data, Tierney's journalistic investigations mainly wrap up a number of facts that were already known, as attested by his extensive bibliography.
The result is laden with the sensationalism and lack of rigor that usually characterize this kind of exercise.

The first criticism of Napoleon Chagnon's pejorative representation of the
Yanomami goes back to the 1970s (Davis 1976), when the Brazilian Yanomami
were experiencing the first invasion of their territory by gold panners. The ethnographic basis for Chagnon's sociobiological theory of Yanomami warfare was
widely challenged, starting in the late 1980s (see Albert 1989, 1990; Ferguson
1989; Lizot 1989). Chagnon's lack of interest in the survival and rights of the
Yanomami and his opportunistic creation of the elusive Yanomamö Survival
Fund [supposedly set up to help the Yanomami] were questioned during this
same period (Albert and Ramos 1989). The impact of his massive distribution
of manufactured goods on the intensification of the Yanomami wars described
in his publications was analyzed in Brian Ferguson's book *Yanomami Warfare*
(1995:chap. 13). Ever since his first writings, Chagnon has candidly exposed his
field methods, which, in Sahlins's words, were conducted "in the mode of a military campaign" (2000). Similarly, the accusations of pedophilia that Tierney's
book directs against Jacques Lizot had already appeared in Yanomami statements
transcribed in Mark Ritchie's book *Spirit of the Rainforest* (1996:chap. 9).

However, no matter how much Tierney's journalistic style in *Darkness in El Dorado* exacerbated these controversial matters, the accusations he compiled against researchers and journalists who worked among the Yanomami in Venezuela most certainly would never have attained worldwide media coverage were it not for chapter 5, "Outbreak." In this chapter, Tierney implies that James Neel and his research team aggravated or even provoked a measles epidemic among the Yanomami by using an obsolete and dangerous vaccine to prove his genetic theories.

The monstrosity alleged in this accusation, namely, human experimentation and decimation of an ethnic minority, to a certain extent minimized the other charges in the book.[1] For the most part, these charges consist of ethical breaches, both professional and personal, such as using objectionable field methods, manipulating data and images, engaging in shady political deals, indulging in sexual exploitation, and precipitating intervillage contagion and hostilities. As serious as these breaches may be, they are not comparable to the harrowing memories aroused by the connotations of eugenic experiments in the "Outbreak" chapter.[2]

Thus, as soon as I heard about *Darkness in El Dorado,* it seemed obvious to me that the main (but not only) ethical questions raised by the book revolved around the biomedical research and experimentation conducted among the Yanomami from the 1950s to the 1970s and the lack of medical assistance which continues to acutely affect the survival of this indigenous people, especially in Venezuela.[3] In fact, an emergency expedition, organized in 1998 by the *Comissão Pró-Yanomami* and the Dutch branch of Doctors without Borders (Médecins Sans Frontières; MSF-Holland) in the region of the upper Rio Siapa (a region extensively covered in chapters 16 and 17 of Tierney's book), found 58 percent of the population examined (550 people in eight communities) ill with malaria, anemia, respiratory infections, malnutrition, and skin diseases.[4]

BIOMEDICAL RESEARCH
AND INFORMED CONSENT

The shocking idea of deadly biomedical experiments on Yanomami subjects prompted me to write a letter to the French daily *Le Monde* (Albert 2000) and to commission a technical evaluation of chapter 5 from a group of four physicians at the Federal University of Rio de Janeiro (UFRJ), two of whom had previous experience with medical work among the Yanomami in Brazil (see the medical report by Lobo et al. 2000).

Their report has several significant findings: that James Neel's research team did not start the 1968 Orinoco epidemic; that their use of the Edmonston B vaccine (the measles vaccine Neel used that Tierney viewed as dangerous) was considered to be adequate at that time and appropriate to administer in that particular context; that the team could not be accused of withdrawing medical care when needed; and, in short, that Tierney's investigative work was totally lacking in rigor.

Nevertheless, the report acknowledges the merit of *Darkness in El Dorado* in providing an opportunity to seriously discuss the implications of biomedical research on minorities and its relation to anthropology. In this context, the investigation by the Brazilian physicians led them to point out technical and ethical flaws in the way James Neel's team conducted the vaccinations and field research among the Yanomami. These flaws, which ought to be thoroughly investigated, can be summarized in three points:

1. *Possible experimentation by comparing the result of injections with and without MIG* (measles immune gamma globulin) during the immunization of the Yanomami while the measles epidemic of 1968 was raging (a comparison published in Neel, Centerwall, and Chagnon 1970);

2. *Inadequate preparation while planning the field trip,*[5] despite their knowledge ahead of time (in late 1967) of the spread of this epidemic from the Brazil-Venezuela border region toward the Orinoco. (Various letters written in November and December of 1967 attest to this knowledge; for instance, D. Shaylor's letter of December 11, 1967, mentions in its P.S. that "there are reports of measles coming from Brazil down the Orinoco.")[6] This lack of preparation, which had a negative impact on the effectiveness of the vaccination program and mortality control,[7] could be attributed to the priority the team gave its research agenda, as James Neel suggested in his fieldwork diary on February 5, 1968 (p. 79): "The measles vaccination—a gesture of altruism and conscience—is more of a headache than bargained for—I would either put this into the hands of the missionaries or place it at the very last."[8]

3. *Disregard for the ethical norm of informed consent in biomedical research with human subjects,* informed consent having been replaced with exchanges in which goods were traded for the Yanomami's collaboration (such as in collecting blood samples). Citing the report by the Brazilian physicians, "the former practice of exchanging gifts for blood (used by the team of Neel and Chagnon with the Yanomami and other groups), or any similar procedure that constitutes a distorted form of 'informed consent' from indigenous populations, is nowadays totally prohibited by national legislation, as well as by indigenous communities and organizations in Brazil and worldwide" (Lobo et al. 2000:19).[9]

One might object to the apparently retrospective character of the above comment made by the Brazilian physicians, since it would be improper to criticize the nonobservance of norms that were not yet codified at the time of the research (1967–68). However, this same report makes it quite clear (Lobo et al. 2000:9, 13, 16) that respect for informed consent in biomedical research and experiments on human subjects has been considered a fundamental bioethical norm ever since it was established in the Nuremberg Code (1947) and reaffirmed in the Declaration of Helsinki, adopted by the Eighteenth World Medical

Assembly in 1964.[10] The first point of the Nuremberg Code says: "The voluntary consent of the human subject is absolutely essential. This means that the person involved should have legal capacity to give consent; should be so situated as to be able to exercise free power of choice . . . and should have sufficient knowledge and comprehension of the elements of the subject matter involved as to enable him to make an understanding and enlightened decision."

Therefore, even if it appears to have been common practice in the United States in the 1950s and 1960s to neglect the norms established by the Nuremberg Code (especially with ethnic minorities and vulnerable persons),[11] the fact remains that such disregard for the principle of informed consent by James Neel's team cannot be discarded today as if it were a secondary or anachronistic issue. This is all the more so as we find out that this type of conduct continued along the same lines the following decade in biomedical research among the Yanomami and various other indigenous groups.[12] Indeed, having biomedical researchers fully respect the principle of informed consent among indigenous peoples is, to this day, difficult to achieve. As late as 1995, Napoleon Chagnon was still trying to collect blood from the Yanomami in Brazil without official authorization and without the prior consent of Yanomami representatives, as was legally required for conducting any research in indigenous territories.[13]

INSTITUTIONAL RESPONSIBILITIES: FROM THE "ATOMIC" TO THE "GENOMIC" ERAS

In this context, it is worth stressing that this ethical question has implications that go far beyond the individual practices of this or that researcher. Hence, the discussion of such an important issue should not be reduced to personal accusations. It is far more productive to turn our attention to the institutional system within which such research projects were framed. Thus, one of the most intriguing results of Tierney's investigation is his probe into the funding of James Neel's multidisciplinary research from 1965 to 1972 by the former Atomic Energy Commission (AEC) of the United States,[14] which amounted to nearly $2.5 million at the time. Tierney also revealed that the blood samples collected from the Yanomami in Venezuela and Brazil were used for comparative purposes in research on the effects of radioactivity on Japanese survivors of the Hiroshima and Nagasaki bombings (see Tierney's chapter 4, "Atomic Indians").

These facts, which also merit further investigation, shift the key of the issue of disregard for informed consent in James Neel's multidisciplinary research from the "mere" context of personal ethics to the wider level of institutional responsibility. In fact, the data presented by Tierney, if thoroughly confirmed, would bring this violation of Yanomami rights (used as involuntary objects of a biomedical research project) into the larger debate of the ethical breaches involving U.S. research on the effects of radioactivity on human beings carried out during the Cold War.

Certainly the Yanomami in Venezuela and Brazil were not submitted to any treatment that might have put their lives at risk (as was the case in many of the appalling experiments described in Moreno 2000). The fact remains that they were used, even if "only" as a control group, without their knowledge or consent in a research project commissioned by the nuclear agency of the United States government. Furthermore, to date, thousands of blood samples of their relatives (the majority of whom are probably dead) are still in the possession of U.S. research institutions—all this in exchange for some machetes, axes, and other trade goods.[15] This is, then, a clear case in which the rights of the Yanomami have been disregarded, since they were used as objects in biomedical research, the protocol and purposes of which they have never been properly informed.

Besides the issue of informed consent, there are two other ethical considerations to be made here. One is the moral and cultural affront represented by stockpiling the blood of the Yanomami's dead relatives, now in the possession of total strangers in a distant country, given the particularly salient role that blood and mortuary taboos play in their ritual life.[16] The other consideration is that these blood samples are now available to the Human Genome Diversity Project (HGDP). This project has been the object of strong criticism since the early 1990s for opening avenues that may lead to commercial patents on genetic resources from members of indigenous peoples. This in itself is sufficient grounds for concern that even more serious breaches of Yanomami rights are yet to come. In fact, a recent evaluation of the activities of the HGDP raises serious worries about the fate of the Yanomami blood (and of other indigenous peoples in Venezuela and Brazil):

> At some point prior to the early 90s, Neel's collection came to rest at Pennsylvania State University (PSU), which has one of the most ambitious genetic diversity research programmes in the U.S. Researchers at PSU sought a way to revive Neel's collected samples. Because the old blood separation techniques were imperfect, some white blood cells remained in the samples. From these, PSU was able to draw DNA—and lots of it. Using Neel's samples and polymerase chain reaction (PCR), PSU created a technique in which 'the amount of [genetic] material that can ultimately be made available is, for many practical purposes, unlimited' (Weiss et al. 1994) (Hammond 2000)[17]

The author of this text concludes by pointing out, very appropriately, the new ethical questions raised by this scientific frontier, which is already being denounced by indigenous peoples:[18] "The ethical questions raised by the technique are monumental. How can dead *people* . . . [or] *peoples* grant consent? Is it right for geneticists to perform new tests unanticipated at the time of collection? Should they go back to seek permission from the donor, and donor people? If the donor is deceased or gone, should they seek permission from relatives? . . . The Neel samples holder, PSU, did not consider consultation with Brazilian indigenous peoples necessary" (Hammond 2000).

Finally, returning to the Cold War years, *Darkness in El Dorado* also reveals (although with scanty details: see chapter 18, "Human Products and the Isotope Men," in Tierney 2000) that another type of biomedical research was conducted on the Yanomami in Venezuela between 1958 and 1968 under the rubric of the AEC. This research was carried out to study Yanomami thyroid metabolism by administering Iodine 131 radioactive tracer. The medical report of the Brazilian physicians (Lobo et al. 2000:12n18) also makes a brief reference to these studies (citing two articles, 1959 and 1961, by Venezuelan endocrinologist Marcel Roche, who conducted them),[19] calling attention to the fact that this research brought no benefit to the Yanomami.

We also know from Lizot (1970), who began his fieldwork as a collaborator in this research, that it continued from January of 1968 to February of 1970, this time also carried out by the French Commissariat à l'Énergie Atomique (CEA). Anthropologists were given the task to "assure the continuity of the scientific mission by administering Iodine 124, collecting regular blood specimens, and measuring thyroid activity during the absence of the biologists" (Lizot 1970:116).

Thus, we have here not only another instance of violation of the principle of informed consent added to that committed in James Neel's genetic research but also two possible aggravating circumstances, which should be carefully investigated. The first is the apparent absence of any medical benefit for the Yanomami, not even the indirect advantage of the hectic vaccination carried out during James Neel's 1968 research. The second is their possible exposure to unforeseen biological risks. Considering the Yanomami's isolation at the time, this was an act of sheer irresponsibility, which nowadays would be utterly inadmissible.

CONCLUSIONS

In light of all these facts, my main conclusion here is that beyond the ethical debate over the conduct of individual researchers, it is still necessary—indeed indispensable, considering the rights of the Yanomami—that more comprehensive investigations be carried out by an independent bioethics committee to provide complete information on the following issues:

1. the institutional and technical-scientific aspects of the research commissioned from James Neel by the AEC in the 1960s and 1970s, and on the circumstances that led to the selection of the Yanomami as a control group in this research;

2. the location, legal status, and current use of the Yanomami blood samples collected during the time of Neel's research;

3. the institutional framework, technical application, and the risk/benefit ratio for the Yanomami of the research on their thyroid metabolism using radioiodine (Iodine 131 and Iodine 124) in projects carried out in Venezuela by the U.S. AEC and the French CEA.[20]

It is essential that Yanomami representatives from both Venezuela and Brazil be duly informed about the terms and progress of these investigations, so that if the case warrants it, they can bring lawsuits (with the support of the public ministry in each of these countries) to obtain compensation for the violation of their rights during those research projects.

The next step might be to channel compensation benefits generated from these lawsuits to health projects for the Yanomami in Venezuela and Brazil. This would be the only ethically respectable way to redress the damage done to them by the U.S. and European nuclear establishments (and by institutions exploring genomic possibilities) in the name of scientific research. While these projects contributed a great deal to promoting their authors' careers, they were never of much use to their unknowing "objects" in guaranteeing their survival and recognition of their human rights.

Last but not least, it is up to anthropologists to think about the consequences of subjecting their work to the logic of a particular kind of biomedical research that reduces the members of indigenous peoples to "human material," thus denying them their subjectivity and agency as recognized by the bioethical codes prevailing since 1947. To do this is to undermine the very foundation of our discipline, which charges anthropologists with the duty of giving preeminence to the "native's point of view" in its ethical, intellectual, and political dimensions.[21]

NOTES

Catherine Howard was responsible for the translation of this paper from Portuguese into English.

1. The description of the filming of a sick Yanomami woman and her baby in agony, without medical assistance, by a BBC television crew accompanied by an anthropologist (Jacques Lizot), as described in chapter 13, surely must be one of the most dramatic passages in the book.

2. The e-mail of Terry Turner and Leslie Sponsel, which triggered the media attention before the publication of Darkness in El Dorado, alerted the president of the AAA to the fact that "Tierney's well-documented account, in its entirety, strongly supports the conclusion that the epidemic was in all probability deliberately caused as an experiment designed to produce scientific support for Neel's eugenic theory" (Turner and Sponsel 2000).

3. In Brazil, a reform in the administration of indigenous health services in 1999 delegated medical care in the Yanomami area to various NGOs, among which the most important is Urihi Yanomami Health, which is now attending approximately 5,250 Yanomami in ninety-six communities, using funds from the Brazilian Ministry of Health. (See the Web site http://www.urihi.org.br for a report on the activities initiated by this association.)

4. "·MSF/Holland 1998, "Expedicion a la región del área Yanomami Venezolana en carácter emergencial. Informe final. Octubre 1997–Maio 1998." The communities of Narimipiwei II and Toshamoshi (see references to "Narimobowei" and "Doshamosha" in Tierney 2000:277, 283–84) revealed the highest rates of malaria (58.3 percent and 50.4 percent, respectively).

5. According to the report of the UFRJ physicians, Neel and his team should have taken "precautions that would have reduced the difficulties encountered in the field, includ[ing] the training of those administering vaccinations, information on complications and treatments, provisions of medications and antibiotics, an itinerary and schedule of villages to visit, etc." (Lobo et al. 2000:18).

6. See references labeled COR 5, 22, 38, 39, and 81 in Turner and Stevens (2001), part II.

7. In the words of the UFRJ physicians' report, "The planning and organization of their movements—whether they gave priority to either medical care or research—probably had a greater impact on the failure of the vaccination (since immunization took place later than 3 days after infection) and

the lack of control over mortality (due to the ill-preparedness of the team for dealing with the serious complications of measles, mainly pneumonia), rather than on the spread of the epidemic" (Lobo et al. 2000:36).

8. See Turner and Stevens (2001), part III.

9. See also Tierney 2000:45–46.

10. See the documents posted at http://www.irb-irc.com/resources/nuremberg.html and http://www.irb-irc.com/resources/helsinki.html.

11. On this matter, see chapter 7 of the impressive book by J. D. Moreno (2000).

12. In Brazil, this included the Krahó, Kayapó-Gorotire, Macuxi, and Wapixana (1974), and the Ticuna, Baniwa, and Kanamari (1976) (see Salzano 2000).

13. This episode is documented in *Darkness in El Dorado* (Tierney 2000:xxi–xxiii and notes on p. 328 citing documents of the Brazilian Indian bureau).

14. More precise information has been furnished by Tierney since the publication of his book, at the site http://members.aol.com/archaeodog/darkness_in_el_dorado/index.htm (see "Independence of the Atomic Bomb Casualty Commission").

15. In *Darkness in El Dorado*, Tierney (2000:51) mentions that twelve thousand blood samples are today under the power of Pennsylvania State University, at the disposition of the Human Genome Diversity Project.

16. See Albert (1985) on Yanomami conceptions of blood and mortuary rituals.

17. For a synthesis on intellectual property and genetic resources, see UNESCO 2000.

18. See the editorial in *New Scientist* 2000.

19. Details and contextual information on Roche's research with radioiodine are provided by Dr. E. Romano of the Instituto Venezolano de Investigaciones Científicas (IVIC) at the site http://www.ivic.ve/ivicspan/darkness.html.

20. See, for example, the recent investigation into studies using radioiodine 131 on the Inuit and Indians in Alaska by the Air Force's Arctic Aeromedical Laboratory in 1956–57, at http://tis.eh.doe.gov/ohre/roadmap/achre/chap12"4.html.

21. For a broader reflection on the relations between anthropology and anthropological advocacy, see Albert 1997.

....

THE POLITICAL USES
OF ETHNOGRAPHIC DESCRIPTION

RAYMOND HAMES

In 1988 Chagnon's publication of "Blood Revenge" in *Science* created a furor in the Brazilian anthropological community and elsewhere. Some of the criticism was of the standard scientific sort, dealing with methods, analysis, and interpretation (Albert 1989; Ferguson 1989). But the most sensational criticism was an accusation of ethical malfeasance. The Association of Brazilian Anthropologists claimed that Chagnon's portrayal of Yanomamö violence served as a critical rationale for Brazilian government officials to develop a plan to partition the Yanomamö area into twenty-one separate parcels as an initial stage to permit gold miners and other economic interests to infiltrate the interstices and ultimately to invade Yanomamö land. That is, Chagnon's descriptions of the Yanomamö as warlike are employed to justify the taking of Yanomamö lands. I believe it useful to examine this issue in some detail because it goes to the heart

---

KEY ACCUSATIONS AND ISSUES
(see also pp. 317–41)

Should Chagnon have responded better to the media's misuse of his work? Chagnon took concrete steps in later editions of the book to address the misuse of his writings by changing the title of his book, deleting certain passages, and adding others. To assert that Chagnon was responsible for Brazilian politicians and generals wanting to limit the Yanomamö reserve is to obscure the larger power plays these people have continually perpetrated against their national minorities. (see pages 121–23)

Additional Comment. Whatever power anthropologists have with people beyond the discipline depends on their providing accurate information rather than politicized ideologies. (see pages 120, 125)

QUESTIONS TO CONSIDER

Did Chagnon do more good than harm in the way he publicized the lifestyles of the Yanomami?

Is Hames correct when he says that a key reason people beyond the discipline listen to anthropologists is that anthropologists provide accurate facts rather than politicized ideologies?

---

of what ethnographers should do: provide accurate and empirically grounded accounts of the behavior, values, and beliefs of others. Traditionally those others are indigenous populations who have a precarious relation with the states that forcefully attempt to incorporate them into their governmental sphere. Whatever power anthropologists have is founded on the explicit belief that we provide accurate information. If we stray from this obligation we will be dismissed as ordinary political actors who distort reality to promote our political aims. I believe too that we have an obligation to ensure that what we produce is not used by others to harm the people we study and, if necessary, we may need to engage in political action to deter injustices meted out to those we study. As I will later note, this ethical precept is difficult to fulfill because superficial differences between "us" and "them" are manifold and can always be employed to bolster ethnocentric rationales designed to justify immoral courses of action.

IS THE CRITIQUE OF CHAGNON JUSTIFIED?

A major theme of *Darkness in El Dorado* is that Chagnon's actions in the field and research publications on the Yanomamö have either directly harmed them or provided a necessary propagandistic rationale for government officials and economic and military interests to destroy the Yanomamö. On page 160 Tierney quotes a public memo sent by the president of the Association of Brazilian Anthropology, Maria Manuela Carneiro da Cunha (in 1989) addressed to the Committee on Ethics of the American Anthropological Association and to the American Association for the Advancement of Science, publisher of *Science* magazine (see Carneiro da Cunha 1989). "Thus, less than a year after the *Time* Magazine piece came out, top level officials of the Brazilian Indian Service (Fundação Nacional do Índio, FUNAI) referred to the Yanomami 'violence' as sufficient justification for a plan to cut up their lands into 21 micro-reserves that were to be surrounded by corridors for the installation of regional economic projects, a plan that was intended to put an end to the aggressive practices of the Indians."

This is extraordinarily weak evidence to underwrite a claim that Chagnon's *Science* publication led to the FUNAI action. The *Time* magazine piece referred to by the ABA does report on Chagnon's *Science* article, but from the information above there is no evidence that the unnamed FUNAI official was swayed by Chagnon's account. Given the numerous accounts of Yanomamö violence prior to and after the action, how are we to know which ones allegedly inspired the statement? Are we expected to believe that prior to Chagnon's publication in *Science*, officials at FUNAI were ignorant of traditional Yanomamö warfare even though it has been systematically documented by modern ethnographers other than Chagnon in Brazil (Albert 1985; Peters 1998) and in Venezuela (Barker 1961; Lizot 1976, 1977) as well as the earliest explorers to the area (Humboldt 1967/1851:294–95; Koch-Grünberg, 1990/1917)? For example, on numerous pages Koch-Grünberg describes how neighboring groups such as the Ye'kwana lived in fear of the Yanomamö because of their propensity to raid (1990/1917:167, 182, 188, 205, 212, 214, and 289). In one instance, upon meeting a Yanomamö in Moromoto he characterized him as "un tipo feroz" (a fierce type of person) (1990/1917:212).

This is not to say that the unnamed FUNAI official did not or could not have employed Chagnon's *Science* article to rationalize bureaucratic plans to divide and control Yanomamö land. Nevertheless, everything we know about state actions against indigenous populations in the New World tells us that whenever it is in the interests and power of the state (or, more properly, in the interests of those who use the state to advance their interests) to expropriate indigenous land or subjugate its people, they will do so, independent of the cultural traditions of those people. Throughout most of their history, the Yanomamö have had little direct contact with outsiders. Consequently, they are little acculturated and are numerous in comparison to other native peoples in the region who have suffered the devastating consequences of contact. In the case of Brazilian Yanomamö, this relative isolation has been breached, as roads were constructed on their southern periphery and gold miners cleared illegal airfields in the heart of Yanomamö territory. I believe that most agree that the fundamental causes of the invasion are the consequences of the Brazilian government's desire to exploit the recently discovered riches of the area mapped by remote surveys and then actuated by the construction of the Trans-Amazon road system, the Calha Norte Project, and other development schemes. These incursions are aided and abetted by FUNAI, a chronically corrupt federal bureaucracy formed to protect Brazilian native peoples. (This corruption occurs at the higher levels. Many rank-and-file workers genuinely care for indigenous peoples.)

That still leaves open the question of whether elements of the image created by Chagnon's portrayals have worked against the Yanomamö. Alcida Ramos, in her useful and comprehensive monograph on the politics of indigenous rights in Brazil, says the following: "Although anthropology may be the major source about the primitive, it should by no means be held responsible for the political use and abuse as the notion of Indians as primitive, as something of the past that should be eradicated" (1998:46).

This statement strikes me as curious, because Ramos, along with Bruce Albert, both of whom are Yanomamö ethnographers, were instrumental in drafting the ABA denunciation of Chagnon in which his portrayals are alleged to have harmed the Yanomamö. Yet Ramos states that ethnographers should not be held responsible. I can devise a sensible way to resolve this contradiction.

Perhaps it is the case that Chagnon has not attempted to combat the evil uses to which his portrayals have been put. An examination of recent editions of his ethnography suggests otherwise and presents the reader with compelling evidence that the opposite is true. In the fourth edition of Yanomamö (1992a) he dropped the subtitle The Fierce People, in part because "government officials in, for example, Brazil, might try to justify oppressive policies against them on the argument that they are 'fierce' and, therefore, 'animal-like'" (Chagnon 1992a:xii). In that same edition, Chagnon expunged considerable information on infanticide because of concerns about how such data could be used against the Yanomamö. In footnote 9 (1992a:93) he notes he has ceased to publish information on Yanomamö infanticide because he was asked by a government official to file a notarized affidavit in the Venezuelan congressional record on infanticide. He did so and claimed that he had never seen an infanticide among the Yanomamö. Five years prior to the ABA denunciation in the third edition of Yanomamö: The Fierce People (1983) he added a section in the final chapter entitled "Balancing the Image of Fierceness" in which he states that his focus on warfare was a consequence of the topic being poorly described ethnographically and he had the opportunity to document it among a still sovereign people. Finally, the final chapter in fourth and fifth editions has grown significantly in size through his documentation of the threats to Venezuelan and Brazilian Yanomamö. I believe these changes and other publications demonstrate that Chagnon is acutely aware of the misuse of his ethnographic descriptions, and he attempts to combat this problem.

DO ETHNOGRAPHIC ACCOUNTS REALLY SWAY GOVERNMENT OFFICIALS?

No matter what precautions ethnographers take to qualify or even sanitize their ethnographic accounts of indigenous populations, ethnographic accounts can always be used against them. At the same time, I would emphasize that such accounts are insignificant explanations of why governments and other powerful interests seek to destroy indigenous peoples. Those who believe such accounts do play a significant role appear to reason in the following way: enemies of Yanomamö self-determination claim that the Yanomamö are so warlike that outsiders must step in and take control, or that because some Yanomamö engage in chronic warfare they do not deserve rights to their land because they do not behave in a civilized fashion and are undeserving of self-determination. As mentioned previously, I do not doubt that some governmental official or general somewhere could have made such a statement to rationalize the expropriation or greater control of Yanomamö land by non-Yanomamö.

Belief that government officials are swayed by ethnographic reports rests on a number of assumptions that I believe are faulty. It first assumes that generals and others not only read scientific reports on indigenous peoples but that such reports affect their decision making processes. By implication it means that if the Yanomamö were described as peaceful then military and economic interests would be inhibited from taking indigenous land because they could not rationalize control, partitioning, or seizure of Yanomamö land. I believe this to be wrong on two counts. First, internal colonialists will seize on anything that differentiates them from the other. This is the simple use of ethnocentrism for political and economic ends. Historically, in the New World not being Christian was used by the conquistadors to rationalize the reduction, enslavement, decimation, or expropriation of native peoples or their land (for the Brazilian case see Hemming 1978 and chapter 2 in Ramos 1998). Anthropologists as objective describers of the people they study are bound to create a large list of potential cultural differentiators that contrast indigenous peoples with their potential conquerors. Differentiating practices such as shamanism, socially approved use of powerful hallucinogens, polygyny, and mortuary endocannibalism powerfully clash with values held (but perhaps not practiced) by the majority population of a nation-state such that any of them could serve as a rationalization for divesting native peoples of self-determination. If the research model proposed by those who truly believe that knowledge of native peoples will be used against them is followed, then the only thing one could describe would be values and patterns of behavior that are identical to those of conquerors.

Furthermore, the ethnographer faces a constantly moving target about which cultural traits may be viewed as unsavory by his or her readership. Ethnocentric standards change through time. For example, in the first edition of *The Isthmus Zapotecs*, Beverly Chiñas did not present information on Zapotec sex/gender variants "because it did not seem to me that I could present such materials to the then homophobic United States so that they could understand and accept it as part of everyday Isthmus Zapotec culture" (Chiñas, 1992:3). Now she feels that her readership is not so homophobic, and the information is presented. One could argue (but I would not) that delaying the publication of information on Zapotec sex/gender variants and how it harmoniously meshes with their culture was counterproductive: in the struggle for sexual civil rights we need examples of cultures of tolerance. But once we publish something, how do we know that at some time in the future that practice will not be condemned and then be used against the people we have studied?

Second, I would argue that even positive or benign portrayal of native peoples does not prevent their annihilation at the hands of conquerors. The foraging San or !Kung of Botswana have been characterized by Elizabeth Marshall Thomas as the "harmless people" (1958), a people who lack indigenous patterns of warfare (Lee 1979). In many ways the San are stereotypically diametrical opposites of the "fierce people." Anyone remotely familiar with the San knows that they have had a long history of violent confrontation with outsiders who enslaved and conscripted them and have steadily reduced their lands and, most recently, in the name of conservation and economic development, have denied them the right to hunt in their traditional areas (Hitchcock 1996). And those San who hunt in their traditional areas with or without a game license are fined, beaten, and killed by game scouts. Rousseauian characterizations have not helped the San. For me the reason is obvious: powerful interests pay no attention to our characterizations of indigenous peoples unless it is in their interests to do so. And even when they do use them, such characterizations are employed as post hoc rationalizations of what they already had planned.

FUNDING NONGOVERNMENTAL ORGANIZATIONS

Negative portrayals of indigenous peoples are of concern to nongovernmental organizations because the NGOs believe the portrayals have negative consequences for their ability to raise money to defend the interests of the Yanomamö and other indigenous peoples. Recently David Maybury-Lewis, president of Cultural Survival, one of the most important NGOs defending indigenous rights, stated this position clearly regarding the Yanomamö. "The ways in which anthropologists portray the societies they study have consequences, sometimes serious consequences in the real world. Indigenous societies have all too often been maligned in the past, denigrated as savages and marginalized at the edges of the modern world and the modern societies in it" (http://members .aol.com/anavanax/darkness_in_el_dorado/documents/0257).

To attract contributors to the cause of protecting the rights of indigenous peoples, ethnic groups must be somehow portrayed as deserving of protection by documenting wrongs done to them and/or demonstrating them as noble people. Both of these tactics depend on eliciting cultural values held by nonindigenous donors about what constitutes virtuous cultural traits (conservation, democracy, local-level directed development, political justice, and sexual equality, just to name a few). Obviously, donors are going to be reluctant to help a people characterized as warlike, sexist, and despoilers of the environment, even if they are the objects of predation by powerful governmental or economic interests. An even more extreme statement of this view comes from Darrel Posey, an Amazonian researcher who has actively defended Brazilian Kayapó land rights. He states "Any evidence of unsound ecological activities by indigenous and traditional peoples undermines their basic rights to land, resources, and cultural practice" (cited in Ridley, 1999:217). The fundamental message here is that indigenous peoples deserve our help only to the degree that they are like us or, more to the point, are like what we want to become. Before I deal with this issue I would like to make it clear that I believe that NGOs do vital work that should be supported because they make an important positive difference in the lives of exploited indigenous peoples. Indeed, John Saffirio and I sought out Cultural Survival as a place to publish our account of the terrible consequence of road building on the Yanomamö (Saffirio and Hames 1983).

At the same time, I believe it fundamentally wrong to paint false pictures of native peoples, even if the goal is noble. The problem is that in the long run you will eventually be found out and you will lose credibility. Consequently, your ability to intervene and help will be compromised. As I have argued elsewhere on Amazonian conservation (Hames 1991:193), indigenous peoples have a prior fundamental and inalienable right to self-determination and their ancestral land. Although they may have values and practices that differ sharply from our own, their human rights are independent of this. NGOs should encourage donors to respect the cultural practices of others, and, at the same time, they should go about their important task of convincing donors and governments about dire threats to indigenous peoples. When that battle is won, or while it is being fought, one can attempt to convince all people, including indigenous people, of the benefits of fundamental human rights that have yet to be fully achieved in any society.

······

THE ETHICAL IMPLICATIONS RAISED BY
DARKNESS IN EL DORADO AND THE BEST MANNER
FOR DEALING WITH THEM

KIM HILL

First and foremost, anthropologists should be aware that although we have multiple intellectual goals, we should share a single priority. Our goals are to study issues of academic interest, but the health and welfare of the study population must always take precedence over any academic goal. Tierney's most notable charges, if true, would indeed constitute major ethical violations. However, we now have enough information to conclude that the most serious of those charges are false. Neel and colleagues did *not* intentionally infect the Yanomamö with measles using a dangerous vaccine in order test certain scientific theories. Tierney claimed that "these zealots of biological determinism sacrificed everything—including the lives of their subjects—to spread their gospel" (2000:17).

KEY ACCUSATIONS AND ISSUES
(see also pp. 317–41)

Did Neel act ethically during the 1968 expedition in the way he balanced his research with the need to treat the measles epidemic? Published and unpublished documentation makes clear that Neel intended both to vaccinate the Yanomamö and to study their reactions to the vaccine. That the vaccination campaign during the measles epidemic took precedence over Neel's research design is clear from the fact that Neel gave vaccinations to villages he never returned to and to people whose names went unrecorded. (see page 127)

Did Chagnon act unethically in collecting genealogies that violated Yanomami taboos? If Tierney's accusations concerning Chagnon's manipulative behavior in gathering genealogies are correct, then the behavior is borderline unethical; but many anthropologists use tricks to collect sensitive data, and journalists are much worse in this regard. (see pages 130–31)

Did Chagnon act unethically when he sought to gain control, with two others, of a large land reserve in Venezuela in what became known as the FUNDAFACI affair? Chagnon allied himself with disreputable characters, but this was a case of bad judgment rather than a serious ethical shortfall. (see pages 130–31)

Given what we now know, are the accusations made against Chagnon and Neel mostly true or untrue? Tierney has distorted the truth to attack and smear his ideological enemies. (see pages 134–35)

QUESTIONS TO CONSIDER

Is it fair to say that Neel held to the standard of "do no harm" in his research among the Yanomami?

Is it fair to say that Chagnon held to the standard of "do no harm" in his research?

Since no such thing ever happened, we must wonder why Tierney was so prepared to try to make such a case with so little evidence. What is his gospel? Indeed the entire case presented in the book is based on leaping to unwarranted conclusions based on insufficient scientific background, assuming the worst about the actors, and backing unwarranted speculations with distorted information. The seriousness of such a charge should have demanded impeccable evidence, and the evidence in the book does not begin to rise to that level. Indeed a good fraction of the footnotes in the book provide no support whatsoever for the assertions in the text. The attempt to ascribe an evil motive (allegedly tied to a scientific viewpoint unpalatable to Tierney) to an event that never happened suggests that Tierney was engaging in ideological warfare and was prepared to misrepresent the truth as one of his tactics. Such behavior is clearly unethical.

ACCUSATIONS AGAINST NEEL

Likewise, Tierney and some of his supporters have sought to "prove" that the measles vaccination program was mainly an experiment rather than a medical procedure designed to save lives. In their simple view of science, it must be either one or the other. Published and unpublished documents, however, clearly show that Neel intended to both vaccinate the Yanomamö and research aspects of the Yanomamö reaction to vaccine. This combination of treatment and research is not remotely unethical and is standard practice in all of modern medicine. In fact, it would have been highly irresponsible of Neel not to collect data about the vaccination program that could later be used in understanding epidemics among other indigenous populations. Neel acquired and delivered the vaccines at a considerable cost to himself (something that government agencies and missionaries failed to do) because prior blood sampling had shown that the Yanomamö had not been exposed to measles (Tierney also alleges that those blood collections were unethical, but in fact they were critical to saving Yanamamö lives).

Ample evidence (especially his own field notes) shows that Neel behaved ethically and tried to get information of scientific value. Because of the urgency and chaos of the field situation, however, the vaccination of threatened villages took precedence over any research design. He gave vaccinations in some villages to which he never returned and gave vaccinations to many people whose names were never recorded. Since research on the vaccine required measuring antibody titers of vaccinated individuals at a later time, clearly this could not have possibly been part of any research protocol. Again, however, the effort by Tierney to vilify Neel's behavior suggests that there were prior motives that directed his interpretation of events. Tierney leaves little doubt in his development of his case against Neel (including irrelevant attempts to connect him to alleged actions of the Atomic Energy Commission) that his smear is motivated by (what Tierney believed to be) Neel's theoretical views on issues that Tierney feels strongly about. This is ideological terrorism, pure and simple. Tierney shows the willingness to use any means necessary, including misrepresentation, to discredit an academic viewpoint that is disagreeable to him. Such behavior has no place in the free market of ideas that is modern academia.

Other charges of unethical behavior by Neel and Venezuelan scientists are based on faulty logic. Tierney asserts that all research done on indigenous populations that is not designed to help those same populations is unethical. I strongly disagree.

Research done on native peoples that can be used to help the world community at large (as in the case of basic medical research) or other indigenous populations (as in the case of Neel's studies on virgin soil epidemics) is absolutely ethical as long as (1) there is informed consent by the study subjects as to the dangers of the data collection procedures; (2) the subjects clearly understand that the research is not being carried out just to help them; (3) there is fair remuneration for the subjects' cooperation; and (4) the procedures are not potentially dangerous. Thus, for example I see nothing unethical about using the Yanomamö as study subjects to research childhood asthma, which is a major killer in the United States but is not present among the Yanomamö. Indeed the lack of this medical problem among the Yanomamö is the very reason why they represent a good study population.

Likewise, Marcel Roche's research on goiter with Yanomamö study subjects using small amounts of radioactive iodine was vigorously denounced by Tierney but was not unethical per se. It did, however, lack adequate informed consent and should not be repeated today under the same conditions. Roche's logic at the time was that much could be learned about goiter that would benefit numerous Venezuelans with the disease, as well as helping indigenous populations and probably the Yanomamö themselves in the future. His research protocol was not dangerous but was too complicated to be understood by the Yanomamö participants and was thus not explained (the Yanomamö couldn't possibly understand radioactive tracers at that time). Such research should always be voluntary, informed, and appropriately rewarded. Roche's lack of informed consent was an error by today's standards but certainly did not represent the callous disregard for Yanomamö welfare that Tierney suggests. Indigenous peoples should not be indoctrinated to believe that all research done with them should benefit only them. Such a view is based on a racist double standard that assumes that native peoples are special in the world. They are not. They are members of a larger world community, and they should cooperate with that community for the common good, just as they expect to receive the benefits from research done on other communities (all the modern medicine they receive is based on prior research with other groups). Most natives with whom I have discussed this issue are proud to be able to contribute to the world community in this way.

ACCUSATIONS AGAINST CHAGNON

Tierney also makes numerous allegations against Napoleon Chagnon that constitute important ethical issues. Most important among these are Tierney's claims that Chagnon's portrayals of the Yanomamö have harmed them, that Chagnon's gifts caused conflict, that Chagnon falsified or misrepresented data to support certain hypotheses, that Chagnon used unethical methods to obtain data from the Yanomamö, that Chagnon allied himself with people who intended to harm the Yanomamö, and that Chagnon did little to help the Yanomamö during his many years working with them. These charges should cause all anthropologists to reflect on their own fieldwork (even if the charges against Chagnon are false). First, it is true that anthropologists should show concern about the ways that information they publish could harm a study population or embarrass them. This is the case even if the portrayals are based on scientific data and are true. Such concern does not imply that we should falsify results to make study populations look flawless but simply that we must be sensitive to potential damage that can come from some types of information.

When M. Hurtado and I published a book about Ache demography, we were careful not to overemphasize high infanticide rates and rampant promiscuity in Ache society even though such patterns were evident. We did not call the Ache "the baby killers" or "the love makers" on the jacket of our book, nor did we emphasize exotic behavioral patterns in the lay media. Instead we put the data in scientific papers and books where they belonged and where they could be discussed by appropriately qualified scholars. In fact we were so concerned about the potential damage of our data that we met with several community leaders before publishing our book. The result of that meeting was an agreement that we would not publish our findings in Spanish. This meant that our work was unlikely to be cited by local media and made available to the close neighbors of the population who might use it against the Ache, but instead the information would be read primarily by a well-educated segment of the world population that was more likely to be sympathetic to the contingencies associated with these behaviors in the first place. This is an example of the type of compromise between scientific findings and image concern that should be a part of modern anthropology. The same commonsense rule applies to embarrassing portrayals. Nobody wants photos published of herself picking her nose, even if that is an actual behavior that she engages in from time to time. Drug-induced dazes and filthy faces are not "cute" to the people being portrayed even if they are "good copy."

Anthropologists have a responsibility to be sensitive to the feelings of their study population as well as to be true to their research results. But fairness on this issue demands that we also reveal the hypocrisy of the Tierney exposé on this account. Tierney criticizes Chagnon for portraying the Yanomamö as excessively violent in print and in film, yet he published a book claiming that Andean Indian populations still practice child sacrifice. There are few other descriptions that could be more damning to the reputation of a native group. Unlike Chagnon's warlike portrayal of the Yanomamö, which is backed up by a good deal of independent corroboration, Tierney's description is not supported by any responsible anthropological study.

Another important issue raised by the Tierney book is the extent to which gifts from anthropologists cause conflicts in the study population. I agree that all anthropologists should be aware of potential problems caused by their gifts, but I do not believe there is much empirical support for the notion that Chagnon's gift giving caused any more conflict among the Yanomamö than that of the missionaries, of the witnesses against Chagnon in this book, or even of Tierney himself. All anthropologists must be willing to reward the cooperation of the study population. Chagnon's gifts were typical and not particularly excessive given the rewards that he gained from his research (it would be unethical not to share such economic success). While it is possible to exercise bad judgment in this realm, and induce social conflict (for example, by giving massive support to one faction in a village and nothing to others), Tierney provides no serious evidence that Chagnon made such errors. The solution that Tierney appears to advocate—that anthropologists should provide no material goods to study populations—is paternalistic and would surely be opposed by all native groups. And again, why was Chagnon singled out for criticism when the Salesian missionaries who hosted Tierney have provided orders of magnitude higher quantities of the same trade goods?

Tierney claims that Chagnon falsified data or engaged in misleading data analyses to obtain a desired result from scientific study. The scientific issue concerns levels of Yanomamö warfare and whether men who have killed have higher reproductive success. The claim of data falsification is clearly a serious ethical issue, but no credible evidence is presented to back this claim. Whether Chagnon's data collection methods, sampling procedures, data analysis methods and conclusions are valid is a proper and important topic for scientific discussion but has no ethical ramifications. If Chagnon's work includes methodological problems, we should point that out to improve future anthropological study, but such errors are not "unethical." I and other sociobiologists have identified some weaknesses in the oft-cited *Science* study, as have many Chagnon opponents. A strong demonstration that killing raises male fitness would require a random sample of men from some time cohort, an analysis of the impact of "having killed" on both fertility and mortality of those men, a multivariate design that would eliminate age effects and other possible covariates of both killer status and fitness, and the coding of killing as a time-variant covariate to establish that killing per se caused the observed demographic effects.

Chagnon's study is preliminary and suggestive and should be treated as such. It is an important result that suggests that in societies where most men go on raids, those men who are successful and survive have more wives. This may partially explain why the willingness to use violence under some conditions is part of the male human psyche. The precise cause of the association, however, is not possible to determine from the data presented, and there are many possible interpretations, including ones that do not imply that men gain wives directly by killing. But such discussions should remain in the scholarly realm of those who understand them and care about getting the true answer (something not characteristic of many Chagnon opponents).

The only ethical issue I see in this debate is whether data are intentionally misrepresented to win a scientific argument. In this light, Tierney's views are both scientifically unqualified and blatantly biased. In his treatment of this topic, evidence is selectively presented and counterevidence available in the same cited sources remains conspicuously unmentioned. While this may not be technically unethical, it is certainly bad science. It is typical of a lawyerly style (to present only the evidence supporting one side) rather than scientific discourse (which includes putting an idea at risk by examining all evidence, pro and con).

In discussing Chagnon's methods, Tierney also asserts that Chagnon was culturally insensitive in obtaining names and genealogies and often tricked informants into providing information, or exploited existing conflicts to get sensitive information from enemies about each other. These charges, if true, seem to be borderline unethical. But many anthropologists use a variety of tricks to obtain desired sensitive information, and journalists are a thousand times worse (Tierney is alleged to have deceived many informants while gathering information for this book). Cultural anthropologists routinely ask for information from children or neighbors and show no reluctance to delve into local gossip networks, opportunistically exploiting social divisions as a way of getting information that would not be obtained from certain individuals voluntarily. The ethics of such techniques should indeed be carefully considered by professional anthropologists. Is obtaining the dirt on an individual from his neighbors unethical? Is obtaining information on sexual activities through secret inquiry a legitimate activity? Does it matter whether the anthropologist has lived with the study population for one week or twenty years?

Many anthropologists explicitly practice a moral double standard here. Any techniques are acceptable when exposing the activities of certain politically incorrect groups (oppressors, etc.), but the same methods are unethical ways to get information on politically correct groups (e.g., the oppressed). This may seem like a reasonable moral position until we consider who decides which groups can acceptably be deceived. Should we conclude that feminist anthropologists can lie and deceive men (whom they view as oppressors) to collect data, but the same tactics of collecting data on women are unethical? I can't judge Chagnon's actions in this realm without access to the Yanomamö that he worked with. One guideline might be that if you have angered the study population through your data collection methods you are doing something wrong. Tierney asserts that Chagnon infuriated the Yanomamö by obtaining the names of adults and dead people. But Peters and Albert also obtained names and genealogies of hundreds of living and dead Yanomamö, and all available evidence suggests that their study populations were quite accepting of these activities. Thus, there is little doubt that there are appropriate ways to obtain such information and that Yanomamö names are not absolutely taboo, as Tierney asserts.

The question here is whether Chagnon used methods unacceptable to a large fraction of the study population. Certainly any data collection can potentially anger a small faction (usually those who want to hide certain truths). But anthropologists routinely collect information that has the potential of upsetting some individuals (often those in power who don't want some of their behaviors revealed). Anthropologists need to develop specific guidelines about what kinds of data collection are acceptable and how this changes depending on who is being studied and what the relationship is between the anthropologist and the study population.

Tierney also alleges that Chagnon allied himself with disreputable characters (Cecilia Matos and Charles Brewer-Carías) who intended harm to the Yanomamö. I too have voiced my own displeasure at these associations, but I think this charge consists of exercising bad judgment rather than a serious ethical shortfall. It is important to remember that both these individuals were "legit-imate" Venezuelan government officials at the time. There was no evidence available to Chagnon at the time that either of these two intended to dispossess the Yanomamö of their land or carry out illegal mining on their lands. Had that been the case, Chagnon's association with them would have clearly been harmful to his study population and thus unethical. But Tierney provides no convincing motive as to why Chagnon would support those who he believed intended to steal Yanomamö lands or engage in gold mining in those areas. Chagnon's only statements on these issues suggest that he has always favored titling Yanomamö lands to the Yanomamö themselves, and he has always opposed gold mining activities on Yanomamö land. Instead it appears that Chagnon simply associated with these characters because they were powerful Venezuelans who could help him gain access to the Yanomamö at a time when it was being denied. Associating with unsavory characters seems like unwise behavior by a scientist who very badly wanted to continue his research, but no ethical violations are apparent.

Another ethical issue that I believe is one of the most important in the Tierney book concerns our responsibilities to provide long-term assistance to study populations and what constitutes a fair redistribution of the economic gains that come from our collaboration with anthropological study populations. When I visited the Yanomamö, I heard complaints that Chagnon had made a great deal of money off the Yanomamö and had done next to nothing to help them or share his economic success with them. Unfortunately I must honestly report that I have heard the same comments expressed about me and my wife, Magdalena Hurtado, at our own long-term field site, despite having provided nearly a quarter million dollars in economic aid for that population during the past twenty years, and the time cost to both of us has been enormous. This included providing long-term medical care; paying for emergency evacuation and hospital bills; building schools, clinics, housing, water and electrical facili-ties; working to obtain land titles; providing long-term employment; and design-ing training programs for the study group. Chagnon himself should address this issue and explain what types of assistance he provided. It is rumored that he made a good deal of money from books and films about the Yanomamö, and we must consider that his entire lifetime academic earnings can be directly tied to the Yanomamö, since his scientific reputation was based solely on his Yanomamö work.

Chagnon paid the Yanomamö for data when it was collected but apparently did not provide any other assistance to the tribe. Is this a fair distribution of the gains that came from the Chagnon-Yanomamö collaboration, or is it exploita-tion? I believe that this is an issue Chagnon should discuss directly with the Yanomamö who helped him through the years. Unfortunately, Chagnon's ene-mies made it impossible for him to return to the Yanomamö for many years, so he couldn't possibly have helped them even if that were his top priority.

Although Chagnon has been singled out here for criticism, this is an issue that applies to many anthropologists. I have seen dozens of field anthropologists over the years work in precisely the same way as Chagnon is alleged to have done. They provide a few gifts to informants and then never again return to share out any of the economic success that comes from a career that was built on that fieldwork. Very few anthropologists could withstand the scrutiny of careful investigation into their own activities on this front.

Likewise, Tierney claims no moral high ground on this account. He was asked directly by Magdalena Hurtado at a press conference at the 2000 AAA meetings in San Francisco if he intended to donate proceeds from his book to help the Yanomamö and he remained silent. In other interviews when asked about his economic motives, he has insisted that he deserves a monetary reward for his years of hard work (how does that differ from Chagnon's claims on his income?). Peters donated all the proceeds from his 1998 book on the Yanomamö. Magdalena Hurtado and I donated all the proceeds from our two Ache books as well as all money we have made during the past twenty years from selling Ache photo and film rights. I would like to hear from the Tierney allies here. I personally observed some of the fiercest Chagnon critics (from the book) in the field. I saw no evidence of their assistance to the Yanomamö beyond the typical anthropological payment to informants. What exactly have they done that allows them to cast the first stone?

THE CAMPAIGN AGAINST SOCIOBIOLOGY

Finally, this essay would be unbalanced if I didn't also comment on the unethical behavior of those who attempted to discredit Chagnon and Neel *only because* of theoretical disagreements with the type of work they were doing. For years Chagnon's enemies have attempted to keep him from gaining access to the Yanomamö because they are displeased with the questions he asks and the results of his scientific research. Those critics engage in the "naturalistic fallacy" of Hume. They believe that "what is" in nature provides moral guidelines for "what should be." They are afraid that a particular scientific finding will undermine their own moral agenda for the world. Their holy war is misguided, since Yanomamö behavioral patterns have no necessary implications for how people in modern society should behave nor what types of behavior might be eliminated or promoted through appropriate social incentives. Whether Yanomamö violence levels are high and whether killers have high reproductive success in that group is irrelevant to any important modern social issue, yet some Chagnon opponents have reacted as if the future of modern society were at stake when assaulting this result. This has led to the manipulation of the Yanomamö themselves as pawns in a perceived political Armageddon.

Chagnon was denied research permits for years because his work was offensive to some and because the Yanomamö supposedly didn't want him to come back. However, Chagnon opponents have incessantly coached a small number of Yanomamö spokespeople to legitimize their own ideological oppression.

Tierney hides this fact although it is easily discovered. When I visited the upper Orinoco I heard the Yanomamö complain about Chagnon's films despite having never seen them. They told me that Chagnon wrote books about them that called them savage animals. When I asked how they knew about this, they told me that Salesian missionaries and other anthropologists had told them. Indeed, they even believed they knew what "sociobiology" was. According to them it was the portrayal of them as nothing more than animals (but implying that civilized people are not animals). In other words, sociobiology was an explicitly racist philosophy that denigrated them vis-à-vis civilized people. This is a sad misrepresentation of an evolutionary view of human behavior, but it also illustrates an obvious fact. Somebody is maliciously coaching the Yanomamö—no Yanomamö ever read anything about sociobiological theory.

The Yanomamö have experienced a massive campaign of propaganda by anti-Chagnon/anti-sociobiology forces. Those same Chagnon enemies later use Yanomamö mouthpieces to insist that Chagnon is not welcome. In 1988 I witnessed a meeting at the Platanal mission in which a Salesian priest and two anthropologists discussed ways to keep Chagnon out of the upper Orinoco. That meeting included statements about Chagnon's alleged evil activities, in front of several Yanomamö witnesses. I take seriously the fact that some Yanomamö are unhappy with Chagnon's work. But I also believe that the intentional distortion of an academic competitor's viewpoint in order to manipulate native peoples to oppose further research by that person is a blatant violation of professional ethics.

Most current cultural anthropologists are very poorly informed about different evolutionary views of human behavior. Some have engaged in a massive ideological hate campaign against such perspectives for many years, based on their own ignorance of behavioral biology and their own religious adherence to certain views about human uniqueness in the natural world. The ferocity of their hatred for the sociobiological threat to their worldview evokes memories of the religious reaction to Darwin in the nineteenth century. Although serious scientific investigation into the relationship between biology and human behavior is now found on almost every major university campus in the United States and in most large anthropology departments, some theoretical "commandos" remain committed to their jihad against sociobiology. Tierney is a part of this terrorist band of self-righteous shock troops against "incorrect" views of human nature.

The furor of his attack in combination with his complete lack of criticism of the Salesian missionaries who hosted him (and who certainly must have made mistakes of their own), and the religious writings in his previous book, suggest that Tierney has his own very nonacademic motive for writing this book. In the process he shows a complete disregard for the truth in order to attack his enemies. He suggested that sociobiological "zealots" sacrificed the lives of their study subjects to "spread their gospel." But he distorted and misrepresented information throughout his book to make a case against his villains that would have almost evaporated if backed with the truth. In his own zealousness to promote *his* world view, he demonstrates that while he may not be willing to sacrifice the lives of his opponents in this battle, he has no qualms about sacrificing a lifetime of their work and destroying their reputations. He is not bothered that James Neel's children and grandchildren must live with friends and neighbors who have heard false accusations that Neel engaged in genocidal experiments. Thus Tierney spreads *his* gospel—with a philosophy that the ends justify the means and "collateral damage" is acceptable in this holy war of ideology. He admits early on in the book that he has abandoned "traditional objective journalism" (2000:xxiv) for a cause that he clearly considers more important than truth.

Had Tierney stuck to the truth in this book, it would have constituted an important contribution to the ongoing discussion of anthropological ethics. If he had identified the true causes of current Yanomamö suffering, we could believe that he was mainly concerned with their welfare. But in this book the Yanomamö are just stage props in an ideological holy war. And that is sadly unethical.

THE SWING OF THE PENDULUM: THE IMPACT OF CHAGNON'S WORK IN BRAZIL

LÊDA MARTINS

I have been working with indigenous issues in Brazil since 1991. Between 1991 and 1995, I worked in the Yanomami health project of the Brazilian government that was responsible for providing medical care and social assistance to the great majority of the Yanomami territory. During that period, I had extensive experience traveling inside Yanomami territory and interacting with different villages, and even more dealing with the politics involving their health and possession of their land. My familiarity with the vulnerability of the situation of the Yanomami is incremented by being from Roraima, the state where most of the Yanomami live in Brazil.

Napoleon Chagnon's portrait of the Yanomami as primitive, fierce, and uncultured and his repetitive attacks on advocates of indigenous rights and Yanomami leaders like Davi Kopenawa (Monaghan 1994) were no small matter in light of the circumstances surrounding the Yanomami. In 1987 their territory was invaded by approximately forty thousand gold miners, five times the estimated Yanomami population (Albert 1999). In the same year, missionaries, researchers, and medical teams were banned from their territory by the government on the pretext that it was unsafe for them. The Yanomami were left to their own luck with the miners. Malaria and respiratory infections became widespread, several villages were practically decimated, and hundreds of Yanomami gathered around the mining camps and FUNAI[1] posts begging for medicine and

KEY ACCUSATIONS AND ISSUES
(see also pp. 317–41)

Should Chagnon have responded better to the media's misuse of his work? Chagnon's characterization of the Yanomami as fierce created a widespread negative impression of them among Brazilians. Chagnon cannot be exempted from responsibility for the repeated use of his work against the interests of the Yanomami. Although Chagnon could have reacted against the use of his writings to take government services away from Yanomami, he did not. (see pages 137, 140)

Was it appropriate for Chagnon to publicly criticize indigenous Yanomami spokespeople (especially Davi Kopenawa)? Chagnon's commentary on the Haximu massacre of Yanomami by miners cast a negative shadow on advocates of Yanomami rights and Yanomami spokespeople. (see page 138)

Additional Comment. It is fair to ask if the Yanomami would have been better off if Chagnon had never worked among them; leaders of one NGO, Survival International, say the answer is yes. (see page 139)

QUESTIONS TO CONSIDER

Who makes the stronger case, Martins or Hill, regarding the degree to which Chagnon followed the ethic of "do no harm"?

Should the American Anthropological Association regulate the professional activity of its members? If so, in what way?

food, too debilitated to feed themselves and without effective medicine to face the sudden influx of new diseases. It is estimated that 15 percent of the Yanomami population died in three years (Urihi Saúde Yanomami 2000). In 1990, owing to repeated media coverage of the massive damage inflicted on the Indian, the Brazilian government began to expel the miners (the so-called Operation Free Jungle) and organized an emergency health plan together with CCPY and the Catholic Diocese of Roraima. Later this plan became a long-term project of FUNASA (National Health Foundation), linked to the Ministry of Health.

THE ARGUMENT OVER THE YANOMAMI RESERVE

During this period, the 1980s and the first years of the 1990s, there was an intense argument in Brazil over the Yanomami territory, its uses and its size. The military, miners, local and national politicians, mining companies, and the local business sector pressured the federal government to demarcate the Indian territory in nineteen scattered islands of land to allow mining to continue in between villages. National and international human rights and environmental organizations and a few sympathizers in congress and in the government advocated for a continuous territory and the expulsion of invaders as the only means to secure the survival of the group. Davi Kopenawa campaigned in favor of the latter alternative. We in the Yanomami health project also supported the latter in the face of the life-or-death meaning of these two proposals. In 1992 the Yanomami territory was finally signed by the president as a continuous piece of land due mostly to international pressure and the work of CCPY, of which the anthropologists Bruce Albert and Alcida Ramos are among the founders.

The Yanomami felt this dispute in very concrete ways even after 1992, since the use of their territory kept being challenged. To this day, their land is still being invaded. The Yanomami suffered the political tug of war through the health project of FUNASA and through the actions of FUNAI, responsible for keeping the region free of miners. When the pendulum swung in favor of the Yanomami, there was a flow of money and administrative benevolence from the Brazilian government that resulted in the improvement of the health service for the Indians and yet another Operation Free Jungle to expel the miners from Yanomami land. Miners and malaria came hand in hand, and the latter was impossible to control with the former coming and going. But the pendulum quite often swung in the other direction, and the health project and Free Jungle ran out of money and institutional support. Miners would return to the jungle, malaria numbers would go up, and so would cases of tuberculosis, respiratory infection, malnutrition, and, consequently, deaths.

THE IMPACT OF CHAGNON'S WRITINGS

But what has all this to do with ethics in anthropology? That depends on what or who made the pendulum swing in one direction or the other. Chagnon, at the very least, helped to push it away from the Yanomami in several moments. The insistence on characterizing the Yanomami as "fierce" since Chagnon started to publish in the 1960s has created a widespread negative impression about this people that, although difficult to assess in its extent, can be pinned down through particular examples, of which I will cite a few.

In 1988 he published an article entitled "Life Histories, Blood Revenge, and Warfare in a Tribal Population" in *Science*, in which he characterized Yanomami society as primarily driven by the men's will and need to kill to acquire social status and more wives, and in consequence to secure a large number of offspring (Chagnon 1988). The article came out at the height of the gold rush and of the debate over the destiny of Yanomami land. As Alcida Ramos, Bruce Albert, Manuela Carneiro da Cunha, and others have pointed out, the major Brazilian newspapers reproduced Chagnon's description of the Yanomami as killers, and his quotation of a Yanomami man calling for law and police among them to stop "their wars of revenge" (see Albert and Ramos 1989; Carneiro da Cunha 1989). His idea fit like a glove with the position for the fragmentation of the Indian territory. Albert and Ramos quote General Bayna Denis, the military chief of staff, declaring at the time that the Yanomami were too violent and had to be separated to be "civilized," although surely the general did not use this term with quotation marks.

In April 1994 Chagnon's work again appeared in the *Folha de São Paulo*, a major national newspaper, in an article by Janer Cristaldo (1994b). The piece was entitled "Os bastidores do Ianoblefe" (Behind the Scenes of the Yanobluff), and it challenged, through gross mistakes and misrepresentation of facts, the very existence of a massacre of a Yanomami village, Haximu, perpetrated by gold miners in 1993. The Haximu massacre shocked not only everybody who worked with the Yanomami but the international community and the Brazilian society in general. It was classified as a crime of genocide by the Brazilian government.

But Cristaldo—voicing the opinions of the military, politicians, and miners' advocates, who from the beginning had cast doubt on the assassinations— argued that the massacre, if it happened at all, was more likely to have been carried out by other Yanomami due to their violent nature and practices. Chagnon's ideas were invoked in detail to support Cristaldo's accusations against pro-Indian rights organizations that, according to the journalist, were behind the so-called fabrication of the massacre, or at least of its explanation. In fact, the overall inspiration of the article seems to be Chagnon's words.

In December 1993, Chagnon published a piece supposedly about the Haximu massacre, which, to his credit, he believed was carried out by miners (Chagnon 1993b). But in reality his main purpose in the text was to attack the Salesian missionaries of Venezuela. Chagnon also took the opportunity to throw rocks at "left-wing anthropologists," Yanomami leaders, and "survival groups" that, according to Chagnon, were profiting from the Indians' tragedy. Chagnon's main point was that Venezuelan authorities should investigate other causes of Yanomami death, in this case, the Salesian influence that he suggested had done more harm to the Indians than the miners had. It is not the occasion here to dig into the long-standing dispute between Chagnon and the Salesians except to point out that Chagnon used this dispute to cast a shadow on advocates of Yanomami rights in general and on Yanomami spokespeople in particular. His accusations were vague and unsubstantiated but were readily picked up in Brazil. Cristaldo's article, indeed, seems merely a logical extension of Chagnon's allegations.

A second article by Cristaldo followed that first one. In this one he wrote, "The savage state of the Yanomami, who have not even reached a social contract like that of the chimpanzees, has been amply proved by the anthropologist Napoleon Chagnon" (Cristaldo 1994a; my translation). I need not say that the accusations formulated by Cristaldo represented a total dismissal of all the violence and abuses suffered by the Yanomami and, in particular, by the Haximu village. One has only to look at the letters to the newspaper that followed the article to see that it made a great impression on the lay audience.

In Roraima those articles came as a blow to work in support of the Yanomami. In the health project I recall that they raised anxiety and an extra burden to deal with the bureaucrats of FUNASA, and the politicians behind them, who where not happy spending their budget taking care of Indians, especially "ferocious" ones. The argument of Yanomami brutality and the allegations against Indian rights advocates increased and justified political interests in withdrawing health and social services from the Yanomami population and in giving incentive to the miners to return to the jungle.

My colleagues and I in the health project knew by experience that this political context would be translated into delays or the cutoff of payments for the use of airplanes and helicopters and for food for the medical teams inside Yanomami territory. Many times we had to evacuate the teams or leave them and their patients without assistance for days or weeks. During those hostile times people would stop you in the grocery stores or in the bank to harass and even threaten you if they knew you were somehow involved with indigenous people. In Boa Vista, the state capital of Roraima, conversations on indigenous issues took place everywhere under the tone that it was too much (rich) land for a few Indians. In conversations with politicians and sympathizers of gold miners I heard arguments echoed from quotes from Chagnon about Yanomami's aggressiveness and the consequent argument that it was to their own benefit if they were rapidly "pacified."

I should make clear that I do not blame Chagnon for the gold rush and the dramatic situation inflicted on the Yanomami. Nor can he be held responsible for the political ideas and actions of the military, politicians, and government bureaucrats in Brazil. Those people would think and act in the same manner without Chagnon's ideas, and the gold rush would have occurred even if Chagnon had chosen to work elsewhere. But it is legitimate to ask if the Yanomami would not be better off without Chagnon. Survival International has recently stated that the Yanomami would be in a better position if indeed Chagnon had gone to work in another part of the world (Survival International 2001). The organization affirms that Sir Edmund Leach refused to support the campaign in favor of the Yanomami territory because "they would all 'exterminate each other'" and that the British government turned down an educational project for the Yanomami on the basis that any program with this Indian people should aim to reduce violence.

TAKING RESPONSIBILITY

Scholars and advocates in Brazil have been vocal in their concern about the impact of Chagnon's work with the Yanomami several times in the past without a proper response from the American Anthropological Association. In 1989, Manuela Carneiro da Cunha, then president of ABA (Brazilian Anthropological Association), wrote in the anthropology newsletter warning of the "the political consequences of academic images and the extremely serious consequences that such publicity can have for the land rights and survival of the Yanomami in Brazil" (Carneiro da Cunha 1989).

The AAA took no effective action to investigate or even address the complaints from ABA.[2] The president of the AAA at the time, Roy Rappaport, took a rather dismissive position, stating that "anthropologists should be concerned about how governments interpret our work, but there is nothing short of not publishing to stop this kind of thing from happening" (Booth 1989). He is right in suggesting that any publication can be used politically by other parties and that anthropologists should be concerned about the use of their writings. But Chagnon's case directly addresses the question of what should be done when scholars are not concerned about how their writings are used, even when their ideas are used with their knowledge against the interests of their subjects.

Chagnon cannot be exempted from responsibility for the repeated use of his work against the interests of the Yanomami people. In the cases mentioned above and in others, Chagnon did not react, although he could have, against the use of his words to support attempts to take land and government services away from the people he studied. It would certainly have deflated the balloons of people like Janer Cristaldo if Chagnon had dissociated his work from their intentions. One could then argue that no reaction by Chagnon would make a significant difference and that politics in Brazil would stay the same. Perhaps this is true, but it is beside the point.

Chagnon deliberately ignored all warnings and complaints that his portrait of the Yanomami was bringing harm to them, and he took no effective action to avoid the political use of his work against the Yanomami. And he even joined the attacks on Yanomami leaders and human rights advocates. There are no excuses for what Chagnon did.

NOTES

1. FUNAI is the equivalent of the Bureau of Indian Affairs in the United States.
2. The ABA discussed responses by the AAA to its complaints in the latest ABA statement about Chagnon's work, read at the AAA annual meeting of 2000.

ETHICS IN ANTHROPOLOGY: A RESPONSE TO PATRICK TIERNEY'S *DARKNESS IN EL DORADO*

JOHN F. PETERS

INTRODUCTION

The discussion of ethics in social science research is certainly not new. And this discussion will not be resolved or exhaust all possibilities after we have nitpicked our way through Tierney's *Darkness in El Dorado*. The pursuit of knowledge, particularly of humans, is an extremely humbling experience. Cultures are contin-

KEY ACCUSATIONS AND ISSUES
(see also pp. 317–41)

Looking at the broad picture, how would you assess the value of Darkness in El Dorado? Tierney did us a service by showing that anthropologists can operate as colonizers. (see page 145)

Did Chagnon benefit unfairly from the royalties earned from his books in relation to what he gave back in compensation to the Yanomami? The incomes of some anthropologists with faculty positions are more than the income of the entire group they studied. (see page 146)

Additional Comment. Knowing the sensitivity of Yanomami to photographs, Peters wonders about the impact on the Yanomami of the films made by Asch and Chagnon in the 1960s. (see page 144)

QUESTIONS TO CONSIDER

What would constitute just compensation to the Yanomami informants who provided information to Chagnon and other anthropologists?

Should the American Anthropological Association become more like missionary societies in the way it regulates the professional activity of its members?

ually changing, and subcultures modify both themselves and the dominant culture. We may therefore ask the author(s) of any written document, of whom do they speak, and for what period of time?

Ethics in research of human subjects is especially sensitive in the anthropologists' field of investigation. In much, but not necessarily all of our research, we deal with subjects who are vulnerable because of their status within large nation-states, people who have restricted freedom, rights, privilege, and power. Many carry a history of such treatment. This is particularly the case when one compares their position to that of the anthropologist. And frequently the researcher appears on the scene with goods the people crave.

The anthropologist arrives with "knowledge" that he or she deems superior to that of the group being researched. Furthermore, the goals of the anthropologist, in terms of the host group, are generally not understood or of any long-term value. (The gap between the two cultures is seen in the following: The research funding agency stipulates that all "subjects" have freedom not to answer any question and freedom to terminate the survey at any point. How does one practice this among a people who do not understand research, or the concept of human rights?)

In my view, the discussion of ethics emerging out of the Tierney book addresses three significant areas. The first relates to the anthropologist as researcher. The second looks at the anthropologist in his field of research, and the third addresses "professionalism." Where appropriate, I will use illustrations specific to my experience with the Yanomami.

THIS WRITER'S STORY

I begin by giving some of my own story, particularly as it relates to the Yanomami and academia. My late-teenage and early-adult years were spent in forested areas in northern British Columbia. After a year at the University of British Columbia (UBC), in addition to courses in linguistics and cultural studies, I thought my life's purpose would be fulfilled by serving with an evangelical mission society in the state of Roraima, Brazil. After some study of Portuguese in 1958, I made contact with the Yanomami on the Mucajaí river, who referred to themselves as Xiliana. I was stimulated by the anthropological questions our mission leader provoked among us. I loved the outdoors and accompanied my rain forest companions in hunting, and ventured to a half-dozen "uncontacted" Yanomami communities, including, in 1961, the Marashi-teri, where miners and medical personnel had become prominent at the Paapiu airstrip. I was married in Brazil and fed my appetite for anthropology by taking several courses by correspondence from UBC and the University of Oregon. After nine years we moved to the United States, where I completed a bachelor's degree in anthropology, then an M.A. and Ph.D. in sociology. In 1969 and 1972 I returned to the Yanomami for research purposes. My earlier years with the Yanomami provided me with an immediate rapport with my hosts, general language and cultural understanding, and specific demographic data. In my Canadian university teaching career my research interests were family, ethnicity, and social change.

Though I frequently referred to the Yanomami in lectures, both on and off campus, I did not do any further research until anthropologist John Early (Florida Atlantic University) contacted me and encouraged me to do collaborative demographic work, a worthwhile collegial endeavor (Early and Peters 1990; 2000). I renewed my field research with trips to Brazil in the late eighties and early nineties. As the Yanomami became more of a centerpiece in anthropology, I felt there was a story that was not being told, and consequently I wrote *Life among the Yanomami*, published in 1998. The heated debate stimulated by Tierney's book has again stirred me to enter the fray.

ETHICAL CONSIDERATIONS

The Anthropologist as Researcher

Every anthropologist enters the field of research with a very Western accumulation of values, attitudes, perspectives, goals, and hopes. While one, or even three, graduate courses in methodology may assist us about sensitive areas in the research of human "subjects," we never attain a value-free stance. In the past two decades feminist research has indelibly reminded us of this fundamental principle, but still we lumber on without adequate regard of the limits of our investigative methods, all the while engaging in the polemics of doing "good social science." We err in not knowing who we really are, especially in relation to our host environment, our impact upon the people in the research, and the total and complete picture of the real people in our research.

We believe our scientific model of investigation provides us with tools to know fully the social structure and organization, as well as numerous layers of the social system under investigation. Our commitment to science has possibly placed us within boundaries that restrict investigation. Is this system of investigation one that limits the broad scope of knowledge? Are some areas of research beyond the parameters of science? Postmodernists raise a question worthy of consideration. (I am struck that no researcher comprehends the Yanomami spiritual world, which is the very core of their everyday life: relationships, conflict, food, and health. This may not be such a strange anomaly, given the absence of the spiritual in the Western world.)

We assume that from our "democratic," capitalistic, technological, nonmystical, and affluent culture we can thoroughly and fully comprehend all or much of the organization of foreign (and strange) cultures. This as an arrogant stance, and one that goes beyond what a member of the host population might attempt to do. We may learn some of this foreign culture as it is described to us by native informants, or as seen through our Western lenses. However, we will never fully sense the multiple layers of the institution of family, governance, religion, dominance, and subordination experienced by the members born into this population. Our understanding will always be partial.

In many cases researchers experience a superior status in the host population, which is undeserving. Our abundance of material goods, our clothing, resources in food and health, availability to easy and comfortable transportation, and possibly color of skin and passport identification give us status that we have not earned. The duration of our stay in the field is often no more than a few years, and this limits, and possibly stilts, reality. When questioned in the field by authorities, we tend to legitimize our findings with careful phrases of "development" or improvement in social conditions, while we honestly know it is primarily the dissertation, or another journal article we want (a point Tierney makes). Let us not fool ourselves!

Most of us in the social sciences are trained to see the "faults," injustices, contradictions, and discrepancies in any given society. We rarely see the wholesome and constructive elements pervasive in the culture of our hosts. Or possibly we do not feel at liberty to analyze and then print this data. Qualities that are disapproved of within our larger society such as patriarchy, socialism, the collective, generosity, or intergenerational interaction do not find an easy place for publication. Anthropologists carry their own tainted glasses. (The next appropriate step in the current interest to develop applied anthropology might be to work toward applying these constructive attributes of the host people into our own culture!).

As anthropologists, we are quick to identify the negative effects of change brought on by other outsiders: entrepreneurs, governments, missionaries, medical staff, and megaprojects like dams and mines. Yet we ignore the impact of anthropologists in the short and long term upon an indigenous group. Why not an anthropology of anthropologists in the field? Why this oversight? Our record does us harm. (Knowing the Yanomami's sensitivity to the still photographs I took of them between 1958 and 1962, I have often wondered how Chagnon and Asch used movie cameras in the mid-1960s, so soon after Chagnon's entry into the field, and in very sensitive settings! Why did the AAA not raise questions much earlier, and why did AAA members make such extensive use of this footage?)

We often consider culture X among preliterate peoples to be sacrosanct. We condemn any aspect of the indigenous culture that is in change, usually attributing such modification to outside national or technological pressures. We go to great efforts to keep the status quo in this indigenous culture, even when leaders within the culture desire and work for change. I encountered this distortion on my 1996 visit in Yanomamiland. One headman asked me why such an effort was being made by an NGO agency to help the Yanomami go "native," the way of life before the Yanomami initiated contact with the wider world in 1956. He said his people will not go back to a life without salt and without clothing! (He could have added axes, knives, matches, and aluminum pots.) This NGO agency was also advocating the full indigenous return to the practice of shamanism, some of which, if the truth be told, is destructive to life.

Frequently we are selective in our portrayal of a culture foreign to the Western public. Chagnon was selective. I was as well. We do this because of our perception of the audience, as well as the specific emphasis or points we wish to make. Academia reinforces this perspective. Our own socialization within our political and university culture has established norms of what is appropriately said of a culture. In some cases we fail to disclose or fully critique the culture. My experience with the Yanomami includes contact with female infanticide, infanticide of deformed infants, and violence against, and rape of, women. I also learned of the centrality of the supernatural in all life, the power of shamanic pronouncements of death upon an enemy, unrelenting determination to seek revenge, and brutality in judging and punishing deviance. I saw frequent drunkenness and its results: slash wounds, fractured skulls requiring hospitalization, and bruises. I also saw gardens depleted when food was needed, the produce used earlier in drinking festivities. This drinking practice was adopted in the late 1960s from a neighboring Yanomami village. In this, Yanomami carry social responsibility.

While anthropologists and NGOs advocate a sensible response from the state and the public, there is little advocacy for what the indigenous peoples themselves might do in terms of the problematic aspects of their society. No anthropologist has disclosed the more inhumane aspects of the culture. (I was publicly criticized at the AAA meeting in 1998 after mentioning that shamanic activity does not always contribute to the health of the Yanomami!)

From my perspective, one of the "black holes" of anthropology research is missionary activity. Most of us lose all objectivity. We show bias at the very mention of "missionary." (One Yanomami researcher refuses to read anything I write because of my earlier vocation.) Our naïveté shows, in that our images of missionary work are based on our readings and hearsay from the early twentieth century: pith helmets, colonizers under a foreign power, cultural insensitivity, and ignorance. A few mission agencies still operate with some of these characteristics, but most do not. Most address poverty, subordination, restricted and limited resources, education, and health. Most avoid issues that are directly political in nature.

Most missionaries are in for the long haul in less comfortable conditions than they would experience in their country of origin. Most of us academic "do-gooders" do not have such a commitment. Christian missions in the past two decades have changed, some radically. Missions now function under very direct observation of governments, and in many cases direct proselytizing is not tolerated. While mission agencies have faults, they likely do not exceed those of academia. Most anthropologists do not recognize that they themselves operate as colonizers under a super power, that of their home government. (Tierney does us a service in identifying this reality.) Chagnon's Venezuelan experience strongly suggests this. Just as medical researchers are seduced by pharmaceutical companies, we are not immune from monetary and status seduction.

The Anthropologist in the Field

The target population of the research is often a vulnerable group, layered with subcultures, gatekeepers, the oppressed, manipulators, official and nonlegitimate rulers—the lot, as found in our own society. While being ready to report how other "outsiders" contaminate the indigenous culture, we do well to acknowledge that we are agents of change, even though we prefer this not to be the case.

We are guests. In terms of our academic project, we have more to gain than they do. In most aspects within the host culture, our mechanized, rational, and impersonal culture has little to offer. On the individual level, a few persons will gain from payments we make, and a few will be pleased that they have social exchanges with an outsider. Our comments about our own families and home country may be partially understood and prove to be interesting and entertaining. Others will not appreciate our close association with our new "friends."

It may be that our established aspirations, well argued and scrutinized in academic offices just months earlier, are only partially going to be realized in the field. There may be ethical issues that have been discovered that we prefer not to trespass. We decide not to violate these codes, at risk even to our own immediate academic goals. It may require creative thinking to form some viable alternative, and even greater energy to operationalize the new direction. We need a new mentality in academia to recognize such possibilities.

There have been, and will be, numerous occasions in which we err. Most will be simple blunders, but there will be some serious ones. (Anthropologists tell these stories only among themselves.) Generally our hosts are extremely forgiving. Most cultural stupidities prove to be points of startling new comprehension. Out of the months we spend with our hosts, there may well be long-term expectations on their part, years after we have received the degree: requests for financial and medical assistance, advice, or simply personal communication. In these matters there may be an expectation to act as a privileged person within their culture would. It is not enough to claim exclusion because we are Western. This is a dilemma.

Increasingly, marginal people are becoming savvy to monetary gains made by outsiders, whether they be entrepreneurs, government agents, or researchers. In 1995 the Yanomami asked me about profits I would make from publishing. At least we now have a few examples of anthropologists who return all book royalties for development in the population studied. We might move this sentiment a bit further. The income of some anthropologists with faculty positions is more than the income of the entire group originally studied. The researched people made the position and status possible for the anthropologist. The royalty "gift" may be mere tokenism.

The Anthropologist as "Professional"[1]

AAA members are not professionals as is the case with doctors, lawyers, dentists, and engineers. Similarly, there are no professional sociologists or historians. We call ourselves professionals because we make our living in this particular branch of scholarship. We are university faculty members, or perhaps employees of research agencies. We call ourselves professionals because we earn our livings in this particular branch of scholarship.

This fact is important in a number of ways. There is no set of criteria by which a person's capability to perform in the field is adjudicated. We become a member of AAA by virtue of paying fees and subscribing to a journal. Therefore, we are uncertified individuals in our research endeavors. The AAA has no power to adjudicate the "professional" conduct of a person. This means that a person can go and do research wherever they wish, as long as they have permission from the government in the jurisdiction in which the research is taking place. Some anthropologists, such as Chagnon, have been stopped in their endeavors. Therefore, as long as anthropology is not a professional body it will have little significance in regulating the activities of its members.

Mission organizations are different from both academic bodies and professional groups such as doctors and engineers. They act in a corporate way in dealing with state governments. As a body, they are accountable. Mission organizations negotiate their clearance to carry on their work. No missionaries are *franc-tireurs* (snipers who don't fall under the jurisdiction of an army), but all anthropologists are. Anthropologists are on their own. Once legitimately in a country, they pretty much ask the questions they wish, in whatever manner they wish, wherever they are, of whomever they choose. No professional body gives any "you shall nots" in terms of dress, participation, recorders, photographs, or movie cameras. There were, and are, no professional bodies that placed this control on any of the anthropologists, medical researchers, or cameramen mentioned in the Tierney book.

We have moved into a new era of social science research in which the norms and rules of the game, public sentiment of human sensitivity and rights, and international communication and understanding have all been altered from the 1970s and 1980s. As students of human groups and of change, we need to sensitively investigate this new direction, with the perspective of making a global contribution. I am convinced this will emerge as we include the marginalized, both within and outside our "professional" group.

NOTE

1. I am indebted to anthropologist and colleague Laird Christie, Wilfrid Laurier University, for this insightful contribution.Ï

....

ETHICAL ISSUES ARISING FROM PATRICK TIERNEY'S *DARKNESS IN EL DORADO* AND THE ENSUING CONTROVERSY

TERENCE TURNER

Patrick Tierney's book *Darkness in El Dorado*, his *New Yorker* article "The Fierce Anthropologist," and the controversy that they have provoked have raised a series of ethical issues, some stemming from the content of Tierney's writings and some from the conduct of those involved in the controversy. Amid the barrage of charges and countercharges, the most important ethical issue, namely, what, how, and why the Yanomami have suffered from the actions of those who have come to study, document, film, convert, aid, and otherwise impinge upon them over the past thirty years, has tended to get lost.

Very few of the messages and postings relating to the controversy have paid serious attention to the condition of the Yanomami themselves or to their views, and most have tended to ignore ethical issues altogether. Instead, the out-

KEY ACCUSATIONS AND ISSUES
(see also pp. 317–41)

Given what we now know, are the accusations made against Chagnon and Neel mostly true or untrue? Some defenders of Neel and Chagnon have attempted to discredit the whole book by focusing on the book's flawed treatment of the measles epidemic while avoiding the many parts of the book that are supported by abundant evidence. Although the broad outlines of Tierney's accusations regarding Chagnon were well known and well established, Tierney has added new details and filled in gaps in the public record. (see page 150)

To what degree did the Neel expedition violate reasonable standards of informed consent? A review of Neel's field notes reveals no attempt to secure informed consent from the Yanomami for Neel's research or vaccination program. (see page 152)

Did Neel act ethically during the 1968 expedition in the way he balanced his research with the need to treat the measles epidemic? Neel's field notes confirm a point made by Tierney: the vaccination of Yanomami against the measles epidemic caused severe reactions among a number of Yanomami that led in some cases to panic and flight from villages where treatment was available. While it would have been prudent to vaccinate as many people in as many places as quickly as possible, Neel did not change his planned research itinerary in any major way when faced with the measles epidemic and hence was less successful at stopping the epidemic (and saving lives) than he might have been. (see pages 152, 154–55)

QUESTIONS TO CONSIDER

How would you evaluate the credibility of Tierney's book?

Who makes the stronger case, Hill or Turner, regarding whether Neel followed the ethic of "do no harm"?

pouring of e-mail messages and postings by defenders of Neel and Chagnon over the past several months has been almost exclusively concerned with defending James Neel and Napoleon Chagnon against Patrick Tierney's allegations. The most common basis for dismissing the criticisms has been the charge that Tierney, and other critics of Chagnon such as Leslie Sponsel and myself, are primarily motivated by some combination of hostility to "science" and an unwillingness to face the hard truths about the Yanomami and other primitive people as revealed by Chagnon's scientific approach. The implicit subtext seems to be that if the critical allegations against Neel and Chagnon can be refuted on scientific grounds, then the ethical questions raised by critics about the effects of their actions on the Yanomami can be made to go away. This tropic use of "science" is epitomized by the attempt of leading partisans of Neel and Chagnon to use Tierney's errors in the chapter on the measles epidemic—concerning such scientific matters as whether the vaccine used by the expedition to vaccinate the Yanomami could itself have caused the ensuing measles epidemic—to discredit his entire book.

ETHICAL ISSUES RAISED

The main issues raised by Tierney's critical accounts of the 1968 AEC expedition and Chagnon's actions, however, concern the ethics of scientific practice: they imply no attack on science as such. Any discussion of the ethical issues raised by Tierney's work ought to begin by giving Tierney credit for raising important ethical issues. Science is not a substitute for ethics, scientific findings do not obviate ethical issues, and scientists, particularly those who work with human subjects, have ethical responsibilities. In this connection, the words of the report of the Brazilian medical team of the Federal University of Rio de Janeiro on chapter 5 of Tierney's book (his account of the epidemic), otherwise highly critical of Tierney, are apropos: "The positive aspect of the polemic raised by chapter 5 of Tierney's book, despite its serious documentary and conceptual failures and its lack of demonstrative rigor, is in the fact that it has made possible a more profound discussion reflecting upon the ethics of research among indigenous populations and minorities in general, not only in biomedical research, but also in other spheres, such as anthropological research, which, in the case under discussion, was strictly associated with biomedical research" (Lobo et al. 2000: section 7, subsection "Ethics of research on indigenous peoples: past and present").

The ethical issues in this controversy, however, have not been confined to the actions of Neel, Chagnon, and others toward the Yanomami. The conduct of the controversy has raised important ethical issues of its own. One ethical imperative is clearly to correct the errors of Tierney's account (and of the memo that Leslie Sponsel and I sent to the leaders of the AAA summarizing Tierney's allegations and calling for their investigation by the association) to prevent the damage to individual reputations they might cause. As the authors of the memo that became the vehicle for the dissemination of these errors (albeit against our wills and without our consent), we have assumed responsibility for researching and publicizing relevant aspects of the conduct of the 1968 AEC Orinoco expedition (see below). Another ethical issue was posed by the leaking of our confidential memo on the Internet by a party or parties unknown. This was a breach of trust as well as a legal breach of copyright. The consequent sensationalized exploitation of the contents of the memo in the media led to a number of distorted and untruthful reports, which Sponsel and I have sought to correct at every opportunity (e.g., in lectures, letters to the editor, postings on the Web, published columns and articles, and media interviews).

Finally, the outpouring on the Web in defense of Neel and Chagnon has not stopped at correcting Tierney's errors but has produced a rich crop of tendentious prevarications and untruthful assertions that raise ethical problems all their own. Some of the loudest defenders of Neel and Chagnon have attempted to discredit the book as a whole by reference to its flawed treatment of the epidemic, while avoiding discussion of the many parts of the book for which there is abundant evidence in the public record and the testimony of other anthropologists, missionaries, and Yanomami. Some of the most violent attacks on Tierney's book, in sum, seem directed as much at distracting attention from the truth of many of its allegations as at exposing its relatively few (but important) errors. There has been a good deal of "spin," in short, along with some well-founded criticism, in the attack on Tierney.

Ninety percent of the controversy over Tierney's book has focused on the less than 10 percent (one chapter out of eighteen) devoted to the measles epidemic and the Atomic Energy Commission Orinoco expedition of 1968. The remaining 90 percent deals with completely different issues, most of which concern Chagnon's activities and their effects on the Yanomami. Tierney's accounts of the more ethically problematical of these actions and effects are on the whole accurate and well founded (e.g., the political damage done by Chagnon's demeaning characterization of the Yanomami as violent savages incapable of peaceful self-government, his unfounded calumnies against Yanomami leaders and NGOs dedicated to supporting and aiding the Yanomami, the disruptive effects of Chagnon's field methods and actions on Yanomami communities, and his joint attempt, in collaboration with Charles Brewer-Carías and Cecilia Matos, to get a large tract of Yanomami territory in the Siapa valley converted into a personal research park under their joint administrative control).

Most of these actions and events were already common knowledge among anthropologists, missionaries, journalists, medical personnel, and government functionaries who have worked among the Yanomami, not to mention the Yanomami themselves, who are rapidly becoming more vocal in their own behalf. Most have been reported in the Venezuelan and Brazilian presses, made the subject of published critiques by other anthropologists who have worked with the Yanomami, and been the object of collective protests by the anthropological associations and professions of those two countries. Because of the intense opposition his practices and statements have aroused, Chagnon has repeatedly been denied permission to enter Yanomami areas in both countries. Tierney's chapters on Chagnon add many new details and fill in many of the gaps in this public record, but the broad outlines of what he reports are already well established and independently documented.

When Leslie Sponsel and I were sent the galleys of Tierney's book by the publisher in July-August 2000, we decided that our responsibility as members of the AAA was to warn the association of the seriousness of the allegations and the need for an investigation. When the memo we sent to the AAA leadership summarizing Tierney's allegations was made public without our permission, the result was a media furor in which exaggerated and sensationalized versions of the allegations we had summarized were presented as assertions of fact by us, rather than as reports of allegations by another that we were reporting to call for their investigation. Apart from the distortion of our own position, this resulted in the circulation of allegations damaging to the reputations of those named in them, without prior investigation by qualified reviewers such as we had called for in our memo. Under these circumstances, it seemed to us that we bore an ethical responsibility to speak out in the media against the distorted, unfounded, and unconfirmed versions of the allegations that were circulating and also to do what we could to investigate the most serious allegations ourselves. These tasks acquired additional ethical urgency as we realized that some of the allegations were not true.

THE 1968 MEASLES EPIDEMIC

The most serious, and also the most questionable of Tierney's allegations, dealt with the 1968 Atomic Energy Commission expedition led by James Neel and the epidemic of measles that broke out among the Yanomami it was vaccinating. Of these allegations, the most serious were that the vaccinations themselves might have caused the epidemic and that this might have been done intentionally as part of an experiment (these suggestions and others in the galley proofs of the book were withdrawn or modified in the published version). I accordingly set out to check with independent medical experts on the possibility that the Edmonston B vaccine used in the vaccinations might have given rise to transmissible cases of measles. The result of these consultations was to confirm the judgment of Dr. Samuel Katz and other medical experts that the vaccine employed by Neel's expedition could not have caused transmissible cases of measles. I immediately sent an e-mail to Dr. Katz informing him of this result (this message was immediately posted on the Web site of the society for evolutionary psychology, presented in such a way as to suggest that I had repudiated Tierney's whole book; a followup message that I sent affirming that I continued to find other parts of Tierney's account to be well-founded was never posted).

The point about the inability of the vaccine to cause the epidemic, of course, was only a first step toward working out what had actually happened. It left unanswered most questions about the nature of Neel's ideas and intentions, and about the conduct of the expedition as it struggled to reconcile its research program with the humanitarian demands of medical prevention and care. The major source of information on these questions was known to be the collection of Neel's papers and correspondence in the archive of the American Philosophical Society (APS) in Philadelphia. I therefore undertook to make a comprehensive search of Neel's papers in the APS archive. I was able to visit the archive in December and go through all the documents I could find relevant to Neel's Yanomami research and the 1968 AEC expedition, including Neel's field journal. Together with my research assistant, John Stevens, I produced an annotated index of the field journal and all the letters and documents. Copies of this index have been furnished to the Venezuelan and AAA investigative commissions and posted on the Hume Web site (see Turner and Stevens 2001).

The picture that emerges from these documents of Neel's motives, ideas, and actions in planning and leading the 1968 AEC expedition, as well as the conduct of the expedition as a whole in carrying out the vaccination campaign and reacting to the epidemic, differs in a number of critical respects from Tierney's account (and therefore also from Sponsel's and my memo, written as a summary of that account) and from the accounts of many of Neel's and Chagnon's defenders on the Web. On the other hand, it converges on essential points with the report of the Brazilian medical experts organized by Bruce Albert. While the new data do not support the more extreme assertions and suggestions of Tierney's original galley text—such as that Neel might have deliberately caused an epidemic of measles or knowingly risked doing so by using a "contraindicated" vaccine [i.e., the Edmonston B vaccine] or that he contemplated or actually executed an "experiment" that he knew risked medically serious or possibly even fatal consequences for some of his Yanomami subjects—they do support other points of Tierney's account, and indicate certain ethical problems with Neel's and the expedition's approach and conduct that neither Tierney nor others have noted.

There was, for instance, a definite research purpose for the vaccinations, as Tierney insisted. The papers also provide negative evidence that supports two other points made by Tierney: there seems to have been no attempt to secure informed consent from the Yanomami either for the taking of biological samples or for the vaccinations, which would have been called for given that the latter also formed part of a research program; and there is no evidence for any formal permission from either the Brazilian or Venezuelan governments for any of Neel's expeditions to either country. The papers also provide confirmation of Tierney's assertions that the vaccine did in fact cause extremely severe reactions that led to social complications (social panic, flight from villages where treatment was available), which did in some respects exacerbate the effects of the disease.

On another disputed point, while the APS papers provide further evidence for Neel's genetics reductionist and eugenic beliefs about a relationship between leadership, reproductive success, and genetic endowment and the central role of this genetically based complex in determining Yanomami social and political organization, they show that the eugenic ideas had nothing to do with the vaccination program and the research purposes it served, as we speculated they might have done in our memo. Finally, they make clear that the expedition routinely provided medical care while it was in Yanomami communities and attempted to extend medical help by providing medicines and vaccine to missionaries, although there were indeed occasions when the expedition moved out of villages where sick people needed care to get on with its scientific itinerary (we had misunderstood Tierney's account of such an occasion to imply that the expedition refused medical treatment on Neel's orders, and mistakenly said so in our memo). We regret that the unauthorized circulation of our memo caused these erroneous claims and suggestions to be disseminated to the general public before they could be properly investigated, as we had called for in the memo, and we regret the pain this must have caused to James Neel's family and friends. As a result of my research on Neel's own papers, I am now in a position to correct these erroneous reports.

NEEL'S PRIORITIES

The controversy that has blown up around Tierney's book has focused so heavily on the 1968 measles epidemic that it came as a surprise to discover from reading Neel's field journal and correspondence that measles and matters associated with it, such as vaccinations and the type of vaccine to be used, held a relatively low priority for Neel, both before and even during the epidemic. This relative lack of importance that Neel attached to medical work and even the research value of the vaccinations by comparison with the other kinds of data he planned to collect affected Neel's (and hence the expedition's) planning and conduct both before and during the epidemic.

Neel originally planned the expedition for the purpose of collecting blood samples and other biological data (specimens of urine, stools and saliva, anthropometric measurements, etc.) that would have a bearing on his research into genetic variation among and within indigenous communities. This research purpose remained his top priority throughout the expedition. He was interested in epidemic diseases, specifically including measles, for some of the same reasons, because as "natural stressors" they exercised important selective pressures, and because by observing the levels of antibodies generated by a "virgin soil" population like the Yanomami to such diseases, or to vaccinations against them, he would be able to test the theory that Amerindians and other isolated populations were equally capable in terms of genetic endowment of producing antibodies for them as long-exposed populations. The vaccinations, in short, were originally planned primarily as a research tool for eliciting the production of antibodies (although Neel also thought of them as serving a humanitarian medical purpose). The specific type of vaccine seems to have been a matter of relative indifference. Far from deliberately selecting the Edmonston B vaccine for its reactive properties, his correspondence leaves the impression that he simply took it because it was what the U.S. pharmaceutical companies with which he was in contact were prepared to give away free (they were probably dumping their inventories to make way for the new Swartz version of the vaccine, which was about to become the new world standard).

It is clear from the papers that Neel planned the measles vaccinations for his own research purposes and began soliciting donations of vaccine months before he heard the first reports of the outbreak of measles among Yanomami on the

Brazilian side of the border with Venezuela. When he received reports of the out-break of the epidemic in Brazil, and then of its advance into Venezuela, he responded by shipping one thousand units of vaccine (without accompanying gamma globulin) to the missionaries with the threatened Brazilian Yanomami villages, but he made no other changes in his plans or preparations. He knew from reports from missionaries, and also from a conversation with the head of the Venezuelan Indian Agency on the night before his departure for the field, that the epidemic was moving down the Orinoco and had also reached the Ventuari, so he had every reason to believe that time was running out before it would reach the villages he was heading for.

From a medical point of view, the prudent move would have been to try to vac-cinate all the villages he could reach immediately upon arriving in the area, leav-ing his blood and stool sampling until later, but he made no such alterations in his previously planned itinerary. He did not even formulate a plan for defend-ing the region against the epidemic by vaccinating at the main points of access to the area until the epidemic actually broke out in the villages where he was working, after he had been in the field for a month. He wrote several times in his journal of how great a burden the vaccinations had become because they were taking too much time away from the research tasks of expedition person-nel. In planning for the last part of the trip, he wrote of the need to set firm pri-orities for the various research tasks, starting with the collection of blood sam-ples, and only after completing them "then vaccinate—if at all."

The Brazilian team, after rejecting Tierney's suggestions that the expedition might have caused or spread the epidemic by its use of the Edmonston vaccine or that it sought to produce heavy vaccine reactions as part of an experiment, presents a plausible alternative theory of the origin and spread of the epidemic. The Brazilians start from the proposition that the epidemic, having originated in Brazil rather than the Orinoco (which now seems established beyond dispute), reached a number of the Orinoco villages a few days before the expedition arrived and began vaccinating. Given that vaccinations applied three or more days after exposure are ineffective in preventing the outbreak of the disease, this meant that in many cases the expedition's vaccinations came too late to do any good. It is also why, the Brazilian experts suggest, measles appeared to break out in reaction to the vaccinations, as the witnesses cited by Tierney testified. Rather than the measles breaking out as an effect of the vaccine, the Brazilian team suggests, it was the ineffectiveness of the vaccinations, owing to their late-ness, that allowed the measles to break out within the normal period for incu-bation of reactions to the vaccine. In the Brazilians' view, in short, it was above all the failure of the expedition to move fast enough to get to many of the villages before they became exposed (or at least within the three-day grace period after exposure, during which vaccinations could still be effective) that was responsi-ble for the failure of many of the vaccinations to prevent the onset of the disease or to stop the epidemic. "if measles reached the region before the team arrived, the planning and organization of their movements—regardless of whether they gave priority to either medical care or research—probably had a greater impact on the failure of the vaccination (since immunization took place later than 3 days after infection) and the lack of control over mortality (due to the ill-preparedness of the team for dealing with the serious complications of measles, mainly pneumonia), than on the spread of the epidemic."

Revising the "planning and organization of their movements"—that is, the research itinerary that called for spending enough time in each village to collect enough samples to reach the target of a thousand blood specimens—to permit the most rapid possible vaccination of all the villages within the expedition's reach would, however, have required giving the vaccinations top priority at the expense of the tightly planned research program, in effect abandoning the target sample sizes for blood and other specimens and settling for less significant research results. As a number of entries in his field journal make clear, Neel never entertained this possibility but single-mindedly pressed on for collecting the maximum possible number of blood samples while sacrificing collection of some other types of data (e.g., anthropometry, dental impressions) to allow more time for vaccinations and medical care.

SUMMARIZING

To sum up: Neel's unwavering prioritizing of the scientific research goals of the expedition over the needs of more effective preventive measures against the measles epidemic (more timely vaccinations) and more effective medical care for patients suffering from reactions to vaccinations as well as from measles itself undermined the effectiveness of the vaccinations and care he did provide and thereby contributed to a "failure . . . to control mortality" (i.e., the death rate from the epidemic). Ultimately this may have contributed to the failure to stop the spread of the epidemic, which despite Neel's claim to have "averted a real tragedy" by the vaccinations, continued to spread and rage on for months after the expedition left the field. This has to be set against the undoubted overall beneficial effect of at least some of the vaccinations in saving many Yanomami lives. Given the time Neel had allotted for the expedition and the quantities of specimens to be collected he had set as its goals, there was no way he could have succeeded as he did in collecting his thousand blood samples and other specimens and also have optimally met the medical needs imposed by the measles epidemic. He ended up making some sacrifices on both sides, but more on the medical than the research side. These sacrifices were ethical choices. In the making of those choices, the scientific requirements of studying the Yanomami as a biological population took relative, though not absolute or exclusive, priority over the requirements of assisting the Yanomami as a people—that is, as social communities of individual persons facing a medical emergency.

This seems to me to be the main point that subsumes the more specific ethical questions that have been raised about the practices of the expedition. All of these specific issues go back to the general problem of the relative lack of importance Neel allotted to medical and social issues in comparison with his own research goals. This attitude, it seems to me, was essentially a matter of Neel's intellectual orientation, although it turned out to have ethical consequences in the context of the epidemic. It is clearly not an intrinsic corollary of scientific research or attitudes per se. To criticize Neel for the ethical implications and consequences of this attitude in his conduct in the epidemic, in other words, is not to attack "science" or to question the value or propriety of scientific studies of human populations at either the biological or the social level. Rather, it is to call attention to the ethical implications of choices and acts of individuals faced by conflicting demands under circumstances that made it impossible to fully satisfy personal goals, scientific interests, and humanitarian values at the same time.

9

ROUND TWO

In Round Two, participants discuss where they agree and disagree with one another's contributions in Round One in the previous chapter. This process allows readers to clarify the strengths and weaknesses of each participant's position.

BIOMEDICAL RESEARCH, ETHNIC LABELS, AND ANTHROPOLOGICAL RESPONSIBILITY: FURTHER COMMENTS

BRUCE ALBERT

Although all of us made efforts in Round One of our debate to rise above the factional Manichaeism of the Chagnon-Tierney dispute that has been raging ever since the galley proofs of *Darkness in El Dorado* circulated and the revised book was published, perhaps we did not entirely get beyond its initial terms. However, it is clear that all contributors demonstrated a deep concern for the Yanomami's condition; as Kim Hill put it so well, "The health and welfare of the study population must always take precedence over any academic goal." If we keep such principles in mind, we will surely continue our progress in discussing ethical questions directly relevant to the rights and survival of the Yanomami (and other indigenous peoples).

Most contributions focused on a major theme of discussion (Terry Turner and I on the aspect of biomedical research, Lêda Martins and Raymond Hames on ethnographic images), while the two other authors (Kim Hill and John Peters) raised a wider range of ethical themes. In this paper, I will comment on these contributions in this same order.

KEY ACCUSATIONS AND ISSUES
(see also pp. 317–41)

Did Neel act ethically during the 1968 expedition in the way he balanced his research with the need to treat the measles epidemic? Tierney's paranoid, nightmarish scenario of Neel's research has been completely and thoroughly discredited. But Turner reviewed Neel's field notes and found that Neel gave a low priority to immunizations compared with his research agenda while the measles epidemic raged along the Orinoco River. (see page 159)

Should Chagnon have responded better to the media's misuse of his work? While the Yanomami do practice warfare, the stereotypical image Chagnon presented is a serious matter, because it showed a minimal concern for the ongoing political threats to the Yanomami's survival. Albert agrees with Hill and Hames that anthropologists should respond to the misuse of their work that harms the people studied, but Chagnon, unfortunately, never did this. (see pages 162–63)

Did Chagnon act unethically in collecting genealogies that violated Yanomami taboos? Chagnon's "hit-and-run" fieldwork—in contrast to the slower-paced traditional fieldwork style—was tied to the frenetic schedule of Neel's research and created the necessity for developing aggressive and less ethical ways for circumventing the Yanomami name taboo to collect genealogies. (see pages 164–65)

Did Chagnon benefit unfairly from the royalties earned from his books in relation to what he gave back in compensation to the Yanomami? A fair redistribution to the Yanomami of the economic benefits Chagnon gained from his work is still awaited; Chagnon should explain what he intends to give back to the Yanomami in return for all their help. (see page 165)

QUESTIONS TO CONSIDER

Is Albert fair in claiming that Chagnon violated the ethic of "do no harm?"

What would be just compensation to the Yanomami for the benefits both Neel and Chagnon received from working among them?

ON THE 1968 ORINOCO EPIDEMIC AND BIOMEDICAL RESEARCH

Questions concerning James Neel's biomedical research and vaccinations in 1968, to which I dedicated a lot of attention in my contribution (and previous efforts), were also the focus of Terry Turner's piece. His document research (along with J. Stevens) on James Neel's papers and correspondence in the archives of the American Philosophical Society (Philadelphia) is a very important initiative. It contributes a great deal toward moving the debate about chapter 5 ("Outbreak") of *Darkness in El Dorado* beyond the unrigorous journalism and biased polemic that have been raging since September 2000. Such was the intention of the research I commissioned (and assisted on anthropological points) from a group of experienced Brazilian physicians of the Federal University of Rio de Janeiro (Lobo et al. 2000). I am thus particularly satisfied that these two research initiatives converge on several fundamental points and complete each other on many others (see my first contribution for a summary of the Brazilian medical report). In fact, these complementary findings substantially alter the way in which Neel's research and vaccinations have been seen and discussed up to now.

The paranoid, nightmarish scenario of experiments and eugenics imagined by Patrick Tierney in the preliminary version of his book—subsequently muddled and attenuated to the point of being self-contradictory in the published version—has by now been completely and definitively discredited. But as Turner and I made clear, several aspects of Neel's expedition in 1968 still need to be evaluated in terms of biomedical ethical norms. The Brazilian physicians' report focused on three main points: possible experimentation during vaccinations with and without immunoglobulin (MIG), inadequate planning and training to cope with the epidemic, and failure to properly obtain informed consent while collecting biological samples. Turner's research sheds further light on these points by demonstrating that the vaccinations were originally planned as a research tool rather than as a health care measure and by confirming the low priority that Neel gave to immunizations compared with his research agenda, even when the measles epidemic was raging along the Rio Orinoco (with the result that most of the vaccinations were not administered in time to reduce mortality).

The question of Neel's official authorizations, at least in Brazil, is getting clarified. In 2001, I consulted a research report on this matter written by an official at the National Indian Agency (Fundação Nacional do Índio, or FUNAI for short) in Brasília (Furtado 2001). This report shows, to the benefit of James Neel and his U.S. and Brazilian colleagues, that official authorizations for their research among the Yanomami were properly granted by different FUNAI presidents in 1970, 1972, and 1974. No documents have been found yet regarding their first expedition in 1967, probably because the files of the government agency that preceded FUNAI, the Indian Protection Service (the Serviço de Proteçno aos Índios, or SPI), were partially destroyed in a fire (1968) and the remaining archives have not been systematically organized. However, the report demonstrates that the president of FUNAI in 1970, General Bandeira de Mello, was informed of Neel's 1967 expedition.

Kim Hill dedicates a part of his contribution in Round One to Neel's Orinoco vaccinations and research. His discussion does not take into account the new information contained in the Brazilian medical report (posted on the Internet since December 2000 in Portuguese, and since February 2001 in English; see reference to Lobo et al. 2000 in the bibliography for the URL), or, of course,

Turner's research into Neel's archives. His approach largely remains within the spirit of earlier stages of the polemics, defending Neel mainly by targeting Tierney's "ideological warfare" and "ideological terrorism." I hope that the new kinds of information brought to our debate will lead to a different way of discussing the issue.

I am not a "Tierney supporter" and, like the Brazilian physicians, I was shocked by his irresponsible and incompetent writing about the history of the epidemic. But as a Yanomami supporter, I do not think that Neel's work among the Orinoco Yanomami in 1968 was merely, as Kim Hill characterizes them, a "combination of treatment and research" or that his blood samples "were critical to saving Yanomami lives." I will wait until the next round of discussions to have, perhaps, an exchange of opinions on this matter with Kim Hill (in response to the contributions by Turner and myself).

Like Kim Hill, I also addressed the issue of radioiodine 131 research in my first contribution, but in very different terms. I do not agree with the idea that since the Iodine 131 research (from 1958 to 1970) may have been too complicated to explain to the Yanomami, this was therefore a justification for not bothering with their rights to informed consent, which, I must insist, are not simply a matter of "today's standards" but were in vigor since the Nuremberg Code (1947). This code does not sustain the idea that if people do not understand the research and experiments to be made on or about them, they are by definition available to serve as human material for these research projects and experiments without informed consent.

This idea is extremely dangerous. It means that the presence or absence of a common communication ground (linguistic or cultural) could legitimately be used as a criterion for granting to, or withholding from, a person or people the right to informed consent in biomedical research. This is essentially the same criterion that is used to justify animal experiments, which are rationalized on the principle that animals are not included in the moral community since they cannot express their interests (classical philosophy restricts the "equality of justice" only to moral beings capable of expression).[1] Let me quote Nadia Farage on this dangerous slide: "Speech, the power of speech, the literal distinction between humans and animals, metaphorically extends to all of us as humans and, as a metaphor, is no longer a question of nature, but, rather, of degree. This explains the fact that experimentation, which is usually restricted to animals, has been applied to social categories whose discourse is confiscated in oppressive political situations" (Farage 1999:6).

Finally, Kim Hill condemns the notion, which he attributes to Patrick Tierney, that research done on an indigenous population that is not designed to help that same population is unethical. It seems to me that the problem is not properly formulated here. The question is, in reality, that once they are fully informed about a research project, indigenous people have the perfect right not to authorize research among their collectivity on the grounds that it is of no direct benefit to them, or to negotiate with the researchers that some part of the research activity or funds be funneled into something that is more directly beneficial to their community. These negotiations are taking place more frequently as the process of indigenous empowerment advances (Albert 1997). To get authorizations from research and government Indian agencies these days, researchers in the Brazilian Amazon have to negotiate the conditions under which their projects will be conducted, as well as with Indian leaders and/or Indian organizations (which number more than 180; see Albert 2001). In fact, this negotiation process is now a matter of official regulation.[2]

Besides, it sounds somehow paternalistic (as if to suggest that "behind every Indian is a white man") to think that indigenous people need to be "indoctrinated" (in Hill's words) to reach the opinion that biomedical research done among them should have some kind of benefit to their families and communities when, in reality, they suffer from precarious or nonexistent health care. This indigenous view does not seem to me to be an affront to science, but a matter of justice. Through their research projects, scientists gain a direct benefit to their careers. Let us admit that their work could also bring a universal benefit to humanity, as Kim Hill insists. If so, scientists would gain double benefits, both direct and indirect, as researchers and as members of humanity. Why couldn't indigenous people be granted the same privilege: a negotiated direct benefit as communities collaborating in the research (if they decide so) and an indirect benefit as members of humanity? Or should they really be left to suffer their horrible health conditions with a few trinkets and the injunction to be proud of contributing to the universal advancement of science?

ETHNOGRAPHIC IMAGES
AND POLITICAL RESPONSIBILITIES

*Implied in Chagnon's finding so far is a notion startling
to traditional anthropology: the rather horrifying Yanomamö
culture makes some sense in terms of animal behavior.*
(*Time* magazine, May 10, 1976)

Studying and publishing works on Yanomami warfare (sociopolitical, cultural, or other aspects), as many of us have done, is one thing. Pinning this ethnic minority with the exoticizing, stereotypical label of the "fierce people" (the subtitle of Chagnon's book from 1968 to 1992), knowing full well how vulnerable they are to dramatic local threats (racial discrimination, land invasion, and physical violence) is quite another.

Nobody maintains that the Yanomami do not practice warfare or that Yanomami individuals are not occasionally violent (as is true for most societies, including the United States, where some kids even shoot up their schools).[3] But many people do maintain that it is unethical and politically damaging to reduce the richness of Yanomami society and culture to the stereotypical image of "the barbaric violence [that] Chagnon documented" (*Time* magazine 1995). It requires only a minimal ethical sensibility and political awareness to understand that such long-term pejorative labeling and its apparent scientific authority can be (and has been) used by anti-Indian agitators to rationalize and encourage violations of Yanomami rights—nobody ever said such labeling caused them. Does one really need to be a left-wing radical to fear the impact of articles like the one in *Time* magazine ("Beastly or Manly?") once they ramify in the Brazilian press, in reinforcing the racist justification of military officials as they plan the dismemberment of Yanomami lands?[4] Does one need to be an enemy of sociobiology to understand that a researcher bears some ethical responsibility if he publishes and invites widespread media coverage of a paper about "blood revenge" and "Yanomamö killers" (Chagnon 1988) during a gold rush into Yanomami lands in Brazil? After all, the invasion in Roraima (1987–90) involved almost forty thousand gold panners trying to expropriate those lands or exterminate their legitimate owners, leading to the deaths of about 1,200 to 1,500 Yanomami.

If the recent reaffirmation by the Brazilian Anthropological Association (ABA) of the contents of its 1988 letters of protest to the American Anthropological Association (AAA) on this case (see Oliven 2000) is not yet considered sufficient evidence,[5] then Lêda Martins's contribution to this debate offers more vivid, direct testimony about the impact of Chagnon's publications in Brazil in the 1990s.

In view of this context, it is clearly reasonable to hold that an ethics of responsibility is involved in creating ethnic labels for the people with whom we work and in contributing to the spread of such labels through mass media. This basic responsibility, which should be the concern of any anthropologist, involves also avoiding and fighting, as much as possible, the misuse of our ethnographies against the societies they describe. In his contribution, Kim Hill expresses a deep concern about this point, which he shares with many so-called "Chagnon opponents." Indeed, his own work, as he described it, is exemplary in this respect. Ray Hames agrees, too, with the principle that "we have an obligation to ensure that what we produce is not used by others to harm the people we study and, if necessary, . . . to engage in political action to defend injustices meted to those we study." Unfortunately, in his (generous) effort on Chagnon's behalf, he gradually shifts the problem away from its original context and onto a generic level where it gets lost. He begins by saying that Chagnon was unduly accused, but that anyway he changed his ways (so then why did this supposed mutation take place if the accusations were irrelevant?). He then argues that whatever forms our ethnographic accounts take, they have no impact on the fate of indigenous people anyway (so then why did he affirm the principle quoted above?). He goes on to criticize pro-Indian NGOs for spreading the image of the "noble savage" and ends his paper by offering them a lesson in human rights. In the end, one wonders where this juxtaposition of arguments is supposed to lead. Does it mean that anthropological writing transcends ethics and that NGOs should heed our armchair preaching and carry out the job for us?

Finally, going back to the Yanomami realities, we need to ask why Napoleon Chagnon never publicly came out to condemn the use of his work by sensationalist journalists and unscrupulous politicians, or to support the international movement in defense of Yanomami survival that began at the end of the 1970s. Instead, he dedicated his time and energy to waging a media war against advocates for Yanomami land and human rights. For instance, consider his three-page interview in *Veja* (the main news magazine in Brazil) in 1995, where he criticized the coordinated actions among NGOs on behalf of the Yanomami as amounting to nothing more than a competition to become the "exclusive owner of the Yanomami cause" just to make money. Consider also his accusation against Davi Kopenawa, a major Yanomami spokesperson, as being no more than "a parrot of human rights groups" (Monaghan 1994:A10).

Adding insult to injury, this reduplication of ethical irresponsibility may even be worse than his original offense of persistently labeling the Yanomami in such negative terms—which resulted in decades of media caricatures of them as savages/prehistoric peoples/primates.

Undoubtedly shaken by the debates swirling around his 1988 article in *Science*, Chagnon suddenly announced in 1989 the creation of a Yanomamö Survival Fund, which remained inactive, at least until 1997 (Rabben 1998:138n7). In 1992, he changed the title of his famous book to *Yanomamö*, including in its final chapter some lyrical statements about his future dedication to Yanomami rights (Rabben 1998:36–37). Will the shallow ethics of such editorial plastic surgery be sufficient to erase the stigma of the "fierce people" label pinned on the Yanomamö for so much time? One can entertain doubts about this.

Writing a few declarations on anthropological advocacy here and there, on the one hand, and trying to transform the dramatic realities confronted by indigenous people through effective forms of social engagement, on the other, are two quite different things. The comfortable confusion of the two is a very common, but no less ethically dubious, artifice.

YANOMAMI ETHICAL MISCELLANEA: TRADE GOODS, GENEALOGICAL METHODS, AND REDISTRIBUTION OF GAINS

Trade Goods and Conflicts

Kim Hill raises the issue of the extent to which trade goods cause conflicts in the population under study. Most of us use trade goods to reciprocate with our informants and others for their many services (food, transport, guiding, etc.) or simply to give presents to our hosts. In a society like the Yanomami, trading is embedded in every social relation, and, as Mauss put it, "le bien remplace le lien" (1991/1925). What is at stake with Chagnon's fieldwork is a very different problem. His research was not the usual type of anthropological fieldwork. He was the "jungle advance man" (Sahlins 2000) of Neel's huge project for the Atomic Energy Commission (AEC) from 1966 to 1972, endowed with a budget of more than $2.5 million. He had to follow an intensive research agenda for collecting blood and genealogies, filming, and performing many other services for Neel's project. For years, he spent his time passing back and forth through some forty to fifty Yanomami villages at a frantic pace, distributing huge amounts of trade goods to the Indians as payment and to gain their goodwill and collaboration with the AEC project. For any ethnographer of the Yanomami or other Amazonian groups, it would not be a surprise that such unusually hectic field-work and forms of compensation could have generated so many conflicts between Chagnon and the Yanomami, and between the Yanomami themselves, as each village competed to get the biggest part possible of this incredible manna from U.S. Atomic Energy Commission funding.

Unethical Name Collecting

As Kim Hill rightly guesses, I began my fieldwork in 1975, like many, if not all Yanomami ethnographers, collecting names of individuals and their relatives to study their kinship. Since the mid-1980s, I have often had to do this again, for more pressing reasons as part of medical emergency field missions (for instance, patients needed personal identification for malaria exams and treatment). The Yanomami never utter their own names when asked, their classical answer being "I don't know. I have no name." Traditional Yanomami names, which are nicknames and frequently pejorative to one degree or another, cannot be pro-nounced in front of a person or his or her close relatives—"to insult" is a syn-onym of "to name" in Yanomami (Albert 1985:394–404). But these nicknames circulate freely at a distance among unrelated people. I described a simple methodology for getting these names during medical missions in a linguistic field manual on Yanomami health published a few years ago. As the following passage demonstrates, it does not involve bribing, tricking, or offending anybody: "If the person does not have a Portuguese nickname, one should find out his or her Yanomami name from another person who is not a relative, preferably coming from another village. The question should be made discreetly, out of earshot of the person named and close relatives. Children or leaders can be of great help in identifying Yanomami names: the former because it is a fun game; the latter because no one is going to complain about being named by them (since publicly naming people is a demonstration of courage)" (Albert and Gomez 1997:182–83).

Here, once again, the atypical "hit-and-run" fieldwork methods used by Chagnon in his frenetic schedule of collecting genealogies and blood for the AEC must have induced him to invent ad hoc measures for getting around Yanomami name secrecy in ways that were more aggressive and less ethical. Had he used the more typical slow pace and low-profile attitude that most anthropologists employ during fieldwork, he would never have found himself in situations of having to resort to bribery, trickery, or offensive behaviors to collect names. The chaotic and peripatetic nature of his AEC agenda probably did force him into such situations. It is crucial to keep in mind that much of Chagnon's core ethnography is a by-product of the work commissioned by the AEC from 1966 to 1972 (mostly genealogical, demographic, and settlement pattern data). This probably also explains why his ethnography is so weak on the cultural and linguistic side of Yanomami reality.

Redistribution of Financial Gains and the "Anti-Chagnon Plot"

A concrete commitment from Chagnon to help the Yanomami (for example, in coping with their extremely precarious, and at times tragic, health situation) and to fairly redistribute the economic benefits he gained from them during his long career is still awaited. I agree with Kim Hill when he writes that Chagnon should clearly explain what kind of assistance (if any) he provided or intends to provide to the Yanomami and how he intends to redistribute what he gained from them: a lifetime career and probably a considerable amount of money on copyrights of books, films, and photos. (I also agree completely with the idea of redistributing the royalties of *Yanomamö: The Fierce People* and *Darkness in El Dorado* to the Yanomami!)[6]

However, I disagree when Hill suggests that the reasons why Chagnon has not contributed anything to the Yanomami cause or welfare is because his enemies prevent him from going back to the field to make agreements with the people he worked with. I disagree, first, because Chagnon seems to have done nothing especially remarkable on this count while he was allowed to do research in Venezuela for many years (and, given his skills in media promotion, we would probably know about it); and, second, because no omnipotent, terrorist antisociobiological enemies are preventing Chagnon from entering the field. In Brazil, for example, it was the government Indian agency FUNAI that did so because he was trying to smuggle blood samples out of Yanomami territory. A new FUNAI document on the subject, entitled "Napoleon Chagnon Case," states: "In 1995, Chagnon was granted authorization to enter the Yanomami area for an article for the magazine *Veja*. He was accompanied by the photographer Antonio Luis Torry. When they began working in the area, he tried to collect blood samples from the Indians. When this was reported, FUNAI intervened and ordered him to leave the area. In 1997, the same anthropologist requested new authorization, in conjunction with the University of Roraima, this time for research. FUNAI denied the request" (Furtado 2001).

As to an "anti-sociobiological plot" against him, my impression is, on the contrary, that the use of Napoleon Chagnon by some as a media symbol of sociobiological studies was not a very productive move for that brand of research. Given his controversial way of speaking about the Yanomami to the media and his ethically dubious field methods, in the final analysis, he probably generated more bad publicity for sociobiology than anything else. If we put aside academic debates over the political ideology underlying sociobiology and the ethnographic validity of its hypotheses, it is not far-fetched to suggest that, in the context of the Yanomami debate, sociobiology has been publicly spurned in Venezuela and Brazil more because of Chagnon's behavior than the contrary.

Anthropological and Missionary Views on Social Change (and the "Spiritual World")

I will end this contribution with a few comments on John Peters's paper. First I want to set his mind at rest: I know and appreciate his demographic work with John Early (a valuable contribution to Yanomami studies), and I won't discriminate against him because he is an ex-missionary of the Unevangelized Fields Mission. Obviously, this does not mean that I agree with the missionary within the anthropologist. However, I must add that I do not hold the absurd view that Indian societies must not change, a notion that he attributes mysteriously to "some NGO."[7] I simply think that indigenous peoples must have the chance to decide for themselves if and how they want to change, and be given the means to keep control over the changes that they (not anthropologists, NGOs, or missionaries) eventually decide to make.

Thus, the notion that we should "keep the status quo in [an] indigenous culture" (supposedly an NGO conception) or practice "advocacy for what the indigenous peoples themselves might do in terms of the problematic aspects of their society" (the missionary position Peters favors) seems to me to be an equally paternalistic and unacceptable view on the subject of indigenous social and cultural change. As an anthropologist and member of pro-Yanomami NGOs, I think—in opposition to these views—that the Indians must have their collective rights respected (to land, health care, adapted education, and to political, cultural, and linguistic autonomy) and that they must have the choice to decide for themselves what they want to do with their lives and their society (which includes the right to go on with their own "spiritual world"). This is also what is established in paragraph 231 of the Brazilian constitution of 1988.

A parenthesis here: John Peters writes that "no researcher comprehends the Yanomami spiritual world." I don't exactly understand what he means here, but perhaps I need to remind him that several people have at least tried to understand the Yanomami shamanic, ritual, and mythological world. For example, Wilbert and Simoneau (1990) published a compilation of 364 Yanomami myths collected by nine Yanomami ethnographers, one of whom is Don Borgman, a fellow missionary of Peters. I personally wrote a doctoral thesis of eight hundred and something pages on the Yanomami ritual system (Albert 1985); also, the health field guide I wrote with Gale Goodwin Gomez (Albert and Gomez 1997) presents many Yanomami concepts on diseases and shamanism. Well before that, Kenneth Taylor wrote about Yanomami shamanism (1974), and young anthropologists in Brazil are still doing so at present (e.g., Smiljanic Borges 1999).

I am not sure that John Peters, here more a missionary than an anthropologist, really contributes much himself to "comprehend[ing] the Yanomami spiritual world" when he writes: "The approach of both FUNAI and CCPY [Pro-Yanomami Commission, our NGO] is to encourage shamanism and not curb sorcery. The missionaries, for their part, see the Yanomami world of spirits as integral to the people's lives, but they believe in another viable option as well. They believe that most Yanomami spiritual forces enslave the people, bringing fear and retaliation, and that God's power liberates. At least a few Xilixana [a Yanomami subgroup] have shown their belief that they have experienced this liberation" (Peters 1998:262). (The rest of the page continues in the same vein of evangelical proselytizing.)

Finally, I agree with the sensitive critique Peters makes of the "arrogant stance" of anthropologists and anthropology (on which an abundant literature has been produced since at least the mid-1980s). However, I was disappointed that he did not exercise the same sensible critical thinking about the effects of missionary proselytizing on indigenous cultures. "Christian missions have changed," he writes. I agree with that. They attenuated the "arrogant stance" of their proselytizing in the field, largely because of pressures from FUNAI and indigenous people, as Peters himself explains in the case of the Brazilian Yanomami (1998:262). But do missionaries actually reflect critically on their own ethnocentric and paternalistic views of indigenous cultures and societies (as anthropologists certainly do; see Albert 1997)? I am not really sure of that when I read, amid John Peters's admirable anthropological mea culpa, an extreme and superfluous condemnation of Yanomami shamanic practices three times on the same page (describing them as "destructive to life," "pronouncements of death," and prejudicial to health!), although these practices constitute a central part of their "spiritual world," culture, and society.

NOTES

1. On this matter, see Elisabeth de Fontenay 2000.

2. Resolution 304 of August 9, 2000, of the National Health Council in Brazil requires that a proposal for research in indigenous communities include: "(1) a commitment to obtain the consent of the communities involved and a description of the process of obtaining this consent; (2) a description of the process of obtaining and recording the Terms of Free and Enlightened Consent, demonstrating the adequacy [of the process] to the cultural and linguistic particularities of those involved."

3. See the impressive cover of *Time* magazine, March 19, 2001.

4. Let me briefly quote a Brazilian military document written in 1977 about the Yanomami: "We see that . . . the group lives in fiefs, each one made up of 50 to 200 Indians, and that each group is hostile to the others, leading us to conclude that the physical relations between man and woman occurs between siblings, father and daughters, mother and sons, and perhaps even between grand-

sons and grandmothers, and granddaughters and grandfathers, constituting true incest, which, over the centuries, has been causing the physical and intellectual atrophy of this indigenous group" (Oliveira 1977). This racist delirium served as the justification for sending a study group to the field in March 1978. This group's report became the basis for a project of dismembering Yanomami lands in Brazil, dividing them into nineteen "islands." The Pro-Yanomami Commission originated in the fight against this expropriation.

5. Hames writes that Alcida Ramos and I were "instrumental in drafting the ABA denunciation of Chagnon." I certainly was consulted at the time as a Yanomami ethnographer and advocate by the ABA president. However, the decision to write the letter and adopt a critical stance was entirely ABA's initiative, taken when its president at the time, Manuela Carneiro da Cunha, was also, like CCPY, at the forefront of the struggle for Yanomami survival.

6. Although not a "Tierney ally," I wish to answer Kim Hill's challenge about book royalties. When Gomez and I published a linguistic and cultural field manual on Yanomami disease conceptions (Albert and Gomez 1997), half of the copies were bought by the French IRD (Research Institute for Development) and distributed to health workers among the Yanomami in the states of Roraima and Amazonas. When Milliken and I published a book on Yanomami ethnobotany (Milliken and Albert 1999), we donated the rights to Survival International. Besides paying my Yanomami informants, I am a cofounder and board member of two NGOs that have been working on behalf of Yanomami rights and welfare in Brazil since the 1970s.

7. Elsewhere he clarifies that this NGO is the CCPY. Peters speaks well of CCPY's health and political work in many places of his last book (Peters 1998), but at the end he states, "They (CCPY and FUNAI) want the Yanomami to retain traditional practices, even to the point of returning to the wearing of the loin cloth for the men and the small apron for the women, but the Xilixana will never return to the form of clothing used before contact" (1998:261). I certainly hope that Peters will admit that, as anthropologists, both Alcida Ramos (president of CCPY, who has worked with the Yanomami since 1967) and I (a member of the CCPY board of directors, having worked with the Yanomami since 1975) have a more sophisticated view of the problem of social change.

....

INFORMED CONSENT AND TELLING IT LIKE IT IS

RAYMOND HAMES

In Round One Albert brings up the important issue of informed consent. As noted by Peters in his Round One contribution, informed consent is a creation of the West initially designed to protect and inform human subjects about the purposes, risks, and benefits of their participation in medical trials funded by government agencies. As noted by Albert, informed consent guidelines were developed at the Nuremberg trials in 1947 and later elaborated in the Declaration of Helsinki put forth by the World Medical Association in 1964. In the United States, the National Research Act of 1974 and the Belmont Report of 1979 created a set of regulations regarding informed consent and requirements for ethical research. This led to the establishment of Institutional Review Boards (IRBs) in 1981 to ensure that local researchers followed these guidelines. Importantly, social and behavioral scientists were included in these regulations because of the realization that some investigations might have negative consequences (e.g., emotional stress) for participants, especially if subject anonymity

KEY ACCUSATIONS AND ISSUES
(see also pp. 317–41)

To what degree did the Neel expedition violate reasonable standards of informed consent? It is clear that the Yanomamö gave their blood in exchange for trade goods, and they did it on a voluntary basis. Chagnon could not give the Yanomamö a crash course in infectious disease, genetics, and epidemiology to fully explain the purpose of the blood collection. (see pages 170–71)

Did Chagnon act unethically in using methods to collect genealogies that violated Yanomami taboos? The pressure to complete research in a limited time can lead ethnographers to use their wealth in an unethical way to get information; they might get that information as a matter of course if they stayed in the field for a longer time. (see page 174)

Should Chagnon have responded better to the media's misuse of his work? To assert that Chagnon was responsible for Brazilian politicians and generals wanting to limit the Yanomamö reserve is to obscure the larger power plays these people have continually perpetrated against their national minorities. (see pages 174–75)

Did Chagnon provide inaccurate representations of the Yanomami, especially regarding their "fierceness"? There are many accounts of Yanomamö violence; Chagnon's is not the only one nor the first one to describe their violence. (see page 175)

QUESTIONS TO CONSIDER

Did Chagnon inform the Yanomami as best he could under the circumstances in gaining their consent for the blood samples, and did the Yanomami, by accepting Neel's trade goods, thereby consent to donating their blood?

Is Hames correct in saying that Chagnon's portrayal of the Yanomami was not central to the Brazilian government's efforts to reduce the size of the Yanomami reserve? Or are Albert and Martins correct in saying that Chagnon's portrayal of the Yanomami did indeed influence the government's deliberations?

was not maintained. There is a growing literature on the nature of informed consent as it applies to research among indigenous peoples, much of it spurred by the implications of the Human Genome Diversity Project (HGDP) (Foster et al. 1997) and the nature of participatory research, where communities help identify research relevant to their needs and interests. The latter is largely a consequence of increased political power of indigenous groups, which require researchers to balance their own professional interests with those of the people they study.

INFORMED CONSENT
AND THE 1968 EXPEDITION

I cannot deal definitively with the issue of whether Neel and his colleagues conformed to developing informed consent guidelines during the measles epidemic
of 1968 or in the course of their routine collection of human biological specimens before or after the measles epidemic. In part, this is a very complex historical issue that can begin to be resolved after Neel's archived materials in the
American Philosophical Society have been thoroughly examined (as Turner is
doing) and after other members of the research team who worked with Neel during the epidemic have been interviewed or have issued statements. I think this
last point is important because characterizations of the epidemic give the mistaken impression that Neel, Roche, and Chagnon were the only participants.
There were others, such as Ryk Ward (the Oxford University professor who actually helped deliver some of the vaccine to Neel's team in Caracas before they
entered the field) as well as pediatrician Hugh Centerwall, dental researcher
Charles Brewer-Carías, linguist Ernesto Migliazza, and the late film maker
Timothy Asch. (Incidentally, Ward has stated that the allegations in *Darkness in
El Dorado* regarding the measles epidemic are "all demonstrably false" [Meek
2000]). Also ignored in the measles epidemic story are the roles played by the
Salesian and New Tribes missionaries and by Venezuelan government officials
who assisted in the vaccination campaign. What really concerns me as an ethical issue are the partially informed speculations about the ethics of the measles
vaccination campaign. I believe that it has been clearly established that Tierney
made numerous, fundamental errors (described to some extent in Turner's and
Albert's first-round contributions) on this issue, yet people continue to specu-
late based on incomplete information colored by Tierney's questionable handling
of the documentary evidence.

Albert claims that the collection of blood samples (largely for the purpose of
population genetics and epidemiological studies) by Neel's team did not meet the
principles of informed consent because a subject "should have sufficient knowledge and comprehension of the elements of the subject matter involved as to
enable him to make an understanding and enlightened decision"; he later suggests they were "used as involuntary objects of a biomedical research project."
First, it is clear that the Yanomamö gave their blood in exchange for trade goods,
and it was done on a voluntary basis.

Albert has no basis on which to judge whether or not the Yanomamö were
informed about the purposes of the research, because he cites no information
from Neel's articles or his diaries that deals with what Neel said to the Yanomamö
about why they were collecting blood. I am convinced that no such information
has been published. Given that this is the case, I called Napoleon Chagnon and
asked him what he said to the Yanomamö about the purposes of drawing blood.
He said that for a year before Neel's arrival and during the collection phase he told

the Yanomamö in all the villages to be sampled that Neel's team wanted to examine their blood in order to determine whether there were things that indicated whether or not they had certain kinds of diseases, especially *shawara* (epidemic diseases) and that this knowledge would help treat them more effectively if they became ill (Chagnon, personal communication, March 18, 2001).

Clearly Chagnon could not give the Yanomamö a crash course in infectious disease, genetics, and epidemiology to more fully explain the purposes of the research. Nevertheless, it seems to me that he gave them information consistent with their ability to comprehend the research. I would also add that the participants in biomedical research done in the West often do not have a very sophisticated understanding of the nature of the research in which they are subjects. The collection of biological materials from indigenous peoples predates and antedates Neel's research. For comparative purposes we need to know how others have managed the complex issue of informed consent. If these comparisons were to show that what Neel did was standard, this would not necessarily settle the issue. We need to know whether there existed some sort of double standard regarding research done on Western subjects.

Albert further notes that blood samples collected by Neel are now being analyzed as part of the Human Genome Diversity Project, a research use unforeseen by Neel, and that this use breaches informed consent. This is a gray area, especially because the standards of informed consent have evolved since 1968 and some (but clearly not all) of the analyses of Yanomamö blood by the HGDP undoubtedly fit the parameters of what Neel asked Chagnon to communicate to the Yanomamö. Most important, as Albert notes, no harm was done to the Yanomamö by having them serve as a control for Neel's investigation.

In the end, Albert calls for an independent bioethics committee to investigate Neel's blood collecting. I think this a useful idea, and I would welcome it to provide us with closure and, more important, with some guidelines for researchers who engage in future work among indigenous peoples. If such an investigation were to be done, I would not limit it to Neel's research but extend it to the research done by a sample of researchers who have collected biological specimens from indigenous peoples. Toward this end I think it would be useful if Albert were to describe the informed consent protocols members of the emergency expedition organized by the CCPY and Doctors without Borders (Médecins Sans Frontiéres-Holland) when they entered Venezuela to investigate epidemiological patterns in eight Yanomamö village in the upper Siapa. Doing so would help provide us with a potential set of ethical protocols.

We really need good ethical models in this area because our notions of medicine, general scientific research, and informed consent are based on cultural assumptions not necessarily held by indigenous peoples. In the first round Peters makes much the same point about our cultural arrogance in this regard. I think we need to find a way to make it relevant to those we study by making sure it does not breach not only national or international ethical standards but also the ethical standards of the people we study. This last point requires that we have a sophisticated understanding of the ethical values held by the people we study. But as we all know, this comprehension develops over time as we continue our research. Oftentimes we learn those standards through blunders in the course of our research. No one has bothered to deal with what the Yanomamö believe about informed consent, risk, and benefit.

One of the charges mentioned by Turner in the first round was that Neel did not obtain proper governmental authorization to vaccinate the Yanomamö. Ultimately, I believe that it will be shown that minimally he had implicit authorization, as evidenced by the cooperation of the Venezuelan government during the vaccination campaign and through his research collaboration with biomedical researchers at IVIC (Instituto Venezolano de Investigaciones Ceintificas), Venezuela's premier government-supported research institute. The evidence clearly indicates that Neel sought permission, although at this point we have no record that it was obtained (National Academy of Sciences 2000; Lindee 2000b). Nevertheless, let us suppose that he did not have authorization. The obvious question is the ethics of waiting for permission, or not acting for lack of permission, compared to rushing into the area to begin the campaign without permission. I believe that most would agree that the vaccination campaign was an ethical as well as humanitarian act and that not acting would be ethically suspect. What would Neel's critics say upon learning that he had measles vaccines in the middle of an epidemic but withheld their use for lack of proper authorization? Kim Hill also made the correct ethical decision when he decided to deal with an epidemic, even though he was initially told by Peruvian officials to provide no treatment.

Regarding Roche's iodine uptake research, Albert complains that there was an "apparent absence of any medical benefit for the Yanomami" and that this is another breach of ethical conduct. This puzzled me because I did not realize that research on a group had to benefit the group being researched. So I called our university's Institutional Review Board (IRB) compliance officer and posed the question to her. She said that biomedical research has to benefit a group (e.g., those afflicted by Parkinson's syndrome) but that the group benefited need not be the group studied. Egidio Romero, the director of IVIC, provides details on how Roche's research benefited Venezuelan peasants living in the Andes, where up to 25 percent of the people show signs of iodine deficiency and associated cretinism. Perhaps the issue of benefit reflects protocols established by the French or Brazilian government. If so, that brings up another complexity to which we must pay attention.

An important issue today is how do we follow our own culture-bound notions of informed consent and ethical research and, at the same time, make sure we respect indigenous protocols about how we should behave in the field and the kinds of investigations we can accomplish. This issue is not discussed much by ethnographers, and one of the reasons Chagnon is the target of criticism is that he has provided rich details of how he collected data and how the Yanomamö reacted to his investigations.

To illustrate some of the issues, I can only draw on my own experiences working with the Ye'kwana and Yanomamö of Venezuela. When I first arrived among the Ye'kwana of Toki in August of 1974, I met with village leaders and described my desire to live among them and study their economic system and how they interacted with the environment. Obviously I did not use those terms but instead said I wanted to know what they grew in their gardens, how much time they worked producing food, how it was exchanged, and the like. I also told them that this information would be published, and that it was the primary purpose of my stay among them. In return for their cooperation with my work, I promised to pay all families with trade goods on a periodic basis and assist the village *enfermero* (local health practitioner paid by the government) in his treatment of the ill.[1] After listening to the offer, a long meeting of family heads was called, from which I was pointedly excluded. After the meeting, the headman and his deputy informed me that my project was approved. Several months later I repeated this process with neighboring Yanomamö. In addition, I was called upon to assist with land registration with the government and to speak with government officials on issues of concern such as the stocking of the *enfermero's* dispensary with medicine. In my opinion, this is fairly standard ethnographic practice. But the real question is: was the consent truly informed?

THE DYNAMICS OF COMPENSATION

What I have described is a classic quid pro quo: informants are compensated by being given goods and services by the ethnographer. The people studied clearly understand what they are getting, and they have the ability to evaluate whether or not the ethnographer is making good on his or her promises. But do the people studied fully understand the benefit the ethnographer gains, and if they did would this affect what they required in the way of compensation? I believe the answer to the first question is no, and I am unsure of the answer to the second. Aside from the publication of scientific articles that advance our careers, we sometimes receive royalties for books, photos, and films. Our informants rarely have knowledge of this. At the same time, most of us profit little in this area, but I think it laudable that both Peters and Hill share royalties with those they have studied. More recently, the patenting of human genetic materials and indigenous botanical knowledge has become another potential benefit for researchers. I believe that we have an obligation to inform the people we study of the possible monetary benefits and share the proceeds. To answer the second question, I am sure that this will have a variable and unpredictable effect on negotiations for compensation.

Peters speaks of the huge power and economic differentials that exist between us and the people we study. This leads me to consider the enormous leverage we have in accomplishing our research and the potential for corruption that the differential causes. Tierney speaks of the thousands of machetes, pots, axes, and other goods routinely distributed by ethnographers to pay for information and cooperation. If you possess such a hoard, the Yanomamö expect such distributions as a matter of course: the Yanomamö reason that a person needs but a few steel goods, and those who have dozens should trade them to those who have none or a few. They don't expect them to be free gifts but rather a means to establish social relations between the giver and the receiver that ultimately provides the giver a kind of social leverage. The Yanomamö desire to gain these goods as quickly as possible, reasoning that if they do not get what you have now someone else may get it soon. This concern is so great that Yanomamö routinely attempt to deter ethnographers from visiting neighboring villages where they know he will distribute goods that they might otherwise acquire. At the same time, a Yanomamö may give something with the expectation of no immediate return and then later use the debt to leverage something from the ethnographer. The pressure to complete research in the allotted time may lead ethnographers to unethically use their wealth to gain information over a short period that they were likely to gain as a matter of course if they had planned to stay in the field for many years. Likewise, Yanomamö's desire to gain goods may lead them to provide information that they would not ordinarily divulge.

More subtlety, we use our powerful medicines to treat all manner of ailments. I believe that most of us regard the treatment of the illnesses as something we do as a kind of generalized reciprocity (using Sahlins's term): a kind of sustained one-way flow from us to them. Still, this leads to an ethical dilemma, since the Yanomamö are chronically ill. We could spend nearly all of our time in the field treating illnesses until we exhausted our medical supplies. At the same time, a visiting Yanomamö is not hesitant to claim there is an outbreak of malaria in his or her home village as a way to induce the ethnographer to visit. When the ethnographer arrives he discovers that the ill have spontaneously recovered and everyone is angry that the ethnographer has brought no trade goods. Finally, most Yanomamö are grateful when you cure them or alleviate symptoms. This gratitude may increase the ethnographer's ability to pursue a topic he formerly was unable to pursue.

CHAGNON'S PORTRAYAL OF YANOMAMI VIOLENCE

Martins in the first round brings up the issue of Chagnon's portrayal of Yanomamö violence being used by Brazilian civil and military authorities to justify control or partitioning of Yanomamö land.[2] This is the central issue I dealt with in my initial contribution to this discussion. Additionally, she notes a conversation Chagnon had with a Yanomamö man regarding the desirability of "law and police" to bring a halt to Yanomamö violence. Following Albert and Ramos (1989) and the Association of Brazilian Anthropologists' (Carneiro da Cunha 1989), she remarks that this also is used by military authorities to justify control of the Yanomamö. Perhaps this is so, but I have my doubts for two reasons. First, it is unclear from either Albert and Ramos or Carneiro da Cunha whether the official involved had read either Chagnon's report or news releases of the report. And second, as I mentioned in my first contribution, multiple accounts of Yanomamö warfare predate Chagnon's research, and use of ethnographic descriptions by powerful bureaucracies are post hoc rationalizations to justify what they were going to do anyway. If Chagnon had never done research among the Yanomamö, Chief of Staff General Bayna Denis could have used ethnographic research by half a dozen other anthropologists to rationalize his position.[3] At the same time, we might ask whether it is true that some Yanomamö believe that police are useful. Salamone's contribution to his own edited volume on the Chagnon-Salesian[4] controversy quotes a Yanomamö man saying this to him: " 'Why do I want the Military to live here? It is because people fight. It is because they take women by force. That is why I want them to come. I said: "Send the military here so that we'll not fight among each other" ' " (Salamone 1997:79).

I have no idea of how widespread this desire is among the Yanomamö. I am sure, however, that most Yanomamö are completely unaware of the numerous downsides of military or police rule. At the same time, it is clear that many of the Yanomamö interviewed by Salamone are appreciative of the role that missionaries play in reducing levels of violence (Salamone 1997:79,81,85). Obviously, unlike police, missionaries do not rely on the use of force to accomplish these ends. Given that Salamone's quote of a Yanomamö voice closely resembles Chagnon, is Salamone also to be accused of facilitating control of Yanomamö land by colonial interests?

NOTES

1. I think it useful to point out that my research was supported by National Institute of Mental Health (NIMH) and National Science Foundation (NSF) grants acquired by Chagnon. Through these grants Chagnon purchased a large quantity of medical supplies and distributed them to expedition members. He explained to us that 95 percent or more of the medicine we expended would be expended on the Yanomamö and what we did not use at the end of our research should be donated to local Venezuelan health authorities or missionaries. When I inventoried the stock of medicines in the *enfermero*'s house, I was shocked to discover that much of what he had was too old to safely use and that he had an inadequate spectrum of antibiotics and other medicines. I was able to remedy this situation by supplementing them with my own supplies, by requesting more from Chagnon, and by making purchases when I left the field to resupply.

2. Euripedes Alcantara, an editor at the Brazilian magazine *Veja*, has been unable to verify any published accounts that Brazilian officials have used Chagnon's writing to justify policy actions on the Yanomamö, according to information posted on Chagnon's Web site at http://www.anth.ucsb.edu/ discus/html/messages/62/63.html (click on "Recent News on Neel/Chagnon Allegations"). See also on the Hume Web site, http://members.aol.com/lithicat/darkness_in_el_dorado/documents/ 0204.htm.

3. Magdalena Hurtado, in a letter to the *Anthropology Newsletter* (1990), correctly to my way of thinking, points out that Venezuelan and Brazilian indigenous policy and government inaction bear primary responsibility for allowing the spread of disease, theft of land, impoverishment, and mortal attacks on indigenous peoples. What bothers me most about this entire discussion of the possible use to which ethnographic facts can be put is that it turns our attention away from the real forces responsible for the unrelenting war on indigenous peoples.

4. This book deals with the controversy between Chagnon and the Salesians over mission policy toward the Yanomamö. Salamone is highly critical of Chagnon and quite supportive of the Salesians.

....

ON THE FIRST ROUND OF DISCUSSION

KIM HILL

I am happy to discover that all commentators made useful and valid observations in the first round of discussion. This is particularly important because some of us have taken very contradictory stances regarding the veracity of the Tierney book, and the tensions between scientifically oriented anthropologists and non-scientific or even antiscientific anthropologists long ago reached destructive levels within the discipline. The debate on the Tierney book has to some extent been symptomatic of these much larger tensions in anthropology, which have in fact led to the division of several anthropology departments along "science" and "non-science" lines in recent years. If anthropology is to survive as an integrated discipline with multiple approaches and multiple areas of interest, greater communication still must be fostered, and both camps must become more introspective concerning their own weaknesses. In this light, I note that two of the commentators focused entirely on alleged ethical misconduct by scientists (specifically biological and biomedical anthropologists) but appear to have drawn no lessons at all from the Tierney book concerning ethical issues that might apply to cultural anthropologists and various types of applied anthropologists. I find that double standard to be unfortunate. Only when each group turns the lens of introspection upon itself as well as others can there be a sincere exchange of ideas.

MISSIONARIES

In general I agree with most ethical issues raised by Peters. In particular I agree that missionaries should be judged individually and according to their current activities and not by some stereotypical notions that are derived from the activities of a half-century or more ago. I also believe that it is critical to recognize that many modern anthropologists involved in advocacy work are in fact missionaries themselves, with their own zeal for evangelization toward a set of values and behaviors that they think best for native groups. Very little differs between them and their missionary adversaries except the religion being preached.

However, I would also suggest to Peters that many anthropologists might be more favorably inclined toward religious organizations if members of those groups were more forthright in their own self-criticism. Many mission organizations are extremely closed, with an "us versus them" mentality toward all who are not members of their organization (including even other missionaries), and many have an explicit policy of prohibiting self-criticism to any outside audience. This, in conjunction with the fact that they set up outposts in remote areas where there are no external controls over their behavior, can lead to problems. I have seen and been informed by native peoples of enough missionary abuses in South

(see also pp. 317–41)

KEY ACCUSATIONS AND ISSUES

Should Chagnon have responded better to the media's misuse of his work? Chagnon cannot be held accountable for all imaginable misuses of his work, and there is little evidence that his work affected Brazilian policy. Martins is correct in saying that we should expect Chagnon to engage in highly visible and energetic attempts to counter the misuse of his work when it takes place. (see pages 178–79)

Looking at the broad picture and all that has happened, how would you assess the value of Darkness in El Dorado? There are relatively few parts of the book that are based on good evidence, and many of the facts that are correct are trivial. The main contribution of Tierney's book should be to focus attention on what can now be done to help the Yanomamö and other South American indigenous populations. (see pages 181, 184)

To what degree should Neel have assumed responsibility during his fieldwork for dealing with medical problems that were imperfectly dealt with by the national governments of Venezuela and Brazil? Neel did far more than the Venezuelan government or the missionaries to fight the measles epidemic, even though these two groups had official responsibility to help the Yanomamö. Instead of suing the American holders of Yanomamö blood samples for the return of the samples, the Yanomamö should sue the Brazilian and Venezuelan governments for their failure to provide adequate medical facilities and protection. (see pages 183, 188)

What should now be done to address Yanomami concerns regarding the Yanomami blood samples? Instead of insisting that the blood samples be destroyed, the Yanomamö should write the holders of the blood and request that research be done that could directly benefit the Yanomamö. (see pages 187–88)

QUESTIONS TO CONSIDER

Can Chagnon be held responsible for the misuse of his work by others in Brazil and Venezuela?

Was Neel morally obligated to compensate for the failures of the Venezuelan and Brazilian governments and missionaries to the degree that he should spend the majority of his time in the field vaccinating Yanomami?

America to cast a deep shadow of sadness upon my own view of human nature. I have seen missionaries lie and deceive in competition with one another and as a tactic to convert natives.

A common trend in the world has been for native groups to evict missionaries from their settlements between fifteen and fifty years after first contact with them. Indeed, one high official of a large missionary organization in a Latin American country admitted to me that his operating plan with a particular tribe was to make several key converts among the Indians before the missionaries were kicked out so that those Indians could then carry on the evangelization work after the missionaries were evicted. Some missionaries want to be viewed as saints and send back glowing reports of their sacrifices and successes to help in fund-raising. They are less candid about admitting that they often fail, that many "conversions" do not constitute any serious incorporation of Christian ideals, and that their work is in fact a "job" that includes economic rewards and that they often lack any other practical skills that would make them marketable back home. In short, both their sacrifices and successes are often overstated. I agree with Peters that there should be an anthropology of anthropology, but I would also suggest to my missionary friends that there should be a missionary study of missionary work. Why do so many native populations reject missionary ideas and missionary presence in their communities and what factors led to missionary success or failure?

THE IMPACT OF CHAGNON'S WRITINGS

I am also highly sympathetic to the frustration expressed by Martins. She is clearly a deeply dedicated individual who has expended a great deal of effort trying to combat some of the forces causing Yanomamö oppression and suffering. She must feel a sense of professional betrayal to discover that a fellow anthropologist, through his ethnographic writing, seems to be supporting the very foes that she battles daily.

But my reaction to her analysis is essentially the same as that expressed by Hames in the first round of discussion (and the same position that was taken by Skip Rappaport when he was president of the AAA). Chagnon cannot be held accountable for all imaginable misuses of his work, and there is actually little evidence that his work affected Brazilian policy. Brazilian politicians, if they read anything before taking action, read only the essays produced by Brazilian journalists. Most of us learn the hard way that we have no control over what journalists say about our work or how they use it to forward their own agendas. Chagnon's portrayal of the Yanomamö as a society in which small-scale raiding (and the potential for being attacked) is an important part of life is congruent with the view that emerges in many other Yanomamö ethnographic works. But Brazilian opinions about Yanamamö warfare are probably more influenced by actual events in which local Brazilian were witnesses than by anything published in stuffy academic journals. There were numerous Yanomamö attacks on Brazilian settlers during the twentieth century (Peters documents a few of these in his recent book), and almost certainly the Brazilian population's image of the Yanomamö was more influenced by these actual instances of violence than by the paper account of an American who never even worked in Brazil. Thus, I doubt that Chagnon's accounts played much of a role in the attitudes of Brazilian politicians, or the local population.

But all this said, I must also agree with Martins that we should expect Chagnon to engage in highly visible and energetic attempts to counter the misuse of his work if he were to discover that it was taking place. The press always has an advantage in these situation because they alone monopolize access to a large audience. But despite these odds, we should do what we can to counter their abuses. For example, recently John Leo used some of my criticism of the Tierney book in a nationally syndicated editorial column in a way that seemed to imply that I thought cultural anthropology was a useless enterprise. Although I myself could not possibly reach all the readers that were exposed to Leo's editorial, I did write a strong letter of protest to the faculty in my department dissociating myself from Leo's views. Ideas in that letter were later extracted by Louise Lamphere, president of the AAA, for use in her *Albuquerque Journal* editorial rebuttal of Leo. Sometimes we can do little to counter the journalistic misuse of our work, but I agree with Martins that we must at least make a concerted effort, particularly if our study population is being harmed through the misuse of our own words.

ESTABLISHING CREDIBILITY

I also agree with almost all that Hames wrote in the first-round discussion. Most specifically I agree with his position that credibility is absolutely essential to be successful in any human rights battle. It has been disturbing to see some anthropologists get carried away in the spirit of well-meaning action and exaggerate or distort the truth about indigenous rights issues in hopes of stimulating more public support for their cause. I believe that such tactics are always doomed to backfire. But my gut feeling is that deception is a tactic that usually produces only short-term gains in any human rights battle. When the deception is discovered, the strength of a morally correct position is heavily undermined. I don't believe that Tierney shares this philosophy.

In keeping with this position about the importance of truth in the battle for indigenous human rights, I disagree with much of what Turner says about the content of the Tierney book. There has not yet been sufficient time to check the accuracy of many charges in the Tierney book (and I certainly don't have time in the four days I have been given to draft this response to check the new information presented by Turner from Neel's APS archive). But if the book contains one hundred allegations and the most important ten are investigated carefully and found to be false, what is the logical reaction of most careful readers? They will conclude that the author has little credibility and discount the remaining allegations as unlikely to be true.

One of the strongest predictors of the validity of information published by an author is the validity of prior information presented by that author. In this sense Tierney has a bad track record, both from the facts that have already been checked in *Darkness in El Dorado* and from some of the highly dubious accounts presented in his previous book on human sacrifice in western South America (indeed I think even most ardent Tierney supporters will dissociate themselves from most of that book after they read it). Turner seems puzzled that Tierney critics have dismissed much of the *El Dorado* book after discovering that its treatment of the measles epidemic is highly distorted and erroneous. He thinks that the misrepresentations and distortions of the book are just small peccadilloes. Indeed he wants to label people like Hames and me as "Neel and Chagnon defenders" rather than "Tierney critics" who insist on the importance of truth.

Turner further observes that some people seem to feel that "if the critical allegations against Neel and Chagnon can be refuted on scientific grounds, then the ethical questions raised . . . about the effects of their actions on the Yanomami can be made to go away." In fact, those of us who have criticized Tierney have refuted his allegations on factual and scientific grounds, and those allegations refuted are specifically about the actions of the two accused and their effects. There are no ethical issues to "dismiss" when the actions presented never took place and the effects on the Yanomamö were never experienced as described. Thus, the facts of the book are indeed central to some ethical discussions, and factual findings can indeed "obviate ethical issues" by rendering the discussions moot. But the discussion of the facts reported by Tierney have been placed outside this forum of debate (we are to consider only ethical issues raised by the book, not evaluate each factual claim in the book). I can only suggest that interested readers consult the numerous Web sites that contain factual assessments of specific Tierney claims. In the most comprehensive Web site about the book (see Hume n.d.) the interested reader will quickly discover that Tierney not only grossly misrepresents the events of the measles epidemic and the motives of the vaccination team, but according to the National Academy of Sciences, he also misrepresents work by the AEC and Neel's connection to that organization. According to Mark Ritchie, he misrepresents events in Ritchie's book (which are heavily cited). According to the Robarchecks, he misrepresents their work on Waorani warfare. According to several prominent ethnographic filmmakers, he misrepresents the authenticity of Asch's Yanomamö films. According to Marcel Roche's wife, he interviewed her husband when Roche was in a relatively advanced stage of Alzheimer's disease and misrepresents him in the reported interview. Finally according to Napoleon Chagnon, "Nearly every damn sentence in the book is a lie."

In short, Tierney has little credibility with many readers at this point, and the fact checking of his book has just begun (the current fact-checking link on the University of California at Santa Barbara's Web site (Chagnon et al. n.d.) is a devastating exposure of Tierney distortions and misrepresentations). I suspect that a year from now his credibility will be even less impressive. But what is more disturbing is not that Tierney made errors but that he appears to have done so intentionally to advocate certain positions. He selectively uses small amounts of information from some sources but ignores other information in the same sources that contradict his favored positions (the most blatant misuse is that he includes selective information about warfare in the Heleno Valero and Mark Ritchie books while ignoring massive evidence in those books that would support the Chagnon views of warfare that Tierney hopes to discredit). And he consciously uses sleazy journalistic devices to imply connections that are nonexistent to support his theses and undermine his villains. This writing style begins on the first few pages of the book when he tries to connect Francisco Salzano's (who is not identified by name) blood collection activities of the 1960s to the Brazilian military dictatorship of that time and implies that Salzano was in collusion with that dictatorship (he was in fact an outspoken opponent of the military regime).

He attempts to mislead the reader from the outset into believing that genetic research is somehow connected to fascist political ideologies, without mentioning that similar blood collection took place in every region of the earth during that period and under every type of political regime, including many democracies and Marxist governments. Tierney's sleazy journalism continues right up to the last chapter, when he attempts to connect James Neel to organizations that he never worked with, to projects that he never participated in and never knew about, and in some cases to studies that never existed.[1] Yes, credibility is an important issue here and Tierney has very little at this point.

I must simply conclude that Turner and I strongly disagree on the overall veracity of the book. He suggests that factual errors are "relatively few (but important)" and that there are many parts of the book for which there is abundant evidence in the public record, consisting of testimony of other anthropologists, missionaries, and Yanomami. My reading of the book is that there are considerably fewer parts of the book for which there is anything constituting good evidence and that many of the correct facts are trivial in nature (such as whether a particular person was in a particular place at a particular time).

A large proportion of the 1,599 footnotes provide no independent corroboration of the assertions they are cited to support. They appear instead to be decorations designed to lend authority to Tierney's assertions. The anthropological testimony referred to by Turner consists mainly of ad hominem attacks through the reporting of unverifiable events supposedly witnessed by two ex-Chagnon students who both parted company with him under hostile circumstances and who both have skeletons hidden in their own closets. However, I don't think further generalizations on my part concerning the factual inaccuracy of the book are useful either. If Turner were specific about which important allegations he considers well supported, I could respond directly as to whether I agree with his assessment of the evidence and whether the allegations are of a serious ethical or professional nature or are simply charges of bad judgment and unadmirable behavior.

THE CONTRADICTIONS OF TURNER'S POSITION

I'm also puzzled that Turner's piece seems curiously self-contradictory. He laments the focus on the measles epidemic rather than other important charges (90 percent of the controversy on 10 percent of the book), but then he returns to the measles epidemic quickly as his main focus (Albert correctly notes that this is because the allegations concerning the measles epidemic are far more serious than anything else in the book). He also appears to apologize for earlier writings suggesting that Neel may have been unfairly attacked, but then he simply mounts a new attack on Neel, which I suspect will also turn out to be misguided.

Turner appears prepared to concede that Neel did not start the measles epidemic either on purpose or inadvertently. However, the investigation into the accuracy of the measles charge (by contacting Dr. Francis Black, Dr. Samuel L. Katz and the Centers for Disease Control [CDC] in Atlanta) was initiated by Tierney critics ("Neel defenders") and seems secondarily verified by Turner only after he realized that this charge would not hold (indeed Katz strongly denounced Turner's initial memo to the AAA president). Turner also sent a memo to AAA officials suggesting that there was strong evidence that Neel's vaccination campaign was essentially an experiment rather than a preventive measure. In that memo he calls for an investigation but also elaborates in several pages his arguments about why he was convinced it was mainly an experiment. It is nice to see that he appears to have now backed off that charge as well. But I do not accept Turner's current summary of the events surrounding the vaccination program either, since I have heard a significantly different account of events from others who have complete access to all of James Neel's notes (especially his son). I will leave that debate to Turner and those who disagree with him, but I do agree with Turner that the question of Neel's priorities during the measles epidemic is an important ethical issue to be discussed.

Did Neel adequately prioritize Yanomamö health needs during his field expedition of 1968? Should we expect people who clearly state that they have come to indigenous populations to do a job (whether it is to collect data or lay down a fence line) to provide medical services that should be the responsibility of national and local government agencies? When carefully contemplated, this question opens a very large can of worms that ultimately contains not worms but a big mirror that must be held up to all field anthropologists (including Turner). In Turner's treatment of this issue there seems to be a blatant double standard developed. Cultural anthropologists can go to the field for years and provide no medical services for their study populations (because they are often unqualified and have no medical skills—a conscious choice that they make before embarking for the field), whereas biomedical researchers are obligated to donate their time and resources to provide help at whatever cost to them personally.

Turner implies that Neel should have abandoned his research (and his ethical commitment to the U.S. taxpayer that contracted with him to do that research and paid him for it) and made vaccination of Yanomamö communities his top priority. Perhaps this is partially true in the case of extreme medical emergencies. My colleagues and I completely abandoned our research for several weeks in Manu Park in 1986 when a respiratory epidemic hit the isolated Yaminahua and Matsiguenga populations with whom we were working. We also flew in medical supplies at our own expense and against the wishes of local cultural anthropologists who threatened to revoke our research permit if we did so (because the supplies came from SIL missionaries and because they "interfered with the natural population regulation mechanisms of the tribal peoples"—i.e., high death rates). In the case of the Yanomamö measles epidemic, it is ironic that Turner seems so quickly prepared to attack the one person in the world who did the most to save Yanomamö lives. I repeat, James Neel's actions saved more Yanomamö lives during this epidemic than any other person on the planet, yet he is roundly criticized for not doing more than he did.

James Neel was a researcher, and his job in 1968 was to collect information on human genetic diversity. The Venezuelan government and the missionaries who lived in the area full-time had much more responsibility than Neel to avert the measles crisis. When physicians from the CDC are called in to a country to research an outbreak of disease, they do their jobs as researchers, not clinical practitioners. They do not and cannot get involved in treating every sick person they encounter in the field; that is the job of local and national government agencies. Most scientific researchers who work in a community doing research either on the human population or on any other nearby phenomenon (weather, geology, ecology, air pollution, cosmic radiation, etc.) would never accept the proposition that it is their responsibility to provide medical care to a population that happens to become ill in proximity to their research. Likewise, very few people believe that they are morally obligated to donate their time and resources to help some other human group just because they receive information about that group's suffering (many will however volunteer help as Neel did). But Turner feels comfortable suggesting that Neel was under just such an obligation, although medical care of the Yanomamö was never his job.

Why exactly Neel should be obligated to donate his valuable time for free to provide medical care to the Yanomamö but anthropologists who hear today that the Yanomamö are suffering from serious health problems (tuberculosis, malaria, etc.) are not "obligated" to give up part of their incomes to help the Yanomamö (since they cannot provide services like Neel did) is unclear to me. Each anthropology student who bought a music CD this month despite knowing about Yanomamö suffering has essentially made the same decision that Neel is accused of here—namely, prioritizing their own needs over those of the Yanomamö. I think that such prioritization is human, and to highlight such difficult human decisions uniquely in Jim Neel's case smacks of hypocrisy.

ALBERT AND INFORMED CONSENT

In my mind the most engaging commentary in the first round was that of Albert, because he opens a dialogue that can be very productive if carried out in a spirit of sincere concern for native peoples. I am in particularly strong agreement that the major contribution of the Tierney book should be to focus attention on what can be done *now* to help the Yanomamö and other South American indigenous populations. I must state from the outset that I disagree with some of what Albert says, but I think that disagreement can illuminate many important ethical issues in anthropology. I do find it a bit troubling that Albert, like Turner, seems primarily concerned with regulation of biomedical research but appears to have thought little about native protections and regulation of mainstream cultural anthropological research (although his last paragraph suggests that anthropologists should subject their work to the logic of biomedical research). This double standard illuminates a fundamental weakness of cultural anthropological training, which leads many practitioners to conclude that only the "other" in their profession (i.e., the people doing scientific research) should be regulated. This mind-set, that cultural anthropological research is generally acceptable but biomedical research is suspect and should be restricted, is clearly at odds with the patterns expressed by native populations who are better educated than the Yanomamö and thus more capable of providing truly "informed" consent. In the United States, one of the few kinds of academic investigation that is regularly encouraged and invited by Native American populations is biomedical research. Cultural research, in contrast, is often strictly prohibited. The concern by some anthropologists to mainly regulate biomedical research seems to derive from an assumption that only scientists exploit native peoples and that only scientific research can be dangerous to native populations. I disagree with both suggestions.

Informed consent, in theory, should include not only information about the potential dangers of the research methodology but also some information concerning the larger goals of the research. While biomedical researchers sometimes fail to carry out this step adequately because of gaps in the educational background of the study population, this oversight is in my experience much more common still in cultural anthropology. Indeed, while biomedical researchers nowadays often have stacks of signed consent forms in their files and provide a basic explanation of what their research goals are, I have never seen such forms for any cultural anthropology project, and the explanations of the research goals are often totally lacking. Do cultural anthropologists fully inform subjects, for example, that their research into oppression is primarily intended to provide ammunition for political battles that may lead to a political system that the native population finds distasteful? Do they explain that research into male and female activities or political power may be used to advocate the imposition of sex roles in society that native peoples find incongruent with their own cultural values? Do cultural anthropologists really explain the deeper theoretical goals of their research the way they insist biomedical researchers must? Did

Claude Lévi-Strauss fully explain to the Brazilian Indians that he studied how he intended to use data on them to advocate a theory of duality about their social organization, and did his study subjects give informed consent for him to put forward such a view? Yes, standards of informed consent need to be developed in anthropology, but they should be consistent across subfields and regardless of whether the research is scientific or nonscientific in goals and methodology.

Regarding Albert's treatment of biomedical ethics, I should start by pointing out that there is a long tradition of protective regulation in biomedical research with humans and that the Nuremberg Code cited by Albert represents only a minuscule part of much more developed and broader protections for human research subjects. Interested readers might consult such documents as the Belmont Report (National Commission for the Protection of Human Subjects of Biomedical and Behavioral Research 1979) of the 1970s, which has been the basis for subsequent biomedical and behavioral research protections developed in the United States (and has heavily influenced IRB regulations), or the Australian national guidelines for research on aboriginal populations (Australia National Health and Medical Research Council 1991) and the Canadian Tri-Council Working Group on Ethics (Canada Tri-Council Working Group on Ethics 1996), which both specifically concern protections that should be implemented when carrying out biomedical research with native groups. A number of other special findings regulating public health surveillance procedures are also relevant (but I don't have time to look them up by the deadline for this second round response). These documents and the numerous discussions generated from them during recent years are far more comprehensive than the Nuremberg guidelines that were highly restricted to dealing with human experimentation.

The Nuremberg Code does not, to my knowledge, attempt to regulate observational research and is not relevant to epidemiological surveillance required in public health emergencies. But, in general, basic moral principles guide all protective measures. First, politically vulnerable groups should not be subjected to dangerous research against their will or through the exploitation of their lack of understanding about the potential dangers of any research. Second, individual and community consent is required for most research among native populations, unless that consent is withheld as a tactic to perpetuate oppression (for example, male leaders refusing to allow research on spousal abuse). And third, when public health is at stake, the need for informed consent and the rights of individuals to refuse to cooperate with research are balanced against the interests of a larger world community.

There is a fundamental difference between experimentation, observational research, and epidemiological surveillance in health research. Experiments require interventions on study populations and can carry some risk to the individual participant. Such research should be thoroughly regulated, with fully informed consent as the cornerstone of any protection policy. I agree with Albert that Roche's research constituted an experiment and should have required completely informed consent (however, he followed standard procedure at the time, and he did not employ a protocol that endangered his study subjects).

Observational research by its very nature does not put study subjects in danger because it includes no intervention (however, some methods like blood sampling may include a slight potential for harm). Observational biomedical research includes activities such as taking blood pressure, checking body temperature, recording skin lesions, collecting blood and fecal samples, and so on. It is important to realize that all advanced health treatment centers immediately begin observational research on any patient admitted to their facility, and the request for treatment at such a facility automatically implies informed consent.

Observational research that is not intended to provide information for clinical treatment is indeed regulated in most cases but can be conceptualized as a business agreement between those who sell information (the study subjects) and those who buy it (the researchers). As such, study populations should be allowed to decide if they want to sell their product (allow the research) and at what price. They must clearly be informed about the dangers of collaboration, but it is not clear that we should expect them to fully understand how their product (data about them) will be used. A Yanomamö artisan does not need to know what will be done with a basket she sells to decide whether or not to sell it. There are, of course, some commonsense limits here—buying a basket to use in a museum display that mocks the Yanomamö people would likely change the seller's mind about whether or not to offer the product. Thus, something about how scientific data are used can be expected to influence native decisions about whether or not to participate in research, and this is the logic for providing basic information about the purpose of the study. Finally, however, when data collection constitutes epidemiological surveillance critical to the public health of a wider community, there is no requirement of informed consent in most countries. For example, in the United States no informed consent is required to collect data on HIV prevalence among patients who are treated in U.S. hospitals. There is a critical public interest at stake in knowing what percentage of our population is infected, and informed consent would invalidate the accuracy of that estimate (if infected groups were more likely to refuse permission). In such cases where research represents a vital public interest, public health officials often supersede the authority of local police and military. I bring this up because Albert seems unaware, for example, that under special circumstances the Yanomamö could be required to provide blood samples (perhaps in a hypothetical scenario where they are the seed population of an extremely infectious type of drug-resistant tuberculosis) whether they give consent or not, and that they would not be compensated for their participation in such research.

In between experimentation (which clearly requires informed consent) and critical public health surveillance (which does not require informed consent), there is a wide range of public health research that is more or less critical to the well-being of the world community. Indigenous populations should have a critical voice in research protocols brought to their communities and whether they wish to participate in any particular study. But they should also be better informed about the potential benefits of such research by people who understand them, and, frankly, many anthropological activists who have attempted to sway indigenous opinion on these matters are not qualified to assess potential benefits of such research.

Albert, for example, sees little value in Roche's study of goiter and insists that such research could not foreseeably benefit the Yanomamö. I disagree. Although the Yanomamö did not have a high prevalence of goiter at the time Roche conducted his iodine tracer studies, there were indications that this problem could become more serious for them in the future. Some populations in Venezuela have very high prevalence of goiter, and one of Roche's goals was to determine why the Yanomamö were generally unaffected by goiter in the 1960s. This research carries the obvious implication that such research could later help to explain why they might begin to develop this health problem. The same analogy could be drawn for the study of any "disease of modern society" (asthma, cardiovascular disease, anxiety and depression, etc.) that was carried out among the Yanomamö, who may not yet be afflicted by such a condition.

Likewise, Albert sees little practical value to the Yanomamö of research into human genetic variation and suggests that the Yanomamö should consider having their blood samples destroyed rather than allowing them to become integrated into the human genome project. I can't imagine more counterproductive advice. First, the samples already exist and thus the beneficiaries do not have to undergo any new procedure to reap future benefits. Although Albert reports that the Yanomamö have a special cultural aversion to allowing their blood to be possessed by strangers, I suspect that most well-informed Yanomamö would quickly make an exception, for example, if they arrived at a hospital with a massive infection and were told that the medical personnel must draw blood to measure their white blood cell count. Cultural aversions can quickly change when important benefits are at stake. (Another explicit example might be gynecological exams, which are probably culturally inappropriate in every society in the world but are often accepted because of their potential value.)

The study of human genetic variation has enormous implications for understanding human disease and pathology, and this is likely to be much more critical for small inbred populations than for members of large Western state societies (this is why groups like the Ashkenazi Jews and the inhabitants of Iceland have been very proactive in encouraging genetic research on their populations). Indeed, as we move into the era of the completely mapped human genome, one of the clearest patterns to emerge is that human genetic diversity is more related to disease adaptation than any other factor (see Ridley's recent book *Genome* for a delightfully clear exposition of this fact). The world community stands to benefit from the analyses of Yanomamö genes, but the Yanomamö themselves are likely to benefit even more. What possible benefit could they gain from the destruction of this material that is already archived? Instead of insisting that previously collected blood samples should be destroyed, I believe that the Yanomamö should write to the guardians of those samples, requesting that research be initiated with them that could benefit the Yanomamö community. Scientists should be co-opted as allies rather than alienated and attacked. I do, however, agree completely with Albert that any commercial use of Yanomamö genetic material must be approved by them beforehand and must include fair compensation and sharing of profits. Unauthorized commercial use of Yanomamö genes should immediately lead to a lawsuit.

LAWSUITS

This brings me to another disagreement with Albert. He suggests that the Yanomamö should consider filing lawsuits against a variety of institutions that were behind previous biomedical research. I believe that such action is not in the best interests of the Yanomamö. In these modern times of absurdly escalating tendencies to litigate over every imaginable issue, there should be commonsense moral guidelines that provide the criteria for justifiable lawsuits. Lawsuits should be filed to compensate for real damages or to punish reckless lack of concern for potential damage. I don't believe previous Yanomamö research meets either criterion. If not, such lawsuits are essentially frivolous and send the wrong moral message to the Yanomamö (that they should be willing to extract resources from anybody they can if they can get away with it, regardless of the ethics of doing so). Filing frivolous lawsuits against researchers or research agencies will only lead scientists to be unwilling to return to the Yanomamö communities, something that would be disastrously counterproductive given their growing health problems. However, if Albert wants to advise the Yanomamö to file lawsuits, I suggest that they first sue those who have truly caused them harm, namely, the Brazilian and Venezuelan governments that failed to provide medical services or adequate protection from rampant infectious diseases introduced by colonists and that have allowed land invasion, environmental destruction, and human rights violations for years.

Finally, I disagree with the last sentence of Albert's essay about "the logic of a particular kind of biomedical research that reduces . . . indigenous peoples to 'human material.'" This returns us to the point made by Peters concerning the anthropological phobia against objective assessment of indigenous culture. I do not believe that anthropologists should award "preeminence" to the "native's point of view" on ethical, intellectual, or political issues. We are in a partnership with native peoples, and we should treat them with respect and as equals. Our views of the world are not superior, but neither are theirs. We both have much to learn from each other. They should not be indoctrinated to believe that they are special and that all outsiders must defer to their worldview—they often make mistakes. Only by working together and discussing what is best for their communities and what is best for all of humanity are we likely to come up with truly "ethical" guidelines for future research.

NOTE

1. A statement from Bruce Albert (National Academy of Sciences 2000).

....

ON THE INFLUENCE OF ANTHROPOLOGICAL WORK
AND OTHER ETHICAL CONSIDERATIONS

LÊDA MARTINS

THE IMPACT OF CHAGNON'S WORK IN BRAZIL

In the first round of papers, Ray Hames and I wrote about the same topic, the political uses of Napoleon Chagnon's ideas in Brazil. However, we stand on opposite sides on the issue. Hames's assertions are misleading in several ways. The first part of his paper deals with the warning letter that Manuela Carneiro da Cunha (1989) wrote on behalf of ABA (Brazilian Anthropological Association) to the American Anthropological Association and to the American Association for the Advancement of Science, *Science* magazine's publisher, in 1988. Hames's account of the controversy that emerged at that time is confusing and needs to be clarified.

ABA's letter was prompted by Chagnon's article published a few months before in *Science* on Yanomami warfare (Chagnon 1988). The article in *Science* was reproduced in American newspapers and then made headlines in the Brazilian media. In the letter, the Brazilian anthropologists call the attention of the scientific community in America, anthropologists in particular, to the negative consequences of Chagnon's work on the welfare of the Yanomami in Brazil. As Hames correctly points out, the main concern of ABA was that Chagnon's depiction of the Yanomami as fierce was being used by governmental officials and generals to divide the Yanomami territory into small pieces of land and to open what was left out to mining and logging. Hames cites a quotation from Patrick Tierney's book (2000:160n19) of this letter, where it mentions an article in *Time* magazine published in 1976 ("Beastly or Manly?" May 10, 1976). Hames then says that the letter is "extraordinarily weak evidence" of the connection between Chagnon's ideas and the decision of FUNAI (the Brazilian Indian Service) to divide and reduce the Yanomami territory. And in response to Tierney's allegation, he says that "the *Time* magazine piece . . . does report on Chagnon's *Science* article, but from the information above there is no evidence that the unnamed FUNAI official was swayed by Chagnon's account."

The *Time* article is from 1976, and Chagnon's article in *Science* came out in 1988. That is why the former does not mention the latter. In *Time* Chagnon compares the Yanomami to "many primates in breeding patterns, competition for females and recognition of relatives." The article states that "like baboon troops, Yanomamö villages tend to split into two after they reach a certain size." In *Science*, Chagnon expands on his theory of the central place of violence in Yanomami society. Echoing Carneiro da Cunha, Tierney argues that the repeated portrayal of the Yanomami as fierce and animal-like posed a threat to the well-being of the tribe.

KEY ACCUSATIONS AND ISSUES
(see also pp. 317–41)

Should Chagnon have responded better to the media's misuse of his work? Those who challenge the impact of Chagnon's writings on the Brazilian Yanomami need to be much better informed about the Brazilian context and especially about the situation in the state of Roraima where most Brazilian Yanomami live. Although Chagnon did make changes in later editions of his book, he could have supported the Yanomami more effectively by protesting in Brazilian newspapers over the misuse of his work. (see pages 190–92)

Was Chagnon unfairly restricted from continuing his long-term fieldwork among the Yanomami? The opposition by a range of people to Chagnon conducting fieldwork among the Yanomami in Brazil in 1995 can be attributed to the association of Chagnon's work with those who oppose Indian rights as well as to accounts of his fieldwork in Venezuela. (see page 193)

QUESTIONS TO CONSIDER

What might Chagnon do to help the Yanomami that he has not already done? Will he remain a scientist if he takes such actions?

Is it true, as Martins argues, that the real issue is not about opposition to science in favor of a sociocultural agenda but about whether Chagnon violated ethical principles that apply to fieldwork?

I find it puzzling that Hames, who did not conduct research in Brazil and seems to have very limited knowledge of politics in the country as a whole and in Roraima in particular, can dismiss up front the claim of the impact of Chagnon's work on the lives of Yanomami in Brazil. Hames is not merely rejecting Tierney's argument; he is negating the analysis of anthropologists with long and extensive experience in the politics of indigenous rights in Brazil, such as Manuela Carneiro da Cunha, Bruce Albert, and Alcida Rita Ramos, and the appeal of the entire association of Brazilian anthropologists. Albert wrote his own contribution to reinforce the ABA letter. Hames did in his paper what the AAA did in 1989, that is, reject the claim from a colleague in Brazil without looking at the issue carefully and with no valid reason to do so.

Hames says that other Yanomami specialists and earlier explorers of the Amazon have described the aggressive aspect of the Yanomami and that is impossible to know who has influenced Brazilians to say the Yanomami are violent and do not deserve special rights. The answer to this argument has two parts. First, I do not claim that there is no violence among the Yanomami. This would be absurd. What many specialists dispute, though, is the emphasis that Chagnon gives to warfare and conflict within that society. Even more serious is that other anthropologists such as Bruce Albert and Jacques Lizot have refuted, with substantial evidence and analysis, Chagnon's data on Yanomami warfare, and Brian Ferguson has suggested that Chagnon provoked some of the conflicts that he later describes as evidence of his findings (see Albert 1989, 1990; Ferguson 1995; Lizot 1989). So it seems that Chagnon not only has overemphasized violence but also does not have reliable data to back up his ideas.

Second, the fact is that none of those other references to violence has made headlines in Brazilian newspapers. As I mentioned in my first contribution to this Roundtable, soon after the media in Brazil had reproduced parts of Chagnon's article in *Science*, the military chief of staff, General Bayna Denis, declared that the Yanomami were too violent and should be separated, the infamous call for reduction of their territory (see Albert and Ramos 1989). In 1994 Chagnon's ideas appeared in two articles (Cristaldo 1994a, 1994b) published in one of the top four Brazilian newspapers. Those articles had concrete effects on the life of the Yanomami, as I described in my first contribution. Why is Chagnon's reference to aggression and warfare more appealing to the media than any other references cited by Hames? It might be because of the sensationalistic way he has dealt with the matter.

I join Hames in his skepticism that military officials and bureaucrats would read scientific texts, especially if they are published in foreign countries and languages. But Hames forgets that military and bureaucrats do read the Brazilian newspapers that have reported on Chagnon's arguments. It was precisely the serious repercussions from media news that prompted ABA and Albert and Ramos to write to American journals warning of the consequences of Chagnon's work in Brazil. Hames also reasons that colonial governments in the past and their successors in the present have broadly carried out the practice of seizing any aspect of native societies—highlighting and using the differences between those societies and the dominant one—to rationalize oppression and exploitation. His idea is that anthropologists are bound to aid this colonialist practice because the result of their research is the production of "a large list of potential cultural differentiators that contrast indigenous peoples with their potential conquerors." So Hames suggests that to the ones "who truly believe that knowledge of native peoples will be used against them" there are two possible solutions: they either lie about or hide the true "nasty" aspects of the societies they study to protect them.

With that discussion, Hames misconceived and misrepresented the problematic aspects of Chagnon's work. The problem is not that Chagnon wrote the "truth" instead of lying or deceiving or that governmental officials in Brazil would or would not have disregarded indigenous rights in the same way with or without Chagnon. The problem is that Chagnon insisted on emphasizing violence as the driving feature of Yanomami society even after being warned of the negative shadow his work cast on the already difficult situation of the Yanomami; that his ideas were openly and broadly used against the Yanomami's rights, and he did not oppose that; and finally that he joined the attacks, usually made by

mining supporters, on Yanomami leaders and their supporters, further compromising the survival of the Yanomami people. These are the ethical breaches
of Chagnon.

My claim that Chagnon did not oppose the use of his ideas in Brazil is based
on the same grounds proposed by Hames, that is, that foreign academic publications are not usually read by Brazilian military and bureaucrats. All the references that Hames gives of Chagnon's reaction to the political use of his words
are from his book *Yanomamö*, famous in America, but not read in Brazil. At the
very least, Chagnon could have written to the Brazilian newspapers that reported
on his ideas to protest or extricate his work from its political uses. But he chose
not to. In a prominent interview in 1995 in *Veja*, the equivalent of *Time* magazine in Brazil, Chagnon said nothing about this matter (see Alcantara 1995). This
interview appeared after Janer Cristaldo had referred to Chagnon's work to discredit a massacre of the Yanomami village of Haximu. Chagnon took the opportunity in *Veja* to launch accusations against pro-Indian rights organizations, suggesting that their primary interest is profit and not defense of human rights.
Once more, he disregarded completely the consequences of his words and the
fact that environmental and human rights organizations are considered by the
military and right-wing politicians as Brazil's number one enemy and as a threat
to the country's sovereignty. The military argue that those entities are part of an
international plot to take the Amazon from Brazil. Behind this nationalist discourse are, indeed, powerful economic interests that want to exploit protected
land such as the indigenous territories and that support the notion that NGOs
are barriers in the path of such economic projects.

In *Veja*, Chagnon states that it is because of power and profit that anthropologists and advocates oppose his work, that is, because Chagnon exposes the
"real Indians" while "survival groups" make a living out of an "imaginary
Indian, an idealization" (Alcantara 1995). Chagnon also makes this accusation
in his account of the Haximu massacre in the *Times Literary Supplement*
(Chagnon 1993b) but gives no evidence to support it in either piece. Hames follows the same argument in his paper. This is an offensive accusation. First, it is
not true. The opposition to Chagnon in Brazil is due to the direct implication of
his words to the welfare of the Yanomami. Second, I do not work for an NGO
and have no personal gain in exposing the impact of Chagnon's work in Brazil.
But I know personally several anthropologists and advocates who do belong to
NGOs and find it an offense to their dedication to the defense of Indian rights
to say their primary concern is power and money. Moreover, neither Chagnon
nor Hames gives any evidence to support these hidden motives. Third, what
Chagnon claims as the "true" notion of Indians is an essentializing concept, a
mere Rousseauian notion with inverted content. When asked in *Veja* to define
the "real Indians," Chagnon said, "The real Indians get dirty, smell bad, use
drugs, belch after they eat, covet and sometimes steal each other's women, fornicate and make war." Is this the great science that some academics are rushing to defend?

SCIENCE VERSUS ANTISCIENCE

Having used much of the space allowed in this response to address Ray Hames's first statement in this Roundtable, I now turn briefly to the issues that I found most provocative in the other participants' papers.

The controversy around Tierney's book has focused attention on the details of episodes that happened in the distant Amazon region of Brazil and Venezuela, and it led to speculation on the participation of the main actors, Indians and non-Indians, many of whom live and work there. The American scientific community has debated why and how vaccinations took place, anthropologists had research permission denied, movies were made, presents were distributed, sexual favors were gained, and so forth. The dispute has spun out from America to other parts of the world, and it has been presented as a war among anthropologists, or better, between sociobiologists (or evolutionary psychologists) and sociocultural anthropologists, science versus antiscience. But does this framework reflect what happened in the jungles of South America?

I cannot answer this question in relation to the Venezuelan context, but I can assure readers that the layout of the debate on Tierney's book does not reflect the events in Brazil. Take, for example, Chagnon's attempt to do research in Brazil in 1995. Chagnon encountered great opposition from Indian leaders, Brazilian anthropologists, Catholic missionaries, and local FUNAI employees, mainly because of the association of his work with the discourse against Indian rights but also in part because of the tales of Chagnon's research in Venezuela that people in Roraima heard from across the border. Despite all this opposition, the headquarters of FUNAI gave Chagnon permission to accompany a photographer and work as a consultant for him. However, he arrived in the airport in Boa Vista, the capital of Roraima to take the plane to Yanomami territory with material to take samples of blood, stools, and urine. Chagnon was watched closely in Yanomami land, and he was not allowed to collect the samples he wanted since he did not have permission to do so (this information was reported to me by the FUNAI officer who accompanied Chagnon inside Yanomami territory).

The opposition to Chagnon was not an opposition to science or to sociobiological research in favor of a sociocultural agenda. The people who took part directly in the event are not aware of such fine divisions within academia and therefore do not take sides. In Roraima Chagnon is known as an anthropologist, and anthropologists and other scientists are usually welcomed by Indians and their supporters. But Chagnon is not, for all the reasons I have extensively discussed here and in my earlier comments. I believe that the people who opposed Chagnon's research trip in 1995 would be very surprised to see their action perceived as a plot against scientific endeavors. Kim Hill finishes his article in the first round of this discussion by saying that there is "an ideological holy war." I participated in several events described in Tierney's book and heard about others from first-hand witnesses, but I did not take part in or hear of a war against

Science. If there is a war, it was created here in America, in academic settings, in publications, and through Internet exchange.

In fact, the ones who brought capital-S Science to the debate were not Tierney but the partisans of James Neel and Napoleon Chagnon, who have shaped the defense of those scientists in the form of a shield around Science against the allegedly anti-Science crusade of Patrick Tierney and his so-called allies. As Terence Turner said in his first paper, the implication of reducing the debate to exclusively scientific grounds is that if Tierney is mistaken on one scientific point, then we should discredit his entire work. One example of this strategy is the article by Magdalena Hurtado et al. in *Anthropology News* (Hurtado et al. 2001). The authors set themselves the task of showing "how Tierney's book promotes anti-science views" but never deliver on the promise. The article is in fact a list of past medical misconduct practiced among Amazonian indigenous people. The authors present the debate on the book as if all allegations by Tierney had been refuted by scientists of prominent institutions, and they do not address a single ethical problem raised by *Darkness in El Dorado*, even problems that had been known and discussed years before Tierney set foot in the Amazon, as Albert reminds us in his article.

I think this is an important aspect to take into account because the science versus antiscience approach has served to blur our view on important ethical issues raised by Tierney's book. The approach is in itself unethical and compromises the ability of anthropologists in general to deal with ethical issues like the violation of human rights and relations of inequality. Anthropologists need to be able to deal and respond adequately to the ethical issues raised by Tierney's book, and deviating from or denying those issues is not the solution.

EMPOWERING YANOMAMI
WITH NEW KNOWLEDGE

Besides the problem with the framework of the debate, Kim Hill raises another relevant point related to the access and use of knowledge. In the same paragraph that inspired me to write on the local context of the resistance to Chagnon, Hill tells of his own experience in Venezuela with what he calls "a massive campaign of propaganda by anti-Chagnon/anti-sociobiology forces." He says that during a visit to the upper Orinoco, he heard some Yanomami complaining that Chagnon created an animal-like image of them in his books and movies, although the Yanomami themselves had not read the books or seen the movies. According to Hill, the Yanomami mentioned the word "sociobiology," and described the way they understood it as the "portrayal of them as nothing more than animals." Hill's conclusion is that the Yanomami have been "coached" by Chagnon's enemies. Hill's story stirs important questions regarding knowledge and indigenous people. First, the term "coaching" is problematic, since it implies that the Yanomami do not have the capacity to think for themselves and that they do exactly what people tell them. Chagnon said at the 1994 AAA meeting that Davi Kopenawa does not write his own speeches (Turner, personal communication, March 21, 2001); it is the same principle. Hill seems to imply that the Yanomami had too much wrong information. But what is wrong for Hill (an interpretation of Chagnon's work) is right for many, and the Yanomami have the right to know about different points of view, particularly on issues that matter to them.

The problem as I see it is not that the Yanomami have too much information about Chagnon and sociobiology, right or wrong, but rather that they have too little. Had the Yanomami read and watched Chagnon's books and movies, and had they had the opportunity to debate with Chagnon and other scientists, this entire controversy would be quite different. But while they have not attained those means and the power to defend themselves from a negative image and controversial data vis-à-vis the interests of the nation-states that surround them, anthropologists and other scientists have to be extra careful with what they write, say, and film. This is what can be expected and required of researchers working with indigenous people, not lying or deceiving as suggested by Ray Hames.

Second, anthropologists, missionaries, physicians, nurses—in sum all who spend a certain amount of time with Indian people—become a major source of information for them. I use my own experience as an example. The Macuxi, with whom I work, have asked me about other researchers who have lived among them, and at least one leader asked if I knew what two anthropologists have said about their villages and their lives. I dutifully responded and gave my own opinion about the publication by those anthropologists, which was positive, but it could just as well have been negative. I expected the Macuxi people to share their individual knowledge with me, and they had a similar expectation of me. Men, women, and children asked all sort of questions about my life, my family, about cities, America, politics, newspapers, fashion, and so on, and I would consider it unethical on my part not to respond honestly to their inquiries since I expected them to do the same for me. I suppose and hope that Hill gave his view of Chagnon's research and of sociobiology to the Yanomami with whom he talked. It is important not to confuse ethics with paternalism.

....

RESPONSE TO MY COLLEAGUES' COMMENTS ON ETHICS IN ANTHROPOLOGY ARISING FROM TIERNEY'S *DARKNESS IN EL DORADO*

JOHN F. PETERS

This has been a fascinating read. The editor has done well in selecting individuals representing a spectrum of perspectives, positions, interests, and concerns. We have the rainbow, and I am aware that readers may choose particular colors

---

KEY ACCUSATIONS AND ISSUES
(see also pp. 317–41)

Did Chagnon benefit unfairly from the royalties earned from his books in relation to what he gave back in compensation to the Yanomami? A researcher's wealth far exceeds that of the Yanomami and should be shared with them at the time of research as well as after he or she has left the field. (see page 196)

Did Neel act ethically during the 1968 expedition in the way he balanced his research with the need to treat the measles epidemic? Placing the health and welfare of indigenous populations above our research interests may well mean revising our research plans in the field. (see page 197)

QUESTIONS TO CONSIDER

What would constitute just compensation to a group of informants that helped an anthropologist in his or her research?

To what degree should anthropologists alter their research plans in the field if they find their research runs counter to the health and welfare of the people they are studying? Who should make that decision and under what circumstances?

---

from the grand spread. We have new information, historical clarifications (Martins, Turner), and detailed exactness in addressing ethnic research (Hill) and writing (Hames). For some writers, attacks against Tierney are seen as being vehement (Albert); for others, his writings are considered ideological terrorism (Hill). Chagnon certainly does not come out clean (Martins and Albert). For other contributors, there is a fundamental desire to move to new horizons, even possibly a restructured science for anthropological research and writing.

I find the themes to be in two areas: health and research. All contributors seek cultural and human sensitivity. No one should gain at the expense of a vulnerable people. The Western researcher's quality of life and resources far exceed that of the Yanomami and therefore should be shared, not only during but after his or her time in the field. Book royalties are not adequate! I fully support this position. Such modeling could have significant and monumental impact upon our students as well as upon the Western world. This is a worthy route, to be set alongside the more democratic voices and demonstrations currently at world free trade conferences. Such considerations challenge perceptions of our "superiority" and right to unlimited resources at the expense of others in the world community. For Albert this includes adequate compensation for blood samples drawn from the Yanomami over three decades ago, now lodged in obscure rooms in Pennsylvania.

I am encouraged by the critique of science. The contributors recognize that poor science (and poor methodology) has, and is, being practiced. I believe it is more pervasive than we recognize. Our scientific goals (an article, a degree) do not justify our practice. A revision of guidelines will address the concern but not totally resolve the problem. Established scholars must exemplify these principles and insist these standards be met. (Here is a small related point on methodology. Hames's mention of Chagnon and infanticide does not prove its absence. There are other ways of recognizing infanticide. In 1958, after being in the field for six weeks I noticed a once pregnant woman was no longer pregnant and was not embracing an infant. Further inquiry led to details of infanticide. I never *saw* the act.) I'll add a further note. Science does have limitations in the anthropological task. However, it may well be the best we have at this time.

I am disturbed that no contributor identifies the Yanomami role in relation to change in the past, present, or future. This is particularly irritating in that those of us with European roots have a shameful history of attempting to "fix" things for indigenous peoples of this continent. No significant, genuine long-term change will take place until Yanomami identify and resolve problems among themselves, as well as with those powers they encounter. We cannot wait for a perfect world or for the day when NGOs have fully socialized the Yanomami to our goals. There are social issues that might be addressed within their communities now.

Contributors have done well to critique the discipline of anthropology as well as science. We recognize that the governments of Brazil and Venezuela have done less than their best. They have done some good, but it has admittedly not been adequate. Despite the bold efforts and victories of NGOs, which Albert identifies, there are areas that the NGOs have not, cannot, and will not address. These are issues on the micro level, where Yanomami at the grassroots level or committed individuals or groups who understand them and who live with them can assist. Institutions are often not good at this kind of thing.

I support Albert's and Martins's pleas that the AAA recognize, evaluate, and support the efforts of other anthropology societies, in this case the Brazilian Anthropological Association.

I find the golden thread in this dialogue to be that we follow the principle of doing good for the health and welfare of indigenous people, even above our research interests. In some instances this will mean sacrificing, and more often, revising our research plans. This is a high standard and a significant break with the past. With such a stance we recognize that we will not always be in agreement as to what is "good health and welfare" for the studied population in terms of both research and writing. There are gray areas, some grayer than others. Our understanding of the culture is often partial. There are both short- and long-term implications. There will be different opinions (and energy) between Ph.D. candidate and supervisor, between government agencies, and between members in the researched population. The impact will vary from time X and Y. Hill's paper carefully examines some of these complexities. He also challenges us to thoroughly think through the concept of ethics, void of bias.

Let us continue the discussion constructively.

．．．．．．．．．．．．．．．．．．．．．．．．．．．．

ANTHROPOLOGICAL RESPONSIBILITIES, SCIENTIFIC
ETHICS, AND THE IDEOLOGY OF "SCIENCE":
WHAT DO WE OWE THE YANOMAMI?

TERENCE TURNER

The first round of papers contributed to this Roundtable raise many important issues and do a good job of presenting different points of view. That my responses to them will be disproportionate in length does not reflect my estimation of their relative value. I thank John Peters for an equable reminder of the importance of the missionary contribution to the situation, indeed to the survival of the Yanomami and other Amazonian indigenous peoples. It is certainly the case with the Kayapó that the UFM/CEM (Unevangelized Field Mission/Calvary Evangelistic Mission) has made the difference between life and death for hundreds of people through the series of contact epidemics beginning with the measles epidemic of 1958–59. That the mission was a reliable, continuous presence, invariably dealt honestly with the Indians, respected them as individuals, and treated them with goodwill thus established as nothing else could have that a decent and humane accommodation with nonindigenous society was possible, which has also been vital to the successful adaptation of the Kayapó to coexistence with Brazilian society.

Hames's and Martins's papers form a complementary pair, speaking to opposite sides of the same question, and I have little to add on either side. One comment on Hames's discussion of the ethical ramifications of Chagnon's statements on Yanomami "fierceness": the main ethical issue involved, as I see it, is not dependent on an estimation of the effects of Chagnon's theories or pronouncements (or silences, for that matter, since these too have become an issue). Ethically, one is obliged to speak out when one possesses relevant knowledge that an act or statement is an abuse or a misuse of the truth (for example, a misuse of one's own research findings that damages one's research subjects) regardless of the effect one's speech may have. The ethical issue, in other words, involves speaking out against the misuse of one's work. This, as I read it, is the main point of the Brazilian Anthropological Association's critique of Chagnon as relayed to the AAA at the San Francisco meeting in November 2000.

The Brazilians recognized Chagnon's right and responsibility to publicly state his research findings but insisted that it was also his responsibility to denounce a misuse of those findings against the interests of the people with whom he had done research. These issues came to a head in the attack on the Yanomami reserve by politicians and media aligned with mining interests between 1988 and 1992. It is good that Chagnon has made some attempts to deal with the general problem in later editions of his book, as Hames records, but as Martins's

KEY ACCUSATIONS AND ISSUES
(see also pp. 317–41)

Given what we now know, are the accusations made against Chagnon and Neel mostly true or untrue? Tierney clearly made serious errors in his chapter on the measles epidemic, and he slips at times into unseemly personal abuse of Chagnon. But Tierney presents data that are supported by publicly available information from a host of other sources, and these data do not appear to be distorted. (see page 204)

Did Chagnon act unethically in using methods to collect genealogies that violated Yanomami taboos? By his own account, Chagnon used field methods that a large fraction of the Yanomami population would find offensive. (see page 206)

Did Chagnon falsify data, especially in his conclusions in the famous Science *article?* Tierney presents a great deal of credible evidence regarding Chagnon's falsification of data that no defender of Chagnon has thus far credibly refuted. (see page 206)

Did Chagnon act unethically when he sought to gain control, with two others, of a large land reserve in Venezuela in what became known as the FUNDAFACI affair? Chagnon was a willing collaborator in actions that he must have known were criminal violations of Venezuelan law and would have damaging consequences for the Yanomami. (see page 207)

QUESTIONS TO CONSIDER

Can Tierney's depiction of Chagnon's ethical violations can be trusted, given the errors in his account of Neel?

Based on the statements by Hames, Hill, and Turner, did Chagnon commit ethically inappropriate acts? If not, why not? If so, what were they?

---

detailed account makes clear, he did not speak out against the most dangerous abuses of his statements and interviews when and where it would have done the most good.

Albert's paper is the only one that focuses on how an analysis of the ethical abuses of biomedical research on the Yanomami in the past might be translated into a basis for actually doing something to help them in the present. His well-documented treatment of the ethical problems of biological sampling without informed consent and some of the less-than-optimal medical treatment accorded the Yanomami by the 1968 AEC expedition has important implications, which he acutely points out, for moral and legal claims for compensation and aid for health and educational assistance in the present.

SOCIOBIOLOGY IN THE WORK
OF CHAGNON AND NEEL

Hill's contribution raises in compelling fashion the issue of how critical analysis and discussion can be debased and rendered effectively impossible when partisans of opposing positions are led to distort reality to suit their passionately held ideological perspectives. The first victim under such circumstances is the truth, or as close an approximation as we can come to it. The second is the capacity for ironic self-awareness, as true believers unself-consciously transform themselves into caricatures of the faults they denounce in their opponents.

As Hill is surely aware, there are a number of scientists (biologists, psychologists, geneticists, and historians and sociologists of science as well as anthropologists) who are critical of sociobiology and its allied tendencies such as evolutionary psychology and meme theory. Not all of these critics are irrationalist fanatics inspired by religious hostility to science. There are reasonable grounds for criticizing sociobiological views that have been stated in numerous publications by respected authorities: Lewontin, Gould, and Ingold, to name a few. My point is not that these critics are right (although I do tend to agree with them) but that many of them make reasonable arguments that should be engaged, and if possible, refuted after taking due account of their strengths. Reducing all criticism to caricature as the expression of ideology, incompetence, or dishonesty, without taking the trouble to consider the arguments and evidence presented by critics on their merits, is a hallmark of the ideological true believer, not of a scientist open to critical debate and capable of revising his views.

The essence of the "evolutionary view of human behavior" offered by Chagnon, which follows in essential respects that of Neel as it applies to the Yanomami, is that the Yanomami exemplify an "earlier" stage in human evolution in which dominant males are able to attain leadership in small breeding isolates by virtue of superior genetic endowment and by virtue of their positions as headmen or leaders to acquire more female breeding partners. Neel believed that there must exist a genetic complex that he called the Index of Innate Ability (IIA), defined as "a quantitative trait certainly related to intelligence, based on the additive effects of alleles at many loci." A superior increment of IIA was the effective prerequisite for leadership, and thus headmanship, in such small, isolated groups. Neel's notion of leadership was relatively diffuse, combining intelligence with hunting ability and the capacity for effective violence when required for the defense of the group. As headmen are said to be universally polygamous, they are therefore in a position to reproduce their superior genes—their greater Index of Innate Ability—at a higher rate than other men. The result is a secular tendency to upgrade the average genetic quality—that is, the quantity of genetic "innate ability"—of the population.

Note that not only headmanship as a central social institution but the structure of society as a whole is, in this view, directly determined by genetics. Neel represents the social organization of the small deme (endogamous breeding population) as a hierarchy of males, with differing numbers of wives corresponding to their relative dominance, which in turn is determined by relative proportions of genetic "innate ability." The more numerous groupings of wives attached to the more dominant men give rise to sibling groups of differing size, which become "lineages" across generations. The differing size of the lineages, a determining factor in the political order of the community, is thus a result of the differing numbers of wives of the adult males, which in turn is a function of their relative dominance, with the headman or headmen having the most. Social structure is thus defined as a dependent variable of the unequal proportions of the right genetic stuff possessed by male competitors for leadership and reproductive advantage (i.e., women).

This conception of "primitive social structure," with headmanship as its central institution directly determined by genetics, is the basis of Neel's explicit claim for the selective advantage, and thus the eugenic effect, of Yanomami-style society. In his article "On Being Headman," he maintained that this form of society was, and is, the common form of social organization in hunting-and-foraging and simple horticultural societies and thus represents the natural social form of the human species. The same ideas and eugenic claims for Yanomami-type society are repeated, in less developed form, in chapter 17 of Neel's autobiography, *Physician to the Gene Pool*.

Neel recognized that there was no empirical evidence for the Index of Innate Ability, and considered his failure to find any measurable objective trait that would serve to indicate different levels of the IIA in individuals the greatest disappointment of his scientific career. In his research trips among Amazonian Indians, he pursued without success the possibility that differential head size or shape might be correlated with headmanship and greater reproductive success (Turner and Stevens 2001: COR 1966, 174, 175, 176) Chagnon, who adopted the general form of Neel's theory, came up with an apparent solution to Neel's dilemma.

Synthesizing his own interpretation of Yanomami society as organized around the violent competition of males for female reproductive partners with Neel's conception of genetically superior, reproductively successful headmen, he proposed that his ethnographic data showed that men who had killed male enemies, thus concretely demonstrating their dominance, had more wives and children than men who had not. Killers could be identified by the Yanomami title *unokai*, denoting one who had gone through a ritual incumbent on all who had killed. *Unokai* status might thus serve as the objective correlative of male dominance in association with greater reproductive success, and thus, presumably, of the possession of higher levels of genetic IIA: in effect, an ethnographic equivalent of what Neel had fruitlessly sought in head measurements.

The importance of "fierceness" in Chagnon's account of the Yanomami was directly connected with his thesis that Yanomami warfare was primarily motivated by male conflicts over women, which in turn was tied to the thesis that competition among males for possession of female breeding partners, and thus ultimately for greater reproductive success, was the central principle of Yanomami social organization. This in turn was central to his and Neel's contention that the Yanomami represented a survival of an earlier evolutionary stage of human social organization, when human society was still organized along the lines of subhuman primate societies organized around "Alpha males" with harems of brood females.

I have taken the trouble to spell out my understanding of the "evolutionary view of human behavior" (Hill's phrase) embodied in Neel's and Chagnon's accounts of Yanomami society to make clear why I think Chagnon's claims about Yanomami "fierceness" have been so important to him and his sociobiological and evolutionary-psychology followers, and why criticisms of the "fierceness" thesis on the basis of mere ethnographic accuracy or the relative discounting of the importance of peaceful, cooperative and female-associated modes of behavior have seemed to Chagnon and other sociobiologists to miss the point.

"Fierceness" and the high level of violent conflict with which it is putatively associated are for Chagnon and like-minded sociobiologists the primary indexes of the evolutionary priority of the Yanomami as an earlier, and supposedly therefore more violent, phase of the development of human society. Most of the critics of Chagnon's fixation on "fierceness" have had little idea of this integral connection of "fierceness" as a Yanomami trait and the deep structure of sociobiological-selectionist theory. The association is all the more important as the Yanomami continue to serve as virtually the sole data on a human society that seems to support the theory. The same considerations account for the tenacious allegiance of some sociobiologists to Chagnon's thesis in his 1988 *Science* article that killers, qua killers, have more sexual partners and offspring, despite its manifold methodological and empirical flaws. Thus, Hill, an otherwise astute critic, who would blow out of the water any interpretation by Tierney with half as many begged questions and unsupported claims, defends Chagnon's basic thesis in the article as "an important result," even after recognizing many of its problems.

There are a number of reasonable grounds for challenging the theoretical foundations of this Neel-Chagnon model of primitive society. To begin with, the Yanomami have been evolving along with everybody else since whatever point in the remote and more apelike past they may be claimed to represent and therefore cannot be considered as a specimens of what they, let alone the rest of humanity, were like then. For another thing, there is no genetic evidence for a connection between any "cluster of alleles" such as the Index of Innate Ability, or its counterpart in Chagnon's conception of the genetic endowment of successful killers, and such a complex social behavior as leadership or success in warfare, let alone a social status like headmanship or *unokai*hood. The attempt to account for human social structure as somehow determined by genetic differences in ability or capacity for leadership, which is fundamental to Neel's and Chagnon's accounts, is simply not defensible in scientific terms. That it is nevertheless defended as "science" by sociobiologists must therefore be understood as a manifestation of ideology. Its ideological character is underlined by its reduction of intrinsically social phenomena to expressions of intrinsically individual properties. It is, of course, for such reasons that most scientists (including anthropological social scientists) view sociobiology as a kind of ideology, not as "science."

Right or wrong, it has to be admitted that these are views held by many reasonable and scientifically well qualified people, including well-reputed human biologists and geneticists, who cannot all be explained away as fanatics engaged in, to use Hill's words, "a massive ideological hate campaign . . . based on their own ignorance of human biology. . . . The ferocity of [whose] hatred for the sociobiological threat to their worldview" turns them into a "terrorist band of self-righteous shock troops against 'incorrect' views of human nature." There should be room for critical disagreement over ideas (and, yes, ethical standards) without leaping directly to "flaming denunciations" like the above. Hill's white-hot rhetoric turns him into a clone of his caricature of Tierney.

PRIORITIES

Quite apart from the issue of the correctness of the Neel-Chagnon conception of the generic foundation of human society is the issue of its potential political implications. If one really believes that Yanomami culture and social organization is a throwback to the evolutionary past, one may easily be led to the view that it is incompatible with contemporary society. Apparent counterinstances, such as the appearance of educated Yanomami leaders able to play NGOs and national government bureaucracies against one another and cultivate allies among sectors of world public opinion, will be likely to seem unauthentic contradictions in terms, engaged only in deceiving their modern supporters by telling them what they want to hear while losing any valid connection with their communities and cultural roots. Looked at in this way, any support for indigenous Yanomami political movements or struggles might well seem pointless at best or counterproductive and hypocritical at worst. An apparently anti-indigenous policy such as that of the Brazilian miners and their representatives in the late 1980s who wanted to break up large indigenous reserves into mutually isolated communities might even seem more suited to the primordial realities of Yanomami culture as well as rendering politically inert and disunited local communities more accessible to research and less able to make self-destructive attempts to break from their immemorial roots.

Hill raises an important point when he says, "Anthropologists should be aware that while we have multiple intellectual goals we should share a single priority. Our goals are to study issues of academic interest, but the health and welfare of the study population must always take precedence over any academic goal."

That actually makes two priorities, not one. Much of the present controversy arises from the fact that while all anthropologists share both priorities in principle, in practice the priorities may conflict and force difficult and ethically fraught choices: not between one or the other but between different combinations of the two. I suggested in my previous contribution that it was a choice of this latter kind that Neel faced in the desperate circumstances of the 1968 epidemic. My reading of his papers and field journal has convinced me that he strove to fulfill both priorities but ended by cutting corners on both sides to meet his basic research goals (Turner and Stevens 2001). I think that the evidence shows that Chagnon, in his drive to fulfill his ambitious research goals with minimal concessions to gaining local rapport, has been led to engage in methods, actions, and statements that have negatively affected the welfare of the Yanomami. It sometimes appears that Hill may also agree with this statement, but he avoids committing himself.

Not so with Hill's opinions on Tierney's ethical problems. Hill makes some valid points against Tierney. Tierney clearly made serious errors in his chapter on the epidemic. He also slips at points into unseemly personal abuse (references to Chagnon's "beer belly") and in his treatment of Neel does seem "to assume the worst" about his motivations. To say, however, as Hill does, of Tierney's whole book that "indeed the entire case presented in the book is based on leaping to unwarranted conclusions based on insufficient scientific background, assuming the worst about the actors, and backing unwarranted speculations with distorted information" is rhetorical overkill. What "entire case"? The book presents many "cases," most of which do not involve "scientific" issues and call for no specialized scientific background. Many, moreover, are not based to any significant extent on unsupported "speculation" but on publicly available information, governmental documents and press accounts, missionary and medical records, and anthropological writings (including Chagnon's). Tierney's use of much of this information does not appear to be "distorted" in any obvious way. Let Hill document his blanket claims with some specific references.

It is important to insist, as Hill does, that medical and other scientific research on indigenous groups is not in and of itself unethical but on the contrary stands to benefit such groups, as well as the rest of humanity, in the short or long run. But to whom is he addressing this admonition? Certainly not to Tierney, who never argued to the contrary and explicitly stated at the San Francisco AAA meeting that he was not opposed to science or vaccinations. There are some other issues related to the 1968 expedition's and Chagnon's subsequent biological research that Hill very properly raises but that he does not fully clarify. He says the collection of blood samples was "critical to saving Yanomami lives." How? This is in the context of rebutting Tierney's charge that they were unethical because obtained without informed consent (an allegation also made by Albert in his paper and by the Brazilian medical group in their report (Lobo et al. 2000). Well, they were obtained without informed consent, and this was contrary to the ethical guidelines laid down by the Nuremberg Code and the Declaration of Helsinki, which were in effect at the time. I fully endorse Hill's contention that using Yanomami as research subjects to study problems like asthma is ethical as long as they are given to understand the purpose of the research. He is right to point out that Roche's experiments with goiter did not meet this criterion; but what he says about Roche applies equally to Neel and Chagnon's blood sampling. Why not say so?

Hill says "in the urgency and chaos of the field situation, . . . the vaccination of threatened villages took precedence over any research design." Neel's papers and field journal, however, show that the reverse is in fact true: the expedition continued to fulfill its original research design and itinerary with only small changes, which with one exception were made for reasons other than the medical needs of coping with the epidemic (see Turner and Stevens 2001). Hill is correct, on the other hand, that the expedition vaccinated many people who were never recorded by name and thus never included on any research protocol. The evidence shows that they had originally planned only to vaccinate half of the population of each village, but in the face of the epidemic they vaccinated everybody they could reach. It is true that Tierney tries to interpret Neel's use of the vaccinations for an experimental purpose (an allegation born out by Neel's own papers) as an indication of unethical motivations. It is also true that Neel's defenders, including in this connection Susan Lindee, have insisted that the vaccinations were undertaken for purely humanitarian motives. Neither is true. The vaccinations were originally planned long before the epidemic materialized as a way of researching the formation of antibodies by the Yanomami as a "virgin soil" population. This was neither unethical in itself nor inconsistent with humanitarian medical motives, as Hill correctly insists. Hill, however, goes on to say that Tierney and "some of his supporters have sought to 'prove' that the measles vaccination program was mainly an experiment rather than a medical procedure designed to save lives. In their simple view of science, it must be either one or the other."

Which "supporters"? Whose "simple view of science"? Or is it really Hill's simple view of these unnamed supporters that is really in question?

THE VALIDITY OF TIERNEY'S ALLEGATIONS AGAINST CHAGNON

Hill lists a series of allegations by Tierney of unethical behavior by Chagnon, then says that "these charges should cause all anthropologists to reflect on their own fieldwork." As indeed they should. But what about reflecting on Chagnon's fieldwork and actions, the original subject of the allegations? Hill somehow doesn't get around to facing that issue. He gives a long and sensitive discussion, with which I fully agree, about the problem of reconciling the scientific obligation to publish and the need not to injure the interests of research subjects but fails to bring it back to the specific issues Tierney and others, such as the Brazilian Anthropological Association, raise about Chagnon. These concern not only the damage his statements on "fierceness" allegedly caused but more important his failure to speak out against the use of his statements by politicians and journalists seeking to obtain the dissolution of the Yanomami reserve. Hill's deflection of the discussion back to a renewed attack on Tierney's "hypocrisy" circumvents this key issue.

Again, when he raises the question of the problems allegedly caused by Chagnon's distributions of gifts, Hill evasively responds by saying that there is in any case no evidence that the effects of Chagnon's gift giving were worse than gift giving by missionaries and also that it was "not excessive given the rewards he gained from his research" (something of an understatement, that). This may be so, but it avoids the point at issue, which is, what was the effect of Chagnon's actions on the Yanomami? Hill claims that Tierney provides no "serious" evidence that Chagnon's behavior in this respect induced social conflict by giving massive support to one faction of a village and nothing to others, but he does in fact give such evidence, citing for example Ferguson's chapter 13 and conclusions, which deal with this issue. One can argue about whether Ferguson's evidence is conclusive but hardly over whether it is "serious." On a related point, Hill justly observes that other anthropologists working with the Yanomami, such as Albert and Peters, have succeeded in obtaining genealogies with the names of dead relatives without causing serious disruptions. As he says, "Thus, there is little doubt that there are appropriate ways to obtain such information and that Yanomami names are not absolutely taboo, as Tierney asserts. The question here is whether Chagnon used methods unacceptable to a large fraction of the study population."

I think that Hill states the issue fairly here. The answer seems obvious, at least in principle: Chagnon did, by his own account (e.g., 1977:10–11) use methods that would be offensive to "a large fraction of the study population." This has been seized upon by many critics of Chagnon, including otherwise critical reviewers of Tierney's book, as a major issue. Hill, however, takes no position and declines to answer his own question. We never do get a straight story on what Hill thinks about Chagnon's ethical problems.

On another important point, Hill notes that Tierney alleges that "Chagnon falsified data or engaged in misleading data analyses in order to obtain a desired result." This concerns the central issue of whether killers have higher rates of reproductive success. As Hill notes, "the claim of data falsification is clearly a serious ethical issue" but says "no credible evidence is presented to back this claim." I cannot agree: chapter 10 of Tierney's book presents a great deal of credible evidence on this point, which no defender of Chagnon has thus far refuted in a credible fashion. Hill's flat assertion that none of Tierney's evidence (drawn in considerable part from published critiques by Lizot and Albert) is "credible" is itself of dubious credibility. Hill notes that "I and other sociobiologists have pointed out some weaknesses" in the study at issue, and notes that Chagnon himself has recognized the seriousness (i.e., potential credibility) of some of the criticisms, such as his initial failure to include the children of dead fathers, to give due weight to age differences, and to note the importance of headman status, and he has promised to produce data from more recent fieldwork that he says will resolve the problems. No such data have appeared. It may be that all that is involved are errors of fact and/or method, in which case Hill is correct to insist that they cannot be considered "unethical." On this point the jury is still out; but to dismiss Tierney's whole discussion, and with it the whole issue, simply by saying that Tierney presents no credible evidence will not wash.

The attempt by Chagnon and Charles Brewer-Carías to set up a personal Yanomami reserve in the Siapa valley under the patronage of Cecilia Matos, the presidential mistress and president of FUNDAFACI (Foundation to Aid Peasant and Indigenous Families), in the early 1990s has been the focus of some of the most serious charges of unethical conduct leveled at Chagnon. It is important to be clear that these charges focus on the illegal activities of Matos and Brewer-Carías, with Chagnon only in an accessory capacity.

Hill notes that he has himself "voiced displeasure" at Chagnon's association with these "disreputable characters" but gives his opinion that this involved "bad judgment rather than a serious ethical shortfall." What it undeniably involved for Chagnon was willing collaboration in actions that he must have known were criminal violations of Venezuelan law and would have resulted in a free hand for Brewer-Carías and Matos to pursue mining operations that would have had damaging consequences for Yanomami health, Yanomami social stability, and the ecosystem. The incident involved illegal actions (e.g., the misuse of military aircraft and personnel) and fraudulent use of funds by Matos, for which she was tried in absentia and sentenced to a substantial jail term. It also led to a parliamentary investigation of Brewer-Carías for illegal gold mining activity on indigenous lands, which produced abundant evidence of illegal mining activities but no indictments.

Hill says that Chagnon at the time had no evidence that Brewer-Carías planned to carry out illegal mining on Yanomami land or that he and Matos intended to dispossess the Yanomami of their land. Chagnon by that time had known Brewer-Carías for more than twenty years and had to have been familiar with his long history of mining activities in Indian areas. He cooperated with Brewer-Carías in drawing up the project for the Biosphere Reserve that would have given Brewer-Carías and himself effective control of the huge slice of Yanomami territory it was designed to contain (and no effective control to the Yanomami themselves). So how can he have had "no evidence" of their intentions? He certainly participated in the illegal flights by air force helicopters and planes into the Siapa valley that Matos funded out of the FUNDAFACI budget, bringing medically unscreened Venezuelan and foreign visitors into contact with "virgin soil" Yanomami communities and damaging Yanomami shelters. In all these ways, it seems plain that Chagnon's association with Brewer-Carías and Matos was indeed, in Hill's own words, "harmful to his study population and thus unethical."

Hill raises the issue of Chagnon's failure to provide any aid or support for the Yanomami aside from the presents he brought as part of his fieldwork. He complains that "Chagnon's enemies made it impossible for him to return to the Yanomami for many years so he couldn't possibly have helped them even if that were his top priority." Couldn't he have opened a bank account in Puerto Ayacucho and hired somebody to act as go-between?

Finally, Hill addresses the issue of Yanomami opposition to Chagnon and suggests that it is due to "malicious coaching" by "somebody" who has been working hard to turn them against sociobiology. No doubt the Salesians have done some such "coaching," but that hardly accounts for the willingness of so many Yanomami to protest against Chagnon's return to their territory and for the other complaints many of them seem to volunteer to whoever will listen. What is missing in Hill's account is any recognition that at least some of the Yanomami may be able to speak for themselves and may be worth listening to on their own account. They cannot all be written off as puppets (Chagnon has recently described the Yanomami leader Davi Kopenawa to a CNN television crew as a "cigar store Indian"), mindlessly repeating the promptings of his puppet masters, the NGOs, Salesian missionaries, and sinister "somebodies" hostile to sociobiology.

When the Yanomami speak, can we bring ourselves to listen to them? Can we take seriously the possibility that they might be able to speak for themselves?

CRITIQUES OF CHAGNON ARE NOT AN IDEOLOGICAL WITCH HUNT

Hostility to science is not the reason for Tierney's criticisms of Chagnon or of Neel and is certainly not for the criticisms of either by myself, Leslie Sponsel, or other anthropologists of which I am aware. Tierney's criticisms of Neel and Chagnon are primarily motivated by partisan zeal for the defense of indigenous people (in this case, the Yanomami) against exploitation and other forms of mistreatment by outsiders of all descriptions: scientists, moviemakers, journalists, and gold miners (although not missionaries, as Hill and others cogently point out). As I have indicated in numerous places, I think that Tierney's zeal led him astray on crucial points in his treatment of Neel and the 1968 expedition. I have done my best to research the disputed issues and publicize my own critical disagreements with Tierney on these points. At the same time, I stand by what I have said all along, that I find most of Tierney's account of the activities of Chagnon and others to be substantially accurate. It is in general agreement with the published and verbal opinions of many anthropologists, medical workers (including missionaries), and NGO workers with the Yanomami whom I know and respect on both the Brazilian and Venezuelan sides of the border and also with the public record (government documents, NGO reports, and media stories).

Hill attempts to make the case that the ethical issues raised by Tierney proceed from a fanatical hostility to sociobiological science are distorted by Tierney's misunderstandings of science in general and sociobiology in particular, and are therefore essentially false. For Hill, it is the ideological opposition to sociobiology, and the willingness to distort the truth that it incites in Tierney and other critics of Neel and Chagnon, that are the true ethical issues raised by Tierney's work. I have given my reasons for disagreeing with Hill's general thesis and many of his specific criticisms. I have made clear some of my general reasons for disagreeing with Neel's and Chagnon's sociobiological views as applied to the Yanomami. Disagreement with the claims of sociobiology (including skepticism about Neel's and Chagnon's genetic reductionism) is, however, not the same thing as hostility to science, and I know that on this point I am in good company with many scientists.

The preoccupation of Hill and other sociobiologists with the threats to their own position they see as posed by Tierney's and other critiques of Chagnon and Neel leads them to substitute the false issue of an attack on science for the real ethical issues in the Yanomami case: responsibility for speaking out against misuses of research findings by third parties damaging to the research subjects; untruthful and damaging statements about indigenous leaders and NGOs; disruptive research methods practiced repetitively and on a massive scale; failure to give appropriate priority to the health needs of the subject population over personal research goals; failure to obtain informed consent or give appropriate compensation for the taking of biological samples and other medical-cum-biological procedures; and collaboration with citizens of the host country engaged in corrupt and criminal acts directly related to personal research activities, among others. These are issues on which scientists and nonscientists, rightists and leftists, cultural anthropologists and sociobiologists ought in principle to be able to agree. Above all, we should be able to agree that when such activities damage the interests and well-being of the people with whom anthropologists work, anthropologists have an obligation to speak out against them as inconsistent with professional anthropological ethics. This at least we owe ourselves, and this is the least we owe the Yanomami.

10

·····

ROUND THREE

What is striking in Round Three is how, despite clear differences, participants also find shared points of reference. It is the weaving back and forth between their agreements and disagreements that makes this final exchange intriguing.

·····

HUMAN RIGHTS AND RESEARCH ETHICS AMONG INDIGENOUS PEOPLE: FINAL COMMENTS

BRUCE ALBERT

I was favorably impressed with the progress of our last round of papers in turning the wild polemics over *Darkness in El Dorado* into a more intellectual and constructive debate oriented toward a wider reflection on essential points of anthropological, biomedical, and missionary ethics. To pursue these issues further, I will first comment on two themes emerging in our last round that are especially relevant to indigenous human rights: cultural relativism versus ethical universalism, and the ethics of truth versus the ethics of responsibility. I will then develop my argument about biomedical and anthropological research ethics, since this topic lies at the core of our debate, and explore the lessons we can learn from the Yanomami case. I will conclude by making some suggestions about the contributions we can make toward improving the Yanomami's current situation, since this has been my first and foremost motivation for taking part in this Roundtable.

CULTURAL RELATIVISM AND HUMAN RIGHTS

I have already expressed my general opinion on missionary work, and I agree, for the most part, with both sides of Kim Hill's last contribution on this subject: on the positive side (since I do not condone stereotypes about missionaries or blind, decontextualized condemnations of their work) and on the critical side (since we are still waiting for a self-reflective analysis from missionaries about

KEY ACCUSATIONS AND ISSUES
(see also pp. 317–41)

How does the discipline regulate professional integrity? Some statements in the
  Roundtable discussion abstractly affirm a particular ethical principle but,
  through convoluted arguments, neutralize its relevance to the concrete case
  being discussed. (see page 214)

To what degree did the Neel expedition violate reasonable standards of informed con-
  sent? Formal informed consent was improperly replaced with the exchange of
  goods to get Yanomami's collaboration in Neel's research. (see page 223)

Were the Yanomami misinformed regarding Neel's collection of blood samples and
  how the samples would help them? Despite promises of medical benefits from
  the collection of blood samples, the Yanomami never gained any such benefits from Neel's research. (see page 224)

QUESTIONS TO CONSIDER

What would have been the best way for Neel and Chagnon to obtain informed con-
  sent from the Yanomami for their research?

What would constitute just compensation for the taking of blood samples or other bio-
  logical specimens from indigenous populations such as the Yanomami?

their ethnocentrism and aggressive proselytizing in the field). However, given
our efforts toward a more constructive debate, his reaction to the information I
provided regarding the sexual abuse of Yanomami women by Brazilian soldiers
in my longer text for this Roundtable was, in my opinion, highly inappropriate.
Hill's answer to this report (also deleted in the editing down of his manuscript)
was to criticize "anthropologists . . . enamored with an ideal of pure cultural relativism, often . . . prepared to ignore or even defend gross human rights violations when committed by members of small oppressed ethnic minorities." This
extraneous and offensive accusation deserves a brief comment.

I have been engaged in defending the Yanomami's rights ever since I began
fieldwork in 1975. This engagement has not been motivated by a naive vision or
a manipulative idealization of the Yanomami. Rather, it has been based on two
fundamental ethical convictions, professional and personal. I consider my
social engagement to be an essential counterpart of my anthropological research
work, and I believe that human rights (including, of course, the universal right
to cultural differences) must be defended in every context in which we act.

This means that if the Yanomami's rights are violated, I maintain that we
must fight these violations in every way possible in the name of the principle of
universal human rights. But this also implies that the Yanomami, whose rights

and duties are part of this universality, must respect these human rights as much as we do when we defend the Yanomami in the name of such universals. We cannot sustain an ethical equivalent of the paradox of Zeno of Elea, who, while walking, negated the existence of motion: that is, we cannot defend the Yanomami in the name of universal human rights and, at the same time, relieve them of their responsibility to observe them.

Therefore, we have no other alternative than to find meaningful ways of affirming cultural particularism within the universalist ideals of our democratic societies. An effective struggle for the former is, in fact, necessarily based on the latter (since our democratic legal systems legitimate indigenous collective rights). Indigenous societies are confronted with the parallel challenges of pursuing their sociocultural reproduction at the same time as they are becoming increasingly aware of the juridico-ethical values that can guarantee them a decent role in the nation-state in which they are included.

I thus contend that the Yanomami must be properly informed about the meaning of the principle of universal human rights and what it entails (because they are defended in its name) and then encouraged to debate the issue among themselves and how they might socially acknowledge such a principle. However, we must avoid adopting an arrogant stance in this process, since our own societies certainly cannot boast a perfect record. Radical cultural relativism or differentialism or, even worse, an opportunistic use of universality will only lead to trouble. I have had pointed discussions (and some heated arguments) with Yanomami men about the abuse of women. Yanomami political representatives, professors, and health attendants are now well aware of this interethnic ethical issue (among others) and are actively promoting a broader discussion and concern about it in their communities.

This being clarified, I am sure that Hill would agree that violence against women, which must be condemned everywhere, is not an exclusive specialty of the Yanomami (again, let us compare the record of the nonindigenous world on this matter).[1] It thus cannot be used to single out Yanomami society, as the media have done for decades, based on Chagnon's ongoing caricature of the Yanomami's "warfare over women," as if the particularity of Yanomami society and culture among those found around the world could be encapsulated in these three words.

I must also underscore the fact that the sexual abuses condemned by the Yanomami assembly of December 2000 involve a system of prostitution set up by Brazilian soldiers at a border outpost, who use food and trade goods as payment to exploit Yanomami women, most of whom are mere teenagers. This constitutes an extremely serious matter, which is currently being investigated by the Human Rights Commission of the Brazilian House of Representatives.[2] I hope that Hill will agree that it deserves more careful attention from anthropologists concerned with human rights than to be used as a polemical maneuver in a purely academic exercise.

Moreover, anthropologists and other researchers should pay more heed to the broader issue of interethnic ethical dilemmas in human rights, since it raises serious questions relevant to indigenous rights advocacy. From this perspective, Hill's point (putting aside its polemical intentions) could be a positive contribution to our debate on ethnographic representations and anthropological ethical responsibilities. However, he could have introduced it in a more sophisticated manner, such as that followed in the special issue of the *Journal of Anthropological Research*, edited by Turner and Nagengast (1997) on this theme.

Nevertheless, Hill has given me a good opportunity to clarify my position on such ethical dilemmas. I believe that the most satisfactory solution is to pursue a progressive intercultural debate on a case-by-case basis to reach the best possible balance between the respect for cultural particularities and the respect for the universal human rights of individuals. This approach represents a kind of mediated and pragmatic universalism, which Todorov (1989) aptly called a *"universalisme de parcours."* I believe that it is unproductive to oppose radical cultural relativism to ethical universalism on a purely theoretical level. These positions form the complementary foundations of the respect for indigenous minority rights, one at the collective level (since cultural differences underpin access to specific collective rights, e.g., to land, religious freedom, and culturally appropriate schooling), the other at the individual level (since universal rights protect members of minority groups against personal abuses within their own societies).

In this context, discussions about one dimension of rights or the other (either particular/universal or individual/collective rights) are relevant only when they take into account the actual contexts in which these rights are to be exercised. This means that we should support Yanomami collective rights in interethnic political contexts (promoting cultural relativism), just as we should help protect Yanomami individuals against abuses in intraethnic contexts (affirming ethical universalism). If we invoke one set of rights in the context of the other (for example, denouncing Yanomami individual abuses when their collective rights are threatened), we end up with intellectually faulty and politically irresponsible results. This confusion undermines our effectiveness in promoting Yanomami collective rights without contributing anything to the rights of any concrete Yanomami individual.

Let me give an example of such a situation. Based on the reputation of the Yanomami in the United States stemming from Chagnon's works, a major Brazilian newspaper, the *Folha de São Paulo* (April 7, 1990), called them a "fierce people who practice wife-beating and female infanticide." The article, entitled "Feminists Attack the Yanomami," was published at the same time as thousands of gold panners were invading Yanomami territory, spreading diseases and violence. It quoted a group of American feminists who described the Yanomami as "a primitive and brutal culture" and asked, "Our question is the following: does this society merit being protected against the twentieth century? Or, to put the question another way: are the gold panners really the outlaws in this story?"

TRUTH AND RESPONSIBILITY
IN HUMAN RIGHTS ADVOCACY

I am pleased that in Round 2 Hill reaffirms a principle on which everybody can agree: anthropologists should make a special effort to get involved "if [their] study population[s] [are] being harmed through the misuse of [their] own words." Besides the first warnings of U.S. anthropologists such as Shelton Davis (1976) or Judith Shapiro (1976),[3] the Brazilian Anthropological Association (ABA) and its members sent two letters to the AAA in 1988 and 2001 in an attempt to call Chagnon's attention to the effects that his stereotype of the Yanomami as "the fierce people" have had as his interviews in the U.S. media have ramified through the local Brazilian press and fed the racist anti-Yanomami campaigns of the Brazilian military, local politicians, and gold miners. If another example is still needed after Lêda Martins's two papers in our debate, see the article "Violence, the Mark of the Yanomami," published in another major Brazilian newspaper, O Estado de São Paulo (March 1, 1988), after Chagnon's article on Yanomami "blood revenge" appeared in Science during the Roraima gold rush. I still hope, after twenty-five years, that Chagnon will realize the harmful ramifications of his portrayals of the Yanomami and engage in energetic, concrete actions to turn them around.

Despite his admirable introduction, Hill keeps on insisting that Chagnon cannot be held accountable for these uses of his negative public portrayal of Yanomami society. I am puzzled by the sophistic structure of Hill's reasoning on this issue. Why does he begin with a reaffirmation of a generic ethical principle but then develop convoluted arguments to neutralize its relevance to the concrete situation we are discussing? Are Hill and Hames really conducting serious discussions when they try to exempt Chagnon of his ethical responsibilities by answering the documented protests by ABA and Brazil-based specialists with simplistic conjectures about the image of the Yanomami in Brazil, quibbles about what Brazilian generals read, and speculations about the esteem that the Yanomami hold for the police and military? I will let the readers of our exchanges be the judge.

In his first round, Hames criticized NGOs for portraying indigenous peoples in an overly positive light. If his point were not embedded in an evasive argument to rescue Chagnon, I could have agreed with him. In fact, I have been quite harsh myself in underlining the dangers of "the questionable use of stereotypical and exoticizing imagery (the ecological and New Age Noble Savage) to which certain NGOs link the recognition of indigenous peoples' rights to guarantee their own legitimacy and boost their fund-raising activities" (Albert 1997:60). But Hill goes much further in Round Two by accusing "some anthropologists" who "exaggerate or distort the truth about indigenous rights issues in hopes of stimulating more public support for their cause."

Besides approaching libel, this argument is irrelevant to evaluating Chagnon's role in fostering negative stereotypes of Yanomami society. Moreover, it is logically self-contradictory. Indeed, if Chagnon bears no ethical responsibility for propagating pejorative images of the Yanomami, why defend him by accusing his critics of doing the same thing in reverse (i.e., propagating positive stereotypes)? Doesn't this symmetrical inversion amount to an implicit acknowledgment of Chagnon's responsibility? But, leaving aside their sophisms, I agree with Hill and Hames that distorting facts on behalf of indigenous peoples' rights is not only unethical but also ineffective in human rights struggles.

Like Hill, I have a personal testimony to offer on this issue. In August 1993, the front pages of every major Brazilian newspaper and magazine, as well as many of those in the international media, carried the story of a massacre of the Yanomami in Brazil. The first alert about the massacre was raised by a letter (August 17, 1993) from a Brazilian nun working for the government health service in the region of Xitei on the upper Parima River in Roraima. She had heard about it from some terrified neighbors of the murdered Yanomami. The president of FUNAI (Fundação Nacional do Índio; the National Indian Foundation) and the Ministry of Justice (on which FUNAI depends) announced the massacre a few days later to the press. During the following weeks, a media war of contradictory statements was waged between pro-Indian groups (including FUNAI, certain congressional members, the Catholic church, and NGOs) and the anti-Yanomami lobby (made up of members of the military and the mining industry, gold panners, ranchers, and their political supporters in the Brazilian congress). These statements either maximized the number of victims (between thirty and seventy-three) or categorically denied that any massacre had taken place. Without any direct testimony or factual evidence, the contest over different versions of the incident served only to fuel the "great divide" of the Brazilian indigenist political scene with renewed vigor.

I was in the field at that time, in Davi Kopenawa's village, near the Pro-Yanomami Commission (CCPY) health post at Demini in northeastern Amazonas. On August 24, a CCPY medical team at a second health post (Parawa-ù) told us by radio that some Yanomami of the upper Demini River had come across a group of wounded Indians heading toward a third CCPY post on the Toototobi River. I radioed a request to the local CCPY office in Boa Vista (the capital of the neighboring state of Roraima) to send a plane to pick me up and fly me to Toototobi. On August 25, I interviewed some of the survivors of the massacre at Toototobi and immediately afterward sent a report to the CCPY office. In the following days, I took part in the official Brazilian inquiry into the case launched by the Federal Police and the attorney general's office. A press release was then issued, stating that sixteen Yanomami had been cruelly massacred by a gang of Brazilian gold panners near a small tributary of the Orinoco headwaters in Venezuela, an episode that came to be known as the "Haximu massacre."

By discovering that the number of victims was much less than the figures of thirty to seventy-three that FUNAI gave to the press, I incurred the antipathy of several native rights supporters. To have shown that the episode was perpetrated in Venezuela by Brazilian gold panners irritated Brazilian authorities. The fact that I proved that a massacre had actually been perpetrated against the Yanomami upset the military, local politicians, and gold panners. A communist member of the Brazilian congress also requested my expulsion from the country. One can understand why I felt quite lonely during this episode. But with the help of a small group of Brazilian colleagues and serious NGOs (such as CCPY and ISA, Instituto SocioAmbiental; the Socio-Environmental Institute, a São Paulo-based organization), I managed to continue collaborating with the attorney general's inquiry and to publish my final report in the major Brazilian and Venezuelan daily newspapers (in early October 1993). Deeply disappointed by the reaction of some indigenist rights groups during the inquiry, I dedicated the report as follows: "To those who think that 16 deaths reduced the gravity of the episode; to those who feared that a 'mere' 16 deaths diverted attention from it, I offer this report as food for thought."[4]

Chagnon's record on this matter was not one of the most ethically edifying. His whirlwind trip to Haximu on September 28, 1993 (see Tierney 2000:chap. 12) took place a month after my first interview with the Yanomami survivors in Toototobi (August 25, 1993) and one day after the final version of my report for the attorney general was transmitted to the press (September 27, 1993). Given his timing, plus the fact that the massacre did not take place precisely inside the Haximu village where Chagnon went but rather in a temporary camp in the jungle, one can easily appraise the validity of his "investigation." His belated and superfluous intervention was irrelevant to the legal case, which had been conducted entirely within Brazil. In fact, he used the press interest in the massacre mainly to redirect its focus to his dispute with members of the Catholic church and his other opponents in Venezuela, whom he accused of covering up the massacre (Chagnon 1993a), even though the Brazilian investigation had already identified the murderers and had arrested some of them much earlier.

My involvement in the Haximu case demonstrates (like Hill's testimony) that it is not easy for anthropologists to stick to their commitment to rigorous research when indigenous rights battles are so heavily loaded with broader political issues. But it also demonstrates that this commitment to truth can obtain effective results only if it is complemented by vigorous social engagement. The detailed documentation of the Haximu massacre that the attorney general was able to produce led to the first legal recognition of an Indian massacre as attempted genocide in the history of Brazil (see the ruling of December 1996 by the Federal Judge of Roraima, confirmed by the Supreme Court [Superior Tribunal de Justiça] in September 2000).[5]

To conclude, handing down anthropological truths with no concrete involvement may be comfortable for anthropological egos, but it does not necessarily convey positive effects for the human rights of indigenous peoples. *Idées-vraies* [ideas that are true] can become *idées-forces* [ideas that effectively shape people's behavior] that are capable of changing human rights situations only when they are backed up by effective social engagement, since, as Spinoza wrote, *"il n'y a pas de force intrinsèque de l'idée vraie"* (there is no intrinsic force in a true idea) (quoted in Bourdieu 2000:68). This is what is at stake in the classic debate over the opposition between an "ethic of ultimate ends" (the duty to truth) and an "ethic of responsibility" (the duty to act), on which Max Weber concluded: "An ethic of ultimate ends and an ethic of responsibility are not absolute contrasts but rather supplements, which only in unison constitute a genuine man" (Weber 1958/1919:127).

BIOMEDICAL AND ANTHROPOLOGICAL RESEARCH ETHICS: FINAL COMMENTS ON NEEL'S 1968 ORINOCO VACCINATION

I will not say much more here about the 1968 Orinoco epidemic and how Neel's research team dealt with it, since I think that the essential points were made earlier in our debate. I will simply insist again on the fact that as I wrote in my first and second papers, both the report of the Brazilian physicians (Lobo et al. 2000) (which Chagnon himself praised)[6] and the preliminary report by Turner and Stevens (2001) on Neel's field papers suggest possible breaches of biomedical ethics in the manner in which blood sampling and vaccinations—which were not merely "observational research"—were conducted among the Yanomami. Their activities may have violated ethical norms in vigor at the time in three ways: by giving priority to a research agenda over vaccinations in the midst of an epidemic; by carrying out inappropriate vaccinal experiments; and by disrespecting the rule of informed consent in biomedical sampling. These indications are serious enough to warrant a full investigation by an independent bioethics committee to bring the discussion of this issue to a close. I do not think that anthropologists have the qualifications to draw final conclusions on the subject of bioethics.

I am glad that Hames agrees that consulting a bioethics committee on Neel's research among the Yanomami is "a useful idea" that may close the case and "provide . . . some guidelines for researchers who engage in future work among indigenous peoples." I also agree that it is "a very complex historical issue" requiring more research by such a bioethics commission. However, I am puzzled when he then suggests including an investigation into the emergency medical expedition by CCPY and the Dutch branch of Doctors without Borders (Médecins Sans Frontières [MSF]-Holland) on the upper Siapa River in 1998. Since he apparently has no information about this medical expedition, let me provide him with some.

Unlike Neel's expedition in 1968, the 1998 Siapa expedition was not a research expedition to collect blood samples or other biological specimens. It was not even an expedition "to investigate epidemiological patterns," as Hames put it in the previous round. It was purely an emergency health operation conducted to rescue dying Yanomami, conducted in full accord with the health and political authorities of Venezuela. Hames's question about informed consent is well answered by the introduction of the report, which also conveys a sense of the dire health situation of the Yanomami in Venezuela:

> At several health posts in Brazil, various requests for help were received from communities that live near the border in Venezuela. These communities frequently cross the border, and the precarious health situation of some of these Yanomami is evident. In the health posts attended by CCPY in the regions of Balawa-ú [Parawa-ù] and Toototobi, the visits of Yanomami coming from communities in Venezuelan territory who gave accounts about their health problems are relatively frequent. This type of request cannot be attended without knowing the location of the communities from which they come.
>
> These mounting circumstances led MSF and CCPY to enter into contact with the health authorities in the state of Amazonas [in Venezuela] to evaluate the possibility of coordinating a mission to the border regions on the upper Orinoco River and the Siapa Valley. This possibility was well received by the Venezuelan authorities who, for their part, shared similar concerns over the health situation of the Yanomami communities in these regions. After negotiations that established the basis of the cooperation among CCPY, MSF, and the Regional Health Council in the state, preparations for the trips were begun (CCPY/MSF-Holland n.d. [1998]:4).[7]

Finally, having cooperated since the mid-1970s with so many Brazilian and foreign physicians and health professionals (from missions, official agencies, and NGOs) and seeing them spend years of their lives at great risk in the forest to deliver medical services to the Yanomami, I was amazed to read Hill's statement that Neel (perhaps because he is a U.S. scientist) is "the one person in the world who did the most to save Yanomami lives."[8] Such overblown and insulting rhetoric could have been avoided.

With these last comments made on the 1968 Orinoco vaccinations, let me move on to deal with several aspects of anthropological and biomedical research ethics raised by Hill and Hames in reaction to my paper in the first round.

A BIOMEDICAL-ANTHROPOLOGICAL ETHICAL "DOUBLE STANDARD"?

Hill seems upset by the idea that biomedical researchers should be held accountable for providing medical assistance when needed to the indigenous people with whom they work. He claims that this is the responsibility of national and local agencies and missionaries. In his eyes, as "researchers, not clinical practitioners," they "cannot get involved in treating every sick person they encounter in the field." The lack of humanity in this statement is quite shocking to me, and I believe no physician would sustain it, since it contradicts medical deontology and the philanthropy of the Hippocratic tradition.[9] But this is probably another unfortunate polemical excess, since in his paper for the first round Hill recognized, to the contrary, that "the health and welfare of the study population must always take precedence over any academic goal." Indeed, he himself acted very properly by interrupting his research during an epidemic in Manu Park in 1986, according to his own account.

However, as if this contradiction were not enough, Hill also protests in his second paper against the fact that sociocultural anthropologists are not expected to give paramedical assistance (stating that they "can go to the field for years and provide no medical services for their study populations"), although he knows that most do so, even if it is not their professional specialty (for instance, in Hames's and my experiences).[10] On these grounds, Hill charges Turner and me with being primarily concerned with the ethical regulation of biomedical research and not with sociocultural anthropological research and thus accuses us of developing a "blatant double standard."

This mixture of contexts is simply absurd. The kinds of research conducted in sociocultural anthropology and biomedicine are obviously different, governed by different codes of ethics and having different implications for indigenous peoples' rights. Does it make sense for Hill to suggest that the recording of mythical narratives or social philosophies by Lévi-Strauss lies on the same level as the collecting of blood samples or administration of radioactive iodine tracers? I don't think so. So let us ask more reasonably for both kinds of researchers to assume their own specific ethical and professional responsibilities toward the indigenous people from whom they get their information.

The knowledge that sociocultural anthropologists gain from indigenous peoples can be reciprocated—beyond simple payments in trade goods—by an involvement in advocacy for indigenous rights (which biomedical researchers could do as well). More specifically, anthropologists can make use of this knowledge to benefit the people who transmitted it (in my previous paper, I mentioned yet another aspect of this issue, i.e., the redistribution of profits from books, photos, and films). Even if sociocultural anthropologists cannot be asked professionally to assume medical care (which biomedical researchers cum physicians certainly can be), at least they can be asked to engage or collaborate in advocacy activities to create medical programs for the indigenous people with whom they work or serve as ethnographic consultants to make health services more effective and less culturally damaging (see Albert and Gomez 1997).

I do agree with Hill's point that any kind of research with indigenous peoples, be it biomedical or anthropological, must be regulated, even if along different lines, to protect the peoples' rights and to contribute to their welfare. As a matter of fact, it is precisely on such grounds that we are devoting equal attention in this debate to the breaches of anthropological research ethics (by Chagnon) and breaches in biomedical research ethics (by Neel and Roche).

I further agree with Hill that indigenous peoples' rejection of the antiquated colonialist style of "hit-and-run" ethnographic research presents a significant challenge to sociocultural anthropologists and must lead them to assume their political and ethical responsibilities toward these peoples in more satisfactory ways. However, indigenous people have expressed greater worries over the abuses of genetic research blood sampling and the patenting of indigenous DNA than over the exoticizing in cultural anthropology (see the Canadian examples in *New Scientist* 2000; Alphonso 2000), a point to which I will return later in discussing the Brazilian situation.

In my view, the social responsibilities of anthropology imply that its research procedures must involve the negotiation of a kind of pact of reciprocity between indigenous peoples and ethnographers. It is precisely in this context that I understand my engagement with the Yanomami since I began fieldwork in 1975. In reflecting on my own experiences, I wrote an article in 1997 about the new conditions of "post-Malinowskian fieldwork" for ethnographic research and anthropological advocacy. I argued that "anthropologists find themselves faced with two ethical and political obligations which were eluded by classical ethnography, but are unquestionable nowadays: on the one hand, being accountable in their work to people who were traditionally the 'object' of their studies; on the other, assuming the responsibility their knowledge entails for these peoples' resistance strategies vis-à-vis the dominant nation-states' discriminatory and despoiling policies" (Albert 1997:56).

Thus, I cannot be suspected of developing any ethical "double standard" or shielding sociocultural anthropology from ethical regulation. The ideas of negotiating research projects and establishing terms of reciprocity with indigenous peoples that I discuss here (which include but go beyond the process of obtaining informed consent) have not yet entered the professional codes of ethics of anthropological associations.[11] But they are making their way in national indigenist legislation and regulations under pressure from indigenous peoples, who are becoming increasingly empowered to assert their rights.

Regarding the Brazilian situation, my previous paper quoted Resolution 304/2000 of the Brazilian National Health Council (see chapter 9, note 2), dealing with biomedical research among indigenous communities; also, the medical report by Lobo et al. (2000: point 4) briefly described the earlier, more general Resolution 196/96. I could also quote FUNAI's 1995 Normative Instruction 01/PRESI (Art. 7), which states that ethnographic research in indigenous areas can be authorized only if it involves a negotiation process with the communities and if they grant their consent to the research project.[12] These regulations give an administrative and juridical frame to the negotiations (mediated by the state) between researchers and indigenous peoples. But the process of negotiation is conducted by the indigenous peoples themselves as they pursue their own social and cultural agendas. They generally carry out open-ended discussions with the researcher, asking first for a public explanation of the project and if they consider it harmless to their rights and welfare, then negotiating for direct benefits from it and recording the agreements on paper. The benefits are material (tools and medicines, payments for intellectual property and image rights) as well as immaterial (generally consisting of the anthropologist's help in land, environment, or health projects or general advocacy work).

Some indigenous organizations are now beginning to think about the issue of "participatory research" on a more ambitious level. A good example in Brazil is the international seminar organized by the Federation of Indian Organizations of the Rio Negro (Federação das Organizações Indígenas do Rio Negro, or FOIRN) (along with the Socio-Environmental Institute) and held in November 2000, to which forty scientists from different fields (anthropology, archaeology, natural sciences, ecology, biomedicine, and nutrition) were invited to negotiate collaborative agreements in the planning of regional research.[13]

I hope that these Brazilian examples also answer Hames's legitimate worries about indigenous peoples' ethical standards for research projects, which he correctly points out are a matter that few researchers bother to consider. These examples demonstrate that one of their preeminent standards concerns tangible and intangible reciprocation for their collaboration in such projects, whether they deal with anthropology, biomedicine, or any other scientific field. The FOIRN seminar established a list of "criteria and procedures for regulating relations between researchers and Indians of the Rio Negro," among which figured prominently the "identification of the forms of recompense (*contrapartida*) for the community/people, which will ensure that their members receive a social return from the work conducted." This makes it clear that the concept of a "social return" for research conducted among them (what I called above a "pact" or "terms of reciprocity") is indeed a crucial point for indigenous people in the Amazon region when negotiating with researchers, since their communities are most of the time politically, economically, and socially marginalized.

To conclude, I agree with Hames that the gradual transformation in the relationship between indigenous peoples and researchers toward a more "participatory research" is a "welcome change . . . largely a consequence of increased political power of indigenous groups, which require researchers to balance their own professional interests with those of the people they study."

MORE ON INFORMED CONSENT
AND BIOMEDICAL RESEARCH
AMONG THE YANOMAMI

This discussion about social returns and the negotiation process between indigenous communities and researchers answers most of Hill's challenges about the differences in obtaining informed consent in ethnographic studies as compared to biomedical research. As has been made clear, sociocultural anthropologists, just like other researchers, must explain and submit their research projects to the communities where they want to conduct them. In Brazil, the regulation of biomedical research is now somewhat tighter than it is for ethnographic research, mainly because these regulations have been revised more recently and have thus integrated the most sophisticated debates on bioethics and informed consent. However, the trend in the country suggests that the criterion of control applied to biomedical research will soon be expanded to all other kinds of research with indigenous people, including anthropological field-work—in fact, it already applies to foreign anthropologists.

As to the complexity of explaining research methodology and goals in the process of obtaining informed consent among indigenous peoples, I have some more comments to make:

1. In my previous paper, I pointed out how ideologically dangerous it is to use the existence of cultural-linguistic obstacles to seeking informed consent as an excuse for exempting researchers from obtaining such consent. I also showed how this unethical logic, challenging the universality of its application, undermines the very idea of informed consent laid out by the Nuremberg Code in 1947.

Administering radioiodine to the Venezuelan Yanomami from 1958 to 1970 without following any procedure for obtaining proper informed consent (as Hill agrees was the case) clearly rested on such morally defective reasoning. It was also an experiment (not simply "observational research") conducted without ever making any proper risk/benefit ratio evaluation of its impact on the Yanomami subjects, although this kind of evaluation was recommended by the World Medical Association in 1964 in the Declaration of Helsinki I. Hames could have consulted that document instead of getting confused over the notion "that research on a group had to benefit the group being researched," which was not the way the problem of the radioiodine experiment was set out in my first paper, had he read it carefully.

Let me quote the relevant point of the Helsinki I Declaration on this issue: "5. Every biomedical research project involving human subjects should be preceded by careful assessment of predictable risks in comparison with foreseeable benefits to the subject or to others. Concern for the interests of the subject must always prevail over the interests of science and society."[14]

If a bioethics commission were to retroactively conduct this kind of risk/benefit analysis, it should include not only a parallel evaluation of Roche's goiter studies[15] (I agree on that with Hames and Hill) but also an investigation into the research agendas of the atomic energy commissions in the United States (the AEC) and in France (the CEA), which funded and organized most of these radioiodine research projects (do Hames and Hill also agree with me?). They may recall (from note 22 of my first paper) that a committee of the U.S. Institute of Medicine and the National Research Council retroactively reviewed the radioiodine 131 experiments on the Inuit and Indians of Alaska, which the Air Force's Arctic Aeromedical Laboratory had carried out in 1956–57.[16] Why not also review the Yanomami experiments funded by American and French nuclear research agencies?

I mentioned the Nuremberg Code in my first paper, not because I am ignorant of more recent developments in biomedical ethics, as Hill seems to suggest, but because (a) it had already defined the norms of informed consent at the time of Neel's and Roche's research and experiments (like the Helsinki I Declaration), and thus it should have guided their work; and (b) in contrast to Hill, who thinks the code is "a minuscule part" of bioethics, I agree with those who see the Nuremberg Code as the symbolic and historical foundation of the protection of human subjects in biomedical experimentation *and research*, since it produced the first definition of the crucial notion of informed consent (see Moreno 2000).

However, I thank Hames and Hill for their documentary research efforts on the developments in bioethics in the United States, Canada, and Australia. I hope that my Brazilian examples will likewise be useful to them. I would also recommend that they take a look at the Helsinki VI Declaration of 2000 (more recent and universal than the U.S. Belmont Report of 1979, which they suggested as a reference).[17]

2. Another notion must be emphasized yet again here: the exchange of blood samples for trade goods can never be an acceptable substitute for informed consent. However, Hames confirms that this is what Neel and Chagnon's team did in the field during their AEC-funded project from 1966 to 1972: "It is clear that the Yanomami gave their blood in exchange for trade goods, and it was done on a voluntary basis." In his second paper, Hames provides more information that is relevant to our debate by reporting a phone conversation he had with Chagnon (March 3, 2001), who discussed how he explained Neel's research to the Yanomami before blood samples were collected in exchange for trade goods. According to Hames, Chagnon told them that "Neel's team wanted to examine their blood in order to determine whether there were things that indicated whether or not they had certain kind of diseases, especially *shawara* (epidemic diseases) and that this knowledge would help treat them more effectively if they became ill."

This testimony is fascinating, since it shows that the explanation of blood sampling for genetic research that Chagnon gave the Yanomami linked it directly to a possible health treatment for epidemic diseases. This may have led the Yanomami to think that the blood drawing in itself could help cure them. The context was indeed perfect for them to draw precisely this conclusion. Chagnon started giving the Yanomami this explanation a year before Neel's team arrived; the team showed up just when the epidemic was beginning and then collected blood samples and administered vaccinations and treatments while it was raging.

Furthermore, given the Yanomami's perception of Western therapeutic practices, Chagnon's explanation probably only *confirmed* to them that blood collecting was indeed part of a treatment practice for the epidemic that was afflicting them at the time. Anthropologists in the Amazon have often noted the preference that many Indians have for injectable medicines, which from their cultural point of view they consider to be more powerful for dealing with intrusive supernatural pathogenic objects or aggressions (Coimbra and Santos 1996:419–20). For the Yanomami, according to my ethnographic observations in Brazil, the body is a mere "skin" (siki), while the "vital essence" (*utupë*) is

located in the "deep interior" *(uuxi)* or "center" *(miamo)* of the corporeal enve-
lope (Albert and Gomez 1997:83, 87–115). Such a cultural conception (or a local
variation of it) must have induced the Orinoco Yanomami to interpret blood-tak-
ing procedures of 1967–68 as therapeutic acts. As Coimbra and Santos aptly
observed, it is precisely because of these kinds of symbolic representations that
Indians are "more 'susceptible,' culturally speaking, to submitting themselves
to blood sampling" and why "researchers rarely report great difficulties in
obtaining blood samples" (1996).

In the final analysis, not only did Neel's blood collecting make no positive contribution to the Yanomami's medical treatment during the 1968 measles epidemic but it probably also had a negative impact in the way he organized it
(indeed, Lobo et al. 2000 and Turner's first paper suggest that the priority he
accorded his research agenda contributed to the ineffectiveness of the vaccinations in curbing mortality).[18] Neel then published a paper in a scientific journal
about the measles vaccinations he conducted or supervised among the
Yanomami in Venezuela and Brazil during the 1967–68 epidemic (Neel,
Centerwall, and Chagnon 1970). To this day, I still do not see how his blood sampling or research significantly helped the Yanomami in treating their epidemic
diseases, as they were promised if they agreed to let their blood be drawn (a
promise that, in their eyes, was reinforced by the delivery of trade goods). The
Venezuelan and Brazilian Yanomami have kept on dying in the same way for
three decades after Neel's project.

So I will grant Hames this point: perhaps I was wrong to think that no explanation had been given to the Yanomami to obtain their consent for Neel's blood
sampling and that all he did was give out trade goods (but see my interview with
Davi Kopenawa cited in chapter 5 that touches on the blood collecting in
Toototobi in 1967). I now realize that the situation was even worse than that. Not
only were blood samples obtained through trade, but the way Neel's research was
explained, the manner in which the Yanomami interpreted it, and the context in
which it was carried out probably encouraged them to think that the blood drawing was part of current or future medical treatments.

So here we are, finally, with a true problem of double standards. When the
issue is justifying why biomedical researchers cannot lose time in medically
treating their "subjects" in the field, Hill tells us that "researchers [are] not clinical practitioners." But when the time comes to convince the Indians to give their
blood, things change. At this point, Hill turns researchers into physicians again
by suggesting that biomedical research can help improve health conditions. This
ambiguous connection between research and health improvements encourages
indigenous "subjects" to think that this statement refers to their own health situation when in fact it refers to some as-yet unforeseen high-tech health benefit
for capital-*H* Humanity (through future applications of advances in molecular
medicine).

Offering this sort of misleading association between blood sampling and
some later ill-defined health care improvement is far from being an archaic pro-

cedure in biomedical fieldwork (nor is the more rustic trading of trinkets for blood). It is apparently still common practice for researchers to present this kind of "explanation" to indigenous people and to keep it sufficiently vague to more easily convince them to impart their consent. In fact, this only provides human genetics scientists with an ad hoc field adaptation of a long-standing "selling point" of their discipline, as illustrated on the Human Genome Diversity Project (HGDP) home page: "The collection and analysis of DNA samples may, in conjunction with epidemiological evidence, help lead to the identification of genetic factors in some human diseases and eventually to ways to treat or prevent those diseases."[19]

Foisting this argument on indigenous people who are in poor health to gain their consent for biological sampling seems all the more cynical in that collecting genetic materials from them was given high priority because (as early versions of the HGDP made it clear) they are "groups with unique attributes that are in danger of extinction" (HGDP n.d.; Santos 2002).

Thus, like Hill, I believe that "indigenous populations should have a critical voice in research protocols brought to their communities and whether they wish to participate in any particular study" (a statement that contradicts the strange scenario he conjured up elsewhere in his second paper, in which the Yanomami could be forced to give blood). I also agree with him that "they should also be better informed about potential benefits of such research by people who understand them." But the problem here is precisely that in the case of the Yanomami and many other indigenous peoples most biomedical field-workers do not bother much with properly informing the Indians about their research (as in Neel's and Roche's cases). Instead of putting their biological sampling at risk, they generally prefer to use vague and deceptive explanations and to substitute consent with trade goods. They then fly back to their careers in their laboratories, leaving local health professionals from NGOs, missions, official health organizations, and mere "anthropological activists" (in Hill's terms) to cope with the critical health situation of their erstwhile research subjects.

Such behavior demonstrates a short-sighted view of the social responsibilities of scientific research, which, I believe, is the principal cause of the growing hostility on the part of local people (indigenous and nonindigenous) against blood collecting and human genetic research in Third World countries. My contention here is that in no time or circumstances should the wider interests of an abstract capital-*H* Humanity as defined by a party of scientists ever justify the unethical treatment of any concrete group of human beings.

3. What is worrisome is that even today many biomedical researchers still do not appear to truly subscribe to the concept of informed consent contained in their codes of ethics, at least as far as indigenous people are concerned. They pay lip service to it, since publicly they cannot do otherwise, but their behavior in the field reveals that they think indigenous people are culturally unable to understand what scientists do (that is, capital-*S* Science). This being the case, the next best way to gain their consent (if not really "informed") is to barter for blood sam-

ples and/or pass out deceptive explanations about health improvements. It is unfortunate to see an anthropologist giving support to such a position, as Hames seems to do, when he writes that Chagnon "clearly could not give the Yanomami a crash course in infectious disease, genetics, and epidemiology to more fully explain the purposes of the research," and that the story about his substitute explanation about improving the treatment of *shawara* epidemics was "consistent with their ability to comprehend the research."

Biomedical scientists ought to make a sincere effort to improve their approach to the process of explaining their research to indigenous people. Let us first consider two extreme views on informed consent. On the one hand is a *degré-zéro* position, in which researchers who believe that linguistic and cultural communication with a subject group is tenuous, if not impossible, conclude that the human right to informed consent of this group can be dismissed for the sake of biomedical investigation. This view is ethically unacceptable, since as I showed in my second paper, it practically reduces research with indigenous (or other vulnerable) people to the standards of animal experimentation. On the other hand is a radical conception of informed consent, which insists on an in-depth explanation of the most technical and theoretical aspects of the methodology and goals of the research. But if such a detailed explanation is required, biomedical research could be carried out properly only on scientists themselves as subjects.

I think (as probably Hill and Hames do) that we must avoid these equally absurd extremes and instead encourage a more respectful process of negotiation and participatory research procedures to be opened up between researchers and indigenous people, as suggested in the FOIRN seminar mentioned earlier. But such a negotiation process cannot be treated as a mere interethnic business of buying and selling information, as Hill put it. It should involve a culturally sensitive and instructive explanation (like those needed for research volunteers from the general public in our society) of the research methods and of the immediate and wider goals of the project (since, as Hill rightly notes, "Something about how scientific data are used can be expected to influence native decisions about whether or not to participate in research"). It should also involve explicit negotiations about the collective health benefits to be obtained by members of the group—not necessarily from the research itself (unless commercial outcomes are planned)—but in compensation for their collaboration in it.

Biomedical researchers must understand that the neocolonial practices of trading goods for blood samples or masking the purposes of blood collecting by linking it to some kind of health care–related practice are unethical and can only be seen as anachronistic means of luring their subjects into consent. Similarly, anthropologists must understand that reciprocating the knowledge they gain through their research by merely paying their "informants" and hosts (or even by redistributing royalties) does not constitute a sufficient form of reciprocation. Through the local knowledge he or she acquired from the people that he or she studies, the sociocultural anthropologist inevitably becomes a special cultural-political link to the outside world for them (see Albert 1997). As Hames's account of his fieldwork negotiations admirably demonstrates, this compensation must also encompass the indigenous community's request that the anthropologist engage in advocacy to support their rights and welfare.

YANOMAMI BLOOD SAMPLES AND DNA EXTRACTION: A NEW FRONTIER OF INFORMED CONSENT

It is unfortunate that Hill begins his answer to my preoccupation with the current use of Neel's Yanomami blood samples by grossly misrepresenting my position on this issue, charging twice that I see no practical value in human genetics research and want to induce the Yanomami to demand that the samples be destroyed. What constructive progress can we reach in this debate with such attempts to caricature opponents as hysterical antiscience obscurantists?

Let me set the record straight. In my first paper, I expressed concerns about the fact that Neel's Yanomami blood samples are apparently stored at Pennsylvania State University at the disposition of HGDP researchers to be processed with new techniques to extract DNA. There is indeed a new ethical issue at stake here, since this genetic material extraction might be conducted without any effort to consult the Yanomami about this new scientific use of the blood of their dead relatives. I therefore recommended that an independent bioethics commission should also investigate the location, legal status, and current use of these samples, and that the Yanomami should be informed about the results of this investigation.

Hill responded that he "believes that the Yanomami should write to the guardians of those samples, requesting that research be initiated with them that could benefit the Yanomami community." I agree with him that negotiations would be an appropriate way of dealing with the situation. However, the responsibility for opening these negotiations should come from the scientists who are now in possession of Yanomami blood samples and may eventually reprocess them. They should contact Yanomami representatives and organizations in Venezuela and Brazil to inform them properly about their research plans and to ask for their points of view about the destiny of these blood samples. My point here, once again, is to defend the Yanomami's right to a decent procedure of informed consent. Whether they eventually ask that the samples be destroyed or whether they overcome their cultural aversion to bodily remains and negotiate some form of compensation for their participation in future research is not up to me to decide.

I am glad that Hill agrees wholeheartedly with me on the necessity of protecting Yanomami blood samples from commercial patents when he states: "Any commercial use of Yanomami genetic material must be approved by them beforehand and must include fair compensation and sharing of profits.

Unauthorized commercial use of Yanomami genes should immediately lead to a lawsuit." Human population genetics studies of the indigenous peoples of Amazonia (among the most studied in the world) were initially based on correlating the frequency of blood markers, which led to findings of a highly academic nature. But times have changed, and recent technical advances in human genome research now permit scientists to study DNA directly, opening the way to commercial uses of genetic materials (Coimbra and Santos 1996:420). My concerns over the possibility of this occurring in the case of the Yanomami's stored blood are thus far from being imaginary, given the considerable number of samples collected by Neel's research team in the 1960s and 1970s and kept in laboratories in the United States (and probably other countries).

As a matter of fact, the commercial circulation of indigenous cell lines apparently takes place without many obstacles, even if it does not often go to the extreme of patenting indigenous genes (which, however, has occurred on several occasions: see Harry 1995; Friedlaender 1996; Cunningham 1998). Such ease reveals the absence of adequate standards regulating their transfer from academic biomedical research circles to the commercial circuit. Alcida Ramos gives a relevant example that recently involved the Karitiana and Surui Indians of Rondônia State in Brazil. These two groups

> were the object of genetic research (unauthorized by the Brazilian Government) by Francis Black, from the Department of Epidemiology and Public Health, Yale University. Black and his team published an article in 1991 in *Human Biology* (Kidd et al. 1991) where they presented their findings among the Karitiana, the Surui and the Mexican Campeche. Candidly as a matter of course, they deposited "for each population five cell lines from unrelated individuals . . . in the National Institute of General Medical Sciences (NIGMS) Human Genetic Cell Repository at the Coriell Institute for Medical Research (Camden, New Jersey) [which were then] publicly available" (1991:778). In April 1996, Coriell Cell Repositories was advertising the sale of Karitiana and Surui DNA samples (Santos and Coimbra 1996:7; *Folha de São Paulo*, June 1, 1997:5–15). (Ramos 2000)

As one can imagine, this episode had widespread negative repercussions in the Brazilian media and public opinion. The Brazilian government's indigenous affairs agency (FUNAI) considered suspending all biomedical research authorizations with indigenous peoples; the Indians filed a formal complaint with the regional office of the federal attorney general; and the Brazilian House of Representatives addressed the issue in 1998 during hearings concerning access to genetic resources (Santos 2002:82–83). Nevertheless, individual cell lines of the Karitiana and Surui are still for sale for seventy-five dollars (DNA samples for fifty dollars), as anybody can check on the HGDP-linked Coriell Cell Repositories Web site (http://locus.umdnj.edu/nigms/cells/humdiv.html, search "Karitiana"). As Santos notes, "Even considering that these funds might aim at maintaining the cell lines and DNA samples," this commercialization "create[s] major discomfort, even more so because health and socioeconomic conditions of the two groups are precarious" (2002:98–99n3).

Let me also give here the example of the Ticuna Indians in the Brazilian state of Amazonas, as described by Hammond:

> Among the collections of the *Alpha Helix*'s 1976 expedition [see Salzano 2000] were samples from the Tikuna (Ticuna), an indigenous people from Brazil's far west (as well as Colombia). Unlike most of the *Alpha Helix* samples, white blood cell lines were established from Tikuna blood by researchers, including former Human Genome Organization (HUGO) head Sir Walter Bodmer of Oxford University and Julia Bodmer of the Imperial Cancer Research Fund (ICRF), both of the UK. Although collected nearly 25 years ago, the cells remain in wide circulation among scientists, travelling the world like few, if any, Tikuna have. Among their adventures, the Tikuna cells have been across Europe and the US, and even shipped back to South America to researchers in Argentina. The cells have been used in research for publications in *Genetics*, the *American Journal of Physical Anthropology*, the *American Journal of Human Genetics*, and others. The Tikuna cells have also been incorporated into a major tool for immunology research, the HLA Diversity Cell Panel. Old stuff? Unlikely, given that, like many *ex situ* plant collections, the cell lines' value seems to appreciate with time. As recently as 1997, Hoffman LaRoche researchers at the company's Roche Molecular Systems division—including the legendary Henry Erlich, one of the creators of polymerase chain reaction (PCR)—were working the cells over and elucidating new information about immunological genetics. The Tikuna are probably unaware of either their important contribution to science or the potential commercial value of their cell lines. They might not even know about their cell lines at all. If they did, would they approve? Is the work done on their cells in accordance with their culture and wishes? There's no way to know for sure until one of the many scientists using Tikuna cells actually takes the trouble to ask them. (Hammond 2000)

As I pointed out in my first paper (also drawing on Hammond 2000), all these facts undoubtedly raise new and fundamental ethical questions that go beyond the issue of obtaining informed consent for blood sampling, such as the population genetics researchers carried out in the 1960s and 1970s. Santos put it well apropos of the Karitiana-Surui samples: "It was considered troubling that blood and DNA samples could be stored, transformed into cell lines and made widely available without explicit individual and community consent for so. There was considerable concern that, while consent may have been given for a particular project, this long-term storage makes it possible to use samples in ways not originally described or intended" (Santos 2002:98–99n3).

The approach to informed consent advocated in the HGDP "Model Ethical Protocol for Collecting DNA Samples" (point IV.C) does not apply to the controversial question of reprocessing old samples,[20] nor does it offer a satisfactory solution for the multiple, circulating uses of new ones: "Samples will be taken to one or more locations to be stored, analyzed, and shared with other researchers from around the world. As part of this last disclosure, the researchers must make clear [in obtaining consent] that the samples may be used for a variety of different projects in the future, including projects that are not currently anticipated."[21]

Supposing that these facts were fully explained, who would be expected to give consent to such a blind agreement for his or her blood DNA to be used in unknown ways, now and in the future, by an unknown number of laboratories around the world? It is obvious in this context that guidelines for negotiating agreements for each stage of research are needed, especially if scientists wish to gain the confidence of indigenous peoples.

As to the possible lawsuit that the Yanomami could file against U.S. institutions that were (and still are) behind past (and present) biomedical research carried out among them without proper informed consent, I want to add some brief comments. In my first paper, I stated that lawsuits could arise from an analysis (preferably by a bioethics commission established to study the case) of the dubious procedures used to gain consent from the Yanomami (among other problems) during Neel's blood collections and Roche's radioiodine experiments. I think that legal actions might also be taken against the extraction of DNA from old blood samples and its present scientific use (not to mention its eventual commercial patenting) that likewise might occur without obtaining any informed or formal agreements with the Yanomami. Thus, instead of accusing me of inducing the Yanomami to pursue "frivolous lawsuits," Hill might consider helping to ensure that a bioethics commission, not only an anthropological debate, will analyze whether these research procedures, past and present, conform to prevailing ethical codes. This would indeed be a great contribution to improving the field practices of biomedical researchers and encouraging them to observe their own professional norms more carefully.

Hill was thoughtful in offering advice that lawsuits should be filed against anyone who threatens Yanomami rights in Brazil. However, he may be happy to learn that quite a number of legal cases have already been initiated by Brazilians to defend the Yanomami. I reported the exemplary juridical proceedings initiated by the Federal Public Ministry and federal judges in the Haximu massacre case. Another judicial case against invasions of Yanomami land by ranchers is currently being pursued in the federal courts, and a lawsuit against illegal tourism in Yanomami territory was recently filed by the attorney general. I must inform Hill that lawsuits on behalf of Indian rights, based on the 1988 Brazilian constitution, are the basic work of the sixth chamber (Indian Communities and Minorities) of the federal attorney general in Brasília, who, being totally independent of the executive branch, fulfills such responsibilities with great competence and courage.[22]

But to end here on a positive note about the relations between biomedical researchers and indigenous people and to make it very clear—if it is still necessary—that I am not advocating any absurd antiscientist position (as Hill seems to suggest), I should point out that, fortunately, socially concerned biomedical researchers do exist. A fine example is the remarkable work of Alexandra de Souza (Souza et al. 1997) on tuberculosis among the Yanomami. Her research was conducted at the request of Brazilian health and indigenist authorities and in close consultation with the Yanomami and local physicians and health professionals. It represented a major step toward increasing awareness of this health calamity and prompting improvements in local-level treatment programs (Fackelman 1998).

As Santos's (2002) analysis demonstrates, the creation of the HGDP project was envisioned as a high-tech molecular biology project for the turn of the twenty-first century; nonetheless, it has remained embedded in an ethical and political philosophy frozen in the 1960s. With its ideological views about vanishing peoples and genetic identity loss, the HGDP has been reluctant to acknowledge the contemporary voices and agency of native peoples. Its ethical parameters were recently revised (1997) under pressure from indigenous organizations and many others. However, its guidelines still lack precision, adequate breadth, and formalization. Even worse, the field practices of most biomedical researchers continue to be a far cry from these norms, no matter how adequate they are.

If biomedical researchers who work among indigenous people want to avoid further rejection or condemnation, they should have the humility to improve their ethical norms in substantial ways and to follow them in field practice with determination. In each and every case, scientists should engage in appropriate procedures for seeking informed consent and negotiating balanced reciprocity with indigenous people. The observance of an improved, fairer, and widely accepted ethical framework for guiding the relationship between researchers and indigenous people must not be seen as a way to thwart research—on the contrary, it is the absence of such guidelines that is becoming an increasing hindrance to it. If the genetic data of indigenous peoples makes them essential for future human genomic research and its benefits for humanity, they should be treated as fully respected social partners, not as natural "populations" for gene mining (Greely 1998:625).

CONCLUSIONS

I wrote at the end of my first paper that anthropologists should avoid collaborating with biomedical researchers when the latter disregard their own ethical norms and dehumanize indigenous people as mere biological "subjects" for research and experimentation. I emphasized that such collaboration represents a serious negation of the foundations of sociocultural anthropology, since its primary commitment is to the "natives' point of view." By this, I mean that ethnographic research should analyze indigenous cultures and societies by using their intellectual categories and models of agency as a point of departure (which does not exclude other data or analytical frameworks). In the ethical domain, this implies that since indigenous peoples are marginalized minorities, anthropologists should support the expression of native political views and promote their individual and collective rights. Hill abruptly labels this an "anthropological phobia against objective assessment of indigenous culture."

Does this kind of irresponsible rhetoric imply that he situates himself outside of sociocultural anthropology and that he recommends replacing it with an ethology of "anthropological populations" (an interesting expression borrowed from Weiss 1976:363)? If so, does this not imply that native (or minority) peoples' cultural and political expressions are insignificant to science and irrelevant to ethics? Or should we instead listen to Hill's earlier, more ecumenical appeal to foster better communication and symmetrical self-appraisals in order for anthropology "to survive as an integrated discipline with multiple approaches and multiple areas of interest"? I definitely prefer this latter, more tolerant approach for our debate. That is exactly why I have tried to make a tangible contribution, based on my personal experiences with the Brazilian Yanomami, toward our collective effort to achieve a more insightful, useful evaluation of the ethical dimensions of conducting biomedical and anthropological research among indigenous peoples.

NOTES

1. In 1993, the *World Development Report* of the World Bank estimated that "women ages 15 to 44 lose more Discounted Health Years of Life (DHYLs) to rape and domestic violence than to breast cancer, cervical cancer, obstructed labor, heart disease, AIDS, respiratory infections, motor vehicle accidents or war." See document posted at http://www.unfpa.org/modules/intercenter/violence/index .htm. See also http://www.hrw.org/wr2k1/women/women2.html.

2. See the report of Representative Marcos Rolim on the case posted at http://www.rolim.com.br/ ASCYANOMAMI.htm.

3. In a letter to *Time* magazine, J. Shapiro (1976), who conducted fieldwork with the Yanomami in Brazil in 1968, wrote: "Now in the light of pop ethology and sociobiology, the Yanomamö are seen not only as 'wild Indians' but as one short step away from a baboon troop. The familiar tendency to look upon other groups of people as being less than fully human than ourselves here masquerades as science. I would like to make clear that the Yanomamö are not the missing link."

4. My final report on the case (September 27, 1993) for the press was published by the Brazilian daily *Folha de São Paulo* on October 3, 1993, and the Venezuelan daily *El Nacional* on October 10–11, 1993 (for an English translation, see Albert 1994). It is posted at http://www.socioambiental.org/ website/epi/yanomami/anexos/haximu.

5. More details on the Haximu massacre and the current legal status of the case can be found in the recent report of Luciano Mariz Maia (2000), a federal district attorney. A summary of this document is posted at the Web site cited in note 4.

6. E-mail of Napoleon Chagnon to CCPY, February 20, 2001: "I read with great interest the excellent article by a group of Brazilian medical experts on the 1968 measles epidemic in Brazil."

7. The deteriorating health situation of the Venezuelan Yanomami in isolated areas along the Brazilian border (outside the zone of the Salesian mission health facilities) has become so grave that the Indians must look for medical help at the health posts run by the Urihi Yanomami Health NGO in Brazil. Data for 2000 indicate that 453 Yanomami from Venezuela received medical treatment in four locations: Auaris, Xitei, Homoxi, and Toototobi (CCPY Bulletin no. 12, April 25, 2001).

8. As one example of the work of indigenist medical personnel in Yanomami territory, the CCPY-MSF expedition involved a forty-five-day trip, walking 350 kilometers in the jungle from the CCPY outpost on the upper Demini (Parawa-ù) in Brazil to give medical assistance to eight Yanomami communities (assisting 550 persons) on the upper Siapa in Venezuela. At the end of the trip, the CCPY-MSF emergency team (conducted by Dr. Cláudio Esteves de Oliveira, who is now president of Urihi Yanomami Health), was airlifted from the region by a Venezuelan Air Force helicopter.

9. Among the Principles of Medical Ethics adopted by the American Medical Association (AMA), we find, for example: "VII. A physician shall recognize a responsibility to participate in activities con-

tributing to an improved community." Posted at http://www.ama-assn.org/ama/pub/category/2512 .html.

10. I began my fieldwork in the Brazilian Amazon during the opening of the northern route of the Transamazonica Highway as part of an assistance project to the Yanomami (Projeto Perimetral Yanoama), organized by the University of Brasília and FUNAI. In those days (1975–76), without any medical program in the area, basic paramedical treatment was a constant part of my activity as a field anthropologist. In the absence of better health care services, anthropologists commonly get involved in this kind of improvised paramedical activities.

11. See ABA's code of ethics, posted at http://www.unicamp.br/aba/secretaria/03_etica.htm.

12. Resolution 304/2000 (specific to indigenous communities) is posted at http://www.ufrgs.br/ HCPA/gppg/res304.htm. Resolution 196/96 (which is more general) is posted at http://www.ufrgs .br/HCPA/gppg/res19696.htm. FUNAI Normative Instruction No. 01/95PRESI is posted at http:// www.ufrgs.br/HCPA/gppg/funai.htm.

13. See a report on this seminar organized in conjunction with the Socio-Environmental Institute, posted at http://www.socioambiental.org/website/noticias/indios/20001127.html.

14. See the Declaration of Helsinki I posted at http://www.irb-irc.com/resources/helsinki.html.

15. Hill unfairly distorts my position on this issue by claiming that I see "little value in Roche's study of goiter and insists that such research could not foreseeably benefit the Yanomami." As any reader of my first paper can verify, I never wrote such a thing.

16. The results are posted at http://tis.eh.doe.gov/ohre/roadmap/achre/chap12_4.html.

17. The Helsinki VI Declaration is posted in Spanish at http://www.ufrgs.br/HCPA/gppg/helsin6 .htm. This same Web site has a good link to a list of "Guidelines, Norms, and Laws in Health Research": http://www.ufrgs.br/HCPA/gppg/diraber.htm.

18. See also Lindee (2001b:274): "I wondered, too, if Neel might have sought the resources and the personnel to make possible a comprehensive and well-coordinated vaccination program instead of a haphazard stopgap program as an add-on to a project focused on other, more important things like blood and data collection."

19. See the HGDP homepage at http://www.stanford.edu/group/morrinst/hgdp/faq.html#Q1

20. Posted at http://www.stanford.edu/group/morrinst/hgdp/protocol.html#Q4.

21. The reference only refers with no precision to a National Institutes of Health (NIH) and Centers for Disease Control and Prevention (CDC) Working Group on Regulations for the Protection of Human Subjects, *Informed Consent for Genetic Research on Stored Tissue Samples* (1995).

22. See the attorney general's Web site at http://www2.prdf.mpf.gov.br/sextacamara/biblioteca/ jurisprudencia/index.html.

························

SOME FINAL THOUGHTS ON WHAT SEPARATES AND UNITES US

RAYMOND HAMES

When I began this project I had scant hope that there would be much that we could agree upon in relation to the ethical issues highlighted in Tierney's work and their implications for anthropological practice. Many issues still powerfully divide us. Nevertheless, I think we all agree that informed consent must be rethought, NGOs and religious missions can be a powerful force for defending the interests of indigenous peoples, ethnographers should attempt to counter the misuse of their reporting by those who would harm the people we study, and in our critiques of one another we ought to focus our analysis on concepts, theo-

KEY ACCUSATIONS AND ISSUES
(see also pp. 317–41)

Should Chagnon have responded better to the media's misuse of his work? Those who accuse Chagnon of not addressing negative images of the Yanomamö ignore how Chagnon has successfully used his media clout to call attention to the plight of the Yanomamö. But Hames does criticize Chagnon's "overall mean-spirited view" of missionaries and NGOs trying to help the Yanomamö as expressed in an interview in the Brazilian magazine *Veja.* (see pages 236–37)

Looking at the broad picture, how would you assess the value of Darkness in El Dorado? Tierney's book forced anthropologists to be more aware of their conduct as ethnographers, but the book itself is a fundamentally flawed work. (see page 240)

Did Chagnon unethically stimulate warfare among the Yanomami, especially through his style of gift giving? There is no convincing evidence that Chagnon's distribution of goods had an impact on Yanomamö patterns of violence. (see page 243)

QUESTIONS TO CONSIDER

Should the AAA, as Hames asks, investigate itself for its complicity in ignoring Chagnon's reputed ethical violations prior to the publication of Tierney's book?

Are Yanomami better off or worse off for having had Chagnon study among and write about them?

ries, and facts and not the motivations behind them. Most important, I think it clear that we all believe that the governments of Brazil and Venezuela need to take steps to ensure Yanomamö control of their traditional lands, assist them in keeping undocumented visitors and colonists out, and render basic medical care to combat the epidemics that deplete their numbers. To a large extent, the situation in Venezuela is much better than that in Brazil. In Venezuela the government has given the Yanomamö some degree of formal control over their land, colonists are unable to penetrate the area, and medical care is available near missions. However, much needs to be done in all three areas. To some extent, the issues that divide us revolve around empirical issues that have ethical implications: What are the political consequences of ethnographic reporting? And how do NGOs use ethnographic images to enhance their ability to assist native peoples in their legitimate struggle for self-determination? There are also some ethical issues that we have not resolved, such as how should we respond to the press's frequently distorted and sensationalistic accounts of our research? There is also the problem of informed consent. I turn to these issues in my final contribution.

THE IMPACT OF ETHNOGRAPHIC REPORTING

An important point I wish to reiterate is that a focus on whether ethnographic reportage may affect policy decisions of national governments in relation to indigenous peoples steers us away from the fundamental causes of mistreatment of native peoples. I think it is clear to all of us that states have committed human rights violations on their native peoples on a par with the terrible violations inflicted in World War II and that these violations continue to the present day. What is happening today with the Yanomamö is but a microcosm of the record of state dealings with ethnic groups lying within their internationally recognized borders. What truly concerns me is that the powerful role played by Venezuelan and Brazilian political and economic interests as primary causes of the current Yanomamö crisis is not addressed.

I do not believe that Martins fully appreciates my position on NGOs. Whether or not my observations about the motivations behind how NGOs portray the tribal people they dedicate themselves to helping is "offensive," as Martins claims, is beside the point. The issue is whether what I have said is correct, incorrect, or somewhere in between. So long as we attempt to falsely portray native peoples as if they were perfect, according to our system of cultural values, as a rationale to assist them in their legitimate struggles to achieve protection and control of their land, we lose credibility as objective analysts. I believe this to be our greatest strength as ethnographers. We are the expert witnesses, so to speak, for the defense of native peoples in the court of public opinion.

To predicate assistance to native peoples on whether or not they emulate our cultural standards is chauvinistic. I believe that native peoples have many cultural values and practices that are worthy of emulation, and one ought to emphasize them in order to encourage support for their legitimate political goals. Nevertheless, I believe that the best and most defensible argument to make on behalf of native peoples such as the Yanomamö is that they have an a priori and legitimate claim to the land on which they have been living for who knows how long. Their land is not terra nullis, open for colonization. This being said, it is clear that the world of politics is quite different from the world of science. Over the short term perhaps, one can acquire more support and sympathy for the Yanomamö by saying they are noble savages. But when this image is found to be misleading, those advocating for the Yanomamö will lose credibility in the long run.

Albert points out an apparent contradiction in my denial that ethnographic reporting makes much of a difference and Chagnon's deletion of the subtitle "The Fierce People" from his ethnography and his decision to temporarily cease publication on infanticide. I pointed this out to show that Chagnon was sensitive to the misuse of his research on the Yanomamö. However, this change was driven more by a concern about accuracy and to avoid confusion. He thought too often people "might get the impression that being 'fierce' is incompatible with having other sentiments or personal characteristics like compassion, fairness, valor, etc." (Chagnon 1992a:xii). Even in his opening chapter he notes that the Yanomamö "are simultaneously peacemakers and valiant warriors." However, I still contend that continuing or not to publish on infanticide or refer to the Yanomamö as the fierce people makes little difference in the political arena. In the case of infanticide, Chagnon clearly believes it does occur, and he did not delete any information on infanticide in the fourth or fifth editions. Any Venezuelan legislator who bothered to read Chagnon's work would discover that Chagnon believes the Yanomamö commit infanticide even though he never saw it happen. Furthermore, it is well documented by others who have written on the Yanomamö (see, for example Eguillor Garcia [1984:50], an ethnographic monograph written by a Salesian nun). As I mentioned at the beginning, fundamental political, social, and economic practices by states are at the root of indigenous problems.

Martins in her second-round contribution cites a specific example of a highly visible and allegedly unflattering image of the Yanomamö created by Chagnon. In the much-discussed *Veja* interview (entitled "Indians Are Also People"), she notes that "When asked in *Veja* to define the 'real Indians,' Chagnon said, 'The real Indians get dirty, smell bad, use drugs, belch after they eat, covet and sometimes steal each other's women, fornicate and make war.'" This quote is accurate. However, in the next sentence after that quote she cites, Chagnon states: "They are normal human beings. And that is sufficient reason for them to merit care and attention." This tactic of partial quotation mirrors a technique used by Tierney. The context of the statement and most of the interview was Chagnon's observation that some NGOs and missionaries characterized the Yanomamö as "angelic beings without faults." His goal was to simply state that the Yanomamö and other native peoples are human beings and deserve our support and sympathy. He was concerned that false portrayals could harm native peoples when later they are discovered to be just like us. The major fault I find in the *Veja* interview is the overall mean-spirited view that Chagnon presents of missionaries and NGOs. While much of what he says is accurate, it is not sufficiently balanced by the positive activities of those seeking to help the Yanomamö.

However, I agree with Martins that we should respond to sensationalistic, distorted, or false characterizations of our work. This can be a difficult task, especially when one may be completely ignorant of how a foreign press is exploiting one's work. It think it would be extremely useful if our fellow anthropologists would inform us of this fact and, if necessary, help us in contacting editors, reporters, and others so we could respond.

What is completely ignored by those who criticize Chagnon's alleged lack of interest in what the press has to say about the Yanomamö is the way in which he has utilized the press to portray the plight of the Yanomamö. Albert faults him for not using his considerable public relations clout to assist the Yanomamö. This is untrue. To cite one example, his knowledge and support were critical to

Spencer Reiss's (1990) article in *Newsweek*, entitled "The Last Days of Eden" (also the subtitle of Chagnon's recent ethnography [1992b] aimed at a general audience). In that report, the world learns of the illegal entry of gold miners into the Yanomamö area and subsequent deaths from malaria and influenza, killings by miners, and the ill-conceived plan by the Brazilian government to partition Yanomamö lands. The article concludes that the Yanomamö need "protection from disease and guaranteed land right" to allow them to decide how they want to integrate themselves into the national life of Brazil and Venezuela. Even more interesting is this quote from Chagnon: "To simply go out and study a people to advance a theory is tantamount to professional irresponsibility (Reiss 1990:49). This statement is immediately followed by a parenthesis by Reiss that notes that Chagnon's description of Yanomamö warfare is being used by some as a rationale for pacifying the Yanomamö. How ironic.

Even more to the point is the fact that Chagnon devotes much of the preface and final chapter of his standard ethnography (Chagnon, 1992a) to detailing the serious problems the Yanomamö face from the introduction of epidemics, massacres by gold miners, Brazilian attempts to separate Yanomamö land in a divide and conquer scheme, and the effects of concentration around missions. Given the enormous readership of his ethnography, my best guess is that his writings have done more to reach the educated public about the serious problems faced by the Yanomamö than those by any other single individual or organization. Again, this is unacknowledged by his critics. Instead, they tend to dwell on some of the details of his analysis (e.g., Salamone's edited volume [1997] on what responsibility Salesian missionaries have in this process). I do not mean to suggest that Chagnon should be immune to this criticism, but the critical point is that he is sending a widely disseminated message that the current crisis among the Yanomamö is not of their making and we must take action to alleviate it.

NONGOVERNMENTAL ORGANIZATIONS (NGOS)

I believe that Martins completely misstates my position regarding NGOs when she says that I believe "their primary concern is power and money." To refresh everyone's memory, here is what I said in the first round: "To attract contributors to the cause of protecting the rights of indigenous peoples, ethnic groups must be somehow portrayed as deserving of protection by documenting wrongs done to them and/or demonstrating them as noble people. . . . I would like to make it clear that I believe that NGOs do vital work that should be supported because they make an important positive difference in the lives of exploited indigenous peoples."

What I mean is that the primary goal of NGOs such as Cultural Survival and Survival International, or the Brazilian CCPY for that matter, is to protect the interests of exploited native peoples. They must raise money to underwrite their publications, lobbying, and direct aid projects. Their work should be supported. The only place where we differ significantly is how I believe native peoples should be portrayed in order to gain funds to help them.

Martins also claims that I provided only one example of an NGO (Cultural Survival) that uses the noble savage image to represent the Yanomamö. I'll give another example, this time from Survival International. In their criticism of Chagnon's portrayal of the Yanomamö, they make the following statement: "The Yanomami are in fact a generally peaceable people who have suffered enormous violence at the hands of outsiders" (Nuñez 2000). The first part of the statement is demonstrably false while the second part is absolutely true. Herein lies the problem as I see it: if you are going to effectively argue for the legitimate rights of native peoples, you cannot mix truth with lies. If an opponent can show the first part of the statement to be false, he can claim that the second part is either false or irrelevant because the first part acts as a premise for the second.

SOCIOBIOLOGY

Turner deals with the role of sociobiological theory as key to Chagnon's interpretation of Yanomamö culture and social organization. Anyone who has basic knowledge of the origins of sociobiology in anthropology will quickly realize that Turner's attempt to show a connection between Neel's allegedly eugenic ideas and Chagnon's analysis of the Yanomamö to be far-fetched. Turner makes the following claim about the importance of the Yanomamö in the context of sociobiological theory: "'Fierceness' and the high level of violent conflict with which it is putatively associated are for Chagnon and like-minded sociobiologists the primary indexes of the evolutionary priority of the Yanomami as an earlier, and supposedly therefore more violent, phase of the development of human society."

I don't know of any "sociobiologists" who regard the Yanomamö as any more or less representative of an "earlier, and supposedly therefore more violent, phase of the development of human society" than any other relatively isolated indigenous society. Some sociobiologists are interested in indigenous populations because they live under social and technological conditions that more closely resemble humanity for most of its history as a species than conditions found in urban population centers. Consequently, groups studied by sociobiologists such as Hill in his work on the Ache and Hiwi, Borgerhoff Mulder in his work on the Kipsigis, or my recent collaboration with Draper on the !Kung San (aka "the harmless people") have equal status with the Yanomamö as representatives of some of the early social conditions of humanity. The claim that the Yanomamö are more representative of "early" humanity than any other relatively uncontacted group is simply false. Each Yanomamö ethnolinguistic group (e.g., Sánema, Ninam, Xiliana, etc.) is simply data points that represent the range of variation found in the context of all indigenous populations studied by anthropologists, and none are specially privileged to somehow represent the archetype of traditional peoples.

I do agree with Turner that certain evolutionary psychologists tend to use the Yanomamö as standard examples of life in the Paleolithic, and this is misleading. They are ignorant of the variation that exists within Yanomamö culture and how it may conflict with their generalizations about life in the Paleolithic. I guess this may be true for two reasons: Chagnon's work is widely known as a consequence of its quality and accessibility, and evolutionary psychologists are not anthropologists and therefore are unfamiliar with cultural diversity.

Nevertheless, I believe that Turner is as guilty as the evolutionary psychologists he criticizes for overemphasizing the importance of the Yanomamö to sociobiological theory when in Round Two he states: "Most of the critics of Chagnon's fixation on 'fierceness' have had little idea of this integral connection of 'fierceness' as a Yanomami trait, and the deep structure of sociobiological-selectionist theory. The association is all the more important as the Yanomami continue to serve as virtually the sole data on a human society that seems to support the theory."

As to the importance of the Yanomamö to sociobiology theory and the relationship between cultural and reproductive success, here is something that I posted on the evolutionary psychology mailing list (September 24, 2001):

> Chagnon's work on the relationship between combat killing and reproductive success is simply part of the larger research by behavioral ecologists on the relationship between cultural success and fitness. It is merely one of the TWENTY-ODD studies done that show that those who are successful culturally tend to have higher than average reproductive success. It is important to realize that what constitutes cultural success varies from society to society. For example, Kim Hill and associates show for the Ache that good hunters have higher RS than poor hunters and Borgerhoff Mulder shows that Kipsigis who have large herds have higher RS than those who have small herds. I would argue that if Chagnon's data were shown to be flawed there would be little damage to the research enterprise of Darwinian anthropologists except among those who strangely believe that the Yanomamö research is somehow central. It is not: the Yanomamö are simply one case.

Finally, I would like to clear up a common misconception regarding Chagnon's beliefs about the causes of Yanomamö warfare. In his second round contribution Turner states, "The importance of 'fierceness' in Chagnon's account of the Yanomami was directly connected with his thesis that Yanomami warfare was primarily motivated by male conflicts over women, which in turn was tied to the thesis that competition among males for possession of female breeding partners, and thus ultimately for greater reproductive success, was the central principle of Yanomami social organization."

In numerous places Chagnon argues that disputes frequently start with conflicts over women (e.g., failure to give a woman promised in marriage) but that raids are overwhelmingly motivated by revenge and that the primary goal of a raid is to kill an enemy and not to abduct a woman. R. Brian Ferguson, Chagnon's most notable scientific critic, documents the misconception that competition over women is the major cause of ongoing Yanomamö conflict held by Turner and others in some detail (Ferguson 2001).

I fully agree with Turner that "disagreement with the claims of sociobiology (including skepticism about Neel's and Chagnon's genetic reductionism) is, however, not the same thing as hostility to science.". . . . Chagnon himself tends to refer to his critics as left-wingers and Marxists (Wong 2001). I believe this sort of name calling to be both counterproductive and irrelevant. At the same time, I think it is true that Tierney is antiscience, and many of Chagnon's critics believe that politics and science are inseparable (e.g., Schepher-Hughes 1995). We need to separate what we believe are the motives of critics from their analyses. To conflate the two is to commit the genetic fallacy. The issue, as I have noted, is whether or not the critics are correct. To refer to someone as "antiscience" or "Marxist" is a diversionary tactic designed to dismiss their claims. Finally, I am greatly concerned with criticism through demonization, a tactic used by Tierney and some of his supporters. One simply claims that the theoretical ideas or empirical findings in another's work are inherently evil or that the findings can be used by evil people for immoral ends.

INFORMED CONSENT

Finally, I think it is clear that we all agree that the issue of informed consent must be rethought. The protocols we are expected to follow, at least in North America, are based on a set of cultural assumptions that are not completely applicable to indigenous populations. We assume that adults are free agents, able to agree or not to agree to participate as subjects in research on a take-it-or-leave-it basis. The situation in corporate indigenous communities encapsulated in a state system is different and much more complex. We need to negotiate our research according to foreign state requirements and then begin a new set of negotiations with corporate indigenous councils and local leaders at the community level. Whether it is social or biomedical research, we need to explain the risks and benefits of our investigations and faithfully live up to our promises. These days, I find there is more interest by the Yanomamö in how the research might benefit me and them. This negotiation not infrequently leads to requirements that we study something they feel is valuable through some form of collaboration. Now, more than ever, native peoples have their own research priorities. And sometimes our research hinges on the expectation that we engage in some sort of bureaucratic or political action on behalf of those we study. The only value I perceive in *Darkness in El Dorado* is that it forces us to become more aware of the consequences of our conduct as ethnographers. My main regret, however, is that this fundamentally flawed work was the impetus for our discussion.

A SHORT REFLECTION AND COMMENTARY
ON THE AAA FINAL REPORT OF THE
EL DORADO TASK FORCE

Obviously, I cannot do justice to such a complex and large report in the space allotted. Consequently, I restrict my comments to issues of why the association decided to investigate Chagnon when the evidence for his malfeasance had existed for decades, why I was invited to participate as a Task Force member and why I subsequently resigned, and what role Chagnon's distribution of trade goods may have played in Yanomamö warfare.

There is deep irony in the creation of the El Dorado Task Force. Chagnon's *Yanomamö, The Fierce People* (now simply *Yanomamö*) was first published in 1968. Today it is in its fifth edition, and it has sold more copies than any other anthropological monograph. In addition, Chagnon's award-winning ethnographic films with Timothy Asch are among the most widely viewed in college classrooms. Before the publication of Tierney's *Darkness in El Dorado*, there were no complaints about Chagnon's ethical conduct in the field, even though much of what Tierney characterizes as unethical behavior is drawn directly from Chagnon's publications and films. Of course, Sponsel (e.g., 1998) and others claimed that Chagnon's exaggerations of Yanomamö aggression and violence were being used against them by powerful national forces. But this is quite different from any claim of unethical behavior in the field. In any event, the AAA had plenty of evidence to launch its own investigation into ethical misconduct by Chagnon decades before Tierney's 2000 publication, but no one seemed to notice. Why did they not investigate him? Even Chagnon's most dedicated adversaries, Leslie Sponsel and Terry Turner, never petitioned the association for such an investigation into unethical fieldwork before Tierney's work.

The answer, perhaps, lies in the fact that the association was embarrassed by the furor created by *Darkness*, especially by the claim that James Neel had deliberately started a deadly epidemic of measles out of scientific curiosity. Even though that monstrous claim was quickly and expertly refuted, and further investigations by experts and eyewitnesses into Tierney's work showed clear patterns of distortion, deception, half-truths, and poorly founded conclusions, the association went ahead with the formation of the task force. One would hope that any investigation would be based on a credible indictment, but much of what Tierney claims is not credible. And again, if much of what Tierney's alleges is based on Chagnon's publications why did it take an outsider to draw the association's attention to it? By not speaking out against Chagnon's methods, is it not reasonable to conclude that the association thought them unremarkable and disreputable? If true, why did the association not investigate itself?

The final report of the Task Force noted my late addition and abrupt resignation. I would like to detail the circumstances of my selection and resignation. Before I was asked to become a member, two other behavioral ecologists were asked to participate in order to provide some sort of theoretical balance by having a behavioral ecologist on the panel. The initial two declined the invitation. When I was asked, my initial reaction was to decline for two reasons. First, I have collaborated extensively over the years with Chagnon and had planned to continue my collaboration. Therefore, my participation would constitute an apparent conflict of interest. Second, a Task Force should not require any sort of balancing of theoretical perspectives. This second issue requires some elaboration, and the first should be self-evident. I strongly believe that regardless of our theoretical persuasions, we all follow the same ethical guidelines established by the association and our local IRB's (Institutional Review Boards). A behavioral ecologist does not operate under different ethical guidelines than a postmodernist or cultural materialist. Since our ethical guidelines do not make distinctions about ethical conduct based on theoretical perspective, my services would not be needed for any "balancing." I told President Lamphere that the only rationale for adding a new member would be to have someone who had worked with the Yanomamö. To this end, I suggested John Peters: he has a deep knowledge of the Yanomamö (see Peters 1998; and Early and Peters 2000) and has no connection to Chagnon or to any of the others such as Turner or Sponsel who were energetically campaigning against Chagnon. My suggestion was not heeded. Consequently, I agreed to become a member to provide needed expertise on the Yanomamö.

One issue the Task Force did not investigate was whether Chagnon "exacerbated violence among the Yanomami through his practices of distributing gifts" (American Anthropological Association 2002, 1:30). I now briefly present my views on this issue. It is well documented (e.g., Valero 1984) that before regular contact by missionaries, government officials, and ethnographers that the Yanomamö were desperate to acquire metal goods of all sorts, axes and machetes in particular. They sometimes raided isolated criollo settlements or other Yanomamö to acquire them. So, Ferguson is correct: in some instances the Yanomamö have been motivated to raid to gain trade goods. In the late 1950s, with the establishment of Protestant and Catholic missions on the Orinoco, a regular flow of metal goods entered the area. As the demand for heavy cutting tools began to become satisfied, desires for aluminum pots, fishing tackle, cotton cloth, and other nonlocal goods increased. Ferguson (1995) develops a thesis that differential access to trade goods by Yanomamö villages led to a situation whereby those who were well situated to trade goods sources attempted to control access, and those who were poorly situated attempted to gain greater access through raiding or the establishment of trading links. This reasonable model shares similarities with the one developed by Secoy (1953) for the United States plains, where trade in guns and horses motivated Native American groups to employ warfare to contest for access to French and Spanish traders. The major way in which Ferguson believes Chagnon is implicated in increases in warfare among the Yanomamö is through his episodic and intense distribution of trade goods. Near the end of a field season in particular villages, Chagnon would sometimes distribute a large cache of trade goods at once. Ferguson claims that this created periodic unequal concentrations of goods in recipient villages, which led to some villages being trade goods poor and others trade goods rich. The have-nots sought to acquire these goods through violence, while the haves attempted to deter the have-nots from gaining access to anthropologists and missionaries.

Both alone and in the company of Chagnon, I have made distributions of goods near the end of a field season, and the immediate reaction of the Yanomamö when they acquire such goods is instructive. As soon as distributions are made, most of the men who are recipients either immediately depart to trade those goods to neighboring villages or make plans to do so in the next few days. Some may even give goods to covillagers who received little from us. So the immediate consequence of payment of trade goods is intervillage trade. They trade these Western goods for traditional items such as hunting dogs, hallucinogenic drugs, cotton, and hammocks. If the distribution of trade goods by ethnographers and others immediately leads to trade, then one would have to conclude that the motivation to attack a neighbor to attain these goods would be sharply diminished.

In the short space allotted I cannot produce a full critique of Ferguson's hypothesis or adequately answer the El Dorado Task Force's charge of evaluating the consequences of Chagnon's distribution of trade goods. As far as I know, no other Yanomamö ethnographer views Ferguson's theory favorably (see Hames 2001a for a list of those ethnographers). Instead of appealing to authority, however, one should read the work of Peters on this issue. Peters (1998: 207–16) uses ethnohistorical and historical data to specifically test Ferguson's theory of Yanomamö warfare. He presents data on the causes of raids from 1959 to 1996 and concludes: "The history of the Xiliana since the time of contact gives no evidence that the acquisition of steel goods was the primary purpose of warfare" (216). This does not mean that the Yanomamö have never raided for trade goods. Peters states that trade goods acquisition was not a "primary" cause of warfare. I would state this even more strongly by claiming that it was only rarely a cause of warfare and was largely restricted to periods when Yanomamö villages were just beginning to acquire steel cutting tools. Those who have studied Yanomamö warfare consistently note that it revolves around a cycle of revenge (e.g., Chagnon 1988; Lizot 1977; Ales 1984). I conclude by stating that there is no convincing evidence that Chagnon's distribution of trade goods had any effect on Yanomamö patterns of warfare.

....

SOME FINAL THOUGHTS ON THE ETHICAL IMPLICATIONS OF *DARKNESS IN EL DORADO*

KIM HILL

The most important consensus to emerge from this interchange is the agreement that the suffering of the Yanomamö and other indigenous peoples is the most important focal point for turning discussion of the Tierney book into a use-

KEY ACCUSATIONS AND ISSUES
(see also pp. 317–41)

To what degree did the Neel expedition violate reasonable standards of informed consent? Although Neel's collection of blood samples was not conducted under today's guidelines for informed consent, it did allow Neel to realize that the Yanomamö had no antibodies to measles and thus motivated him to acquire a vaccine for the Yanomamö to fend off any future measles epidemics (which in fact did occur). Neel's early blood samples allowed him to take steps that saved many Yanomami lives. (see page 246)

To what degree should Neel have assumed responsibility during his fieldwork for dealing with medical problems that were imperfectly dealt with by the national governments of Venezuela and Brazil? Common sense suggests researchers cannot be held responsible for the failings of national governments. (see page 245)

Was Chagnon unfairly restricted from continuing his long-term fieldwork among the Yanomami? Chagnon's enemies unfairly restricted his access to the Yanomamö because they were displeased with his research questions and results. (see page 250)

Looking at the broad picture, how would you assess the value of Darkness in El Dorado*?* There is a blatant antiscience attitude in the book that explains the negative reaction of many readers. (see page 253)

QUESTIONS TO CONSIDER

Neel made only limited efforts to gain informed consent for his research. But the blood samples he collected prior to 1968 led him to bring measles vaccine on his 1968 expedition. Did this positive result absolve Neel of failing to properly follow informed consent guidelines?

Hill stresses that Yanomami suffering today is mostly the result of a larger historical trend in which nation-states mistreat their ethnic minorities. Is it the anthropologist's responsibility to try to correct such mistreatment? What should indigenous groups such as the Yanomami expect of anthropologists?

ful exercise. Anthropologists and those we try to reach with our writings need to be aware that the vast majority of Native Americans were driven to extinction during colonial conquest and that this process did not end hundreds of years ago—it is ongoing. Indeed, as Peters points out in a recent book, data on Brazilian Indians show that 36 percent of all indigenous groups that were contacted around or after 1900 were already extinct by the late 1950s (note Ribeiro 1967). Indigenous peoples are plagued by poor health and poverty, and programs in these two areas, along with education, land rights, and political protection are the keys to their survival.

THE ROLE OF THE STATE

I join Albert in his support for Yanomamö land rights and the rejection of any "readjustment" of the Yanomamö boundaries by Brazilian politicians with "reformist" ideas about indigenous territories. Brazil does not need indigenous lands to solve its own problems of poverty, and it is not in Brazil's interests to continue an immoral conquest that began five centuries ago by further reducing indigenous land holdings. Instead the Brazilian people need education and technological development to make more effective use of the land that has already been expropriated from prior indigenous peoples through extermination and slavery. If Brazil cannot figure out how to raise the standard of living of its poor with two million square kilometers of Amazonian forest, it will not solve those problems with four million square kilometers of forest. And of course the same is true for all other Latin American countries: there is no justification whatsoever for further land expropriation from native inhabitants, and it must be stopped now and forever.

Albert focuses on pragmatic steps that lead to a reduction of indigenous suffering. I wholeheartedly support that approach, though he and I don't always agree on the details. Albert suggests that there are still three issues of biomedical ethics that should be investigated here: (1) possible experimentation during vaccinations without immunoglobulin, (2) inadequate training and planning to cope with the epidemic, and (3) failure to obtain informed consent while collecting biological samples. I believe, however, that looking at the present and future situation is likely to help native peoples more than reexamining the past. I agree that the vaccinations without immunoglobulin should be investigated if this will bring closure to the issue, though I am fairly certain that the procedure was an accidental result of packing vaccines and immunoglobulin separately (the explanation given by those familiar with the situation). The issue of inadequate planning of the vaccination program really concerns the appropriate balance of help versus research that should be required by visiting researchers. Should Neel have assumed full responsibility for counteracting the measles epidemic just because he was informed about it and was planning to be in the area? I don't think this issue can be settled by an investigation.

Common sense suggests that researchers cannot be held responsible for doing the job of governments. Neel did what he felt he could, and that was a lot more than any other anthropologist, missionary group, or government agency working in the upper Orinoco did at the time. In this light it is important to remember that Neel also shipped a large supply of measles vaccine in 1967 to Brazilian missionaries who never administered it, because the Brazilian government denied them permission to do so (Headland n.d.). If someone is to be investigated, should it be Neel or the Brazilian government? Likewise, Albert suggests there should be a fuller investigation of the issue of informed consent while collecting 1968 biological samples? I doubt that an investigation of that specific event would be useful. The blood samples collected by the first Yanomamö expedition clearly were not collected under *today's* guidelines of informed consent although the blood collection allowed Neel to discover that the Yanomamö had no antibodies to measles and thus motivated him to acquire and deliver the measles vaccine that saved many lives. It is important to note that Neel began plans for vaccination before hearing that an actual epidemic had started, and he did this because of information that he obtained through systematic blood sampling.

INFORMED CONSENT

Although investigation may uncover very little new information about this past event, it would indeed be useful to have more discussion about what sufficiently "informed" consent should consist of in the present and future given that the Yanomamö do not have an advanced education in molecular biology and medicine that might be required for a complete understanding of the significance and utility of research that could be conducted among them. On other biomedical ethics issues I agree with Albert. He seems to mistakenly suggest that my position is that informed consent was not required for the radioiodine studies conducted by Roche because the Yanomamö couldn't fully understand the research. I do not hold that position. Instead I believe that informed consent is and was required for all experimentation carried out on indigenous populations. This is true of Roche's iodine tracer studies, although they posed little hazard to the study population and had the potential of benefiting the Yanomamö (El Nacional 2000a, 2000b, Nuñez 2000.).

But I think that it would be useful to consider the levels of information required in order to label consent as "informed." I suggest that a perfectly informed opinion about the implications and significance of any particular research project requires one to be a specialist in that research area—something unrealistic for Yanomamö or even American populations. Instead, "informed consent" should include a complete understanding of the potential risks of a research protocol and a more general understanding of the purpose of the research (and this is the gray area that I think needs to be carefully considered). I don't believe that the Yanomamö have a full understanding of the implications of any of the anthropological or medical research conducted among them, but I do think that the general research goals can be adequately explained to them and that perhaps knowing that is sufficient for "informed" consent.

Finally, I also agree fully with Albert's reformulation of my original suggestion that when research is not designed to directly help a native population, they should know that fact and should be expected to negotiate the terms of the research accordingly. It is logical and wise that indigenous populations request technical and material assistance from the same scientists who carry out such research in payment for their collaboration. The only departure between Albert and me on this point is whether the natives have more to gain by adopting a friendly stance of seeking allies or an adversarial stance of threatening lawsuits when negotiating with biomedical researchers.

I also want to join Martins in a call for more effective education of native peoples. It is not appropriate that we as a "panel of experts" debate the pros and cons of specific types of research on indigenous people for years into the future. Instead, the native populations themselves must receive an education that allows them to assess the trade-offs inherent in any research protocol and allows *them* to determine whether they think there are potential long-term benefits or risks associated with any research plan. This is indeed a tall order, but we must begin somewhere. Indigenous peoples cannot remain at the mercy of outsiders (with their own agendas) who attempt to sway them one way or another on a given scientific program. I believe that the Human Genome Project would be a great place to start this process, because it has many implications for native peoples concerning both their health and their history and relationships to other native groups and because native DNA is currently held by many scientists around the world. This will require a basic education far beyond anything currently available for any South American indigenous population (or even most peasant populations in Latin America).

I agree with Martins's suggestion that I should be careful not to label the education of native peoples "coaching." But unfortunately it remains coaching as long as native populations hear only one side of every issue and are given incomplete information, and as long as some ideologues remain committed to obstructing indigenous access to all points of view in the modern world. Native peoples are "coached" when words are placed in their mouths that they repeat without a full understanding of their significance or implications. Sadly, there are examples of this in many recent debates concerning indigenous issues in South America. And ironically this process of ideological persuasion by incomplete information and deception now practiced by some anthropologists is directly analogous to methods that have been denounced by anthropologists when practiced by some missionaries (religious conversion based on deceit or incomplete information).

NONGOVERNMENTAL ORGANIZATIONS (NGOS)

Both Martins and Albert mention the good work of NGOs in the indigenous rights struggles of South America, and Martins suggests that criticism of such groups is "offensive." I agree that many NGOs do a great job and serve an important function in countries where governments have ignored indigenous needs and human rights. I am very sorry that some criticism may indeed be unfair to many people who have sacrificed for worthy causes. But no institutional system can be placed above criticism.

Modern indigenous rights and development NGOs are a mixed bag that unfortunately does not always serve the interests of native groups. We must criticize this system if it is ever to improve. Recent analyses of NGOs in Africa has suggested that some of these groups may intentionally exacerbate and exaggerate conditions of hunger to generate public economic support for their famine relief organizations. We cannot be naive about the fact that many NGOs have paid staff and that those people might sometimes show more concern for their careers than for the targets of their programs. We should not forget, for example, that a recent head of UNICEF resigned in disgrace for embezzling funds despite an obscene yearly salary paid to him so that he could oversee programs for the needy children of the world.

NGOs that concern themselves with indigenous peoples' causes come in two basic flavors: those that channel technical advice and help programs (educational, health, economic) to indigenous populations and those that claim representational authority for indigenous populations. I believe that the first type of NGOs should be supported unconditionally as long as the funds and help they claim to provide are actually delivered to native peoples. The second group is more problematic. They sometimes contain foreign nationals (especially expatriate failed anthropologists) or nonindigenous advisers who set the agenda for a collection of indigenous puppet leaders. This, ironically, is the same colonial model that most anthropologists have criticized when practiced at the national level during western colonialism. Puppet leaders can be cultivated from native groups as easily as they are cultivated in colonized nations. In some cases the "indigenous leaders" showcased by these NGOs are highly acculturated, city-raised opportunists who do not represent in any way the views of the native populations among whom they claim membership.

Despite agreements on the foregoing issues, I believe there is also an ethical issue raised by this book that concerns the practice of anthropology in recent years and how we want to proceed in the future. This is the ethical issue concerning legitimate tactics of academic debate. Should anthropologists condone theoretical censorship and oppression and professional behaviors designed to silence those who hold unpopular theoretical views?

THE PROBLEMATIC ACCURACY
OF TIERNEY'S BOOK

There remains a debate about the truthfulness of this book that has dual ethical implications, which I pointed out in the first two rounds of discussion. First, if the book is full of distortions, then we are morally bound to point that out. As Turner says, "Ethically, one is obliged to speak out when one possesses relevant knowledge that an act or statement is an abuse or misuse of the truth." Second, if the book is full of misrepresentations, there is an ethical issue concerning why Neel and Chagnon were targets of this untruthful piece of work. This is related to the disturbing ethical question of why some anthropologists have attempted to stop Chagnon from carrying out research for many years (and long before any Chagnon association with alleged gold miners, etc.). The ethical issue here is censorship based on theoretical disagreement, and it was in that context that I introduced to this discussion the persecution of sociobiology by Tierney and his associates.

Let me treat these points in turn. First is the factual basis for many of Tierney's charges, particularly about Chagnon (since most of us seem prepared to accept that Tierney botched much of his treatment of James Neel's activities). As I suggested in both earlier rounds, I do not consider much of Tierney's account of either Neel's or Chagnon's activities to be well established, and his credibility is very low given the fact that the pieces of his book most thoroughly checked to date have been shown to be marred by misrepresentations and distortions.

Despite an impressive number of footnotes, my opinion is that many of those provide no support for assertions they are associated with and some directly contradict the passages in the text where they are cited. New examples of this appear with each successive week that the text is scrutinized. For example, an essay recently published by Paul and Beatty concerning Neel's eugenic views (Paul and Beatty n.d.) notes in the first paragraph that Tierney claimed Neel was denied the Nobel Prize because he was considered a "pariah" in the field of human genetics. The Tierney footnote to back that assertion refers to Neel's own autobiography, in which nowhere in 320 pages does he mention the Nobel Prize nor any indication that he was considered a "pariah" by his peers. This is typical of Tierney's sloppy and dishonest use of footnotes. I have seen preliminary copies or heard of reports by Jim Neel Jr., Ryk Ward (a geneticist who worked with Jim Neel during the measles vaccination period), and Napoleon Chagnon, who all suggest that various aspects of Tierney's book are packed with gross misrepresentations and that even Turner's recent archival research and the Federal University of Rio de Janeiro's investigation still contain some errors.

Thus, while I am certain that some parts of the book have now been thoroughly discredited, I continue to withhold judgment on other parts of the book until more information is available. This appears to frustrate Turner, who wants all readers to immediately denounce Chagnon regardless of the fact that we have not heard his side of the story, nor has there been time before this discussion to carefully fact check all chapters in Tierney's book (something that Turner interprets as proof that those sections are accurate).

SOCIOBIOLOGY

The second point of clear disagreement concerns the issue of "sociobiology" and its role in this controversy. Turner points out that many intelligent and careful scientists do not accept some sociobiological theories or approaches as useful in the search for understanding about human culture and behavior. This is quite correct but irrelevant to a discussion about ethics. Indeed, Turner has provided his own confused and muddled understanding of sociobiology and then demolished that straw man with obvious satisfaction, but this too is irrelevant to a discussion of ethics. Most scientists who disagree with sociobiological theories are not actively trying to block sociobiological research and censor the research findings of sociobiologists.

That is an ethical issue, one concerning academic freedom. I suggested in Round One that sociobiology was relevant to the discussion of ethics because the book is an attempt to smear sociobiologists with untrue charges only *because they are sociobiologists*. Turner appears to simultaneously reject that charge and then reaffirm its accuracy, launching into a discussion that attempts to convince the reader that sociobiology is so misguided that the attacks on its practitioners are justified. Indeed he concludes by suggesting that sociobiological theory leads its adherents to reject legitimate modern indigenous leaders. This suggestion is malicious slander that has no basis in reality (where most sociobiologists not only accept modern indigenous leaders but work together with them to help solve modern indigenous problems).

I believe that there is good evidence that Chagnon was denied research access to the Yanomamö only *because* he espoused sociobiological theories (particularly about warfare) and that some anthropologists were actively engaged in this theoretical persecution because of their own muddled ideas about the implications of Chagnon's research. Furthermore, I think the record is clear that Chagnon has often been attacked by those who mainly wish to discredit sociobiology and that hypocritical attacks on him and not others (who engaged in similar field practices described in the Tierney book) have been motivated only by that desire to discredit sociobiology—not because his behavior is exceptionally unethical (which I do think would constitute legitimate grounds for criticism if true).

Many of those who have defended Chagnon from theoretically motivated attacks have done so not because they necessarily agree with his views or because they like him as a person or because they think his behavior has always been admirable but *because* he has been the target of theoretical persecution that amounts to academic censorship. I think that Albert makes an interesting point when he suggests that the cause of sociobiology may have been more hurt than helped by Chagnon's association with that cause. I have heard the same point of view expressed by a variety of sociobiologists who recognize that Chagnon made an extraordinary number of enemies in his career compared with most other sociobiologists. However, Albert should realize that the flip side of his observation is also valid. If attacks on Chagnon had focused on his personal behavior and specific activities that were considered unacceptable instead of attacking his sociobiological theories as inherently evil (and the dangerous nature of his data and interpretations), perhaps Chagnon would be answering entirely for himself in this debate.

I will not accept the degrading labels that try to blame the sufferings of modern indigenous people on "immoral sociobiologists." Sociobiologists are not fascists (most are typical left-of-center academics), they are not racist (there are many minority sociobiologists), they are not sexist (there are many female sociobiologists), and there is no justification whatsoever for the mention of Nazis in a sentence that discusses sociobiology (in fact many sociobiologists are Jewish). Those of us who are interested in exploring what evolutionary biology can tell us about human diversity are fed up with this unethical slander. I intend to call attention to such persecution whenever I see it (and the Tierney book qualifies).

I do not wish to correct Turner's confused and mistaken notion of what constitutes "a modern evolutionary view of human behavior." Modern researchers in this area usually designate themselves as either "evolutionary ecologists" or "evolutionary psychologists," with some small but important differences in the two schools of theory (Smith, Borgerhoff Mulder, and Hill 2001). The term *sociobiology* has effectively been dropped from the vocabulary except when used by outsiders to refer to all the different evolutionary perspectives collectively. For those who are interested in knowing what types of behavioral anthropological research are done under an evolutionary framework, there are several good review articles and books that cover the past twenty years of this research in anthropology [Smith and Winterholder, 1992; Borgerhoff Mulder 1991; Cronk, Chagnon, and Irons 2000). Most anthropologists who have read this type of work are impressed by the quantitative empirical methods and focus on behavioral sampling techniques, even when they disagree with the evolutionary interpretations of some of the results.

For those who have read the Tierney book, it is useful to point out that while Tierney tries to weave Neel and Chagnon together into some unholy sociobiological alliance out to sacrifice their study subjects in order to prove their repulsive theories, in fact Neel was never much of a sociobiologist at all (but Chagnon was and is). Neel was primarily a geneticist who was interested in questions of human genetics and had very little interest in the growing fields of behavioral research that made up sociobiology.

The article that Tierney and Turner use to build their case for Neel as a "pariah" eugenicist is primarily about the implications of the measured mutation rate for the genetic well-being of modern society. The article starts with Neel reviewing available data concerning the probability that any allele undergoes mutation per generation and the number of total genes that are required for the healthy functioning of a human being. Contrary to Turner's assertion, Neel shows no interest in that article in how genetics might impinge on social structure, but instead he focuses on how social structure affects the genetic composition of a population. He points out that mutation rates are high (and even higher in modern polluted environments) and that something must counter this genetic load of deleterious alleles in order for populations to stay healthy. He notes that headmen generally are not defective individuals and also usually have high genetic fitness, thus partially explaining why the accumulation of deleterious mutations has not been a serious problem in human history. He does not attempt to model how "superior" alleles are constantly introduced to populations due to headman reproductive rates, but instead he explains why deleterious alleles do not become overly abundant (because the Index of Innate Ability is unlikely to be high for those with blatantly defective genes). Indeed, as Neel would have easily realized, any strong positive selection for "superior" genes in headmen would have long ago driven those genes to fixation (in an additive genetic system) and *all* members of the population would have the "superior headman genes"; thus there would be no genetic basis for new headmen. Instead Neel points out only that when deleterious mutations arise in the population that affect certain capabilities ("deficient speaking ability, poor knowledge of tribal lore, lackluster hunting ability, ineptness in tribal raids, etc."), individuals having those mutations are unlikely to be headmen and are therefore unlikely to have high fitness. Thus, the traditional relationship between headmen and polygyny is part of the explanation in human history for why deleterious mutations do not accumulate through time. Neel mentions in the same article (Neel 1980) that childhood viability and differential female fecundity also must contribute to populational genetic well-being as well but that these factors are less well studied than the polygynous mating advantages of headmen (something that neither Tierney nor Turner mentions in their confused rendition of Neel's paper).

Neel was a type of eugenicist like many other geneticists who consider it unwise for people with severe genetic defects to reproduce and pass on that burden to their families and society. Indeed, all modern genetics counseling is driven by the same concerns that Neel expressed. But Tierney and Turner have grossly misrepresented Neel's eugenic views in an attempt to connect one allegedly sinister worldview (sociobiology) with another allegedly sinister academic interest (eugenics). In short, James Neel saw himself as a "Physician to the Gene Pool," just as his autobiography suggests, but this was nothing like the distorted view that Tierney and some of his allies try to convey to readers not familiar with Neel's work.

Not only does the Tierney book assert that sociobiologists are immoral but it also develops the theme from the first chapter to the last that scientists in general are immoral people because of their interest in research (rather than just helping). This too, unfortunately, is a theme that has been developed in some circles of modern anthropology. Tierney is careful to inform the reader early on that he himself has abandoned his own "objectivity" to advocate indigenous causes more effectively (2000:xxiv). He asserts that those who do research with Indians are engaged in an unethical enterprise unless that research is directly designed to help the Indians who participate in the study. In short, the subtext of his book is that scientists are evil people because they engage in inquiry rather than advocacy.

This attitude takes on a smug holier-than-thou character as Tierney continually reminds the reader that he and his friends do nothing more than provide services to native peoples—the only proper activity for anyone visiting native communities—while other evil scientists are engaged in the unethical enterprise of trying to find answers to questions (allegedly for their own career gain). This position represents the ultimate moralizing that pervades this book. Only Tierney's lifestyle is moral and ethical and all who deviate from his standards are evil. Not surprisingly Tierney sees little value of scientific research because he doesn't understand the significance of most scientific studies he discusses in this book. It hardly escapes notice that many strong Tierney allies in this debate also have little or no scientific background or ability to understand scientific research. I don't object to their lack of interest in scientific methods and research, but I do object to them trying to force everyone into their mold.

Rather than the scientists being selfish and misguided, I suggest that it is these antiscience activists who have a very shortsighted view of what will ultimately provide most help for native populations. Yes, direct assistance is important and should often be a priority. But scientific research can also provide important benefits to the native populations and to the world community (which includes them and many other people). There is indeed a blatant antiscience tone in this book, and that tone explains the negative reaction by many readers outside sociobiology or anthropology who are unfamiliar with the details but recognize the tone of the argument. Tierney's travels to Venezuela to convince the government to ban all scientific research on native populations (see El Nacional 2000a) are the logical final step in this process and should surprise no one who has read the book.

SUMMARIZING

How are we to summarize the experience of this discussion? For those of us who took time out from our own busy schedules of research, teaching, and involvement in indigenous development projects, there has to be some justification for this use of our time. I don't believe this discussion has been just about posturing and displays of cleverness. Instead, all of us are concerned about native peoples and whether the activities of anthropologists are helping or hurting their struggles for survival and respect. We are also concerned about our discipline—about improving it and correcting past mistakes. We must continue to strive to work in an ethical way, while simultaneously discovering important anthropological principles in the world that can help promote a deeper understanding of our fellow human beings.

Native peoples are partners in this process and have every right to be heard. I disagree strongly with the description of "real Indians" attributed to Chagnon by Martins (and which Turner implies that all "sociobiologists" must adhere to). I have spent more than half my life working with "real Indians," and I know that their authenticity is not derived from being dirty and smelly, nor is it derived from wearing pretty feather adornments and body paint and going naked, nor from taking drugs and invoking spirits to heal illness caused by infectious agents. "Real Indians" are people who have hopes, dreams, goals, fears, doubts, and disappointments. They care about their children and their friends, and they hope to improve their material well-being and standard of living. They have lives driven by the same forces as the rest of us: they want happiness for themselves and their families, they want respect, and they are willing to cooperate with those who cooperate with them. They are proud of their past and the successful lifestyles of their ancestors but are also prepared to adopt solutions to their problems even if those solutions are not part of their traditional culture. They are interested in the world and their place in it. They want to know why some groups of people are different from them and why some traits present among their people are also found in all human groups.

This means that native people *are* in fact anthropologists, and they should have input into anthropological theories and conclusions. Indeed native peoples are our partners in this process of learning and inquiry because they are us. Let's make sure we as anthropologists invite them permanently into the process and never again stand accused of exploiting or deceiving them for our own career gain.

....

FINAL COMMENTS ON ETHICAL ISSUES RAISED BY *DARKNESS IN EL DORADO*

LÊDA MARTINS

A recent trip to Brazil and interviews with several Yanomami leaders have highlighted for me some aspects of this controversy more than others (see the interviews in chapter 5). The themes brought up by the Yanomami revolved around the research expeditions organized by James Neel and Napoleon Chagnon and the collection of specimens, especially blood. In that regard, it is crucial to discuss the question of informed consent and compensation. The principle of this Roundtable is a serious commitment to a discussion of ethics in academic endeavors, although it is clear that the dialogue has gotten off track at some points. It appears in general that most of us agree in broad terms but have deep divergences when we descend to the details and applicability of broad notions. I hope that the ideas presented in this contribution will advance the debate on ethics in anthropology and academic research in general.

INFORMED CONSENT REGARDING THE COLLECTION OF BLOOD SAMPLES

The interviews with Yanomami leaders showed that the collection of blood samples is for them the most important issue in the wide range of topics that Tierney's book stirred up. It was only recently that the Yanomami began to learn about the research done with those samples and the fact that the blood is still

KEY ACCUSATIONS AND ISSUES
(see also pp. 317–41)

To what degree did the Neel expedition violate reasonable standards of informed consent? The Yanomami were not informed as to what their blood was going to be used for, which means that the Yanomami were not fully informed when their consent was obtained. Martins suspects that it was the implied but ultimately false promise of medical help that convinced the Yanomami to allow Neel to take blood samples. (see pages 256–57)

To what degree should Neel have assumed responsibility—during his fieldwork—for dealing with medical problems that were imperfectly dealt with by the national governments of Venezuela and Brazil? Neel needed to do more to help the Yanomami than was usually called for in such circumstances because the Yanomami were in the midst of a devastating epidemic and no one else was around to help. (see page 260)

Looking at the broad picture, how would you assess the value of Darkness in El Dorado? Tierney's book leads us to reflect on how we relate to the people we study. (see page 261)

Was it appropriate for Chagnon to publicly criticize indigenous Yanomami spokespeople (especially Davi Kopenawa)? Chagnon improperly participated in media attacks on Yanomami leaders and human rights advocates. (see page 262)

QUESTIONS TO CONSIDER

Are the original gifts given to the Yanomami enough to compensate for their blood donations? Or is something more needed today, since the Yanomami feel they had been misled by Neel? If so, what would this be?

How might the American Anthropological Association hold members accountable for violations to its code of ethics?

being stored in refrigerators in American research institutions. The interviews presented at the end of this text touch on this and other issues.

The lack of knowledge among the Yanomami of the destiny of the blood collected during several expeditions organized by Neel and Chagnon makes informed consent the most crucial question to be addressed in this debate. Chagnon and several scholars argue that the Yanomami gave consent for them to draw blood, that the Yanomami were not coerced. But the statements given by Yanomami leaders now raise some questions: What type of consent did the Yanomami give to the medical expeditions? What was the explanation provided by the medical teams? Was the consent fully informed? Were the Yanomami paid for the blood? Are they satisfied with that payment? What is the correct attitude to be taken now by the parties involved?

Hames's second contribution to the Roundtable started with a discussion of this topic. Although he subscribed to the principle of informed consent, Hames concluded that he could not have a definitive position on the case involving Chagnon and Neel because he needed more information. Despite his indecision, Hames proceeded in an attempt to exonerate Neel and Chagnon of any charge of not complying with norms of informed consent that had been internationally established in 1964. Hames had three main arguments. One was that "the Yanomamö gave their blood in exchange for trade goods, and it was done on a voluntary basis." The second came in the form of a recent conversation between him and Chagnon in which Chagnon explained what he told the Yanomami on the occasion of the blood sampling: "He [Chagnon] said that for a year before Neel's arrival and during the collection phase he told the Yanomamö in all the villages to be sampled that Neel's team wanted to examine their blood in order to determine whether there were things that indicated whether or not they had certain kinds of diseases, especially *shawara* (epidemic diseases) and that this knowledge would help treat them more effectively if they became ill." Hames added that Chagnon could not provide more accurate information to the Yanomami because it was impossible to give them a "crash course in infectious disease, genetics, and epidemiology." The third argument was that this type of information, that is, "information consistent with their ability to comprehend the research," was standard for research done with indigenous populations (and even for research done in the West).

Hames's arguments denied the Yanomami people any say on current and future research on their blood samples that now have been integrated into the Human Genome Diversity Project. But his opinions were also confusing. Did the Yanomami give blood because they were paid for it with trade goods? Or because they accepted the research purposes? If yes is the correct answer for both, as Hames implied that it is, he should have explained better what the deal was. Perhaps pots, machetes, and fishing hooks were used as more persuasive arguments with those who were not convinced by Chagnon's explanation, or the goods were thrown in as an extra for everybody, or perhaps the team gave out more goods when no explanation was given at all, for lack of time, for example. I call attention here to an important distinction made by Kim Hill on the different types of medical research (experimentation, observational research, and epidemiological surveillance). He explained that observational research (taking blood temperature, collecting blood samples, recording skin lesions, etc.) "can be conceptualized as a business agreement between those who sell information (the study subjects) and those who buy it (the researchers). As such, study populations should be allowed to decide if they want to sell their product (allow the research) and at what price." We are left to wonder which kind of "business agreement" Neel's team and the Yanomami really had, if any at all.

The real problem is that whatever the deal was, Chagnon and other members of the expeditions did not get close to giving a reasonable explanation to the Yanomami about the purposes of the sampling. In consequence, any deal was invalid. Indeed, I think that Chagnon's statements were deceptive and not instructive. In my view, to say to a group of people with very limited knowledge of Western medical science and suffering from ravaging diseases that giving their blood will help to determine if they have certain illnesses and in consequence provide some kind of treatment is to lure them with implied clinical assistance for their current situation and not to simplify the explanation of a research project. It seems that it was exactly the implied promise of clinical treatment in the short run that convinced the Yanomami to give away their blood. In recent interviews, some Yanomami leaders have touched on this issue. Those interviews are presented in chapter 5.

The Yanomami specimens collected in Neel's project have not resulted in any treatment to alleviate their suffering from any illness to the present day. The Yanomami population has been blasted with diseases in the last two decades because of the encroachment of miners and settlers on their territory. Tierney affirmed in his book that the Yanomami blood samples were used in the past for comparative purposes in research on radioactivity with Japanese survivors of the Hiroshima and Nagasaki bombings and later turned over to the Human Genome Diversity Project. The ethical problem is not that the research on Yanomami blood samples has not benefited the Yanomami directly but rather that the Yanomami gave their blood under the impression that they would receive medical treatment because of such research. In other words, clinical help became an ethical issue because it underlined the very act of the donation of the blood, when the researchers knew that treatment for the Yanomami was not the primary goal of the study, or at least that treatment was not certain and immediate.

And let us consider as a reasonable argument for a minute that the Yanomami did not have the grasp of epidemiology, genetics, and infectious diseases to receive a detailed account of the research and fully comprehend its aims and consequences. Chagnon could have given nonscientific information that the Yanomami would have understood easily and that he, as a cultural anthropologist, knew would be relevant in their decision making process. For example, why did not Chagnon tell them that their blood was going to be kept under refrigeration for a long, long time (perhaps forever)? In the first round, Albert called attention to the moral and cultural problems of storing blood from deceased Yanomami in light of "the salient role that blood and mortuary taboos play in their ritual life." In a similar direction, Hill stated that "something about how scientific data are used can be expected to influence native decisions about whether or not to participate in research, and this is the logic for providing basic information about the purpose of study." In recent interviews the Yanomami indicate that this simple information would have made a significant difference for them (see chapter 5).

The last part of Hames's argument appealed to the idea that half-disclosure or sometimes no disclosure at all was standard procedure in medical research in the 1960s and 1970s when most of the Atomic Energy Commission project was carried out among the Yanomami. Hill suggested a similar idea and went even further to state that the Nuremberg Code does not "attempt to regulate observational research and is not relevant to epidemiological surveillance required in public health emergencies," suggesting that blood sampling does not come under the Nuremberg principles. Soon after making this statement, Hill seemed to remember Marcel Roche's goiter study and the experiments with iodine 131 radioactive tracer carried out with the Yanomami. And he added that Roche should have sought complete informed consent for the experimentation, but then later he dismissed his own claim by saying that the iodine study presented no danger to the Yanomami and followed standard procedures for the time.

Again I am left with the impression that Hill agrees with the general principle as long as it is not applied to anything related to the cases in question here. More problematic is his notion that norms can be bent without any accountability if no supposed harm is caused to the subjects of the studies. It is a very dangerous notion, because there is no definition or regulation of who is doing the assessment of possible harm and why. Hill? Me? Hames? Are we entitled to do that? International norms like the Nuremberg Code and the Declaration of Helsinki were created precisely to ensure the participation of subjects in the assessment of harm and benefits of research and to give them the freedom to say no. Subjects who participate in studies that were not fully explained to them must have the right to take a stand on the assessment of damage caused by those studies, especially when such undertakings have consequences for the future, as in the case of the Yanomami blood samples. Scientists who work with those groups or communities should welcome this type of assessment.

Complaints and disputes over biological materials and intellectual property rights—and it appears that a large proportion of the specimens was taken without adequate consent—are bound to become the most important issue in the agenda of indigenous people in the near future; for some it already is (see, for example, Lewin 1993). The Yanomami are not an isolated and archaic case. An illustrative glimpse at the controversy over genetic studies is provided by a recent editorial in the *New Scientist*: "Should scientists who take blood and tissue samples for research be allowed to use them for other studies without permission? Will the original donors care if they do? Getting the answer right is a big deal for geneticists who are beginning to link diseases to genes in the newly sequenced human genome. . . . One group of indigenous people in British Columbia is feeling particularly let down. Members of the Nuu-Chah-nulth claim research was done on their blood without their consent. They are angry, and want their samples back." In his conclusion, the editor states that "clearly people have the right to decide how their own genetic material will be used and it doesn't have to be a bureaucratic nightmare. Volunteers could simply tick a box on the consent form if they want to know what their DNA is intended for. Or they could be asked to specify areas of research they don't want to be part of, such as studies on alcoholism, race, or intelligence. If they object, they must have the right to withdraw" (*New Scientist* 2000).

Indigenous and human rights organizations have paid special attention to genetic studies and patents on human tissue since the Human Genome Diversity Project was made public or perhaps since the 1995 patent case of a

DNA sequence of the Hagahai, a group of Papua New Guineans (Salopek 1997b). Indian spokespeople and advocates have stated their concern about collection and use of human specimens without the informed consent of the donors, which some call "biopiracy," and the disregard for cultural practices and beliefs. They have also emphasized the financial disadvantage that indigenous people might have in deals proposed by research institutions or multinational pharmaceutical laboratories. Paul Salopek gave an overview of the different positions involved in the discussion of the HGDP. He wrote, on the opinions of indigenous people, that "as the gigantic scale of the survey begins to lumber into the public eye, a growing number of aboriginal groups, who are the main if not exclusive target of the study, see the project as simply another form of high-tech exploitation—scientists arrogantly using tribes as guinea pigs while offering nothing tangible in return. 'It's biocolonialism, plain and simple,' said Jeanette Armstrong, a member of Canada's Okanagan Nation. 'First, they take our land, then they take our culture and now they want our genes'" (Salopek 1997a).

In response to Hames's line of reasoning on the standard of research in the 1960s and 1970s, I would like to add that Chagnon attempted to take blood samples without adequate informed consent in 1995. Albert and I recalled the episode in our statements in Round Two. Hill's contention that studies like the ones conducted by Neel and Chagnon are not subject to the Nuremberg Code is likely to be disputed by physicians and other professionals in the field. The doctors in Rio de Janeiro cited the Nuremberg Code and the Declaration of Helsinki as guidelines that should have been followed by Neel, Chagnon, and Roche. In fact, the Helsinki principles adopted by the World Medical Assembly in 1964 make no distinction between different types of research.

Another point brought up by Hill is that indigenous people have a moral obligation to participate in research that may not benefit them directly, since they also gain from results of studies carried out with other groups of people. I agree with him on this point, although I think potential research subjects have the right to refuse any study, as necessary as it may seem. But I do not see the reason for bringing to our debate nightmarish hypotheses of situations when the Yanomami would be forced to donate blood. We already have concrete and complex cases to discuss here. Imaginary dramas of infectious diseases coming out of the jungles of South America and, for that matter, Africa or Asia to infect the entire world (and always starting with the United States) should be restrained to Hollywood.

ETHICAL DECISIONS

We all seem to agree that the well-being and interests of the people we work with should be put above any scientific objective. Hill said in Round One, "Our goals are to study issues of academic interest, but the health and welfare of the study population must always take precedence over any academic goal." I believe that all the other participants endorse Hill's statement, as do I. But the ideas of some participants become cloudy in the second round. Hill, for instance, stated that doctors who "are called in to a country to research an outbreak of disease . . . do their jobs as researchers, not clinical practitioners. They do not and cannot get involved in treating every sick person they encounter in the field." Was he suggesting that Neel's team had no obligation to assist the Yanomami because they were on a research mission? I think a distinction needs to be made between studying an epidemic when there are other medical teams providing care, and doing research in the middle of an outbreak when the research team is the only clinical help around. While the first case is not likely to raise ethical problems, the second involves precisely the general principle stated by Hill. Neel's expedition in 1968 falls into the second case.

The subject gets even more divisive when we touch on the details of the case under discussion, that is, the ethical decisions taken by Neel and his team during the measles outbreak in 1968. Did Neel give priority to research over medical treatment to the Yanomami during his research expedition? Turner's conclusion after examining Neel's documents and field notes is that Neel tried to balance the sampling and the vaccination and that he even compromised some aspects of the research to give more time to inoculation. But Neel ended up sacrificing to a larger degree the necessary measures of vaccination and health care needed in face of the epidemic to meet his goal of bringing home a thousand Yanomami specimens. I find it striking that it appears that Neel did not alter the route previously designed or the schedule of stays in each village in the face of all the panic, chaos, and illness in the Yanomami villages around him. It is illustrative that Neel brought back the thousand blood samples he wanted, and the films that Chagnon and Timothy Asch were scheduled to make were completed.

Discussing the specifics of the case, Hill first said that Neel tried both to vaccinate and to research, then in the second round he affirmed that Neel's job in the 1968 mission was to "collect information on human genetic diversity." In addition, Hill dismissed Turner's findings without any explanation for doing so. Hames did not address the question directly and preferred to restate that Neel had some kind of permission to vaccinate and that is what he did. Peters did not refer to the issue at all. The circumstances of the case are very complex, and it seems that this Roundtable is not the forum to put the case to rest. In my opinion, then, the appropriate conclusion is Albert's proposition for the creation of an independent bioethics commission to examine the research projects headed by James Neel in the 1960s and 1970s involving the Yanomami. Turner and Hames have directly endorsed Albert's proposal.

LAWSUITS

In the first round Albert mentioned the idea of possible lawsuits against the institutions that were responsible for the research done among the Yanomami without their informed consent. Hill reacted strongly against the idea, arguing that the Yanomami should not file "frivolous" lawsuits that would only serve to scare away scientists from doing further research with the Yanomami, which for him would be disastrous (to the Indians, of course). Hill's opinion is simple: the blood is already in the laboratories; let science do its crucial job and let the Yanomami wait for an uncertain future of medical benefits and—who knows— some profit.

I think Hill missed the point. The question is about ethical principles: the Yanomami did not give permission to have their blood stored indefinitely and to have the samples participate in the Human Genome Project. So ethically the institutions responsible for past and present research with Yanomami specimens are required to inform them of the purposes of the sampling and subsequent procedures done to the samples and must ask permission now, as late as it is. And the Yanomami, considering all the information available, have the right to make a wide range of decisions, including proceeding with a lawsuit.

I am not advocating for a legal dispute over the Yanomami blood samples, but I think that it is unacceptable that Hill has attempted to shame the Yanomami out of seeking a court solution to the case. Hill has no credentials to state that no "real damage" was done to the Yanomami. It is up to attorneys and judges to decide if a case involves damage of any sort or not. I think it would be educational to see someone explaining to the Yanomami that the pots and fishing hooks they got out of the deal are enough in the face of the money involved in the collection of and research on their blood and the fortune that may be made with genetics discoveries through the HGDP. But mostly I think Hill went too far when he suggested that this would be frivolous and would send a "wrong moral message" to the Yanomami, suggesting that the Yanomami would be puppets in such an act.

We should remind ourselves that the Human Genome Diversity Project is far from enjoying a consensus in the scientific community. Hill gives the impression that the HGDP holds the key to the complete understanding of human disease and pathology and that this knowledge will bring infinite and direct benefits to everybody, including the Yanomami. However, it appears from the extensive debate among renowned scientists that the project is iffy, to say the least. Several scientists dispute the publicized therapeutic benefits of genetics studies like the HGDP and the Human Genome Project. There is no consensus about when, how, at what cost, and even if the HGDP and HGP will deliver what they promise (Lewontin 2000).

HOW WE RELATE TO THE PEOPLE WE STUDY

I believe that one of the promising results of the debates triggered by *Darkness in El Dorado* is a serious reflection on how we relate to the people we study. I will attempt here to make some contributions to this debate, which I hope becomes a continuous process.

I disagree with Kim Hill on several points regarding the work of cultural anthropologists. His generalizations and attacks on advocates of indigenous rights, which he seems to direct in particular to cultural anthropologists who are involved with human rights issues, are gross generalizations of complex and variable situations. It is chilling the way Hill insists on broadly attacking human rights organizations. He gives a few examples that lack adequate specific references to people or institutions and then generalizes his experiences to a large number of organizations and activities. His discourse is very close to the arguments used by the military and right-wing politicians in Brazil (and I would guess also in other South American countries) to undermine the legal rights of Indian people. Hill must know this, and I wonder why he insists on these generalizations.

It is true that NGOs in general struggle with ways to present a deromanticized image of indigenous people without hurting public support for their causes and running the risk of obstructing legal claims for land and assistance for Indians. It is even a fact that there are advocates with an idealized view of indigenous people who oppose any sort of data that go against that Rousseauian notion or that they perceive as a threat to Indian rights. But in any of those cases, the participation of anthropologists in advocacy work certainly has been more on the side of supporting or pushing for nonromantic treatment of Indians, showing the complexity of their societies and fighting the easy, one-label solution. In this sense, I see and have experienced myself (from both sides) that the interaction between anthropologists and lay advocates is extremely positive and necessary to the defense of the rights of indigenous people and to anthropology, because both sides are forced to confront facts and ideas that they otherwise would not. It pushes anthropologists to deal with concrete problems and advocates to rethink their concepts. Good results of the interaction between anthropology and advocacy can be seen in the work of ISA (Instituto SocioAmbiental) (see, for example, Ricardo 2000).

Another charge made by Hill is that cultural anthropologists and activists defend indigenous rights on the basis of human rights laws and principles but fail to apply those principles to the lives of Indians. In fact, many anthropologists and scholars from other areas have addressed the challenge of rendering universal human rights meaningful and relevant to different cultures without obliterating the right to cultural diversity, the right to be different (Turner 1997). Moreover, many Indian rights organizations and activists (including anthropologists) deal in a nonpaternalistic way with violations of individual rights such as the abuse of women, infanticide, and incest, but most do not use religious proselytism. Hill seemed to favor the missionary approach that he called "moral cultural criticism," but which can be more accurately referred to as moral cultural judgment. Missionaries have been criticized for condemning Indian people's beliefs and banning certain practices that go against their religious dogmas, such as shamanism (although I would not generalize this statement to all missionaries). In contrast, human rights advocates prefer secular education as the approach to deal with abuses of individual rights within Indian societies. The Pro-Yanomami Commission (CCPY), for example, has an educational project that involves lawyers, anthropologists, linguists, and teachers and that introduces Yanomami students to aspects of Western laws, Brazilian social norms, market practices, and so on.

The engagement of anthropologists and other scientists with ethics and indigenous rights is very welcome, but what Hill and Hames (in Round One) have done is to blur the problem and paint a misleading picture of the participation of anthropologists in human rights advocacy. In fact, my impression in reading their statements is that cultural anthropologists are easily corrupted or seduced to join an army of advocates committed to lie and hide the truth to achieve their purposes. It seems that only "hard-core" scientists, like Hill and Hames themselves, are immune to such corruption. This whole scenario is so stereotyped that it leaves no space for a dialogue. Anthropologists and lay advocates are not naïfs or terrorists, and the objectivity that Hill and Hames proclaim is conditioned by their own biases and limitations. I have been involved for eleven years with indigenous rights and have been working as an anthropologist for the last two. But I refuse to be taken hostage by the generalized accusation that Hill and Hames spread and be forced to defend myself. Unfortunately, a dialogue on the ethics of human rights advocacy is not possible in the terms established by them.

The other part of Hill's argument on the relationship of anthropologists-advocates and indigenous people is even worse than the first: his accusations about the "coaching" of indigenous leaders. Throughout Hill's statements he makes several references to a supposed manipulation of Indian leaders or an absence of the agency of Indian people in their own affairs. He wrote in Round One that "somebody is maliciously coaching the Yanomamö," and in Round Two that "such lawsuits are essentially frivolous and send the wrong moral message to the Yanomamö."

Again, Hill's ideas are similar to those of the Brazilian military and Amazonian politicians who say the Indian spokespeople who defend their land are manipulated by the Catholic church or by activists on behalf of foreign countries (that want to take control of the Amazon). The suggestion that Indian leaders are puppets of human rights advocates is the modern version of the colonial idea that Indians cannot think for themselves, that a "white" person is always behind their reasoning. This is the easiest and most efficient way to silent indigenous people when one does not want to hear what they say or does not like what they say. It happens every day in my home state, Roraima. Indian leaders are considered authentic when they say what people expect. It happens in academia too; Chagnon has repeatedly called Yanomami leaders who criticize him puppets of NGOs.

Hill also brought up questions regarding informed consent in anthropological research. He suggests that we cultural anthropologists do not contemplate the ethics of our methods and academic production. I think Hill has forgotten all about postcolonial, postmodernist and feminist critiques in anthropology, as well approaches that seek to foster a more engaged relationship with our subjects and produce locally relevant theories such as applied anthropology and participatory action research. With as much debate as there is in relation to those theories and methods within the discipline, it is absurd to suggest that nothing has changed or has been challenged in cultural anthropology since Lévi-Strauss's first fieldwork. And contrary to what Hill suggests, cultural anthropologists are also required to fill out research permission forms and receive approval from their sponsoring institutions and from the appropriate institutions in the country in which they carry out the study.

Despite all my disagreements with Hill, I have to admit that challenges to the ethical norms of anthropology are not totally groundless. The AAA has an ethical code that is very encompassing and progressive, but the mechanisms by which anthropologists are held accountable for their work are not clear. What happens when an anthropologist breaks the code? What is supposed to be done? What accountability exists? I am afraid that if we do not respond to these questions, the burden of dealing with our ethical problems will be always passed to the people who should have the least to be responsible for: the people we choose to study.

Hill also touched on a key aspect of anthropological research that deserves more attention within the discipline, that is, the disclosure of our academic theories to our subjects. I think the point is not simply disclosure but the opening of a dialogue about our ethnographic writings with our subjects and a subsequent change of the nature of the relation between us and them. Such dialogues, including disputes and joint publications, between anthropologists and their subjects have already started in other parts of the world, but the process is incipient with indigenous peoples in South America. Indigenous peoples have started to transform their perception of anthropologists, and in consequence the discipline will need to adjusts its methods, its publications, and so on to contemporaneous fieldwork realities. The traditional beads, pots, machetes, and, more recently, cash as exchange for hospitality and data might see their last days sooner rather than later. Indigenous peoples are beginning to expect and require that anthropologists engage and assist them in their political struggles and with health projects, education programs, and so on. Not that this type of engagement is anything new. For decades some anthropologists have been assisting indigenous peoples in their political and economic agendas, but this has been more in consequence of the researchers' personal political orientation and interests. The difference now is that indigenous peoples have started to factor this kind of involvement in the trade-off for research.

I am not the first to perceive this change (see, for instance, Albert 1997), and I think that the relation between indigenous people and anthropology is heading for further transformation. Beyond a transaction of exchange, the payment of material goods or professional assistance in given projects, Indian leaders seem increasingly more interested in the subject of our research and publications. My recent fieldwork illustrates this point. I was not asked for financial or intellectual help and then left alone to do what I wanted. Instead, the very theme of my research was the object of discussion; it became in some sense a part of their own agenda and vice versa. Luckily for me, my academic goals and their interests were very similar. Some Macuxi leaders expect a long-term commitment of my academic work to issues they consider relevant and want to be able to discuss what I write about them. The Yanomami indicate a very similar expectation in their interviews.

....

FURTHER REFLECTIONS

JOHN F. PETERS

The Roundtable discussions have created glowing heat and at the same time show considerable agreement. In Hill's words, later affirmed by Albert, this common ground is unequivocally that "the health and welfare of the study population must always take precedence over our academic goals."

The dialogue has been rich, stimulating, helpful, and a bit creative. Although more than three decades have passed since the first published Yanomami research, we have come closer to twenty-twenty vision but have not yet achieved it. The Roundtable discussions have not only addressed ethical matters but penetrated some areas of challenge to the discipline and to social science. This challenge captures my attention the most. If we wish to incorporate the ideas and proposals, it will require a bit of redirection. This will alter our orientation toward fieldwork, impacting researchers as well as academic and sponsoring institutions.

REFLECTIONS ON WHERE WE NOW STAND

This dialogue of three rounds shows that each participant makes different interpretations and chooses spheres of discussion he or she considers significant. Other areas are unimportant to him or her but prime for another colleague. Our struggle to hear and be heard, with tolerance for the other's perspective but without being political or defensive, is a stringent exercise. Imagine this forum if the participants in the dialogue had a wider representation of cultural diversity, including Yanomami!

On a research level, it appears that in the field we have an intense exposure to a vastly different culture, then transfer back to our domain of Western academia, which is swamped in a culture of privilege, comfort, elitism, consumerism, power manipulation, technology, nationhood, and individualism. (The people and culture in our field of study have some of these characteristics as well.) We seek to survive in our home milieu and often readily forget the earthier and more commonsense aspects in the social life where we did our fieldwork. (I have friends in the academic community who avoid visiting people in Latin America because they fear the impact this exposure would have upon the

KEY ACCUSATIONS AND ISSUES
(see also pp. 317–41)

Should Chagnon have responded better to the media's misuse of his work? Peters agrees with Martins that Chagnon could have done more to squelch media reports that unfairly affected the Yanomami. (see page 267)

Did Neel act ethically during the 1968 expedition in the way he balanced his research with the need to treat the measles epidemic? Researchers might do all they can medically, given their resources, to help indigenous peoples, but this does not relieve national governments of their responsibilities in this regard. (see page 267)

Did Chagnon provide inaccurate representations of the Yanomami, especially regarding their "fierceness"? Anthropologists should not err in excluding destructive aspects of a culture, such as the suppression of women, in their reports. (see page 269)

QUESTIONS TO CONSIDER

Given the considerable financial differences between anthropologists and the people they study, how might the discipline address the issue of just compensation?

What ethical lessons about fieldwork should people take away with them from this controversy?

indigenous people.) Martins reminds us (in Round Two) again of the stratospheric gap between our academic culture and the Yanomami. It would be appropriate now to initiate similar discussions of researcher and practice in the anthropologist's field of study where the perceived distance is not that vast, such as in Bosnia, China, or Colombia. The gap is still significant and worthy of careful consideration.

Serendipitously, the dialogue has stretched some of our previously held Yanomami ethnographic and historical understandings. We now realize the centrality of gift giving, people's names, relationships with the deceased, and something more of their sphere of the spirit world. (I still contend that while research on the Yanomami spirit world has been documented, we do not fully comprehend its pervasiveness and depth.)

The ethics of Neel's and Chagnon's medical work, is thoroughly discussed by Hill, Turner, and Albert. I feel uncomfortable in this exhaustive discussion because much of the initial activity relating to medical research of 1968 goes beyond the pale of anthropology. We might learn from investigating the codes of ethics and problems encountered by international medical research bodies. Hill and Albert have indicated some appropriate sources. AAA might take its recommendations, meet with medical counterparts, and apply the principles deemed appropriate from such an exchange.

Should the AAA have responded more aggressively twenty years ago in addressing Chagnon's research? Gray areas were evident. Some issues were discussed at AAA annual meetings. The concerns of colleagues could have stimulated much more debate on ethics and been in print. I am in agreement with Martins that Chagnon could have made efforts to squelch media reports that unfairly affected the Yanomami. I do not feel AAA's mission is to serve as a police agency or to scrutinize an anthropologist's research on a "pass-fail" basis.

But what of the AAA in a judgmental role toward nations? What are the boundaries of when to raise a voice and when to remain silent? Why single out study A or nation X and avoid situation B and nation Y? Furthermore, it is somewhat presumptuous to expect a foreign country, such as Cambodia, Benin, Iran, or any other, to heed a reprimand from an American academic body. A well-respected international academic body, with membership from within the country under scrutiny, would carry much more legitimacy.

I stand with Hill in muting Albert's zeal to have the Yanomami gain from the blood slides currently held in America. Our practice of litigation for every aspect of wrongdoing is an unacceptable model and in particular for less-privileged peoples. In this statement I am not compromising indigenous peoples' land claims.

PROVIDING HEALTH CARE

Turner and Albert focus concern toward health needs for the people in the field of study. Hill tempers this position, placing direct responsibility upon governments, in this case Brazil and Venezuela. Researchers might do all they medically can, given their resources, even at their inconvenience. At the same time the nation has responsibility. We need to bear in mind that as in our own nation, medical resources are unequally distributed and would similarly be limited in the hinterland of any nation in the Latin America.

There is another matter of cross-cultural behavior in health care, a matter with far-reaching implications. Our discussions prod me to comment on Western treatment of the sick and dying in another culture. In the absence of Western practices of medicine, traditional beliefs of health have been operational for centuries among the Yanomami. Some of these may not be good health practices. I identify such areas as conception, reproduction, sanitation, and methods of healing, which include shamanic practices. Western ideology and practice is vastly different from that of indigenous societies. In general, in matters of life and death, the westerner usurps the native's cultural values and uses his own methods. The Western methods of treatment have developed out of rational thought and careful and costly research that has proven successful for many maladies. It is easy to see that the use of injections (the needle) and blood and stool sampling is intrusive, as Albert has shown. Yanomami know the first two items to be very serious and the latter extremely humorous.

Diseases foreign to the culture, such as measles, tuberculosis, and new strains of malaria, enter, and immediately even more radical intrusion is ex-

ercised. There is no time to negotiate and ponder cultural norms and misunderstandings. Add to the blood sampling and injections rigor in exact time-
sequenced pill consumption, some of which are big and bitter, air flights to
Boa Vista or a larger city more distant, and lengthy absences from Yanomami
people and the forest environment. AIDS is only a hairbreadth away from the
Yanomami. The Casa dos Indios in Boa Vista is a center where patients and relatives hang out for weeks and months. These contacts have helped build wider
Yanomami solidarity. Romances between individuals in disparate villages have
been initiated here, resulting in later migration and new alliances. Are such radical means of health care negotiable? Such practices have saved human life. But
they have also been intrusive to the culture. Do we really know what we are
doing? Anthropologists do not administer such medical assistance, but we operate in societies where the above description fits. It was true for the Yanomami
from the 1950s to the 1970s. This is not a statement of condemnation but an
area where cultural disruption takes place, which we deem as acceptable. Such
activity is rarely critiqued. Cultural practices have been altered, and new forms
have been adopted by the Yanomami.

SCRUTINIZING OUR OWN BEHAVIORS

I do hope we have been sensitized to the degree of power anthropologists have,
along with NGOs, entrepreneurs, government agents, health care services, and
missionaries. Each of us would do well to scrutinize our own behavior and ideology and seek some dialogue and understanding of the other and work toward
cooperation. Though with good intention, no one organization addresses all the
complex needs of the Yanomami in this millennium.

Obtaining informed consent is complex. Even Hames's helpful illustration of
using terminology in comprehensible terms for indigenous peoples allows considerable latitude for the researcher's manipulation and interpretation. We adjust
our words, depending upon the audience. One segment of the population may
agree to the study while another may not. In the name of democracy, what group
gets our ear? In many cases the researcher is not aware of the full implications the
research project will have during and after the researcher's presence. There is risk.

Researchers in the field encounter the self-interests of groups, whether they
be subordinate or superordinate. Hill's examples with the Ache are enlighten-
ing. Some seemingly expedient temporary deviations from truth made by the foreign researcher may have serious short- and long-term consequences in the
future ambitions of the researcher. I'll stick to truth. In another culture I may
not know the full consequences of such action.

Albert and Hill are critical of the actions of missionaries. Hill recognizes the
"us" and "them" distinction practiced by missionaries, which I agree to. I endorse a critical evaluation by missionaries of their enterprise and their work done
in recent decades. This critique, as Hill states, could also include the institutions

now administered by local people. Competition with other agencies and territorial positioning could also be critiqued. It would be beneficial if anthropologists would give evidence of constructive and culturally sensitive work done by missionaries. It would be helpful to report some satisfying dialogue that has occurred between missionary and anthropologist. (Christian institutions of higher education, of which there are many in the United States, often have an AAA member teach classes to students who anticipate going abroad. If one does not see a direct positive relation between these students and their practice in the Latin America, we are in deep trouble!)

THE BAD, THE GOOD, AND THE HOPEFUL

While I have high respect for, and friendships with, the Yanomami, my research will not exclude the destructive aspects of the culture. Hill and Hames make the point that as anthropologists we err in presenting only a perfect or near-perfect culture. Among the Yanomami, specific areas omitted in research and publications have been identified. The status of women continues to be suppressed by the patriarchal structure. I include aspects of shamanism as a further area of critique, because I know that black magic is used to maim or "kill" a disliked person in another village. Traditional beliefs and practices of power and revenge are not constructive among the Yanomami. The two murders in February of this year are a blatant example. To my knowledge these are the first adult cases of homicide between Yanomami at Mucajaí in the past forty-five years.

Good research is a challenging enterprise. Status differentiation is shifting among the Yanomami. The aged have less prestige, and a few younger males who know the ways and language of the Brazilian or Venezuelan now have status (and possibly the only motor-driven canoe in the village). There are gatekeepers, authoritative peoples and/or groupings, and powerful persons who manipulate and control and may not speak for the wider community. This creates an additional dilemma for the Western anthropologist in a foreign culture.

This dialogue shows consensus for a greater sensitivity on the part of the researcher, both during the research period and after. This covers two areas: (a) actions while in the field, and (b) some forms of moral and possibly material assistance in the months and years after we have done our research. Indigenous people have helped us in our academic careers, and we can reciprocate. Such behavior would impact a future generation of students, as well as global relationships in a meaningful, constructive, and more equitable manner.

The goal of achieving a fair society, as chosen by the Yanomami within a Brazilian or Venezuelan context, is not simple. While Roundtable members show agreement on the Yanomami's right to land and resources, as well as to medical care, the process and inclusion of other matters will vary.

This dialogue, stimulated by cross-cultural activity of human research by Westerners among one South American tribe over a thirty-five-year period, has forced us to look not only at ethics but also at other horizons such as science, methodology, justice, and cross-cultural relations. Let the dialogue and action continue.

....

NEW LIGHT ON THE DARKNESS:
NEW EVIDENCE AND NEW READINGS IN THE
TIERNEY/NEEL/CHAGNON CONTROVERSY

TERENCE TURNER

We arrive at the final round of this discussion having found ourselves able to agree to the extent of identifying some of the issues that need to be discussed. The participants have addressed the points in question in ways that have usefully brought out further aspects of their positions. However, the discussion has so far been limited to only a few of the many issues raised by Tierney's book— mainly those arising from the 1968 AEC expedition and the measles epidemic, Chagnon's statements (and silences) about the chronic Yanomami penchant for violence ("fierceness"), and his attacks on the NGOs and missions that were struggling to prevent the breakup of the Brazilian Yanomami reserve during the crisis of the late 1980s and early 1990s.

These issues are important, but they are only a fraction of the issues arising from the conduct of Neel and the 1968 AEC expedition and do not even touch upon the more serious allegations concerning Chagnon's conduct and writings since the 1968 Orinoco expedition. Surely we can all agree that no discussion of Tierney's book can be considered complete without some attention to the chapters dealing with Chagnon's work.

We can also agree, I trust, on the importance of taking fuller account of the important new evidence that has become available from sources such as Neel's papers in the archives of the American Philosophical Society and the work of the Brazilian team of medical experts assembled by Albert. Albert has mentioned some of the main Brazilian findings, but the Neel papers have up to now remained almost entirely outside the discussion. These new sources afford independent evidence on most of the major issues raised by Tierney's book. They thus open up fresh critical perspectives on Tierney's allegations and findings, and, more important, on the conduct of Neel, Chagnon, and others involved with the Yanomami over the past three decades. I have attempted to synthesize the main findings and implications of these two important sources in my extended third contribution to this volume, which has been reduced for this publication. That longer contribution has been separately published as an Occasional Paper of the Latin American Studies Program of Cornell University (T. Turner, "The Yanomami and the Ethics of Anthropological Practice" 2002), and is available from the Cornell Program as well as on the Hume Web site (members.aol.com/archaeodog/darkness_in_el_dorado).

KEY ACCUSATIONS AND ISSUES
(see also pp. 317–41)

Did Chagnon act unethically? Chagnon violated the American Anthropology Association's code of ethics by repeated, untruthful attacks on Yanomami leaders, missionaries, and NGO activists; failing to speak out against uses of his statements that proved damaging to the Yanomami; eliciting genealogical information in ways that significantly exacerbated tensions among the Yanomami; giving gifts on such a massive scale that it led to conflict among the Yanomami; participating in the FUNDAFACI project, especially because of the way the project, if implemented, would have harmed a significant number of Yanomami; and not giving benefits to the Yanomami in return for their help. (see pages 274–77)

Given what we now know, are the accusations made against Chagnon and Neel mostly true or untrue? The American Anthropological Association's El Dorado Task Force Report confirmed a number of Tierney's serious allegations against Chagnon. (see page 278)

QUESTIONS TO CONSIDER

How many of the accusations Turner makes against Chagnon do you accept? Which ones? Why?

Does the American Anthropological Association have a role to play in ensuring that American anthropologists act in ethically proper ways during fieldwork? If so, what is its role? If not, why not?

WHAT DOES "SCIENCE" HAVE TO DO WITH IT?

I will summarize the findings of the final report concerning Chagnon later in this chapter. First, however, I must respond to comments addressed to me and other participants by Hill in his second-round paper. His opening statement that "the debate on the Tierney book has to some extent been symptomatic" of the "destructive level of tension" between what he calls "scientifically oriented anthropologists and nonscientific or even antiscientific anthropologists" has indeed been exemplified, in microcosm, by Hill's own comments, which demonstrate how the fundamentalist cult of scientism he espouses functions as a filter to distort beyond recognition the issues and interlocutors he purports to address. There is not enough space here to take on the tedious and unproductive task of dealing with Hill's irrelevant stereotypes of "scientific" and "antiscientific" positions, which have little to do with the ethical or empirical issues with which those of us at whom he aims them (Albert, Martins, and myself) are concerned. Hill's fantastic allegations about our supposedly "antiscientific" views, ethical "double standards," and "cultural relativism" have led to essentially sterile arguments that have deflected much of our discussion from developing into a genuinely critical dialogue on the real issues at stake.

These are, as I see them, the ethical issues arising from the impact of science as a social activity on the human subjects who are the objects of scientific investigation. This includes providing medical assistance in cases of medical emergency. It also includes the moral, ethical, and professional obligation to represent the human (social, cultural, and political) reality disclosed by ethnographic research as truthfully as possible and to avoid untruthfully distorting that reality to conform to theoretical or ideological preconceptions in ways that damage the public image of the people with whom one does research, or to serve as a basis for false charges against political or scientific enemies. It entails the responsibility to refrain from field methods and conduct that disrupt the social peace of communities in which one carries out research. It also implies the obligation to do what one can to help those with whom one has done one's research, in reciprocity for the hospitality and cooperation they have given to make possible one's research.

There are other ethical and scientific issues in question, but these seem to me to be the most important. It is because the conduct of Chagnon, Neel, and other researchers among the Yanomami appears to have violated these principles, not out of any supposed antipathy to "science," that I and my colleagues have criticized them. Our criticisms, and the findings of our independent research, have often converged with Tierney's allegations, although we have also made clear our critical reservations about some of Tierney's assertions, particularly about the involvement of Neel and the vaccine he used in the 1968 measles epidemic.

QUESTIONS OF VALIDITY AND ETHICS

It is time to call the bluff of those who have tried to dismiss Tierney's book by extrapolating from the flaws of his chapter on the epidemic to discredit the book as a whole. The authors of the University of California, Santa Barbara, Anthropology Department's Web site (see Chagnon et al. n.d.) have claimed to have revealed that the other chapters of the book are a mass of errors or worse, but they have in fact done no such thing. Many of the major allegations and general points in the book apart from the chapter on the epidemic remain unchallenged and appear to be well attested in the writings and statements of other anthropologists, journalists, NGO workers, government functionaries, medical workers, missionaries, and government records. Many of them have now acquired new support from the final report of the AAA El Dorado Task Force.

Hill, in his second contribution to this Roundtable, has countered that "there are considerably fewer parts of the book for which there is anything constituting good evidence [Which parts? It would be interesting to know which ones Hill does consider well founded.] and that many of the correct facts are trivial in nature." He adds, quite inaccurately, that "the anthropological testimony referred to by Turner consists mainly of ad hominem attacks through the reporting of unverifiable events supposedly witnessed by two ex-Chagnon students who both parted company with him under hostile circumstances." On the contrary, Tierney cites many anthropologists and one biologist who have either worked closely with the Yanomami in the field or made scholarly studies of the historical and ethnographic literature on them—in effect, the great majority of contemporary scholars working with the Yanomami. They include Bruce Albert, Leslie Sponsel, Jacques Lizot, Brian Ferguson, Lêda Martins, Alcida Ramos, Nelly Arvelo, and Irenäus Eibl-Eibesfeldt. Tierney draws heavily on writings and comments by all of these scholars, as well as ex-students of Chagnon like Kenneth Good, Raymond Hames, and Jesus Cardozo, and ex-collaborators like Timothy Asch. That Good and Cardozo (whom I assume are the two ex-students alluded to by Hill) "parted company with [Chagnon] under hostile circumstances," like other ex-Chagnon associates, including Tim Asch and James Neel, does not necessarily invalidate what they have to say, as Hill seems to imply. Hill to the contrary, many of the correct facts reported in the body of the book are far from "trivial in nature," as the following list reveals at a glance.

Hill remarks in his Round Two paper, "I must simply conclude that Turner and I strongly disagree on the overall veracity of the book. . . . If Turner were specific about which important allegations he considers well supported, I could respond directly as to whether I agree with his assessment of the evidence and whether the allegations are of a serious ethical or professional nature or simply charges of bad judgment and unadmirable behavior." Fair enough. I do indeed "strongly disagree" with Hill's estimate of "the overall veracity" of Tierney's book, despite my recognition of its serious errors. I do, however, agree with him that it is essential to specify which points in the book are well founded if useful discussion is to proceed. This part of my paper offers an outline of such a reading of Tierney's text.

I think that the best way to proceed is to attempt to identify and summarize in a concise manner the main allegations of ethically questionable conduct from the parts of Tierney's text that have thus far remained outside the purview of critical discussions, which have focused primarily on Neel and the epidemic. This means dealing primarily with the parts of Tierney's text that treat the actions, writings, and public statements of Napoleon Chagnon, although others— Charles Brewer-Carías, Jacques Lizot, Helena Valero, and a BBC film crew, for example—get a chapter apiece. Given the relatively peripheral relevance of these latter figures to the current debate, however, I will have to pass over Tierney's discussions of them, although I generally endorse what he has to say about them.

The shortcomings of Tierney's account of the 1968 measles epidemic are by now generally recognized. There has been no corresponding effort to recognize the major claims and analyses that appear to be well founded, let alone evaluate their ethical implications. An honest appraisal of the book will recognize that it is a mixed bag but that a lot of what it has to say is well founded and important. One contribution that even a necessarily abbreviated summary like this can make is to try to sort out the forest from the trees.

I am mindful that this Roundtable is supposed to focus on ethical issues rather than questions of fact or interpretation in and of themselves. I will therefore proceed by listing instances of ethically problematic behavior from Tierney's text that seem to be sufficiently well documented and analyzed and/or attested from other sources. I emphasize that instances of all of these ethically problematic modes of conduct were relatively well known among specialists before Tierney's book appeared. Most had already been subjects of criticism and controversy in Brazil and Venezuela. Whatever else they may be, they are not private fantasies or "deliberate frauds" on the part of Tierney, as the authors of the Santa Barbara Web page claim. They would all be around to confront the profession of anthropology with the same ethical issues even if Tierney had never written his book—as the El Dorado Task Force has now recognized in its report.

I now present a concise topical outline of the main types of ethically fraught actions described by Tierney that I deem to be well founded. My standard for judging an action, statement, or inaction as ethically fraught is the code of ethics of the AAA. At the beginning of the outline I list the six provisions of the AAA code of ethics that are specifically relevant to the actions I include. For ease of reference, each provision is identified by its numerical designation in the text of the code. The numerical designations are then included in the topical outline of types of actions with each issue to which they pertain. Each topic in the outline carries chapter and page references to places in Tierney's text and some other sources where it is mentioned and described. Each of these actions is more fully discussed in my Occasional Paper, The Yanomami and the Ethics of anthropological Practice, but there is no space to include these fuller discussions here.

OUTLINE SUMMARY OF ETHICALLY
PROBLEMATIC ACTIONS REPORTED BY TIERNEY

Relevant provisions of the "Code of Ethics of the American Anthropological Association," listed by their headings in the code

III. Research: Introduction. ". . . Anthropological researchers should be alert to the danger of compromising anthropological ethics as a condition to engage in research, yet also be alert to proper demands of good citizenship or host-guest relations."

III.A. "Responsibility to people and animals with whom anthropological researchers work and whose lives and cultures they study"

III.A.1. "Anthropological researchers have primary ethical obligations to the people, species, and materials they study and to the people with whom they work. These obligations can supersede the goal of seeking new knowledge, and can lead to decisions not to undertake or to discontinue a research project when the primary obligation conflicts with other responsibilities, such as those owed to sponsors or clients."

III.A.2. "Anthropological researchers must do everything in their power to ensure that their research does not harm the safety, dignity or privacy of the people with whom they work, conduct research, or perform other professional activities. . . ."

III. A. 4. "Anthropological researchers should obtain in advance the informed consent of persons being studied, providing information, owning or controlling access to material being studied, or otherwise identified as having interests which might be impacted by the research. . . ."

III. A. 6. "While anthropologists may gain personally from their work, they must not exploit individuals, groups, animals, or cultural or biological materials. They should recognize their debt to the societies in which they work and their obligation to reciprocate with people studied in appropriate ways."

III. B. "Responsibility to scholarship and science"

III. B. 2. "Anthropological researchers bear responsibility for the integrity and reputation of their discipline, of scholarship, and of science. Thus, anthropological researchers are subject to the general moral rules of scientific and scholarly conduct: they should not deceive or knowingly misrepresent (i.e., fabricate evidence, falsify, plagiarize), or attempt to prevent reporting of misconduct, or obstruct the scientific/scholarly research of others."

III. C. "Responsibility to the public"

III. C. 1. "Anthropological researchers should make the results of their research appropriately available to sponsors, students, decision makers, and other nonanthropologists. In so doing, they must be truthful; they are not only responsible for the factual content of their statements but also they must consider carefully the social and political implications of the information they disseminate. They must do everything in their power to ensure that such information is well understood, properly contextualized, and responsibly utilized. They should make clear the empirical bases upon which their reports stand, be candid about their qualifications and philosophical or political biases, and recognize and make clear the limits of anthropological expertise. At the same time, they must be alert to possible harm their information may cause people with whom they work or colleagues."

Types of ethically problematic conduct
described by Tierney: a topical outline

[Reference code: Chapter and page numbers in italics refer respectively to chapters and pages in *Darkness in El Dorado*, except where indicated otherwise. References to works by other authors as indicated.]

I. Statements and silences by Chagnon damaging to the Yanomami (pertinent provisions of code of ethics: III.A.2., III.B.2., III.C.1., with specific relevance as indicated)

I. A. Statements and silences (failure to speak out against uses of statements about "fierceness" or violent aggressiveness as a dominant feature of Yanomami society damaging to the Yanomami (*xxi, 8, 13–14, 160, 164, 232*) (pertinent provisions of code of ethics: III.A.2., III.C.1.)

I.B. Repeated and untruthful attacks on NGOs, anthropological activists, and Yanomami leaders

I.B.1. Untruthful attacks on NGOs and anthropological activists (pertinent provisions of code of ethics: III.A.2., III.B.2.) (*xxii, xxiii, 9–11*)

I.B.2. Untruthful attacks on Yanomami leaders: (pertinent provisions of code of ethics: III.A.2., III.B.2.) Davi Kopenawa (*xii, 11, 201, 227*), (Chagnon 1997:252–54); Alfredo Aherowe (*292–94*)

I.C. False accusations against missions and NGOs of "killing" Yanomami or otherwise being responsible for raising their death rate (pertinent provision of code of ethics: III.B.2.)

   1. Deceptive statistics on mission death rate (*ch. X; appendix: 317–26*)

   2. The massacre at Haximu (*ch. XII: 195–214*)

   3. "The guns of Mucajaí" (*ch. XII: 210–13*)

   4. The Lechoza massacre (*ch. XII: 238–40*)

I.D. Misrepresentation of ethnographic reality (noncorrespondence of data and theoretical claims supportive of theses on "fierceness," violence, and warfare) Tierney's critique of Chagnon's article "Life Histories, Blood Revenge, and Warfare in a Tribal Population" [*Science* 239: 985–92(1988)] (*26, Ch X*) (pertinent provision of code of ethics: III.B.2.)

I.E. Misrepresentation of Yanomami reality in films: "choreographed violence," misrepresentation in films (ch. XIV: *85–88, 101–4, 114–19, 216–17*) (pertinent provision of code of ethics: III.B.2.)

II. Field methods disruptive of Yanomami society (pertinent provision of code of ethics: III.A.2.: applies to all the following subheadings)

II.A. Elicitation of pedigrees in ways that exacerbate tensions among enemies, factions, and communities (e.g., obtaining names of dead from enemies, then telling relatives of deceased) (*30, 32, 33, 42, 45–68; 185*)

II.B. Resort to threatening methods by Chagnon to secure cooperation by informants (e.g., brandishing and shooting of firearms, performances as "vulture-spirit" shaman, etc.)

   1. Use of firearms to intimidate (pistol, shotgun) (*31, 46, 89, 232, 283, 362n21*)

   2. Shamanic vulture spirit child-killing performances (*46–47, 89*)

II.C. Gift giving on massive scale as cause of conflicts. (*ch. III, 18–35*). See also Ferguson 1995, chs. XIII, XIV

II.C.1. Wars between villages attached to sources of trade goods (anthropologists or independent Yanomami cooperative organization, SUYAO [United Yanomami Communities of the Upper Orinoco]).

   a. Between "Chagnon's village" and "Lizot's village" (*141–43*);

   b. Between "Chagnon's village" and "SUYAO village" (*227*)

II.C.2. Personal participation by Chagnon in raids (providing transportation to raiding parties) (*33, 166*)

III. Failure to get informed consent (and obtaining consent with misinformation) for research on human subjects (pertinent provision of code of ethics: III.A.4: applies to both the following subheadings)

III.A. No informed consent for research practices, including vaccinations (failure to explain that there was a research motive for collecting specimens and vaccinations; failure to explain that the blood would be stored indefinitely, potentially outlasting the lives of the donors) (43–45)

III.B. Misinformed consent: Yanomami and missionaries led to believe that taking blood was for medical help (44–45)

IV. The Siapa Biosphere Project in collaboration with Brewer-Carías and FUNDAFACI: alliances with political and extractivist interests hostile to Yanomami control of land and resources; active collaboration in projects potentially harmful to Yanomami rights and interests (pertinent provisions of code of ethics to all three of the following subheadings: introduction excerpt; III.A.1.; III.A.2.; III.A.4.)

IV. A. Brewer-Chagnon project for research reserve in the Siapa valley, FUNDAFACI support. This project was intended to exclude "acculturated" and "mission" Yanomami, leaving more than 80 percent of the Yanomami area and population contained in the previously projected biosphere reserve unprotected (*ch. XI, 181–94*)

IV.B. FUNDAFACI flights with unquarantined journalists and political figures: illegality, medical risks, damage to shelters and persons from helicopters (3–5, 282, 290–91, 294)

IV.C. Misrepresentation of Siapa "first contact" to generate press support for Siapa preserve (187, 290)

V. Failure to reciprocate, return benefits to Yanomami: (pertinent provision of code of ethics: III.A.6.) Yanomami Survival Fund apparently inactive since founding or soon thereafter (188–89)

THE BEARING OF THE "FINAL REPORT OF THE EL DORADO TASK FORCE" ON THE ALLEGATIONS OF UNETHICAL CONDUCT BY NEEL AND CHAGNON

Since writing the original draft of this chapter, a major new source has appeared in the form of the "Final Report of the Task Force of the American Anthropological Association" appointed to investigate the allegations of Patrick Tierney and related issues concerning the Yanomami and anthropological ethics. This document is excessively long and internally inconsistent, oscillating between whitewash, tendentious distortion of evidence and strategic omission in its section on Neel, and reasonably accurate critical review and commentary in some of its discussions of Chagnon's statements and activities.

The Task Force often appeared to be more concerned with defending the American researchers accused by Tierney than with getting at the truth of his allegations, even to the extent of attempting to stack the membership of the group by adding a blatant supporter of Chagnon (who was eventually obliged to resign on grounds of conflict of interest) under political pressure from Chagnon partisans. Its preliminary report—which completely omitted discussion of many of the main issues, suggested that there was no evidence to support Tierney's more serious allegations, and predicted that the final report would arrive at the same conclusion—aroused a storm of protest at the 2001 AAA meeting. Two members of the Task Force refused to sign the report, and the Society of Latin American Anthropology voted unanimously to demand its recall. Strenuous criticisms were also voiced at the business meeting later the same evening.

The storm of criticism obviously took the chair of the Task Force and the president of the association by surprise. To their credit, they responded flexibly by assenting to the demands of members to open the Task Force's Web page to comments and to research inputs from non–Task Force members. A large number of critical comments, some lengthy and well researched, were submitted. The more important of these were duly included as appendices of the final report, and clearly had an affect on the preparation of its final draft. This rebellion by the membership against the attempt of the association's leadership to sweep the controversy and the ethical issues it had raised under the rug, and its effective contributions to researching a number of the allegations that became integrated to a degree as appendices in the report, was a momentous event in the history of the association. It evidently put some steel in the backbone of the Task Force leadership and some members, and is doubtlessly responsible for the strength of some parts of the final report (particularly those dealing with Chagnon).

However this may be, the final report does conclude that most of Tierney's more serious allegations against Chagnon (and some made by other researchers that Tierney missed), including those summarized in the six points of the preceding outline, are borne out by the evidence, and concurs that some do indeed constitute serious violations of professional ethics. Among the specific allegations of unethical conduct by Chagnon that the report finds have validity are that he made damaging and unfounded public statements about the Yanomami and organizations that were working to help them that undermined the struggle to create the Brazilian Yanomami reserve; that he failed to speak out against misuses of these statements by Brazilian politicians, military leaders, and journalists to block the formation of the Brazilian Yanomami reserve; that he made damaging and unfounded attacks on Yanomami leaders and spokespeople, threatening the political effectiveness of these leaders and thus endangering the interests of the Yanomami communities they represented in relations with non-indigenous groups; that he made misleading statements and false assurances of medical benefits to induce the Yanomami to allow the collection of blood and other biological specimens; that he collaborated in the 1990s with corrupt Venezuelan politicians engaged in criminal activities related to a scheme to set up a much reduced Yanomami reserve in the Siapa Valley, which would have allowed illegal mining to go forward on Yanomami land excluded from the new reserve, and would have given him and his collaborator, Charles Brewer-Carias (a right-wing politician implicated in illegal gold mining schemes on indigenous lands, whom Chagnon represented as a "naturalist"), control over the area; and that he brought many outsiders into this area without the mandatory quarantine precautions, risking, and probably causing, outbreaks of disease among previously uncontacted Yanomami (AAA 2002, vol. I, part I:2.2.1, 2.2.C).

What some Chagnon partisans have stigmatized as mere charges of Chagnon's "guilt by association" (referring to academic critics of his collaboration with Brewer-Carias and Cecilia Matos in the Siapa valley affair) were made in more concrete terms by the Venezuelan military pilots who eventually refused to fly Chagnon and his associates into Yanomami areas, on the grounds that they were illegally misusing public funds and military equipment and personnel for their private purposes, as well as violating other national laws for the protection of indigenous peoples against mining and the taking of biological samples without permission from the proper government bodies. Chagnon's associate Cecilia Matos was tried and found guilty for crimes including her involvement in activities in which Chagnon participated (2202, vol. I, part I:2.2.C).

The report further concludes that Chagnon has misrepresented Yanomami ethnographic and historical reality in ethically consequential ways. Contrary to the claim of certain partisans that "the panel [Task Force] did not seriously contest the accuracy of his [Chagnon's] portrayals or demonstrate any material damage that the villagers might have suffered from them" (Gregor and Gross 2002, B:11; cf. refutation by Sponsel and Turner 2002, B:13) the Task Force report does both (AAA 2002, vol. I, part I:2.2.1). The section of the report entitled "The Problem of Representation" criticizes Chagnon's representations of the Yanomami as specimens of a prior stage of human evolutionary history, which it terms the "denial of coevalness," as fundamentally erroneous both in theoretical and empirical terms, that itself represents an ideological throwback to an earlier stage of anthropological development (2002, vol. I, part I:2.2.b.3). This discredited interpretation is fundamental to Chagnon's representations of the Yanomami as "fierce" savages. These are precisely the statements that are at the center of the allegations of his violations of anthropological ethics by making damaging statements that he knew would be used to damage Yanomami interests by those opposed to Yanomami struggles to retain their territorial rights and failing to speak out against these misuses when they duly occurred. This point about empirical and theoretical "accuracy" is thus inseparable from the allegations about the unethical character of Chagnon's statements and silences (on this topic, see also documentation by Survival International on their Web site or the Hume Web site).

The report lists still other instances of unethical conduct by Chagnon. It presents considerable documentation of another serious allegation, that Chagnon in various ways actually caused or helped cause much of the fighting that he made the focus of his studies of the "fierce" Yanomami. This documentation includes charges by Yanomami that Chagnon actually paid them to go out on raids against other Yanomami (2002: vol. 2, part V:5.8; Appendix: Interview with Davi Kopenawa Yanomami, "Davi Kopenawa responds to William Irons").[1] It also includes evidence that he facilitated a raid on an enemy village by providing motorboat transportation to the raiding party. The Task Force failed to reach a conclusion on the validity of these charges because the member who had been responsible for this section (Raymond Hames) resigned on grounds of conflict of interest before completing his inquiry, so the question is left open in the report. That the chair of the Task Force had assigned Hames the sole responsibility for reporting on this extremely sensitive issue despite the conflict of interest which forced his resignation is in itself a telling comment on the political weakness and propensity for appeasement of the sociobiology–evolutionary psychology lobby that pressured a weak president to appoint Hames in the first place, with the collaboration of the chair of the Task Force (2002: vol. 1, part I:1.3.2; part II:2.2)

Besides these general issues, the report also mentions numerous specific actions actually or potentially damaging to Yanomami social, cultural, and/or physical well-being, such as damaging village shelters and injuring villagers by landing helicopters in the central courtyards of the shelters; ignoring quarantine precautions before entering Yanomami communities vulnerable to outside diseases; carrying cans of chemical mace and other antipersonnel weapons for defense against members of host communities; manipulating children as informants; and repeatedly violating local customs and taboos such as speaking the names of the dead in indiscrete ways calculated to arouse resentment and hostility. The report also raises the issue of Chagnon's failure to reciprocate to the Yanomami for the benefits he has derived from his research among them. Finally, the report recognizes a "pattern" in Chagnon's repeated violations of local laws and requirements for permission from governmental authorities in his clandestine attempts to take more blood samples from Yanomami communities (2002, vol. 1, part II:2.2; vol. 2, part V:5.8).

When it became obvious in the final weeks before the release of the report that the Task Force was going to be critical of Chagnon on a number of serious issues, his supporters reverted to their initial strategy of attacking the memo that Leslie Sponsel and I had originally sent to the leaders of the association to warn them to prepare to investigate the allegations in Tierney's book and their scandalous implications. They sent a coordinated salvo of memos to the association's Web page accusing us of "bearing false witness" in our original memo (which we had not done). It was a bankrupt strategy. Once the Task Force of generally reluctant colleagues had finished their work and collectively put their names to the report's long litany of charges of unethical conduct by Chagnon, and some by Neel, the cat was out of the bag, and no amount of killing the messengers would be able to force it back in. No amount of hammering our two-year old memo has been able to distract attention from the extensive research carried out by us and many other scholars and critics, as well as the voluminous valid evidence presented by Tierney that is now supported by the report. We are still waiting for the partisans of sociobiological "science" to confront and deal with this evidence, as some at least of the authors of the report have done.

In supporting so many of Tierney's allegations, the report has vindicated the value and importance of Tierney's work for anthropology, even while recognizing its shortcomings, as well as much of the new research produced by other critics of Neel, Chagnon, and colleagues, both here and in Brazil. The scale and gravity of the unethical conduct the report examines and confirms, and in some of the worst cases considers but leaves undecided, fully justifies the association's undertaking this investigation, and thus also Sponsel's and my action in alerting the leadership to the need for the inquiry through our original memo. Despite clamorous pressures and intimidation by the highly organized Chagnon and Neel partisans, and the weakness and vacillations of the association and Task Force leadership epitomized by the shameful Hames affair, the authors of the report, supported by important elements of the membership, found the courage and will to examine important parts of the evidence and to speak the truth about their implications. After an uncertain start they ended by acting as a truth commission, demonstrating for the first time in a case of this magnitude that the association's code of ethics can be effectively applied to evaluate and sanction unethical conduct that violates its principles. The public announcement of the judgment of a duly constituted investigative body that such violations occurred is in itself an effective sanction—otherwise the partisans of Neel and Chagnon would not have gone to such lengths to prevent it. This is a salutary precedent with implications for the association and the practice of anthropology far beyond the specific case of the Yanomami.

NOTE

1. The thirty-one appendixes to the report, consisting of comments by members generally critical of the interpretations of issues presented in the preliminary draft of the report, are listed in the report's table of contents but were unfortunately not included in the printed version of the report. They remain on the Web page of the Task Force, within the overall Web page of the AAA (www.aaanet.org/committees/ethics/ethcode.htm).

11

....

THREE ASSESSMENTS

In drawing the book's themes together in this final chapter, we turn to three assessments of the Yanomami controversy. The assessments consider the following questions: What are the key issues at stake in the controversy? How do we ethically assess what the various participants did (and did not) do—from Neel, Chagnon, and Tierney on the one hand to American anthropology and the American Anthropological Association on the other? And, most critically—since assessing blame for past actions is less important than trying to ensure that we do not repeat the ills so openly displayed in the controversy—where do we go from here? How might we develop a more publicly concerned and just anthropology?

The first assessment involves a joint letter written by the Roundtable's six participants and myself. As the El Dorado Task Force was being formed during the spring of 2001, a call went out for information. The seven of us decided to send the Task Force the Roundtable discussion (of chapters 8, 9, and 10) along with a letter emphasizing our shared concerns. The joint letter offers a counterpoint to the exchanges of the previous chapters because it emphasizes points the six participants hold in common. The problem is that these agreements are abstractly phrased. Participants in the Roundtable could concur on a number of critical points as long as major figures in the controversy—Neel, Chagnon, and Tierney—were not mentioned. Agreement broke down when one or another participant sought to discuss specific actions by specific people.

Still, important points are raised. The letter discusses (a) professional integrity, (b) just compensation, (c) "doing no harm," (d) the need to address complaints of non-American anthropologists regarding work done in their countries, and (e) the importance of having the Task Force's deliberations a public, educational process. There is an honest effort to consider what needs to be changed in anthropology and how we might do that.

The second assessment involves the El Dorado Task Force reports. I refer to "reports" (rather than "report") because, as mentioned in chapter 3, there were two reports prepared by the El Dorado Task Force that was commissioned by the American Anthropological Association to investigate the accusations in Tierney's *Darkness in El Dorado*: a preliminary one (that caused an uproar among critics of Chagnon) and a final one (that directly addressed Chagnon's actions). The final report is the most direct assessment of Neel's, Chagnon's, and Tierney's actions that we are likely to see by the AAA. Whether one agrees or disagrees with the assessment—and there are anthropologists in both camps—one should view the final report as an act of courage. Not since 1919—when the American Anthropological Association censured Boas—has the AAA formally criticized a famous member of the discipline so publicly.

One might examine the two reports independently of each other. But I think it makes more sense to compare them. If we use the reports as a case study of how American anthropology ethically regulates itself in the face of public pressure, we might consider the following question: what did the preliminary report assert regarding the controversy's key accusations and to what degree these statements were (or were not) changed as a result of public pressure in the final report?

I have enclosed summaries of the two reports as well as a sampling of comments from people who e-mailed in their comments. As previously noted, I believe that what brought the change between the two reports was the more than 170 comments that flooded into the AAA Web site between March 1 and April 19, 2002. Since many of the experts' positions in these commentaries were well known (and had been mostly discounted by the other side before this), I deduce that it was the outpouring of the student comments that led the Task Force to make significant changes in the preliminary report.*

The third assessment is your own. In chapter 6, I outlined a number of questions anthropologists need to grapple with—relating to informed consent, "doing no harm," just compensation, professional integrity, and establishing credibility. After reading parts 1 and 2 and the two assessments in this chapter, it is reasonable to ask where you, the reader, stand? What do you perceive as the central concerns involved in the controversy? Would you assess blame, and if so in what ways regarding which people or groups? And, most critically, how would you set things right?

....

I. AN OPEN LETTER
TO OUR ANTHROPOLOGICAL COLLEAGUES

October 8, 2001

Dear Colleagues,

This is an open letter addressed to the American Anthropological Association's El Dorado Task Force by the members of this Roundtable. Despite our clear disagreements regarding Tierney's *Darkness in El Dorado*—disagreements

---

*One hundred nineteen students sent in e-mails versus 36 professional anthropologists. Since some people sent in more than one comment, the 119 students constituted 77 percent of the total number of commentators.

EXCERPTS FROM THIS SECTION

"If the AAA is to be a self-regulating profession—rather than an organization regulated by outside authorities—it needs to make effective ethical assessments of its members' behaviors during and following fieldwork. Certain issues raised by Tierney had been brought before the AAA in the late 1980s and early 1990s. . . . But the AAA proved unable or unwilling at that time to address them in a fair and open manner. While Tierney's *Darkness in El Dorado* contains clear errors, the public uproar his book caused has proved critical in forcing the AAA to address a set of ethical issues it should have addressed on its own well prior to the book's publication."

"We would offer the following as guidelines for [just compensation]. . . . A mutually agreed upon equitable division of all royalties . . . Given that most anthropologists gain little in the way of royalties they might share, . . . there are still a variety of ways they might redress the basic asymmetries of research. The key . . . is working with informants and their communities to address their collective needs as they stipulate them—not as an anthropologist stipulates them. . . . The essential point is that anthropologists must provide help in terms that the people themselves directly perceive and directly appreciate."

"Anthropologists are morally responsible to counter abusive uses of their work when it is made known to them by local officials and/or anthropologists. They need to speak out in clear and public ways in the countries involved that they oppose the implications others draw from their work, particularly when such implications harm informants in ways the anthropologist never intended."

"The American Anthropological Association should . . . invest both time and energy in encouraging American graduate programs to include a substantive course in ethics prior to fieldwork. Further, the schools that conduct such courses should be placed publicly on the association's Web site."

"The Association's members need to collectively participate in the deliberations [of the El Dorado Task Force]. . . . The inquiry needs to be a collective process in which, through our shared wisdom as anthropologists, we shape our shared future as a profession."

---

which reflect the arguments the book has provoked within the profession as a whole—we collectively affirm it raises important ethical issues which are central to the current discussion. These call for a renewed discussion of general principles of research ethics and the responsibilities of anthropologists to the peoples they study. We would draw the El Dorado Task Force's attention to several points in this regard.

First, the American Anthropological Association has to date proved ineffective—by its own admission—in adjudicating ethical issues relating to the behaviors of its members. As the 1995 "Final Report of the Commission to Review the AAA Statements on Ethics" states: "To be useful a[n] adjudication system must: [a] Ensure due process, which involves collection of data, interviews, hearings, etc., [b] have the ability to impose meaningful sanctions, [c] have moral, if not legal standing, [d] be willing and able to take on all appropriate claims, [and e] be able to deliver what it promises. The Commission found that the AAA adjudication process failed to meet all of these tests" (*Anthropology Newsletter*, April 1996:13).

Yet if the AAA is to be a self-regulating profession—rather than an organization regulated by outside authorities—it needs to make effective ethical assessments of its members' behaviors during and following fieldwork. Certain issues raised by Tierney had been brought before the AAA in the late 1980s and early 1990s, well before the book's publication in the fall of 2000. But the AAA proved unable or unwilling at that time to address them in a fair and open manner. While Tierney's *Darkness in El Dorado* contains clear errors, the public uproar his book caused has proved critical in forcing the AAA to address a set of ethical issues it should have addressed on its own well prior to the book's publication.

Second, the dynamics of fieldwork often reinforce a broader political/economic asymmetrical relationship between "First" and "Third World" peoples. Anthropologists travel abroad, collect socially significant information through the goodwill of informants, return to write papers and/or books based on this information, and through such writing gain a professional position with, often, a professional salary. The informants, who provided the information, tend to remain in the same political/economic subordinate condition as before. Simply offering gifts during fieldwork does not compensate for the asymmetrical advantages that accrue to the anthropologist from the field-worker-informant relationship.

Related to this problem is another: Researchers commonly face conflicts between meeting personal research objectives and addressing the needs of the people studied. Researchers should attempt to balance these demands as far as possible so as, on the one hand, to keep faith with the sponsors of their research and, on the other, to acknowledge their ethical responsibilities to the people they work with—particularly recognizing and respecting their human rights.

Building on this point, we would note anthropologists collecting biological samples often explain these collections as benefiting the people involved. This may hold true in an abstract sense, since in collecting such biological samples we may learn more about the health of human beings. Clearly, however, this is not the same thing as providing medical assistance to the actual people who are asked to donate the samples. One might well argue that framing benefits in these abstract terms—as helping humanity rather than helping the particular people involved—constitutes another case of the political/economic asymmetry noted above: researchers advance their careers through fieldwork; informants do not. The principle that should regulate informed consent and ethical practice alike in the collection of biological samples is that the health and welfare of the study population must always take precedence over any academic or scientific goal.

Central to providing both balance and justice, within this context, is a negotiated contract among the parties involved regarding the benefits accruing to each as a result of their relationship. Whether interpreted within the framework of gifts or exchanges, there needs to be clearly defined rewards. Yet because of the noted political/economic asymmetry, anthropologists often are at an advantage in such negotiations—having a clearer sense of the value gained in relation to the rewards returned. As a rule of thumb, one might follow John Rawls's "veil of ignorance" in which anthropologists consider what constitutes a just balance without presuming to know which side— informant or anthropologist—they are on. As Rawls phrases it with the veil of ignorance, "the parties are not allowed to know the social positions . . . of the parties they represent." What would anthropologists claim to be fair— under these circumstances—for all parties concerned?

We would offer the following as guidelines for answering this question:

(a) A mutually agreed upon equitable division of all royalties that accrue to an anthropologist through the publication of works relating to the people involved. Such remuneration might take a range of forms: in the case of the Yanomami, for example, it could involve reimbursing individuals and groups or using the royalty payments to support projects directed by Venezuelan and Brazilian Yanomami and non-Yanomami specialized NGOs to improve medical, economic, educational, and environmental conditions. (b) A mutually agreed upon equitable division of all royalties drawn from biological specimens—either from the indigenous group itself or from flora and fauna in the area where the group resides—in a manner similar to that noted above. (c) Given that most anthropologists gain little in the way of royalties they might share with their communities of study, there are still a variety of ways they might redress the basic asymmetries of research.

The key here is working with informants and their communities to address their collective needs as they stipulate them—not as an anthropologist stipulates them. For example, informants may be eligible for governmental assistance but, for a variety of reasons, are unable to gain access to it. Informants may request anthropologists, given their skills in dealing with bureaucracies, to lobby on behalf of their communities. Likewise, communities may be short of medicines, such as antimalarial drugs, which the anthropologist can purchase. The anthropologist can, then, offer these medicines to the people themselves and/or restock local dispensaries. The essential point is that anthropologists must provide help in terms that the people themselves directly perceive and directly appreciate.

Third, anthropologists should take care to avoid constructing gratuitously damaging images or accounts of their subjects in their publications and media contacts to prevent possible harm to the dignity and welfare of the individuals and groups they study. Having taken such care, anthropologists cannot be held responsible for the diverse and, particularly abusive, use of their publications. That is a matter of free speech. But, by the same token, anthropologists are morally responsible to counter abusive uses of their work when it is made known to them by local officials and/or anthropologists. They need to speak out in clear and public ways in the countries involved that they oppose the implications others draw from their work, particularly when such implications harm informants in ways the anthropologist never intended.

Fourth, there are a variety of reasons why the American Anthropological Association should maintain collegial relations with other national anthropological associations: as a sign of professional respect, to facilitate international cooperation among anthropologists, and to gain these associations' support for fieldwork in their countries. It is, therefore, critical that the association treat these other associations' concerns and complaints, regarding American anthropologists and American anthropology, in a formal and professional manner. The American Anthropological Association failed to do this in respect to the complaint lodged by the Brazilian Anthropological Association in 1988 concerning Napoleon Chagnon's writing. Specifically, it did not have a structure in place by which to deal with the Brazilian Anthropological Association's complaint at an organization-to-organizational level. The American Anthropological Association should now (a) establish a means for addressing such organizational complaints in the future and (b) write a formal letter of apology to the Brazilian Anthropological Association regarding AAA's failure to address their earlier complaint that will be published in both associations' newsletters.

Fifth, the American Anthropological Association needs to more vigorously pursue its own self-proclaimed educational efforts in the field of ethics. The American Anthropological Association's Executive Board accepted the Commission to Review the AAA Statements on Ethics' "recommendation that the AAA focus on an ethics education program for the American Anthropological Association and no longer seek to adjudicate claims of unethical behavior" (*Anthropology Newsletter* April 1996:14). What is certainly disturbing is that such educational efforts, if they exist, are barely recognizable by association members. The commission listed as the "objectives of the ethics education program . . . (1) to increase the number of candidates for all degrees in anthropology receiving training in ethics before graduating, (2) to provide ongoing education in ethical issues for all AAA members, and (3) to provide advice to AAA members facing/raising ethical dilemmas." To support this program, the Commission offered the following suggestions:

> The AAA should (a) produce and periodically update a publication of case studies of ethical dilemmas anthropological researchers, teachers and practitioners might face, suitable for use in graduate training, postdoctorate training, and continuing education. [We would stress, the only publications widely familiar to the profession on ethics were published well before the Commission's report.

The publication listed on the association's Web site, Cassell and Jacobs' *Handbook on Ethical Issues in Anthropology*, was published in 1987. Fluehr-Lobban's *Ethics and the Profession of Anthropology* was published in 1991.] (b) The AAA should provide departments technical assistance in establishing educational offerings in ethics. (c) The AAA should conduct ethics training workshops at annual meetings and during the year. (d) The AAA should seek a joint grant with one or more other social science organizations to develop a basic ethics teaching module which could be used by all social sciences, calling on resources from across the campus, and which would be supplemented with department training specific to the discipline. (e) The AAA should develop broad guidelines to help departments determine the appropriate minimum of ethics training which should be offered to different levels of students (*Anthropology Newsletter*, April 1996:14–15).

Clearly, this has not occurred. The American Anthropological Association should therefore—in line with its own recommendations—now invest both time and energy in encouraging American graduate programs to include a substantive course in ethics prior to fieldwork. Further, the schools that conduct such courses should be placed publicly on the association's Web site. Certificates of completion might be issued to students who have performed satisfactorily in such courses. These certificates can then be presented to the relevant authorities, anthropological associations, and/or indigenous associations, if requested, in the countries of proposed research.

Finally, given that the American Anthropological Association, by its own admission, has proven ineffective in adjudicating ethical cases relating to the behaviors of its members, it should encourage the wider participation of its membership in its ethical deliberations. The open, public discussion of specific ethical problems—as has occurred in our Roundtable—allows association members to personally grapple with serious ethical issues in ways that abstract reports from the association do not. The experience is far more empowering, far more educational.

But to do this, the American Anthropological Association needs to make the materials used in its deliberations more public. The secrecy that presently shrouds the association's inquiry into Tierney's *Darkness in El Dorado* contradicts the insistence enshrined in fundamental American democratic principles that (a) the presentation of evidence should occur in open court and (b) the "Sunshine Laws" of many states that require important government committees, boards, and council meetings be open to the public. This openness fits with the association's own code of ethics: "III.B.5. Anthropological researchers should seriously consider all reasonable requests for access to their data and other research materials."

The El Dorado Task Force should (a) make available for public release, at the earliest possible moment, an annotated bibliography of all the documents used in their deliberations. (b) Documents that can be released for general consumption, should be. (c) In respect to documents which, because of their personal nature, need remain private, the Inquiry should provide a clear, written justification for such action in each case. The deliberations themselves may remain private but the materials used in arriving at decisions should be a matter of public record.

It would be a disservice to AAA members and to anthropology, more broadly, if the association—which, by its own admission, has proven ineffective in such matters to date—should now take upon itself sole responsibility for making judgments, in complete secrecy, on such a heated subject. To repeat, the process needs to be a shared, educational one for AAA members. The association cannot produce future ethical guidelines from on high. The association's members need to collectively participate in the deliberations. And to do this, the membership needs the documents the El Dorado Task Force uses to draw its conclusions. A formal report—without an annotated bibliography of all the evidence collected, without a chance to ponder the evidence before being requested to vote on accepting the Inquiry's report—simply will not do. The inquiry needs to be a collective process in which, through our shared wisdom as anthropologists, we shape our shared future as a profession.

Whatever intellectual differences on matters discussed in the Roundtable, our joint letter represents clear agreement on these critical ethical issues. We collectively urge the El Dorado Task Force to address them.

> BRUCE ALBERT *(Research Institute for Development-IRD—São Paulo, Paris)*
> RAYMOND HAMES *(University of Nebraska)*
> KIM HILL *(University of New Mexico)*
> LÊDA LEITÃO MARTINS *(Cornell University)*
> JOHN PETERS *(Wilfrid Laurier University)*
> TERENCE TURNER *(Cornell University)*
> ROBERT BOROFSKY *(Hawaii Pacific University)*, *Roundtable Convener*

II. THE EL DORADO TASK FORCE REPORTS

[Note: Citations in this section refer to page numbers in the preliminary report or volumes I and II of the final report.]

As noted in chapter 3, the El Dorado Task Force was formally set up by the American Anthropological Association to inquire into the accusations presented by Patrick Tierney in *Darkness in El Dorado*. A preliminary report was presented at the American Anthropological Association's 2001 annual meeting and was soundly criticized. That criticism led the Task Force at its February meeting to make clear which members had written what sections. The preliminary report summarized here is basically the report as it stood in February 2002. The final report summarized here is the version presented on the AAA Web site, dated May 18, 2002. I have excerpted quotes from the reports and commentaries so authors can speak for themselves. Obviously, there is editing in this and, equally obvious given the partisan nature of the arguments, some would wish for more quotes, more space. The summary that follows is only a guide to the more than five hundred pages of the report.*

Let me add three further comments. First, in the final report's summary below, the focus is on the "Introductory Statements by the Entire Task Force" (vol. I:21–47). Here Task Force members were able to reach—openly and publicly—a consensus.

Second, the request for information called for in the "Open Letter to Our Anthropological Colleagues" reproduced earlier in this chapter was only partly addressed in the Task Force's final report. The report lists over 170 references, but few are cited in the "Introductory Statements by the Entire Task Force." Although certain individuals were interviewed (see I: 11–12 of the report), the details of what they said remains unclear, and the final report's interview list is noticeably missing "many of the key anthropologists mentioned in the [Tierney's] book" (*Anthropology News*, April 2001:59); Tierney himself was not interviewed. Such interviews were called for when the Task Force was established. The Task Force has certainly done extensive and thoughtful research in preparing the final report. But the report does not enable readers to follow the specific data that contributed to the members asserting particular conclusions. That story remains to be told.

Third, we might reflect, as we read the summary, on what the final report's ultimate goal was. Was it to simply make public what its members agreed on? Or was it to spur the AAA to action? As noted in chapter 7, the AAA affirmed that it would take a number of actions in light of the El Dorado Task Force's final report. To date, *most* of these have not been carried out. But the Task Force certainly deserves credit for achieving the first goal—reaching consensus on a number of important points. Given the politics involved, this was a major accomplishment.

The final report was written by Jane Hill (Task Force chair), Fernando Coronil, Janet Chernela, Trudy Turner, and Joe Watkins. Raymond Hames, as indicated in chapter 3, participated in the preparation of the preliminary report.

INTRODUCTION

The introductory sections to the preliminary and final reports overlap in numerous ways, with both making many of the same points. As the final report

---

*Because the two Task Force reports were published on the Web in Adobe's PDF format, I include volume numbers and page numbers for the citations. This is not feasible for the comments. But specific quotations can easily be found by searching for the individual under the El Dorado Task Force Report on the AAA's Web site at www.aaanet.org. The final report can be found at http://www.aaanet.org/edtf/index.htm. Although the preliminary report was removed from the AAA Web site when the final report was published, a partial copy of it, dated November 19, 2001, is located on the Hume Web site at http://members.aol.com/archaeodog/darkness_in_el_dorado/papers.htm. The Hume Web site copy of the report presently is missing the section on "Allegations and Case Studies."

"Darkness in El Dorado has served anthropology well in that it has opened a space for reflection and stocktaking about what we do and our relationships with those among whom we are privileged to study." (Final Report)

"We must attend carefully to the responses of colleagues internationally, who have asked why American anthropologists are moved to action by an attack from outside the profession, but not by the collegial inquiry and concerns of our fellow anthropologists in other countries." (Final Report)

"I asked six specialists who have worked with the Yanomami if they had been - approached by the Task Force [for information], and none had." (Commentary: L. Sponsel)

states, the American Anthropological Association's Executive Board's charge to the Task Force "to conduct an 'inquiry' is unprecedented in the history of the association, so that the Task Force had to think about what an 'inquiry' might be. The term implies reflection on the truth or falsity of allegations—and also of reflection of a moral and theoretical kind as well. In no sense did we consider our work to be an 'investigation.' Nor did we consider the materials that we developed to be 'evidence.' Where we found that it was possible to suggest something about the truth or falsity of allegations (or of the approximate location of an allegation in the large zone that exists between these two poles) we have done so" (I:9).

The final report goes on to state:

> We concur with the findings of the AAA Executive Board, based on the report of the Peacock Committee [the Ad Hoc Task Force], that the allegations in *Darkness in El Dorado* must be taken seriously. *Darkness in El Dorado* has served anthropology well in that it has opened a space for reflection and stocktaking about what we do and our relationships with those among whom we are privileged to study. But the required reflection goes beyond these matters. For instance, we must attend carefully to the responses of colleagues internationally, who have asked why American anthropologists are moved to action by an attack from outside the profession, but not by the collegial inquiry and concerns of our fellow anthropologists in other countries. We are aware that many of the allegations raised by Tierney's book have been raised before by other scholars and journalists, including Brazilian and Venezuelan colleagues. We are thus moved to reflection about our relationships with our colleagues around the world and especially in Venezuela and Brazil. (I:9).

Both the preliminary and final reports continue: "All anthropological practice is implicated in what went wrong in 'El Dorado' [i.e., the Yanomami region]— and we believe that things did go wrong" (I:10). The allegations examined are grouped into five categories: "(1) fieldwork practices of anthropologists, (2) representations and portrayals of the Yanomami that may have had a negative impact, (3) efforts to create organizations to represent the interests of Yanomami or efforts to contribute to Yanomami welfare that may have actually undermined their well-being, (4) activities that may have resulted in personal gain to scientists, anthropologists, and journalists while contributing harm to the Yanomami, and (5) activities by anthropologists, scientists, and journalists that may have contributed to malnutrition, disease, and disorganization" (I:8).

The introductory material also offers an overview of the Yanomami (written by Janet Chernela, Raymond Hames, and Jane Hill) that focuses on their present condition. Chernela adds a human rights update. Jane Hill discusses the AAA's role "in advocacy for the Yanomami" as well as "debates on Yanomami anthropology." Hill states that the AAA has, through the Yanomami Commission (headed by Terry Turner) and the Commission on Human Rights ("led by its first chairperson, Leslie Sponsel"), been a strong advocate for Yanomami rights, especially for establishing the Yanomami land reserve. She observes that there has been continuing debate about Chagnon's work, such as in the *Anthropology News*. She adds that while one letter (by Bruce Albert criticizing Chagnon) was refused publication in the newsletter, a letter that "characterized Brazilian concern about the impact of Chagnon's work as motivated by 'confused grievances'" was published. "Members of the Task Force concur," Hill writes, "that it is regrettable that this language appeared in the *AN*" (II:11).

Sample Commentaries

Leslie Sponsel (professor, University of Hawaii) focuses on two issues. First, he observes:

> The Task Force claims "All members have made every effort to become thoroughly acquainted with the anthropological literature on the Yanomami in the specific area that they were assigned, consistent with their expertise" (p. 3). However, the Task Force cites a relatively obscure 1983 publication by J. Saffirio and Raymond Hames, but does not cite a more wide-ranging and far more influential and accessible earlier report by Alcida Ramos and Kenneth Taylor (1979) which first drew attention to the plight of the Yanomami in Brazil, following the devastating consequences of the construction of the northern perimeter highway deep into their territory.

Second, he questions the Task Force's competence in producing an objective report. He notes that the fourth charge of the AAA Executive Board asserts:

> "It is expected that the Task Force will seek information from AAA members, the author, and key anthropologists mentioned in the book" (AAA 2000b). In its Preliminary Report the Task Force asserts that "We have conducted a number of interviews, emphasizing interviews of persons with first-hand knowledge of the Yanomami" (p. 3). Several months ago, I asked six specialists who have worked with the Yanomami if they had been approached by the Task Force, and none had. . . . Why

has the Task Force ignored most Yanomami specialists? Could it be because the over-whelming majority of them have repeatedly been critical of Chagnon for decades?

Juan Villarías-Robles (professor, Consejo Superior de Investigaciones Cien-tíficas, Madrid, Spain) also questions the Task Force's objectivity. After men-tioning the scandal that surrounded Boas (the "father" of American Anthropol-ogy and the only person ever to be censured by the American Anthropological Association) exposing American anthropologists working in Central America as U.S. government spies, Villarías-Robles queries whether a similar prejudicial investigation was under way. He notes, "In the 'Background' of the [preliminary report's] Introduction . . . it is stated that Tierney's book is 'deeply flawed, but nevertheless [highlights] ethical issues that we must confront.' I have taken sen-tences [such as this] as a subtle confession of bias against Tierney as a guiding principle—which is obviously unacceptable in any dispassionate inquiry."

ASSESSMENT OF ALLEGATIONS
AGAINST JAMES NEEL

Because the question of whether Neel's vaccination program spread measles among the Yanomami has been dismissed by all parties concerned (except per-haps Tierney), the controversy concerning Neel really centers on two issues: (1) Did Neel have informed consent from the Yanomami when he conducted his research? (2) When the measles epidemic arose during Neel's research and Neel was under time constraints, did he focus sufficiently on the Yanomami and their health needs or did he give greater priority to his own personal research at the expense of the Yanomami?

Did Neel Have Informed Consent for His Research?

Preliminary Report *(Primary Research Responsibility: Trudy Turner)*

The key questions regarding informed consent are (a) did the 1968 Neel expe-dition follow 1968 standards for informed consent, and (b) in what ways did their efforts at informed consent fall short by Yanomami standards as well as by ours today. Trudy Turner concludes:

> Informed consent procedures today . . . would usually offer subjects an opportu-nity to be informed of the results of the study. The Yanomami believe that they should have been informed about results, and believe that they were not so informed. We are not aware of any efforts by Neel to "follow up" with information on study results designed to be intelligible to interested Yanomami.
> In summary, judged against the standards of 2002, the "informed consent" pro-cedures used by the Neel expedition were minimal. However, judged against the standards of 1968, the use of procedures such as an explanation of the purpose of

EXCERPTS FROM THIS SECTION

"The Yanomami believe that they should have been informed about results, and believe that they were not so informed. We are not aware of any efforts by Neel to 'follow up' with information on study results designed to be intelligible to interested Yanomami." (Preliminary Report)

"Neel not only vaccinated the Yanomami without their consent, he did so without the ability to successfully control their symptoms." (Commentary: M. Dalstrom)

"The Task Force has found no evidence that Neel and his team were unusual in the cursory and misleading nature of their consent procedure. Nonetheless it cannot be condoned . . . The research procedures did, however, pose another kind of risk, which we can identify today in the sense of betrayal and injustice shared by many Yanomami." (Final Report)

the research provided to subjects, considerable care in determining appropriate compensation, and the provision of some follow-up medical attention, were appropriate and even advanced. The Task Force observes that at this period many citizens of the U.S. and Europe were the unwitting and uninformed subjects of medical research; the Yanomami in fact received more explanation and compensation than was typical at that period (p. 4).

Sample Commentaries

Jennie Campana (student, Bucknell) writes: "It is easy to see the difficulties that Neel and Chagnon faced in attempting to obtain informed consent from the Yanomamo during the 1968 expedition. The language barriers that existed were extensive. Although Chagnon had a certain command of the language, concepts such as atomic energy, genetics, etc. would have been difficult to explain. But the fact that truly hits home with this aspect of the El Dorado debate is the fact that the members of the Yanomamo community who were subject to the sampling felt, and still feel, that they were misled by the scientists. . . . Could it be deduced from this episode that anthropologists and scientists consider research more important than the desires of the people who are subjected to this type of study? What kind of message is this sending to the international community??"

Matthew Dalstrom (student, unspecified affiliation) comments: Neel "knew that it was possible that the vaccine could cause the patient to experience strong enough symptoms to put their lives in danger. Neel not only vaccinated the Yanomami without their consent, he did so without the ability to successfully control their symptoms. If consent was properly acquired then the Indians would not have taken "off in fright when they heard we [Neel and colleagues] were giving inoculations." . . . Since he did not have enough gamma globulin to treat his patients . . . he should have researched the Yanomami indigenous medical system. Then he could have adequately determined if they had the ability to deal with the symptoms the vaccine would create."

Final Report

The Final Report discusses this issue under the general heading "2.1.1. Consent, Research and Humanitarianism: James V. Neel and the Yanomami Then and Now." The section begins by noting "a contrapuntal alignment"—a fancy term for disagreement—between Janet Chernela's Yanomami interviews and Trudy Turner's interviews with the original researchers who participated in the 1968 expedition. The former indicate that Yanomami feel deceived by Neel; the latter, that the researchers felt they made an honest, but imperfect, effort to explain their project to those involved. Quoting from the report:

> The consent procedures of the Neel expedition were not in compliance with official standards for informed consent in force at the time of the expedition (and would not, of course, meet today's standards). In this failure, however, they reflect practices that were then common. . . . It would have been possible and desirable to explain to the Yanomami in understandable language that the main goal of the expedition involved improving understanding of genetically-inherited differences between Yanomami individuals and villages, and between Yanomami and other people around the world. . . . While this research goal was potentially of general benefit to humanity, it would yield no immediate health benefit to the Yanomami. Yet the Yanomami might very well have been interested in these broader scientific goals of the expedition and even been willing to participate in them for their own sake, had they been given information that would have permitted them to make an informed decision (I:22).
>
> . . . Neel's expedition collected samples of bodily materials (blood, sputum, urine, feces), using standard procedures that had proven over many years with many populations to have an extremely low risk of complication. They had no reason at the time to suppose that these procedures would pose risk to Yanomami donors, and they had reason to believe that the minimal risks were balanced by benefit, medical care provided by physicians on the research team to a disastrously under-served population. The Task Force has found no evidence that Neel and his team were unusual in the cursory and misleading nature of their consent procedure. Nonetheless it cannot be condoned" (I:23).

The report continues: "The research procedures did, however, pose another kind of risk, which we can identify today in the sense of betrayal and injustice shared by many Yanomami" (I:23).

How Did Neel Balance His Concern to Pursue His Research Objectives with Administering Help to the Yanomami during a Devastating Measles Epidemic?

Preliminary Report *(Primary Research Responsibility: Trudy Turner)*

Trudy Turner and Jeffrey Nelson's "Turner Point by Point" (2001) presents a critique of an earlier paper by Terry Turner ("The Yanomami and the Ethics of Anthropological Practice," Terence Turner 2001b).

"Once he [Neel] was aware of the magnitude of the epidemic he immediately took steps to prevent further spread of measles. . . . It must be remembered that no matter what Neel felt, he did vaccinate." (Preliminary Report)

"The arrival of the epidemic . . . made medical demands on the expedition that it was not prepared to meet, unless it had been willing to put aside more of its research activities temporarily to allow it to vaccinate as many people as possible before they were exposed." (Commentary: Terry Turner)

"The Task Force recognizes that Neel faced a structural conflict between his research program as approved and funded by the AEC, and the vaccination campaign. His notes are full of his frustrations in this regard. . . . Some members of the Task Force argue that the research program, by funding the team's presence in the region, made the vaccination program possible. Other members of the Task Force, however, argue that the question must be kept open, given the possibility that the vaccination program might have been more efficient had it been uncomplicated by the many dimensions of the AEC-funded research that Neel continued to pursue. We are unable to reach agreement on this matter." (Final Report)

Trudy Turner and Jeffrey Nelson state: "Much of what [Terry] Turner says [regarding this matter] . . . is based on conjecture. He uses his interpretations of the material as fact. His major complaint is that Neel gave his first priority to research and the second to the humanitarian effort" (p. 17).

The key statement regarding Neel's intentions comes from Neel's notes: "At Patanowä-teri we will also make our principle [sic] collections of biologicals, and I will concentrate on this while Bill does PEs [physical exams]. Thus, I will get stools and soils while Bill does PEs for 3–4 days—then we get blood, saliva, and urine . . . then inoculate if at all" (p. 13).

Trudy Turner and Jeffrey Nelson state:

> [Terry] Turner makes much of the "if at all" statement in Neel's journal. We have another interpretation and an alternate reading of the material: "if at all" (p. 48). It is important to note that Neel addresses the vaccinations specifically as "a gesture of altruism and conscience" (5 February 1968 entry in field notes: 79). Likewise, he notes how frustrating this vaccination process is: "more of a headache than bargained for." However, he never suggests that he ever "seriously considered jettisoning the 'altruism and conscience' of the vaccination campaign and [abandoning] the vaccinations altogether" (Turner 2001b:32); he does, however, clearly state in frustration that he would like to put the vaccinating into the "hands of the missionaries." Moreover, the context of "if at all" must account for the fact that the Indians had a history of fleeing those administering the vaccinations: "they took off in fright when they heard we were giving inoculations" [1 Feb. 1968 entry in field notes: 76]. Vaccinating "if at all," administering the vac-

cinations "at the very last" [5 February 1968 entry in field notes: 79], or placing the vaccinations into the hands of the missionaries may be indicative of this "flight" problem alone. It should also be noted that this was all written before Neel was aware of the magnitude of the epidemic and before the all-Orinoco plan [for fighting the epidemic] was devised. Once he was aware of the magnitude of the epidemic he immediately took steps to prevent further spread of measles. At this point, he gave preventative doses of MIG [measles immune globulin] to those exposed, but who were not yet sick, but not vaccinated. He also administered penicillin to those who were the most ill. It must be remembered that no matter what Neel felt, he did vaccinate (p. 14).

Sample Commentaries

Terry Turner (professor, Cornell University), in responding to Trudy Turner and Jeffrey Nelson's response to his paper, asserts:

"Turner Point by Point" [Turner and Nelson 2001] is an extraordinary document, considering its context. It is an attempt by a member of a supposedly objective and impartial commission of investigation, with the help of a research assistant, to refute and dismiss in every significant particular an extensive compendium of new research findings dealing with the allegations the commission is supposedly investigating, supplied in good faith to the commission in response to an appeal by its chair for exactly such contributions to aid the commission in its work. . . . It is clearly an attempt to deal with the findings of my research . . . by killing the messenger.

As such, "Turner Point by Point" can only be understood as a product of the peculiar structure of the El Dorado Task Force, which has put individual partisans of the principal figures under investigation in charge of preparing the sections of its report dealing specifically with them. This "division of labor" has given us an investigative commission in which Raymond Hames, a defender and partisan of Napoleon Chagnon, has been assigned to write the section of the report on Chagnon, and Trudy Turner, a biological anthropologist committed to the categorical defense of James Neel against any and all allegations of ethical conflicts or of harboring embarrassing eugenic ideas, has been placed in charge of the part of the report dealing with James Neel. . . .

The Brazilian medical team [see pages 113–114], Albert and I have each challenged the ethics of Neel's attempt to split the difference between his medical and scientific goals during the epidemic on the grounds that it led to failure to move quickly enough to vaccinate some groups of Yanomami before they were exposed to the measles. This rendered the vaccinations ineffective as immunization. . . . The arrival of the epidemic, in other words, made medical demands on the expedition that it was not prepared to meet, unless it had been willing to put aside more of its research activities temporarily to allow it to vaccinate as many people as possible before they were exposed. . . .

My point about the relation between Neel's medical and research goals is not, as [Trudy] Turner and Nelson try to make out. . . . [Turner and Nelson 2001], that Neel had no humanitarian concerns. It is that while Neel had both medical and research objectives for the vaccinations, and that while these objectives are mutually compatible in principle, they did come into conflict in the context of the epidemic.

After questioning Trudy Turner and Jeffrey Nelson's interpretation of "if at all" (as referring to Yanomami possibly fleeing inoculations), Turner goes on to state: "In my analysis of the question I give the most weight to the evidence of Neel's itinerary for the expedition, and his unwillingness to make serious modifications in the routing and rate of the expedition's movements to make possible more effective measures against the epidemic, such as more timely vaccinations and the possibility of not going to relatively remote and unexposed places on the original itinerary where this would mean exposing them [the villagers] to disease carriers who might accompany the expedition."

Ryk Ward (professor, University of Oxford) writes in reply to a commentary by Frechione that Neel was more interested in observing than treating the measles epidemic:

> The message of Frechione's posting is transparently clear: It represents an accusation that Neel deliberately wanted to withhold vaccines from the Patanowä-teri, so he could observe the consequences of a measles epidemic in an unacculturated population. . . . As a member of [the] 1968 expedition, who was present throughout the entire time that Neel and (Willard) Centerwall were in the field, including the visit to the Patanowä-teri, I categorically deny this accusation. . . . Before arriving at a village, Neel was in the habit of making a detailed plan of action, and discussing this with the members of his team. In advance of arriving at the Patanowä-teri, Neel decided that the FIRST task to be undertaken was to vaccinate. . . . Accordingly, soon after arriving in Patanowä-teri late morning of February 21st ("after a hard 3-hour slog through the jungle" — Neel's words), Neel and Centerwall spent the afternoon vaccinating, and carrying out physical examinations. Apart from completing the vaccinations and physical examinations, no other fieldwork was done that day. . . . Not only is this schedule . . . clearly documented in field notes and Asch's film, but [it] is even detailed on page 96 of Tierney's book. It is abundantly clear that Neel's first priority in Patanowä-teri was to do his best to prevent an epidemic.

Final Report

The final report seems to detour away from the question of Neel's priorities during the epidemic, paying much attention to a question not particularly emphasized in the controversy: was the 1968 vaccination campaign organized for research, as a humanitarian program, or both? This issue considers the purpose behind Neel bringing measles vaccine on his research trip. Was it simply to help the Yanomami, or did he have a research motive as well? The far more crucial question, discussed here, is, what did Neel do when confronted by the measles epidemic? The final report turns to this question in one paragraph: "The Task Force recognizes that Neel faced a structural conflict between his research program as approved and funded by the AEC, and the vaccination campaign. His notes are full of his frustrations in this regard. . . . Some members of the Task Force argue that the research program, by funding the team's presence in the region, made the vaccination program possible. Other members of the Task Force, however, argue that the question must be kept open, given the possibility that the vaccination program might have been more effi- cient had it been uncomplicated by the many dimensions of the AEC-funded research that Neel continued to pursue. We are unable to reach agreement on this matter" (I:27).

Beginning to Mend the Damage

The Task Force concludes its collective comments on Neel in a section entitled "Beginning to Mend the Damage." It highlights the Yanomami's sense of betrayal regarding the espoused goals of Neel and colleagues' research and offers guidelines for trying to positively address the problem.

> The Task Force takes seriously the evidence that there has been long-term social and psychological suffering among the Yanomami as a result of the 1968 Neel expedition. According to independent interviews conducted among bilingual Yanomami by Janet Chernela . . . there was consensus that the Yanomami were misled by the promise of health benefits in the "consent procedure" of the Neel expeditions and this promise was not fulfilled. . . .
>
> Obviously many Yanomami who report feeling betrayed by this unfulfilled promise were barely touched by the expedition or were not even alive when it occurred. However, the sense of having suffered an injustice is no less real among them. This sense of injustice comes from the fact that the Neel expedition treated the Yanomami as if they were less than fully capable of understanding and of deter- mining their own destiny. . . .
>
> Janet Chernela and Fernando Coronil have spoken to Yanomami representa- tives who want the sample materials that were collected by the Neel expeditions, especially those that were collected from people now deceased, to be destroyed or returned to them for appropriate disposition. . . . (I:29)
>
> The Task Force recommends that other scholars follow Weiss [who has stopped all research involving the Yanomami blood samples in his laboratory] in imposing an immediate moratorium on scientific work with materials collected from the Yanomami during the Neel expeditions. The moratorium should remain in place until new agreements can be worked out between the scholarly community and the Yanomami under contemporary procedures of informed consent. One of the results of such new agreements may very well be return of the original biological materi- als under terms specified by the Yanomami. Ultimately, though, we believe that bet- ter communication and informed decisions expand possibilities and lay the begin- nings for new collaborations between the Yanomami and the research community, in which the Yanomami are full decision-makers. Moreover, we believe that these agreements should include a commitment by the anthropological community to full collaboration with the Yanomami to see that adequate medical care is provided to Yanomami communities, especially in Venezuela where the need is greatest. This effort should not take the form of vague promises that, for instance, genetic research may ultimately facilitate finding cures or prophylactics for infectious dis- eases. Instead, it should take the form of working with colleagues internationally

"We believe that [there] . . . should [be] . . . a commitment by the anthropological community to full collaboration with the Yanomami to see that adequate medical care is provided to Yanomami communities, especially in Venezuela where the need is greatest. This effort should not take the form of vague promises." (Final Report)

toward immediate and material benefit in the form of training, equipment, medical supplies and medicines, clinical access and personnel, and other benefits that will be accessible to Yanomami throughout their homeland. Many barriers to the success of such efforts exist, but the effort must be sincerely made. (I:30)

FIVE ADDITIONAL ALLEGATIONS IN THE PRELIMINARY REPORT

The Task Force, in its preliminary report, focused on a relatively narrow set of issues relating to Chagnon. The final report makes an effort to examine and assess the accusations against Chagnon in a more global way. As a result, one cannot neatly move from the preliminary report through the commentaries to the final report.

Chagnon's Collecting of Yanomami Names

Preliminary Report *(Primary Research Responsibility: Raymond Hames, Supplemental Editorial Responsibility: Jane Hill)*

Ray Hames assesses the tactics Chagnon used in collecting genealogies: "Among the Yanomamö, use of personal names for maturing males, mature men, or the dead regardless of sex is subject to a number of stringent regulations (Lizot 1985:125–36). In a public context, it is inappropriate and insulting to address a man by his name or mention the name of a dead relative to a close kinsperson. In a private setting these rules change depending on the social relations and context that exist between speaker and listener" (p. 2). He goes on to cite Bruce Albert to affirm that, as a researcher, "one is able to legitimately collect personal names" (p. 2). Hames also observes that a slew of other ethnographers besides Chagnon collected and published Yanomami names—"from Bruce Albert [to] other Yanomamö ethnographers such as Jacques Lizot, Alcida Ramos, Eguillor Garcia, and Marco Ales. . . . Tierney (2000) contains many Yanomamö personal names, some accompanied by photographs" (p. 11).

"The more interesting claim about the collection of names," Hames suggests, "is that Chagnon used unethical methods in his genealogical research by rely-

EXCERPTS FROM THIS SECTION

"The use of [Chagnon's fieldwork] techniques was a consequence of the Yanomamö providing Chagnon with false information. . . . This of course does not excuse Chagnon for the tactics." (Preliminary Report)

"When he was lied to . . . he [Chagnon] should not have thought of a way to deceive them, rather to gain trust from them." (Commentary: E. Hopkins)

"Should we go out and coerce children into giving us names in order to complete our research?" (Commentary: K. Peer)

ing on local pariahs, enemies, and children. To some extent, the use of these techniques was a consequence of the Yanomamö providing Chagnon with false information during the initial six-month period of field research. This of course does not excuse Chagnon for the tactics he may have employed to gain correct genealogies, but it does provide a relevant context. Of these three specific accusations it seems to us that the use of children and 'bribing' of children is the most questionable" (pp. 2–3).

He concludes by suggesting that "it is our sense that many of the mistakes Chagnon made around names were honest and unintended and that he learned from these errors. We are, however, concerned about the use of children as informants as well as the use of aberrant and abnormal individuals. While these are 'classical' anthropological field techniques, we believe that in today's environment, of increasing concern for the dignity and autonomy of human subjects, we should open a new dialogue on such methods" (p. 3).

Sample Commentaries

Elizabeth Hopkins (student, California State, Hayward) writes: "As I read about the Yanomami tribe, it never really occurred to me that the way Chagnon went about getting members' names was wrong. On the other hand, when I read the accusations and the reasoning why the way the Yanomami names were gotten, I changed my mind. I really do feel that the Yanomami were disrespected by being tricked into telling their sacred names. . . . He could have really gone about it in a different way. When he was lied to by the tribe for six months, he should not have thought of a way to deceive them, rather to gain trust from them. Manipulating children to get the names of men, women, and deceased tribe members showed that Chagnon did not respect the Yanomami way of living."

Karisa Peer (student, Middlebury) states: "Chagnon was so desperate to attain 'successful' research that he employed some obviously unethical methods. How does Chagnon feel . . . to be a role model for current anthropology students? Should we go out and coerce children into giving us names in order to complete our research?"

Chagnon's Involvement in Yanomami Political Affairs

Preliminary Report *(Primary Research Responsibility: Raymond Hames)*

At issue in this section is the impact Chagnon's fieldwork had on Yanomami affairs. Rather than focus on the broad issue of whether Chagnon stimulated warfare through his distribution of extensive trade goods, this section considers the narrower "allegation in *Darkness in El Dorado* that Napoleon Chagnon put Yanomamö lives at risk in a peace-making negotiation in one instance, and by aiding a raiding party in another" (p. 1). Regarding the former, Hames concludes, "It is clear from Chagnon's writing that the Yanomamö want to use Chagnon as an instrument of peace and that he obliged them at great personal risk to himself" (p. 1). As for the latter, Hames notes, "Tierney, and to some extent Ferguson, seem to suggest that the failed raid would not have occurred without Chagnon's assistance. Chagnon's text clearly states that the Yanomamö had decided to make the raid and then asked him to help. There is no indication that the raid was contingent on Chagnon's assistance" (p. 1).

Hames concludes: "We believe that ethnographers should not, with premeditation, directly or indirectly involve themselves in hostile acts. But one could imagine other circumstances where involvement in hostilities is unavoidable. . . . That Chagnon assisted the Bisaasi-teri in brokering a successful peace treaty with the Mishimishimaböwei-teri is clearly praiseworthy. However, we believe that the proper stance for anthropologists is to encourage those we study to make peace and not war, and to avoid direct or indirect facilitation of hostilities except in an emergency" (p. 2).

Sample Commentaries

R. Brian Ferguson (professor, Rutgers University, Newark), who suggested Chagnon's distribution of Western goods intensified Yanomami warfare (in *Yanomami Warfare: A Political History*), begins by stating "It is surprising that a former student of Napoleon Chagnon, Raymond Hames, was chosen to write some of the reports [on Chagnon]. Dr. Hames is a strong supporter of Dr. Chagnon." He continues: "I doubt any commission, any few scholars brought in to fact-find on a deadline, could completely untangle all these events [related to how Chagnon's gift giving stimulated Yanomami warfare]. But they are not even mentioned. The effort devoted by this Task Force to considering anthropologists' involvement in Yanomami political affairs is far less than that centered on Neel's activities involving biomedical issues. It barely scratches the surface, and for the record, it must be made clear just how limited this investigation has been. One could read this report by Hames without getting any idea that the role of distributed Western goods in political conflict and war is even an issue. That is pretty amazing."

Dominic Gaccetta (student, Hawaii Pacific University) writes: "Political decisions for any society are heartfelt beacons of values, principles, and ideals. An ethnographer's presence should not disrupt the natural flow of events. . . .

EXCERPTS FROM THIS SECTION

"Ethnographers should not . . . involve themselves in hostile acts." (Preliminary Report)

"One could read this [preliminary] report . . . without getting any idea that the role of distributed Western goods in political conflict and war is even an issue. That is pretty amazing." (Commentary: B. Ferguson)

"Perhaps a counter task force should be made to evaluate . . . how well the task force and the AAA followed through on whatever is decided." (Commentary: D. Gaccetta)

Chagnon had no ties to the area. Whatever damage he caused by . . . [his] actions, he gets to leave and return to his shiny home. . . . Now the Task Force has a situation in front of them where it looks like they will go in one of two directions. The most likely seems to be in favor of providing excuses for what happened, saying it will not be allowed to happen again, but really doing nothing. I could be mistaken though and the Task Force might take a stand and provide guidelines for ethnographical research that would keep researchers in check. I would stress that there is nothing now in place in the AAA to make sure the Task Force's decisions are upheld. Perhaps a counter task force should be made to evaluate the task force in place now, and evaluate how well the task force and the AAA followed through on whatever is decided."

Chagnon's Public Dialogue with Members of Study Communities

Preliminary Report *(Primary Research Responsibility: Jane Hill)*

This topic refers to Napoleon Chagnon's negative statements regarding the noted Yanomami activist Davi Kopenawa. Hill states:

> We are unable to confirm that Chagnon ever referred to Davi Kopenawa . . . as a "parrot"; this language is quoted by Tierney from an article by Peter Monaghan in the *Chronicle of Higher Education* (Monaghan 1994:A19) and is not there attributed to Chagnon directly. Monaghan states "Mr. Chagnon and his supporters dismiss [Davi Kopenawa] as a parrot of human-rights groups and say he does not speak for the tribe." However, the above citation [and the one in chapter 2] are the only published writings by Chagnon on Kopenawa . . . that we have seen cited, or identified ourselves. They are carefully worded and say nothing about "parrots." However, we suggest that Chagnon's remarks were problematic in their context. They were written at a time when there was the most serious threat to Yanomami lands; between the mid 1980's and 1992, when Yanomami lands in Brazil were finally demarcated with their present boundaries, Brazilian anthropologists, accompanied by other anthropologists, . . . international NGOs such as Survival International, and the

EXCERPTS FROM THIS SECTION

"To raise questions, in very widely-distributed publications, about the authenticity of a person who had unquestionably become a very positive symbol of the Yanomami and an important political asset in this fight could not fail to undermine Yanomami interests." (Preliminary Report)

"When the anthropologists . . . begin criticizing the Yanomami as being 'inauthentic,' they only become another one of the puppet masters attempting to influence and direct the future of the Yanomami. . . . [Since the] Yanomami have been subjected (without consent) to over 40 years . . . of . . . questioning, 'experiments' and bombardment . . . they were more or less forced to take sides and form alliances with certain groups who support their cause." (Commentary: H. Ficker)

Yanomami themselves were engaged in an extremely difficult and dangerous fight to protect these lands. To raise questions, in very widely-distributed publications, about the authenticity of a person who had unquestionably become a very positive symbol of the Yanomami and an important political asset in this fight could not fail to undermine Yanomami interests (p. 2).

Sample Commentaries

Harvest Ficker (student, Middlebury) writes: "When the anthropologists . . . begin criticizing the Yanomami as being 'inauthentic,' they only become another one of the puppet masters attempting to influence and direct the future of the Yanomami. Instead, anthropologists need to look at the greater picture that will help lead the Yanomami to a state less influenced by outside forces. It is important to keep in mind the fact that the Yanomami have been subjected (without consent) to over 40 years of observations, questioning, 'experiments' and bombardment from scientists and anthropologists. Therefore, they were more or less forced to take sides and form alliances with certain groups who support their cause."

Nirvi Shah (student, San Diego State) observes: "There is no evidence to show that Chagnon said Davi [Kopenawa] was a 'parrot' for his tribe. There is no evidence in this paper to show what Chagnon's exact opinion was at all. However, if we accept Chagnon's remarks as specified by Hill, Turner et al., then his remarks are, indeed 'unusual as well as condescending.' "

Allegations of Inappropriate Sexual Relationships with Yanomami

Preliminary Report *(Primary Research Responsibility: Jane Hill)*

This section deals with the sexual behaviors of anthropologists in the field—both in the Yanomami case and in a more general sense. Regarding the Yanomami, two cases in particular are mentioned: Kenneth Good's marriage to Yarima and Jacques Lizot's relations with teenage boys. Hill states, "The El Dorado Task Force believes that the allegations about Lizot's activities among the Yanomami made in *Darkness in El Dorado* are well-founded."

She also discusses sexual relations more generally: "In reflecting on the Lizot case, we observe that anthropologists, like other human beings, are sexual creatures. Inevitably, sexual attraction and sexual relationships will develop between anthropologists and those they encounter during field work" (p. 2).

Sample Commentaries

Diana Mabalot (student, Hawaii Pacific) comments: "I do think that it is unprofessional for anthropologists to have sexual relations with a group that they are studying, because in a way, it makes the researcher seem disrespectful to their society, especially if it is against 'cultural' values, morals, and beliefs. It also makes the researcher seem uncaring, and less concerned with the people that . . . [he or she is] studying. I agree that anthropology field work should have guidelines and rules regarding the anthropologist's behavior because it might affect their research and their relationship with the people. It is just like the rule that teachers can't date students, or not dating, more generally, in the workplace. It's just professional. But on the other hand, if an anthropologist becomes interested, not in sex, but in love, and has a close relationship with a 'subject,' I can understand why an affair might take place. It is hard to fight back feelings, especially when it's deep like love."

Amy Vance (student, Gettysburg) writes: "In Lizot's book *Tales of the Yanomami: Daily Life in the Venezuelan Rainforest*, he provides extremely vivid accounts of Yanomami sexual activity—describing young males as frequently engaging in sexual activity . . . ([including] copulation with animals), homosexuality as . . . prevalent in Yanomami society, and incest as condemnable yet frequent. . . . Here is where I have to question the credibility of Lizot's findings. . . . If the allegations against Lizot of unethical sexual behavior are true should we, or more fundamentally can we, accept his conclusions on normative sexual behavior among the Yanomami as fact (or truth)? Are the activities he described really normative or did the presence and actions of outsiders (military personnel, miners, and of course himself) create an environment that transformed Yanomami sexuality into the sexual behavior he witnessed?"

Regarding the Film *Warriors of the Amazon*

Preliminary Report *(Primary Research Responsibility: Jane Hill)*

This portion of the report refers to the staged production of *Warriors of the Amazon*, and the fact (noted in chapter 2) that "a film crew allegedly watched a woman and child die" (p. 1). Hill states,

> The Task Force concurs with Tierney that the film is profoundly problematic. . . . First, the film, made in the 1990's, is obviously staged. (Tierney enumerates a number of pieces of evidence for this [Tierney 2000:216–17].) The film is incongruous in that while it shows many trade goods, the Yanomami wear almost no western clothes (one or two men in shorts are shown). (p. 18)
>
> "The images of the dying young mother and her baby are problematic. . . . It is filmed as a moment in 'nature.' Tierney states that the film was made only an hour by motorboat from the infirmary at the Mavaca mission (Tierney 2000:221). Hames states that this is an exaggeration; the distance might be as much as 3 1/2 hours, depending on conditions and mode of transportation. Nonetheless it would have been easy to take the woman, who is quite young, perhaps even still a teenager, to the hospital. (p. 18)
>
> There is a grim lesson here for us all: decent ordinary people, in the grip of a racializing representation that the film reproduces in almost every dimension, can behave in ways that deeply shocked members of the Task Force as well as Tierney and his informants and that must have been a dehumanizing experience for the Yanomami. (p. 19)

Sample Commentaries

Wes Cadman (student, Gettysburg) comments: "I am embarrassed . . . [by] what Lizot and "Warriors of the Amazon" have done to represent the anthropological community. The sad thing is I can almost understand letting a woman die while filming IF you go into the film with the intention to be as unobtrusive as possible and really get what their way of life is all about. But this film was not even close to catching the natural Yanomami culture. By bribing them with trade goods and setting up the whole movie like some high school play, you immediately lose all realism of the situation and therefore in my eyes have a responsibility to help out the people you are studying, especially medically."

Andrew Ulrich (student, Idaho) writes: "In anthropology . . . there are three things a person is accountable to. The first . . . is the people being studied. The second . . . is the people funding . . . [the research], and the third . . . is people in

EXCERPTS FROM THIS SECTION

"The Task Force concurs with Tierney that the film [Warriors of the Amazon] is profoundly problematic. . . . the film . . . is obviously staged. . . . There is a grim lesson here for us all: decent ordinary people, in the grip of a racializing representation that the film reproduces in almost every dimension, can behave in ways that deeply shocked members of the Task Force." (Preliminary Report)

"By bribing them with trade goods and setting up the whole movie like some high school play, you immediately lose all realism of the situation and therefore in my eyes have a responsibility to help out the people you are studying, especially medically." (Commentary: W. Cadman)

the same profession. This film crew may have stayed within the boundaries that their employers set, and they may have even stayed within the morals of most of the colleagues of the profession of photography and cinematography, but their behavior toward people of the Yanomami was demoralizing. . . . Two out of three in this standard is not good at all. . . . They watched a woman and an infant die when the community of the woman and infant clearly saw this as inappropriate."

THE FINAL REPORT'S ASSESSMENT OF THE ALLEGATIONS AGAINST NAPOLEON CHAGNON

Regarding topics missing from the final report, the Task Force indicates that it "has missed . . . [Ray Hames's] specific expertise about the Yanomami [since his resignation], which prevents the Task Force from completing its work in at least one important area, an inquiry into the allegations that Napoleon Chagnon instigated violence among the Yanomami; there was not enough time between Hames' resignation and our deadline for another member to undertake research on this matter." No explanation is offered for why the "Allegations of Inappropriate Sexual Relationships with Yanomami" is not dealt with in the Final Report.

"Professor Chagnon," the Task Force observes,

> has refused to talk to any member of the Task Force, which we regret. Colleagues (Irons, Hames) who have talked to him have from time to time shared his views with the Task Force. We know that he objects to this inquiry in the strongest terms. We hope that we have proceeded in the spirit of trying to learn from mistakes that he has often modeled in his own work. (I:31)
>
> Chagnon has been exceptionally frank in discussing his mistakes in his textbooks, and we believe that criticism of his work should give proper credit to his openness in matters such as his mistakes in collecting Yanomami names. . . . Members of the Task Force know how easy it is to make mistakes in the field, and we recognize that most careers do not come under such close scrutiny. (I:31)

A major allegation against Chagnon is that he exacerbated violence among the Yanomami through his practices of distributing gifts. This is a major argument of Ferguson (1995), and it is adopted by Tierney 2000. The Task Force finds this to be a very complex matter, and one that it could not address fully without Hames' expertise. (I:31) [Note: Hames gives his assessment of Ferguson's argument in chapter 10.]

The Task Force focuses on two sets of allegations against Chagnon in the final report. There are "first, allegations that his representations of Yanomami ways of life were damaging to them and that he made insufficient effort to undo this damage, and second that his association in the early 1990's with FUNDAFACI, a Venezuelan foundation that sponsored his research, represented an unethical prioritizing of his own research concerns over the well-being of the Yanomami. We concur with both these allegations" (I:31).

Allegations Relating to Problems of Representation

The final report states:

> Insofar as Chagnon's role in these debates has affected the Yanomami, the important question for the Task Force is, were Chagnon's representations damaging to the Yanomami, and, when the possibility of such damage was brought to his attention, did he respond adequately to this concern? The conclusion of the Task Force is that it is likely that these representations have been damaging to the Yanomami, and that Chagnon has not adequately addressed his responsibility to try to undo this damage.
>
> Despite changing the characterizations of the Yanomami in his published works, Chagnon has never spoken out clearly and unequivocally to attack misuses of his work by journalists. Instead he has repeatedly used precious opportunities provided by contexts like *New York Times* op-ed essays and interviews in major magazines to attack professional enemies rather than to render clear support to the Yanomami. The Task Force is concerned by the fact that Chagnon has never found it possible to speak out effectively and unequivocally in support of Yanomami human rights in a context where such statements would receive wide circulation. Rather than allying himself with groups with an established record of advocacy for the Yanomami, he has repeatedly attacked such groups as romanticists who manipulate the Yanomami for their own purposes. (I:33)

Changes in Chagnon's Textbooks. A point emphasized by supporters of Chagnon is that Chagnon did indeed make significant changes in editions of *Yanomamö* in response to criticisms. The Task Force observes: "We review a number of changes in Chagnon's monographs that support the conjecture that he was indeed responding to the widespread perception among his colleagues that there was a potentially damaging overemphasis on violence in the first edition of his textbook. As the editions of his textbook are revised he increasingly tries to balance his discussions of Yanomami warfare and violence with attention to more

EXCERPTS FROM THIS SECTION

"The conclusion of the Task Force is that it is likely that . . . [Chagnon's] representations [of the Yanomami] have been damaging to the Yanomami, and that
Chagnon has not adequately addressed his responsibility to try to undo this
damage." (Final Report)

"Chagnon has from time to time had the opportunity to discredit . . . [negative] representations, and unfortunately has not used these opportunities effectively. One
example of such a missed opportunity is Chagnon's 1995 interview in the important Brazilian magazine *Veja*." (Final Report)

"Anthropologists have a responsibility to resist the siren call of simplifying essentialism[s] and to work to create public appreciation for the world in its full complexity. Anthropologists will not always be able to control the forces that work
against such appreciation. However, they have a responsibility . . . to speak out
when publishers and journalists advance simplistic and damaging stereotypes,
and they especially have this responsibility when their own work may be the unintended source of these." (Final Report)

cooperation-oriented forms of Yanomami politics. In the fourth (1992) edition
of his textbook he eliminates the subtitle *The Fierce People*. Furthermore, the
more stereotypical characterizations in the prefaces to his books by his editors,
George and Louise Spindler, and other authors, are softened and eliminated"
(I:34).

Chagnon's Interview in Veja. Regarding a much-discussed interview with the popular Brazilian magazine *Veja*, the Task Force writes:

> Chagnon has from time to time had the opportunity to discredit . . . [negative] rep-
> resentations, and unfortunately has not used these opportunities effectively. One
> example of such a missed opportunity is Chagnon's 1995 interview in the impor-
> tant Brazilian magazine *Veja*. . . .
>   In the interview, Alcantara quotes Chagnon as saying that "Nobody is interested
> in the real Indian. Western society needs an imaginary Indian, an idealization."
> When Alcantara asks Chagnon, "What is a real Indian like?", Chagnon is quoted
> as replying: . . . "Real Indians sweat, they smell bad, they take hallucinogenic drugs,
> they belch after they eat, they covet and at times steal their neighbor's wife, they
> fornicate, and they make war. They are normal human beings. This is reason
> enough for them to deserve care and attention." An extract from this quotation is
> used as the boldface caption under the photograph on the first page of the article.
>   The problem faced by advocates of the Yanomami in Venezuela and especially
> Brazil is, unfortunately, not to combat romantic images of Indians, but to deal with
> a public—and, most importantly, powerful national and regional politicians and
> businessmen—that sees Indians as worthless savages who block the development

of Brazil. Chagnon's remarks about sweating, smelling, belching, and fornicating, in this context used precisely the terms of this popular image, which can be found reproduced in films, television programs, cartoons, and other sites where the most vulgar images of Indian "savagery" are reproduced for public consumption. And, most unfortunately, much of the rest of the interview attacked NGOs, other anthropologists, and missionaries who have advocated for the Yanomami. About them, Chagnon is quoted as saying that their motives are ignoble, aimed at recruiting the fame of the Yanomami—derived (he notes "without false modesty" [p. 8]) in part from his own work—for purposes that have nothing to do with their well-being. It is unclear on what basis Chagnon founds these attacks. (I:37)

The Denial of Coevalness and the Image of the Yanomami as an Endangered People. The Task Force criticizes Chagnon for his

> representation of the Yanomami as a 'Stone Age' people. . . . In the 1968 edition of the textbook, we find Chagnon characterizing the Yanomami as "unacculturated" and "primitive" (the latter term was already disappearing from much anthropological discourse in 1968 but was used frequently in this work). . . . Especially in the new sixth chapter, devoted to "change" and "acculturation," it is clear that Chagnon believes that "change" is something new for the Yanomami (Chagnon 1977:164) (I:38).
>
> The systems of classification and metaphors that Chagnon uses into the 1990's fall directly into the discursive system that Fabian (1983) has called the "denial of coevalness." Fabian and others have clearly demonstrated the objectifying and racializing implications of this discursive system. Promoting critical understanding of the limitations of these ideas should be a major goal of any introductory course. Any use of Chagnon's books in anthropology courses should include, in our view, a full discussion of these usages and their implications with this goal of critical understanding in mind (I:38–39).

Responsibility and Representation: A Reflection. In its concluding remarks to this section, the Task Force writes: "Anthropologists have a responsibility to resist the siren call of simplifying essentialism and to work to create public appreciation for the world in its full complexity. Anthropologists will not always be able to control the forces that work against such appreciation. However, they have a responsibility . . . to speak out when publishers and journalists advance simplistic and damaging stereotypes, and they especially have this responsibility when their own work may be the unintended source of these" (I:40).

Allegations Relating to FUNDAFACI

Regarding the FUNDAFACI project to set up a private Yanomami reserve in Venezuela, the Task Force writes: "Tierney claims that throughout his career Chagnon took advantage of his professional status, personal connections and

EXCERPT FROM THIS SECTION

"Chagnon's involvement in FUNDAFACI was unacceptable on both ethical and professional grounds. It violated Venezuelan laws, associated his research with the activities of corrupt politicians, and involved him in activities that endangered the health and well-being of the Yanomami. Chagnon apparently chose to overlook these problems in order to pursue his own research questions. For this reason the Task Force believes that a charge of a breach of ethics is proper under the AAA Principles of Professional Responsibility, the code of ethics then in effect, which required that the best interests of the study population should always be the first consideration of the anthropologist. It would also constitute a breach of the current Code of Ethics, which states that 'anthropologists must do everything in their power to ensure that their research does not harm the safety, dignity or privacy of the people with whom they work.'" (Final Report)

material resources to gain access to the Yanomami and to advance his own career as their major ethnographer. While scholars have disagreed concerning the validity of many of these claims, they are in fundamental agreement about the impropriety of Chagnon's involvement in FUNDAFACI. In a field deeply divided by critics and supporters of Chagnon's work, this remarkable consensus suggests that this allegation may be well founded in this particular case. The evidence the Task Force has gathered thus far supports this consensus. On the basis of the evidence we have gathered we feel that Tierney's account of Chagnon's participation in FUNDAFACI is accurate" (I:41).

In analyzing the reasons why Chagnon got involved in this project, the Task Force notes:

> Napoleon Chagnon, who by the late 1980s was a polemical figure in anthropological circles in Venezuela and Brazil, had been unable to obtain stable institutional backing for his research among the Yanomami in Venezuela for many years (Venezuelan law since 1975 required foreign scholars working in border areas such as Amazonas to have an affiliation with a Venezuelan institution). . . . However through his association with Brewer Carías in FUNDAFACI, Chagnon managed to gain access to the Yanomami through FUNDAFACI. Thus, while technically Chagnon had Venezuelan support for his research, this support overrode the objections of the government agency and officials directly charged with regulating research access to indigenous groups in Venezuela. (I:42)

Tierney's (2000:188) claim that the FUNDAFACI proposal would have established a "private biosphere [that] would have given Brewer and Chagnon a scientific monopoly over an area the size of Connecticut" cannot be proven, since the plan was eventually aborted. Yet the evidence suggests that their aim was indeed to develop significant personal control over this area through FUNDAFACI. By placing this area under the control of the foundation, Brewer Carías would have

been able to pursue his mining interests and Chagnon to advance his anthropological research unhampered by their lack of local support and or by professional
or governmental controls. The activities that they carried out in preparation of this
project lend support to this assessment (I:43).

Is There a Pattern? The Task Force concludes:

> Chagnon's involvement in FUNDAFACI was unacceptable on both ethical and pro-
> fessional grounds. It violated Venezuelan laws, associated his research with the
> activities of corrupt politicians, and involved him in activities that endangered the
> health and well-being of the Yanomami. Chagnon apparently chose to overlook
> these problems in order to pursue his own research questions. For this reason the
> Task Force believes that a charge of a breach of ethics is proper under the AAA
> Principles of Professional Responsibility, the code of ethics then in effect, which
> required that the best interests of the study population should always be the first
> consideration of the anthropologist. It would also constitute a breach of the current
> Code of Ethics, which states that "anthropologists must do everything in their
> power to ensure that their research does not harm the safety, dignity or privacy of
> the people with whom they work" (I:44).

TOWARD COLLABORATIVE MODELS
OF ANTHROPOLOGICAL RESEARCH

The final report states:

> Members of the Task Force believe that anthropological research with indigenous
> peoples should deepen the informed consent model in the direction of fully "col-
> laborative" models of research. Collaborative research involves the side-by-side
> work of all parties in a mutually beneficial research program. All parties are equal
> partners in the enterprise, participating in the development of the research design
> and in other major aspects of the program as well, working together toward a com-
> mon goal. Collaborative research involves more than "giving back" in the form of
> advocacy and attention to social needs. Only in the collaborative model is there a
> full give and take, where at every step of the research knowledge and expertise is
> shared. In collaborative research, the local community will define its needs, and will
> seek experts both within and without to develop research programs and action
> plans. In the process of undertaking research on such community-defined needs,
> outside researchers may very well encounter knowledge that is of interest to
> anthropological theory. However, attention to such interests, or publication about
> them, must itself be developed within the collaborative framework, and may have
> to be set aside if they are not of equal concern to all the collaborators. In collabo-
> rative research, local experts work side by side with outside researchers, with a fully
> dialogic exchange of knowledge (that would not, of course, preclude conventional
> forms of training). . . .
>   The Task Force has learned from Yanomami interlocutors that they need
> improved health care, better access to education, fairer access to their rights of polit-

EXCERPT FROM THIS SECTION

"Members of the Task Force believe that anthropological research with indigenous peoples should deepen the informed consent model in the direction of fully "collaborative" models of research. Collaborative research involves the side-by-side work of all parties in a mutually beneficial research program. All parties are equal partners in the enterprise, participating in the development of the research design and in other major aspects of the program as well, working together toward a common goal. . . . We suggest that the future of anthropology among indigenous peoples lies primarily within the collaborative model, with its intrinsic recognition of their full and unfettered right to define their own futures." (Final Report)

ical involvement as citizens, the guarantee of security of their lands, and adequate protection against violence from within and without. We believe that anthropological research among the Yanomami should have as an early goal to help them put in place political frameworks that will permit definition and articulation of these needs, assuming that the Yanomami concur that such development is important. In any case, we believe that anthropological work among them in the foreseeable future should be developed in collaboration with them to address questions that are to a great degree defined initially within Yanomami communities, and elaborated in consultation with such outside researchers as the Yanomami may invite as consultants (I:46).

The final report concludes, "We suggest that the future of anthropology among indigenous peoples lies primarily within the collaborative model, with its intrinsic recognition of their full and unfettered right to define their own futures" (I:47).

III. WHERE DO YOU STAND?

In a concluding chapter such as this, the author frequently sets out where he or she stands on the key issues discussed in the book. It constitutes a way for drawing various themes together.

But the goal of this book is not to simply highlight what I (or the Round-table participants) think. The problems exposed by the Yanomami controversy run too deep to be resolved by the wave of a single wand—by which I instruct readers on what to do and they do it. Academia does not work that way. Such declarations often lead to counterdeclarations and these, in turn, lead to debates that, while producing piles of publications, rarely lead to social change.

This book seeks to do more. It began, in the dedication, by listing the students who got involved in the politics of the El Dorado Task Force reports and made a critical difference in what that Task Force ultimately produced. It ends by asking readers to now get involved in reshaping anthropology as we reflect, through the lens of the controversy, on where we need go from here.

My plea to you, the reader, is to do more than simply passively take in my (or the Roundtable participants') perspectives. My views on the controversy are woven into the various chapters of part 1 as well as into the very structure of how the book is organized. And the Roundtable participants' views are apparent throughout the part 2 discussion. You, the reader, should now decide where you stand on the issues raised.

Here are four sets of questions you might ponder:

1. What do you perceive as the central concerns raised by the controversy? Where do you stand on them?

2. Would you assess blame and, if so, in what ways regarding which people or groups?

3. What is your opinion of the Roundtable's collective letter and the Task Force's final report? How would you improve on them if you were to write them yourself?

4. How might we go about changing the structures that fostered the controversy and the disciplinary ills so openly displayed in it? How would you set things right?

I would offer two notes of caution and one note of hope as readers proceed to answer these questions.

First, there will always be more references, more data, one could cite regarding the controversy. But essentially all the information you need to form your views is right here in this book. To allow others to intimidate you at this point with data that they possess but you lack is only to perpetuate academic status games.

Second, as suggested in chapter 6, readers might frame their assessments less in terms of absolutes—especially since various points remain in doubt—than in the pragmatic terms of what would help the people we work with (and others beyond the academy) to address the critical problems they face. We must remember that there is a world beyond the academy, and that world makes anthropology possible. It provides places to go, people to visit, money for research. Surely we should ask how we might serve this wider world's interests as well as our own. We cannot focus only on our own self-interests, leaving a concern for the broader good to others. Who will trust us—abroad or at home—if we pursue only our self-interest? This is one of the clear messages of the Yanomami controversy. To revitalize the discipline, we need to renew our responsibilities to others.

My note of hope derives from how the 119 students responded to a call for action. It can happen again, only on a larger scale.

I indicated in part I that the Yanomami controversy is part of a continuing tension within the discipline. Anthropology embraces a noble ideal. No other intellectual project in world history has mobilized so many scholars with such energy to understanding others different from themselves with less concern for conquest or financial gain. But when we turn from abstract affirmations to concrete actions, it is clear that the project has been imperfectly realized. Anthropology tends to be embedded in societies with imperialistic aims, and at times the discipline has reflected those aims. Anthropologists have not always demonstrated—in actions as well as words—their responsibilities to others beyond the academy.

The tension between aspiration and action is not going to go away. But recognizing it, understanding it, provides a foundation for change. The goal is to make the anthropological vision of engaging with others with respect and fairness a pervasive reality. Bringing change to anthropology will not be a spectator sport; it will involve courage, action, and persistence. We have the means to move ahead, applying the tools available at the Public Anthropology Web site, www .publicanthropology.org, to widen the discussion beyond coteries of specialists and beyond the discipline itself. And, using such efforts as a foundation, there is the possibility for, if not changing the world, at least holding out a beacon of hope, an affirmation of possibility, of the direction in which relations between First World and Third World countries, between the rich and the less rich, between the more powerful and the less powerful, might move regarding mutual respect and fairness for all.

The Yanomami controversy constitutes a call to action. Highlighting what is wrong, it challenges us to set things right. "Never doubt that a small group of thoughtful, committed citizens can change the world," the anthropologist Margaret Mead once wrote. "Indeed, it's the only thing that ever has."

SUMMARY OF THE ROUNDTABLE
PARTICIPANTS' POSITIONS

This appendix provides a summary of participants' views on the key topics covered in chapters 8, 9, and 10 of the Roundtable. Readers can use the summary as a guide for exploring a particular participant's position or a particular issue. (Citations refer to page numbers in part 2 of this volume.)

QUESTIONS OF POWER

Informed Consent

B. Albert

- Ch. 9: Indigenous groups have the right to withhold informed consent and if a project does not directly benefit them, decide what compensation they should receive for their participation. (160–61)
- Ch. 10: The 1968 expedition misled the Yanomami into believing that collecting blood samples would benefit them in terms of better treatment for the diseases that afflicted them. (223)
- Ch. 10: Informed consent is a continuing process, not a one-time event. (230)
- Ch. 10: We need to include indigenous views of consent in dealing with issues of informed consent. (221)

R. Hames

- Ch. 9: Chagnon sought to do the best he could under the circumstances in explaining Neel's research to the Yanomamö. (170–71)
- Ch. 9: We need to include indigenous views of consent in dealing with issues of informed consent. (172)
- Ch. 9: In accepting trade goods, Yanomamö were giving a form of consent for the blood samples Neel collected. (170)

K. Hill

- Ch. 9: Consent to participate in medical experiments, which are inherently risky, is clearly different from consent to be medically observed where there is minimal risk. (185–86)

- Ch. 10: Fully informing people is often a difficult process, but the people involved must have enough information to make a reasoned assessment of the risks involved. (246–47)

L. Martins

- Ch. 9: Yanomami have a right to hear different views—beyond those of the researcher—in evaluating the impact of particular research on them. (195)
- Ch. 10: Chagnon and others misled the Yanomami regarding health benefits they would receive as a result of Neel's research. (256–57)

J. Peters

- Ch. 10: An ambiguity exists within the concept of informed consent regarding what being "informed" means. (268)

T. Turner

- Ch. 10: False claims were made regarding the health benefits the Yanomami would receive from Neel's blood samples. (277)
- Ch. 10: The American Anthropological Association's Code of Ethics requires informed consent, and this was not obtained, especially regarding the fact that Yanomami blood would be stored indefinitely. (275, 277)

Present Yanomami Perceptions of the 1968 Expedition

B. Albert

- Ch. 8: Yanomami are upset regarding the continued storage of their relatives' blood in a distant country. (116)

L. Martins

- Ch. 10: Yanomami feel deceived by the explanation offered to them for collecting the blood samples in the 1968 expedition. (255–57)

Consensus on Informed Consent

- Ch. 11: "The principle that should regulate informed consent . . . is that the health and welfare of the study population must always take precedence over any academic or scientific goal." (286)

Doing No Harm as a Standard for Researchers

B. Albert

- Ch. 9: Calling the Yanomami the "fierce people" fostered negative stereotypes that hurt the Yanomami when they were particularly vulnerable to outside forces threatening them. (161–62)
- Ch. 9: Why did Chagnon never condemn the negative use of his work by others or support the international movement to defend Yanomami survival but instead waged a media war against advocates of Yanomami land and human rights? (163)
- Ch. 9: Chagnon was drawn into the manipulative practices he used to

gather information against people's wishes by the frenetic schedule he had for collecting genealogies for Neel's Atomic Energy Commission Project. (164–65)

R. Hames

- Ch. 8: Through revisions in later editions of his *Yanomamö* book, Chagnon sought to combat negative uses of his work. (122)
- Ch. 8 and Ch. 9: There are multiple accounts of Yanomamö warfare that predate Chagnon's research; it is unclear whether key military authorities ever read reports about Chagnon's work. (121, 175)
- Ch. 10: Anthropologists should respond to distorted characteristics of their work, and Chagnon did this in the way he mobilized the press to take note of the Yanomamö's plight. (236)
- Ch. 10: The major fault with Chagnon's interview in the Brazilian *Veja* magazine is the mean-spirited way he portrayed missionaries and NGOs. (236)
- Ch. 10: Before the publication of Tierney's book, there were no ethical complaints about Chagnon's conduct in the field. The AAA had plenty of evidence from Chagnon's own work to launch an investigation, but no one seemed to notice. Even Sponsel, a dedicated adversary, did not petition the AAA to conduct an investigation. (241)
- Ch. 10: There is no convincing evidence that Chagnon's distribution of trade goods had any effect on Yanomamö patterns of warfare. (242–43)

K. Hill

- Ch. 8: Although anthropologists use various tricks to obtain sensitive information, journalists often use these tactics to an even greater extent. (130–31)
- Ch. 8: That Yanomamö accepted Peters's and Albert's collecting of genealogies suggests that, contrary to Tierney, there are allowable ways to collect Yanomamö names. (131)
- Ch. 8: Chagnon allied himself with disreputable characters in the FUNDAFACI affair, but this was bad judgment rather than a serious ethical shortfall. (131–32)
- Ch. 9: Chagnon cannot be held responsible for all misuses of his work, and there is little evidence that his work affected Brazilian policy. (178)
- Ch. 9: That said, we should expect Chagnon to energetically attempt to counter misuses of his work when he discovers it is taking place. (179)

L. Martins

- Ch. 8 and Ch. 9: Chagnon insisted on emphasizing violence as a driving feature of Yanomami society despite being warned of its negative repercussions on negotiations over the establishment of a protective Yanomami land reserve. (136–38, 140, 191–92)
- Ch. 9: Chagnon did not speak out in Brazil to oppose the use of his ideas by those fighting against the Yanomami land reserve. (191–92)

- Ch. 9: Although there is violence among the Yanomami, Chagnon has overemphasized it. (190–91)

J. Peters

- Ch. 10: The ethical concerns raised about Chagnon's research over the years could have stimulated more debate within the discipline than they did. (267)
- Ch. 10: Chagnon could have done more to squelch the media reports that unfairly affected the Yanomami. (267)

T. Turner

- Ch. 9: Although Chagnon made some effort to deal with misrepresentations of his work in later editions of his book, he never spoke out against the misrepresentations where it would do the most good: in Brazil. (198–99)
- Ch. 9: Chagnon was a willing collaborator in the FUNDAFACI affair, and he must have known that some of his actions were criminal violations of Venezuelan law. (207)
- Ch. 10: Chagnon violated the American Anthropological Association's Code of Ethics by publicly attacking and misrepresenting Yanomami leaders, activists, and missionaries. (276)
- Ch. 10: Chagnon violated the American Anthropological Association's Code of Ethics by misrepresenting Yanomami reality when he choreographed violence in films and used field methods that exacerbated tensions among Yanomami. (276)

Consensus on Doing No Harm

- Ch. 11: "Anthropologists should take care to avoid constructing gratuitously damaging images or accounts of their subjects in their publications and media contacts to prevent possible harm to the dignity and welfare of the individuals and groups they study. . . . Anthropologists are morally responsible to counter abusive uses of their work when it is made known to them by local officials and/or anthropologists." (286–87)

What Constitutes Just Compensation for Those Who Help Anthropologists?

B. Albert

- Ch. 8 and Ch. 10: The collection of blood samples by American researchers has to date failed to help the Yanomami. (118, 224)
- Ch. 9: A fair compensation to the Yanomami for the economic benefits Chagnon has gained from their help in facilitating his career is still awaited. (165)
- Ch. 10: Anthropologists need to negotiate a pact of reciprocity with the people who help them and use both sensitivity and respect in doing so. (220, 226)
- Ch. 10: Cultural anthropologists can provide help that is comparable

to that offered by doctors by doing advocacy work on behalf of the group with whom they are working. (219)

R. Hames

- Ch. 9: In Neel's research there was a voluntary exchange by the Yanomamö of blood samples for trade goods. (170)
- Ch. 9: In considering just compensation, informants can assess to what degree they get fair compensation for their help in the field, but they often do not understand the academic contexts that reward anthropologists later on in their careers. (173)
- Ch. 9: It is laudable when anthropologists share royalties from their writings with those they have studied. (173)

K. Hill

- Ch. 8: Very few anthropologists could withstand careful scrutiny of whether they have fairly shared the income gained from a career built on fieldwork with the group they studied. (132–33)
- Ch. 8: Chagnon needs to discuss directly with the Yanomamö his limited assistance to them to date. (132)
- Ch. 8 and Ch. 9: Helping others beyond the community with whom an anthropologist works is a form of just compensation if this goal is explained and accepted by that community. (127–28, 187)
- Ch. 9: Instead of asking that the Yanomamö blood samples in America be destroyed, Yanomamö should insist that further research be done on the samples to directly help them. (187–88)
- Ch. 9: There is a double standard in fieldwork whereby medical doctors (like Neel) provide direct help to communities they study, while cultural anthropologists provide little direct help. (182)

L. Martins

- Ch. 10: The blood specimens collected by Neel did not result in any treatment to help alleviate Yanomami suffering from ongoing illnesses. (257)

J. Peters

- Ch. 8: The research conducted on indigenous peoples makes it possible for anthropologists to acquire faculty positions and status. (146)
- Ch. 8: The income an anthropologist makes from his faculty position may be more than the entire income of the group he studies; hence, offering the group book royalties may be a mere token payment for the anthropologist's financial rewards as a result of his research. (146)

T. Turner

- Ch. 8: Neel was faced with conflicting demands regarding how to balance humanitarian and research goals and chose to emphasize his research over humanitarian goals. (155–56)
- Ch. 10: The American Anthropological Association's Code of Ethics

specifies that researchers have primary ethical obligations to the people they study that supersede the goal of pursuing knowledge or continuing with a research project. (274)

- Ch. 10: The Yanomami Survival Fund, organized by Chagnon to help the Yanomami, has apparently been inactive since soon after its founding. (277)

Consensus on Just Compensation

- Ch. 11: There needs to be a negotiated contract between the researcher and the group studied, with clearly defined rewards that follow Rawls's "veil of ignorance" model. A division of royalties is important but, even more important, the researcher must help the researched community in ways the community itself requests and appreciates. (286)

Additional Points

B. Albert

- Ch. 10: Since indigenous groups are often marginalized minorities, anthropologists should support the expression of their perspectives as well as their individual and collective rights. (231)

R. Hames

- Ch. 8: More positive portrayals of indigenous peoples does not prevent their annihilation at the hands of outsider powers. (124)
- Ch. 10: There is more interest today among the Yanomamö in ways in which outside research might benefit them and in which collaborative efforts might emphasize Yanomamö's research priorities. (240)

K. Hill

- Ch. 9: If the Yanomamö were to file lawsuits against anyone, it should be against the Venezuelan and Brazilian governments that have failed to provide adequate medical services against the rampant diseases introduced by outsiders. (188)
- Ch. 10: What is happening among the Yanomamö today is a reflection of larger historical trends in the ways in which nation-states mistreat ethnic minorities within their borders. (235)
- Ch. 10: Researchers cannot be held responsible for doing the job of governments: although the Venezuelan government had responsibility for helping the Yanomamö in the measles crisis, it was Neel who actually offered the most help. (245)

L. Martins

- Ch. 10: Chagnon's suggestion that Yanomami leaders are puppets of NGOs is simply a continuation of an earlier colonial theme that whites dominant Indians and Indians are not authentic unless they speak in white ways. (263)

T. Turner

- Ch. 9: Some Yanomami are quite able to speak for themselves and should not be written off as "puppets" of outsiders. (208)

ENSURING PROFESSIONAL INTEGRITY

How Does the Discipline Regulate Professional Integrity?

B. Albert

- Ch. 8: Albert commissioned a report by experienced Brazilian physicians to objectively assess the validity of Tierney's accusations regarding Neel. (113–14)
- Ch. 10: Some of the Roundtable discussion abstractly affirms an ethical principle, but the principle's relevance to the concrete case being discussed is neutralized by convoluted arguments. (214)
- Ch. 10: Offering up anthropological abstractions while limiting one's efforts to help may build egos of anthropologists, but it does not assist the people affected. (216–17)

R. Hames

- Ch. 10: Many of Tierney's allegations were based on Chagnon's own publications. Why did it take an outsider to draw the AAA's attention to them? Might one conclude that the AAA thought Chagnon's behavior was reputable? And if the AAA is so upset about Chagnon's actions now (but not before), why does the AAA not investigate itself? (241)
- Ch. 10: Hames initially preferred not to join the El Dorado Task Force because he had worked with Chagnon in the field and his participation would be seen as involving a conflict of interest. He agreed to join only because John Peters was rejected as a candidate by the AAA president and there was no one else with expertise on the Yanomamö on the Task Force. (242)

L. Martins

- Ch. 8: The American Anthropological Association took no effective action to investigate the complaints against Chagnon by the Brazilian Anthropological Association. (140)
- Ch. 10: Although the American Anthropological Association has a progressive Code of Ethics, the mechanisms for holding anthropologists accountable to it are not clear. (264)

J. Peters

- Ch. 8: While anthropologists are quick to identify the negative effects of outsiders on indigenous peoples, they tend to ignore the long- and short-term impacts of anthropologists on the people they study. (144)

- Ch. 8: Unlike religious organizations in their dealings with individual missionaries, the American Anthropological Association has no power to "adjudicate" the "professional" conduct of its members, which means that anthropologists can do as they wish as long as they have government permission to do research. (146–47)
- Ch. 10: Anthropologists should scrutinize their own behavior and ideology and work more cooperatively with other organizations concerned with helping indigenous groups. (268)

T. Turner

- Ch. 10: The El Dorado Task Force—set up to investigate Tierney's accusations—initially appeared to be more concerned with defending American researchers than with getting at the truth of Tierney's allegations. (277–78)
- Ch. 10: A rebellion by the membership against the Task Force's preliminary report finally put "steel in the backbone" of the Task Force and made it critically address key issues relating to Chagnon. (278)
- Ch. 10: After an uncertain start the Task Force was able to demonstrate that the American Anthropological Association's Code of Ethics could be applied to evaluating unethical conduct. (281)

Consensus on Professional Integrity

- Ch. 11: The uproar surrounding Tierney's book proved critical in forcing the American Anthropological Association to address the ethical issues raised by Tierney regarding Chagnon and Neel. (285)
- Ch. 11: The American Anthropological Association needs to more vigorously pursue its own self-proclaimed educational efforts in the field of ethics. (287)
- Ch. 11: The American Anthropological Association has, by its own admission, proved ineffective in adjudicating ethical cases, despite its progressive Code of Ethics; it should therefore encourage the wider participation of its membership in its ethical deliberations. (288)

ESTABLISHING CREDIBILITY

Ideological Politics and the Search for Scientific Truth

B. Albert

- Ch. 9: One might suggest that in Venezuela and Brazil sociobiology has been spurned because of its association with Chagnon's work rather than it being the case that Chagnon's work has been spurned because of its association with sociobiology. (166)
- Ch. 10: Hames is correct in saying that NGOs sometimes use overly

positive stereotypical images of indigenous peoples to support the
NGO's fund-raising. (214)

- Ch. 10: Albert is not advocating an antiscience position. (230)

R. Hames

- Ch. 8: Whatever power anthropologists have with others beyond the
discipline depends on their providing accurate information rather than
politicized ideologies. (120, 125)
- Ch. 8 and Ch. 10: Instead of emphasizing the nobility of indigenous
groups or the wrongs done to them in a distorting manner, the justification for indigenous rights should be based on their prior and legitimate claims to the land they live on. (125, 235)
- Ch. 10: Disagreements with sociobiology should not be viewed as
hostility toward science more generally, and the misrepresentation
of opponents (as Chagnon and Turner have done) is counterproductive.
(240)

K. Hill

- Ch. 8 and Ch. 10: Chagnon was denied research access to the Yanomamö
because of his sociobiological views, and Chagnon has been attacked unfairly by those seeking to discredit sociobiology. (133–34, 250)
- Ch. 9: The science and nonscience camps in these debates need to
more honestly communicate with one another if anthropology is to
survive as an integrated discipline. (176)
- Ch. 10: Tierney asserts not only that sociobiologists are immoral but
that scientists, more generally, are immoral. (252)

L. Martins

- Ch. 9: The opposition to Chagnon should not be seen as opposition to
either scientific or sociobiological research in favor of a sociocultural
agenda. (193)
- Ch. 9: The science versus antiscience debate has tended to blur the
important ethical issues raised by Tierney's book. (194)

T. Turner

- Ch. 8 and Ch. 10: To criticize Neel and Chagnon is not to attack science
but to call for greater concern with ethics. (156, 272)
- Ch. 9: Certain sociobiological positions are simply not defensible in
scientific terms and hence must be understood as manifestations of
ideology. (202–3)

Ways Anthropologists Seek to Establish Credibility

B. Albert

- Ch. 8: Most of the accusations against Chagnon in Tierney's book are
not new and precede the book itself. (112)

R. Hames

- Ch. 9: To get a clearer sense of the degree to which Neel and his colleagues conformed to developing guidelines of informed consent in
  their 1968 research, not only must Neel's field notes be thoroughly
  examined (as Turner is doing) but Neel's colleagues on the expedition
  who are still alive must also be interviewed. (170)

K. Hill

- Ch. 8: Tierney accuses Chagnon of falsifying his data in the *Science*
  article, but Tierney offers no credible evidence to support this claim.
  (130)
- Ch. 9: If Tierney's book contains a hundred allegations and the ten
  most important are carefully investigated and disproved, it is reasonable
  to assume that the rest lack credibility as well. (179)
- Ch. 9: Turner's summary of events surrounding the vaccination program should be accepted cautiously because Hill has heard significantly
  different accounts from others who have complete access to Neel's
  notes. (182)

L. Martins

- Ch. 9: Those who challenge the impact of Chagnon's writings on the
  Brazilian Yanomami need to be much better informed about the Brazilian context and especially about the situation in the state of Roraima
  where most Brazilian Yanomami live. (190)
- Ch. 9: Reputable anthropologists have refuted, with substantial
  evidence, Chagnon's overemphasis on violence. (190–91)

T. Turner

- Ch. 8, Ch. 9, and Ch. 10: Tierney has really only filled in the gaps in a
  story that has been well established and independently documented by
  others. (150, 204, 273)
- Ch. 9: No one has refuted Tierney's evidence regarding the falsification
  of data in Chagnon's *Science* article. (206)
- Ch. 10: The El Dorado Task Force confirmed many of Tierney's allegations against Chagnon. (278, 281)

Consensus on Establishing Credibility

- Ch. 11: "While Tierney's *Darkness in El Dorado* contains clear errors"—
  especially regarding Neel's role in causing the 1968 measles epidemic—
  the public uproar Tierney's book caused "has proved critical in forcing
  the American Anthropological Association to address a set of ethical
  issues it should have addressed on its own well prior to the book's publication." (285)
- Ch. 11: "The open, public discussion of specific ethical problems . . .
  allows members of the American Anthropological Association to
  personally grapple with serious ethical issues in ways that abstract

reports from the association do not." The association's members need to collectively participate in the ethical deliberations surrounding the controversy. And to do this, the membership needs the documents the El Dorado Task Force used to draw its conclusions. "The inquiry needs to be a collective process in which, through our shared wisdom as anthropologists, we shape our shared future as a profession." (288–89)

SPECIFIC QUESTIONS REGARDING TIERNEY'S, NEEL'S, AND CHAGNON'S BEHAVIOR

Patrick Tierney

What are the main inaccuracies in Tierney's book?

B. Albert
- Ch. 9: Tierney's paranoid, nightmarish scenario of Neel's research has been completely and thoroughly discredited. (159)

R. Hames
- Ch. 9: Tierney made many fundamental errors in his discussion of the measles vaccination campaign. (170)
- Ch. 10: Tierney's work shows clear patterns of distortion, deception, and half-truths. (241)

K. Hill
- Ch. 8: We now have enough information to know that Neel did not intentionally infect the Yanomamö with a dangerous vaccine. (125)
- Ch. 8, Ch. 9, and Ch. 10: Tierney's case is based on distorted information, unwarranted conclusions, misleading footnotes, and misrepresentations. (126, 181, 249)
- Ch. 8: Tierney engaged in a smear campaign against Neel because of Neel's theoretical views. (127)
- Ch. 9: Tierney consciously uses sleazy journalism to imply nonexistent connections to support his case and undermine his villains. (181)

T. Turner
- Ch. 8: The new data that Turner himself has gathered from Neel's field notes indicate that Neel did not intentionally cause the measles epidemic or conduct an experiment that might have had serious medical consequences for the Yanomami. (152)
- Ch. 9: Tierney clearly made serious errors in his chapter on the measles epidemic, and he slips at times into unseemly personal abuse of Chagnon. (204)
- Ch. 10: It is generally recognized that there are shortcomings in Tierney's account of the 1968 measles epidemic. (273)

Given what we now know, are the accusations made against Chagnon and Neel mostly true or untrue?

K. Hill

- Ch. 8: Tierney has distorted the truth to attack and smear his ideological enemies. (134–35)
- Ch. 9: If the book contains a hundred allegations and the ten most important are investigated and found to be false, one can suspect that there is little credibility in the remaining allegations as well. (179)
- Ch. 9: Not only did Tierney make errors but he appears to have made them intentionally to advocate certain positions. (181)
- Ch. 10: While Hill is certain some parts of Tierney's book have been thoroughly discredited, he is willing to withhold judgment on other parts until more information is available. (249)

T. Turner

- Ch. 8: Some defenders of Neel and Chagnon have attempted to discredit the whole book by focusing on the book's flawed treatment of the measles epidemic while avoiding the many parts of the book that are supported by abundant evidence. (150)
- Ch. 8: Although 90 percent of the controversy has focused on 10 percent of the book, the remaining 90 percent of the book, focusing on Chagnon, is mostly accurate and well founded. (150)
- Ch. 9: Tierney presents much data that are supported by publicly available information from a host of other sources, and these data do not appear to be distorted (204).
- Ch. 10: Tierney draws on the work of other researchers to support his accusations against Chagnon. (273)
- Ch. 10: The American Anthropological Association's El Dorado Task Force Report confirmed a number of Tierney's serious allegations against Chagnon. (278)

Looking at the broad picture, how would you assess the value of *Darkness in El Dorado*?

B. Albert

- Ch. 8: Though Tierney's accusations against Chagnon were not new, they would never have gotten the notice they did if it were not for the accusations Tierney lodged against Neel. (112–13)

R. Hames

- Ch. 10: Tierney's book forced anthropologists to be more aware of their conduct as ethnographers, but the book itself is a fundamentally flawed work. (240)

K. Hill

- Ch. 9: There are relatively few parts of the book that are based on good evidence, and many of the correct facts are trivial. (181)

- Ch. 9: The main contribution of Tierney's book should be to focus attention on what can *now* be done to help the Yanomamö and other South American indigenous populations. (184)
- Ch. 10: There is a blatant antiscience attitude in the book that explains the negative reaction of many readers. (253)

L. Martins
- Ch. 10: Tierney's book leads us to reflect on how we relate to the people we study. (261)

J. Peters
- Ch. 8: Tierney did us a service by showing that anthropologists can operate as colonizers. (145)

T. Turner
- Ch. 8: Tierney should be given credit for raising important ethical issues. (149)
- Ch. 8: Although the broad outlines of Tierney's accusations regarding Chagnon were well known and well established, Tierney has added new details and filled in gaps in the public record. (150)
- Ch. 9: Tierney's account regarding Chagnon is substantially correct. (208)
- Ch. 10: The American Anthropological Association's El Dorado Task Force Report confirmed the importance of Tierney's work for anthropology. (281)

James Neel

Did Neel facilitate the spread of measles during his 1968 expedition?

[NOTE: As indicated in chapter 2, in the prepublication galleys of his book, Tierney suggested that Neel's use of the Edmonston B vaccine might itself have caused cases of measles, but this was toned down in the published book to the vaguer suggestion that Neel had worsened the measles epidemic through his actions. It is the prepublication suggestion that is referred to here by Hill and Turner.]

B. Albert
- Ch. 8: The report Albert commissioned indicated that Neel's team did not start the 1968 measles epidemic, and the use of the Edmonston B vaccine was a reasonable decision at the time. (113)
- Ch. 9: Tierney's accusations against Neel in this regard have been thoroughly discredited. (159)

R. Hames
- Ch. 9: It has been clearly established that Tierney made many fundamental errors in his discussion of the measles vaccination campaign. (170)
- Ch. 10: The accusation against Neel has been expertly refuted (241)

K. Hill

- Ch. 8: We now have enough information to know that Neel did not intentionally infect the Yanomamö with a dangerous vaccine. (125)

T. Turner

- Ch. 8: Contrary to Tierney's accusation, the vaccine Neel employed could not have caused transmissible cases of the disease. (151)

To what degree did the Neel expedition violate reasonable standards of informed consent?

B. Albert

- Ch. 8 and Ch. 10: Neel disregarded international codes for informed consent during his expedition. (114–15)
- Ch. 9: Hill's suggestion that communication difficulties with the people being studied is sufficient reason for dispensing with the protocol of informed consent in research is extremely dangerous. (160)
- Ch. 10: Formal informed consent was improperly replaced by the exchange of goods to get Yanomami's collaboration in Neel's research. (223)
- Ch. 10: Hames is correct that a formal investigation of informed consent in Neel's research is appropriate, as is the establishment of better guidelines for anthropological forms of informed consent. (217)
- Ch. 10: Roche's radioactive iodine experiment with the Yanomami violated the norms of informed consent. (222–23)

R. Hames

- Ch. 9: To what degree Neel and his colleagues violated reasonable standards of informed consent is a complex issue and requires not only an examination of his field notes (as Turner is doing) but an effort to interview other members of his research team. (170)
- Ch. 9: It is clear the Yanomamö gave their blood in exchange for trade goods, and they did it on a voluntary basis. (170)
- Ch. 9: Chagnon could not give the Yanomamö a "crash course" in infectious disease, genetics, and epidemiology to fully explain the purpose of the blood collection. (171)
- Ch. 9: No harm came to the Yanomamö as a result of their participation in Neel's research. (171)
- Ch. 9: A bioethics committee should be established to formally investigate the charges against Neel regarding informed consent and to establish better guidelines for informed consent. (171)
- Ch. 9: Researchers today follow the ethical requirement that their research needs to help some group of people but not necessarily the group of people studied; this is the standard that Roche's research followed. (172)

K. Hill

- Ch. 8 and Ch. 9: Roche's research on the Yanomamö using radioactive iodine, while not unethical per se, lacked informed consent and should not be repeated today. (128, 185)
- Ch. 10: While the collection of Neel's blood samples was not conducted under today's guidelines for informed consent, it did allow Neel to realize that the Yanomamö had no antibodies to measles and thus motivated him to acquire a vaccine to help the Yanomamö fend off any future measles epidemic (which in fact did occur). Neel's early blood samples allowed him to take steps that saved many Yanomami lives. (246)

L. Martins

- Ch. 10: The Yanomami were not informed as to what their blood was going to be used for, which means that the Yanomami were not fully informed when their consent was obtained. (255–57)
- Ch. 10: It was probably the implied, but ultimately false, promise of medical help that convinced the Yanomami to allow Neel to take blood samples from them. (257)

T. Turner

- Ch. 8: A review of Neel's field notes reveals no attempt to secure informed consent from the Yanomami for Neel's research or vaccination program. (152)
- Ch. 10: Neel violated the American Anthropology Association's Code of Ethics by not properly explaining his research motives for collecting blood samples as well as by failing to inform Yanomami that this blood might be stored for longer than the lives of the donors. (277)
- Ch. 10: Chagnon and Neel violated the American Anthropology Association's code of ethics by getting "misinformed consent": leading the Yanomami and missionaries to believe the collection of blood samples would result in medical help for the Yanomami. (277)

Did Neel act ethically during the 1968 expedition in the way he balanced his research with the need to treat the measles epidemic?

B. Albert

- Ch. 8: The Brazilian doctors' investigation (commissioned by Albert) revealed that Neel had not adequately prepared for the expedition, especially once he knew of the Yanomami measles epidemic; they also indicated that Neel gave a greater priority to his research than to helping the Yanomami. (114)
- Ch. 9: Turner's data indicate Neel gave a low priority to immunizations compared with his research agenda while the measles epidemic raged along the Orinoco River. (159)

R. Hames

- Ch. 9: Neel acted ethically in providing treatment to the Yanomamö during the measles epidemic; not providing vaccinations would have been the unethical act. (172)

K. Hill

- Ch. 8: Published and unpublished documentation make clear that Neel intended to both vaccinate the Yanomamö and study their reactions to the vaccine. (127)

- Ch. 8: The vaccination campaign during the measles epidemic took precedence over Neel's research design, as is clear from the fact that Neel gave vaccinations to villages he never returned to and to people whose names went unrecorded. (127)

- Ch. 9: Turner's accusation against Neel of misplaced priorities cannot be accepted because significantly different accounts of events are told by others who are familiar with the same field notes Turner has examined. (182).

- Ch. 10: Neel's failure to provide immunoglobulin to all Yanomamö who were vaccinated—a step that would have lessened Yanomami reactions to the vaccine—was likely an accident of available supplies rather than an intentional attempt at experimentation, but a formal investigation of the question might help to resolve the issue. (245)

L. Martins

- Ch. 10: What is most striking about Neel is that he did not alter his research route (from what he had previously planned) in coping with the measles epidemic. (260)

J. Peters

- Ch. 9: Placing the health and welfare of indigenous populations above our research interests may well mean revising our research plans in the field. (197)

- Ch. 10: Researchers might do all they can medically, given their resources, to help indigenous peoples, but this does not relieve national governments of their responsibilities in this regard. (267)

T. Turner

- Ch. 8: Neel's expedition routinely provided medical care while it was in Yanomami villages and provided medicines and vaccines to missionaries to continue that help. (152)

- Ch. 8: Neel's field notes confirm a point made by Tierney: the vaccination of Yanomami against the measles epidemic caused severe reactions among a number of Yanomami that led, in some cases, to panic and flight from villages where treatment was available. (152)

- Ch. 8: Even before he knew of the measles epidemic, Neel was concerned to vaccinate Yanomami to explore Yanomami production of antibodies. (153–54)

- Ch. 8: Neel wrote several times in his journal that vaccinating Yanomami had become a burden and was taking time away from his research activities. (154)
- Ch. 8 and Ch. 9: While it would have been prudent to vaccinate as many people in as many places as quickly as possible, Neel did not change his planned research itinerary in any major way when faced with the measles epidemic and hence was less successful at stopping the epidemic (and saving lives) than he might have been. (154–55, 205)

What should now be done to address Yanomami concerns regarding the Yanomami blood samples?

B. Albert

- Ch. 8: The location and legal status of the Yanomami blood samples should be determined, and if lawsuits are appropriate, the resulting income should be channeled back to the Yanomami. (117–18)
- Ch. 10: Hill is correct in saying that there should be negotiations regarding what should be done with the stored blood samples, but it is the scientists' responsibility, not the Yanomami's, to begin such negotiations. (227)

K. Hill

- Ch. 9: Instead of insisting that the blood samples should be destroyed, the Yanomamö should write the holders of the blood and request that research be done that could directly benefit the Yanomamö. (187–88)

Were the Yanomami misinformed regarding Neel's collection of blood samples and how the samples would help them?

B. Albert

- Ch. 10: The Yanomami never gained any medical benefit from Neel's research despite promises of such benefits. (224)
- Ch. 10: Hames's description of how Chagnon explained Neel's blood collection program to the Yanomami makes clear that Yanomami would deduce that they would get health benefits from the research. (223–24)

R. Hames

- Ch. 9: Clearly the Yanomamö gave their blood in exchange for trade goods, and they did it on a voluntary basis. (170)
- Ch. 9: Chagnon did explain to the Yanomamö that the purpose of the blood collection was to see what diseases they had in their blood so medical practitioners could more effectively treat the Yanomami when they became ill. (170–71)

L. Martins

- Ch. 10: Chagnon and others misled the Yanomami regarding health benefits that would result for the Yanomami from Neel's expedition. (257)

**To what degree should Neel have assumed responsibility during his fieldwork
for dealing with medical problems that were imperfectly dealt with by the
national governments of Venezuela and Brazil?**

K. Hill

- Ch. 9: It is unclear why Neel should be obligated to help the Yanomamö
  with their medical problems but cultural anthropologists, who have also
  worked with the Yanomamö but lack medical competence, are not obligated give up some of their income to help the Yanomamö medically.
  (183)
- Ch. 9: Turner criticized Neel for having the wrong medical priorities
  during his fieldwork, but the same could be said of anyone who fore-
  goes helping the Yanomamö by giving his or her own desires—say for
  personal goods—a higher priority than helping the Yanomamö. (183)
- Ch. 9: Instead of suing the American holders of Yanomamö blood samples for the return of the samples, the Yanomamö should sue the Brazilian and Venezuelan governments for their failure to provide adequate
  medical facilities and protection. (188)
- Ch. 9 and Ch. 10: Neel did far more than the Venezuelan government
  or the missionaries to fight the measles epidemic, even though these
  two groups had more official responsibility to help the Yanomamö than
  Neel. (183, 245)
- Ch. 10: Common sense suggests that researchers cannot be held
  responsible for the failings of national governments. (245)

L. Martins

- Ch. 10: Neel needed to do more to help the Yanomami than was usually
  called for in such circumstances because the Yanomami were in the midst
  of a devastating epidemic and no one else was around to help. (260)

Napoleon Chagnon

**Did Chagnon act unethically in using methods to collect genealogies that
violated Yanomami taboos?**

B. Albert

- Ch. 9: Chagnon's hit-and-run fieldwork—in contrast to the slower-
  paced, traditional fieldwork style—was tied to the frenetic schedule
  of Neel's research and created the necessity for developing aggressive
  and less ethical ways for circumventing the Yanomami name taboo to
  collect genealogies. (164–65)

R. Hames

- Ch. 9: The pressure to complete research in a limited time can lead ethnographers to use their wealth in an unethical way in order to get information that they might get as a matter of course if they stayed in the field for many years. (174)

K. Hill

- Ch. 8: If Tierney's accusations concerning Chagnon's manipulative behavior in gathering genealogies are correct, then the behavior is borderline unethical; but many anthropologists use tricks to collect sensitive data, and journalists are much worse in this regard. (130–31)
- Ch. 8: Tierney asserts that Chagnon infuriated Yanomamö by obtaining the names of dead people, but Peters and Albert also collected dead people's names among the Yanomamö, and the evidence suggests that Yanomamö were quite accepting of their activities. (131)

T. Turner

- Ch. 9: Chagnon, by his own account, used field methods that a large fraction of the Yanomami population would find offensive. (206)
- Ch. 10: Chagnon violated the American Anthropology Association's Code of Ethics by eliciting genealogical information in ways that significantly exacerbated tensions among Yanomami. (276)
- Ch. 10: The American Anthropological Association's El Dorado Task Force Report indicated that Chagnon had manipulated children as informants. (280)

Did Chagnon unethically stimulate warfare among the Yanomami, especially through his style of gift giving?

B. Albert

- Ch. 9: Chagnon's emphasis on visiting forty to fifty Yanomami villages and distributing a considerable amount goods to them to gain their support understandably generated many conflicts, as people competed for Chagnon's goods. (164)

R. Hames

- Ch. 10: There is no convincing evidence that Chagnon's distribution of goods had an impact on Yanomamö patterns of violence (243)

K. Hill

- Ch. 8: Chagnon's gifts did not cause any more conflict than the gifts given by the missionaries or Tierney. (129)

T. Turner

- Ch. 10: Chagnon violated the American Anthropology Association's Code of Ethics by his gift giving on such a massive scale that it led to conflict among the Yanomami. (276)

- Ch. 10: The American Anthropological Association's El Dorado Task Force Report provides support for the allegation that Chagnon helped precipitate much of the fighting that Chagnon recorded in his fieldwork. (279–80)

Was it appropriate for Chagnon to publicly criticize indigenous Yanomami spokespeople (especially Davi Kopenawa)?

R. Hames

- Ch. 10: Chagnon's interview in the Brazilian magazine *Veja* can be criticized for its "overall mean-spirited view" of missionaries and NGOs trying to help the Yanomamö. (236)

L. Martins

- Ch. 8: Chagnon's commentary on the Haximu massacre of Yanomami by miners cast a negative shadow on advocates of Yanomami rights and Yanomami spokespeople. (138)
- Ch. 8 and Ch. 10: Chagnon participated in the media attacks on Yanomami leaders and human rights advocates. (140, 263)

T. Turner

- Ch. 10: Chagnon violated the American Anthropology Association's Code of Ethics by repeated, untruthful attacks on Yanomami leaders, missionaries, and NGO activists. (276)

Should Chagnon have responded better to the media's misuse of his work during a critical period in Brazil when the Yanomami reserve was under consideration?

B. Albert

- Ch. 9: Albert, Hill, and Hames agree that anthropologists should respond to the misuse of their work that harms the people studied, but Chagnon, unfortunately, never did this. (162–63)
- Ch. 9: Chagnon's dropping of "The Fierce People" as the subtitle of his book (in the fourth edition) did not necessarily erase the stigma pinned on the Yanomami by previous editions of the book. (163)

R. Hames

- Ch. 8 and Ch. 9: To assert that Chagnon was responsible for Brazilian politicians and generals wanting to limit the Yanomamö reserve is to obscure the larger power plays these people have continually perpetrated against their national minorities. (121, 123, 174–75)
- Ch. 8 and Ch. 10: Chagnon took concrete steps in later editions of his book to address the misuse of his writings by changing the title of the book, deleting certain passages, and adding others. (122, 235–36)
- Ch. 10: Those who accuse Chagnon of not addressing negative images of the Yanomamö ignore how Chagnon has successfully used his media clout to call attention to the plight of the Yanomamö. (236–37)

K. Hill
- Ch. 9: Chagnon cannot be held accountable for all imaginable misuses of his work, and there is little evidence that his work affected Brazilian policy. (178)
- Ch. 9: Martins is correct in saying that we should expect Chagnon to engage in highly visible and energetic attempts to counter the misuse of his work when Chagnon discovers it is taking place. (179)

L. Martins
- Ch. 8: Chagnon's characterization of the Yanomami as fierce created a widespread negative impression of them among Brazilians. (137–39)
- Ch. 8: The negative results of Chagnon's characterization of the Yanomami as fierce can be seen in specific articles by Cristaldo in a Brazilian newspaper. (138)
- Ch. 8: Chagnon cannot be exempted from responsibility for the repeated use of his work against the interests of the Yanomami; although Chagnon could have reacted against the use of his writings to take government services away from Yanomami, he did not. (140)
- Ch. 9: Chagnon insisted on emphasizing Yanomami violence even though he was warned of the negative consequences that characterization might produce for the Yanomami. (191–92)
- Ch. 9: While Chagnon did make changes in later editions of his book—a book famous in America—he could have supported the Yanomami more effectively by protesting in Brazilian newspapers over the misuse of his work. (192)

J. Peters
- Ch. 10: Martins is correct in saying that Chagnon could have done more to squelch media reports that unfairly affected the Yanomami. (267)

T. Turner
- Ch. 9: While Chagnon did make changes to his book in later editions, he did not respond to misuses of his work where it would do the most good—in Brazil. (198–99)
- Ch. 9: Chagnon did not speak out against the misuse of his work by politicians seeking to dissolve the Yanomami reserve. (206)
- Ch. 10: Chagnon violated the American Anthropology Association's Code of Ethics by failing to speak out against uses of his statements that proved damaging to the Yanomami. (275)

Did Chagnon provide inaccurate representations of the Yanomami, especially regarding their "fierceness"?

B. Albert
- Ch. 9: While the Yanomami do practice warfare, the stereotypical image Chagnon presented is a serious matter, because it showed a minimal

concern for the ongoing political threats to the Yanomami's survival. (161–62)

R. Hames

- Ch. 8 and Ch. 9: There are many accounts of Yanomamö violence, Chagnon's is not the only one or the first one to describe their violence. (121, 175)
- Ch. 10: While it is important for NGOs to positively portray the Yanomamö in order to raise funds, it is important for anthropologists not to mix truth and lies in their portrayals of the Yanomamö. (238)

K. Hill

- Ch. 8: Tierney criticizes Chagnon for describing the Yanomamö as excessively violent, yet Tierney's own book discusses the practice of child sacrifice among Andean Indians. (129)

L. Martins

- Ch. 9: Chagnon not only has overemphasized violence among the Yanomami but has no reliable data to back up his assertions. (190–91)

J. Peters

- Ch. 10: Anthropologists should not err in excluding destructive aspects of a culture such as the suppression of women in their reports. (269)

T. Turner

- Ch. 9: Chagnon's depictions of Yanomami "fierceness" are related to a broader intellectual perspective emphasizing sociobiological ideas involving males competing for women. (201–2)
- Ch. 10: Chagnon violated the American Anthropology Association's code of ethics by misrepresenting Yanomami's "fierceness," warfare, and violence in his writings as well as films. (276)
- Ch. 10: The American Anthropological Association's El Dorado Task Force Report concludes that Chagnon misrepresented Yanomami reality in ethically consequential ways. (279)

Did Chagnon act unethically when he sought to gain control, with two others, of a large land reserve in Venezuela in what became known as the FUNDAFACI project?

K. Hill

- Ch. 8: Chagnon allied himself with disreputable characters, but this was a case of bad judgment rather than a serious ethical shortfall. (131–32)
- Ch. 8: There is no evidence that Chagnon and his two partners intended to dispossess the Yanomamö of their land or carry out illegal mining. (132)

T. Turner

- Ch. 9: Chagnon was a willing collaborator in actions that he must have known were criminal violations of Venezuelan law and would have damaging consequences for the Yanomami. (207)
- Ch. 10: Chagnon violated the American Anthropology Association's Code of Ethics by his participation in the FUNDAFACI project, especially because of the way the project, if implemented, would have harmed a significant number of Yanomami. (277)

Did Chagnon falsify data, especially in his conclusions in the famous *Science* article?

K. Hill

- Ch. 8: Tierney's accusation regarding the falsification of evidence is serious, but there is no credible evidence to support the claim. (130)
- Ch. 8: Whether the methods of data collection that led Chagnon to his conclusions are valid or not is an important topic, but it is not an ethical issue per se. (130)
- Ch. 8: Tierney's presentation of his own data regarding Chagnon is scientifically unqualified and blatantly biased. (130)

T. Turner

- Ch. 9: Tierney presents a great deal of credible evidence regarding Chagnon's falsification of data that no defender of Chagnon has so far credibly refuted. (206)

Did Chagnon benefit unfairly from the royalties earned from his books in relation to what he gave back, in compensation, to the Yanomami?

B. Albert

- Ch. 9: Chagnon established a Yanomamö Survival Fund in 1989, but the fund was apparently inactive until at least 1997. (163)
- Ch. 9: Chagnon's declarations of advocacy for the Yanomami were never substantial enough—in terms of what he actually did—to be significant. (163)
- Ch. 9: A fair redistribution to the Yanomami of the economic benefits Chagnon gained from his work is still awaited; Chagnon should explain what he intends to give back to the Yanomami in return for all their help. (165)

R. Hames

- Ch. 9: Peters and Hill are correct that it is laudable when anthropologists share their publication royalties with the people they studied. (173)

K. Hill

- Ch. 8: Chagnon paid the Yanomamö for the data he collected but apparently did not provide any other assistance to the tribe. (132)

- Ch. 8: Chagnon needs to discuss with the Yanomamö further compensation, but unfortunately Chagnon's enemies have made it impossible for him to return to the Yanomamö to discuss this important issue. (132)
- Ch. 8: Very few anthropologists could withstand careful scrutiny concerning whether they have fairly shared with a group the income that comes from a career built on fieldwork among that group. (132–33)
- Ch. 8: There appears to be little evidence that anthropologists besides Chagnon who have worked among the Yanomamö have offered assistance to the Yanomamö beyond the typical payments to informants. (133)

J. Peters

- Ch. 8: The income of some anthropologists with faculty positions is more than the income of the entire group they studied. (146)
- Ch. 9: A researcher's resources far exceeds those of the Yanomami and should be shared with them at the time of research as well as after he or she has left the field. (196)
- Ch. 10: Indigenous people have helped us in our academic careers, and we can reciprocate with moral and material assistance after we have left the field. (269)

T. Turner

- Ch. 9: Chagnon does not need to return to the Yanomami in order to help them; he could open a bank account in a Venezuelan town and have someone else distribute the funds. (208)
- Ch. 10: Chagnon violated the American Anthropology Association's Code of Ethics by not providing benefits to the Yanomami for their help; his Yanomami Survival Fund has apparently been inactive since its founding or soon thereafter. (277)

Was Chagnon unfairly restricted from continuing his long-term fieldwork among the Yanomami?

K. Hill

- Ch. 8 and Ch. 10: Chagnon's enemies unfairly restricted his access to the Yanomamö because they were displeased with his research questions and results. (133–34, 249–50)

L. Martins

- Ch. 9: The opposition by a range of people to Chagnon conducting fieldwork among the Yanomami in Brazil in 1995 can be attributed to the association of Chagnon's work with those who oppose Indian rights as well as to accounts of his fieldwork in Venezuela. (193)

Additional Points

B. Albert

- Ch. 8 and Ch. 9: As late as 1995, Chagnon was trying to collect blood samples from the Yanomami without consent from Brazilian officials or from Yanomami representatives. (115, 165)

L. Martins

- Ch. 8: It is fair to ask if the Yanomami would have been better off if Chagnon had never worked among them; Survival International says the answer is yes. (139)
- Ch. 10: Chagnon sought to take blood samples from Brazilian Yanomami in 1995 without adequate informed consent. (259)

J. Peters

- Ch. 8: Knowing the sensitivity of Yanomami to photographs, Peters wonders about the impact on the Yanomami of the films made by Asch and Chagnon in the 1960s. (144)

REFERENCES

All Web references were accessed June 2004 unless otherwise indicated.

YANOMAMI INTERVIEWS

Hawarixapopitheri, Alexandre
    2001   Interview by Lêda Martins, April 19. Electronic document, http://www
          .publicanthropology.org/Yanomami/InterviewsFromBook.htm.

Kopenawa, Davi
    2001a Interview by Bruce Albert, April 8. Electronic document, http://www
          .publicanthropology.org/Yanomami/InterviewsFromBook.htm.
    2001b Interview by Janet Chernela, June 7. El Dorado Task Force Final Report,
          vol. II:30–40. Electronic document, http://www.aaanet.org/edtf/
          final/vol_two.pdf.
    2001c Translator for interview by Lêda Martins, April 19. Electronic document,
          http://www.publicanthropology.org/Yanomami/InterviewsFromBook.htm.

Krokonautheri, Carlos
    2001   Interview by Lêda Martins, April 19. Electronic document, http://www
          .publicanthropology.org/Yanomami/InterviewsFromBook.htm.

Kuesitheri Yanomami, Geraldo
    2001   Interview by Lêda Martins, May 18. Electronic document, http://www
          .publicanthropology.org/Yanomami/InterviewsFromBook.htm.

Parawautheri, Geraldo
    2001   Interview by Lêda Martins, April 19. Electronic document, http://www
          .publicanthropology.org/Yanomami/InterviewsFromBook.htm.

Pirisitheri, Roberto
    2001   Interview by Lêda Martins, April 19. Electronic document, http://www
          .publicanthropology.org/Yanomami/InterviewsFromBook.htm.

Porapitheri, Peri
    2001   Interview by Lêda Martins, May 18. Electronic document, http://www
          .publicanthropology.org/Yanomami/InterviewsFromBook.htm.

Seripino, José
    2001   Speech, George Washington University, September 7. El Dorado Task Force
          Final Report, vol. II:41–45. Electronic document, http://www.aaanet.org/
          edtf/final/vol_two.pdf.

Wawanawetery, Ivanildo
    2001   Interview by Lêda Martins, April 19. Electronic document, http://www
            .publicanthropology.org/Yanomami/InterviewsFromBook.htm.
Wichato, Julio
    2001   Interview by Janet Chernela, November 24. El Dorado Task Force Final
            Report, vol. II:46–52. Electronic document, http://www.aaanet.org/edtf/
            final/vol_two.pdf.
Yanomami, Toto
    2002   Speech, Cornell University, April 6. El Dorado Task Force Final Report,
            vol. II:53–54. Electronic document, http://www.aaanet.org/edtf/final/
            vol_two.pdf.

BOOKS AND OTHER REFERENCES

Albert, Bruce
    1985   Temps du sang, temps des cendres. Représentation de la maladie, espace
            politique et systeme rituel chez les Yanomami du sud-est (Amazonie
            Brésilienne). Doctoral dissertation, Université de Paris X Nanterre.
    1989   Yanomami "Violence": Inclusive Fitness or Ethnographer's Representation.
            Current Anthropology 30:637–40.
    1990   On Yanomami Warfare: A Rejoinder. Current Anthropology 31:558–62.
    1994   Gold miners and Yanomami Indians in the Brazilian Amazon: The
            Hashimu Massacre. In Who Pays the Price? The Sociocultural Context
            of Environmental Crisis, B. Johnston, ed. Pp. 47–55. Washington, DC:
            Island Press.
    1995   Anthropologie appliquée ou 'anthropologie impliquée'? Ethnographie,
            minorités et développement. In Les applications de l'anthropologie. Un
            essai de réflexion collective B partir de la France, J.-F. Baré, ed. Pp. 87–118
            (see also bibliography on Minorities, pp. 259–69). Paris: Karthala.
    1997   "Ethnographic Situation" and Ethnic Movements. Notes on Post-
            Malinowskian Fieldwork. Critique of Anthropology 17(1):53–65.
    1999   Yanomami. Electronic document, http://www.socioambiental.org/website/
            epi/yanomami/yanomami.htm, accessed March 10, 2001.
    2000   Letter to the editor. Le Monde, October 1, http://www.tamu.edu/
            anthropology/Albert.html.
    2001   Associations amérindiennes et développement durable en Amazonie
            Brésilienne. Recherches Amérindiennes au Québec XXXI(3):49–58.
Albert, Bruce, and Alcida Rita Ramos
    1989   Yanomami Indians and Anthropological Ethics. Science 244:632.
Albert, Bruce, and G. Goodwin Gomez
    1997   Saúde Yanomami. Um manual etno-lingüístico. Belém: Museu (Collection
            Eduardo Galvno).
Alcantara, Eurípedes
    1995   Índio Também é Gente. Veja, December:67–9.
Ales, C.
    1984   Violence et ordre social dans une société amazonienne: Les Yanomami du
            Venezuela. Etudes Rurales:89–114.

Anthropology News
   2002   AAA Executive Board Actions: May 18–19, 2002. September:11.
Alphonso, C.
   2000   Natives and Doctor Locked in Blood Feud. The Globe and Mail, September
           22:A1, A5, http://www.ufrgs.br/HCPA/gppg/canada.htm.
American Anthropological Association (AAA)
   n.d.   Statement on Allegations Made in the Book Darkness in El Dorado.
           Electronic document, http://members.aol.com/nymiiiiiii/darkness_
           in_el_dorado/documents/0012.htm.
   1971/   Statements on Ethics: Principles of Professional Responsibility. Electronic
   1986   document, http://www.aaanet.org/stmts/ethstmnt.htm.
   1995   The Commission to Review the AAA Statements on Ethics. Final Report.
           Electronic document, http://www.aaanet.org/committees/ethics/ethrpt.htm.
   1998   Code of Ethics of the American Anthropological Association. Electronic
           document, http://www.aaanet.org/committees/ethics/ethcode.htm.
   2000a   Darkness in El Dorado Controversy: Questions and Answers. Electronic doc-
           ument, http://www.aaanet.org/press/qa.htm.
   2000b   El Dorado Interim Report/Request for Information. Electronic document,
           http://www.aaanet.org/press/eldoradoupdate.htm.
   2000c   The American Anthropological Association Executive Board Has Resolved
           to Take the Following Actions on Allegations Made in Darkness in El
           Dorado. November 15. Electronic document, http://members.aol.com/
           nymiiiiiii/darkness_in_el_dorado/documents/0228.htm.
   2001a   American Anthropological Association Launches Formal Inquiry into
           Allegations Made in Darkness in El Dorado. February 9. Electronic
           document, http://www.aaanet.org/press/ebmotion.htm.
   2001b   Preliminary Report of the American Anthropological Association El Dorado
           Task Force. The Anthropological Niche of Douglas W. Hume. Electronic
           document, http://members.aol.com/archaeodog/darkness_in_el_dorado/
           papers.htm. (This copy of the report is presently missing the section
           "Allegations and Case Studies.")
   2001c   El Dorado Interim Report/Request for Information. Electronic document,
           http://members.aol.com/anavanax/darkness_in_el_dorado/documents/
           0459.htm.
   2002   El Dorado Task Force Final Report. 2 vols. and preface. Electronic
           document, http://www.aaanet.org/edtf/index.htm.
Appiah, K. Anthony
   2000   Dancing with the Moon. New York Review of Books. November 16:55–60.
Arvelo Jimenez, N.
   2001   La saga de los Yanomamö. Reflexiones en torno al libro Darkness in
           El Dorado. Interciência 26(1):32–38. Also available online at http://www
           .interciencia.org/v26_01/arvelo.pdf.
Asad, Talal
   1973   Introduction. In Anthropology and the Colonial Encounter, Talal Asad, ed.
           Pp. 9–19. Atlantic Highlands, NJ: Humanities Press.
Athias, Renato, and M. Machado
   2001   Indigenous People's Health and the Implementation of Health Districts in

Brazil: Critical Issues and Proposal for a Transdiciplinary Dialogue. Cadernos de Saúde Pública, pp. 425–32.

Australia National Health and Medical Research Council
  1991   NHMRC Guidelines on Ethical Matters in Aboriginal and Torres Strait Islander Research. Electronic document, http://www.health.gov.au/nhmrc/publications/humans/pts91011.htm.

Barfield, Thomas
  1997   The Dictionary of Anthropology. Oxford: Blackwell.

Barker, J.
  1961   Incursiones entre los Guaika. Boletín Indigenista Venezolano 7(1):151–167.

Barth, Fredrik
  1994   A Personal View of Present Tasks and Priorities in Cultural and Social Anthropology. In Assessing Cultural Anthropology, Robert Borofsky, ed. Pp. 349–60. New York: McGraw-Hill.

Bellah, Robert N., Richard Madsen, William M. Sullivan, Ann Swidler, and Steven M. Tipton
  1985   Habits of the Heart: Individualism and Commitment in American Life. New York: Harper and Row.

Booth, William
  1989   Warfare over Yanomamö Indians. Science 243:1138–40.

Borgerhoff Mulder, M.
  1991   Human Behavioral Ecology: Studies in Foraging and Reproduction. In Behavioral Ecology: An Evolutionary Approach, J. R. Krebs and N. Davies, eds. Pp. 69–98. Oxford: Blackwell.

Borofsky, Robert
  1997   Cook, Lono, Obeyesekere, and Sahlins (with commentaries by H. Kane, G. Obeyesekere, and M. Sahlins and Robert Borofsky's reply to them). Current Anthropology 38(2):255–82.
  2002   The Four Subfields: Anthropologists as Myth-Makers. American Anthropologist 104:463–80.

Borofsky, Robert, ed.
  2000   Remembrance of Pacific Pasts: An Invitation to Remake History. Honolulu: University of Hawaii Press.

Bourdieu, P.
  2000   Propos sur le champ politique. Lyon: Presses Universitaires de Lyon.

Brenneis, Donald
  2002   On the El Dorado Task Force Papers. Anthropology News, September: 8. Also entitled "Preface for El Dorado Task Force Papers" and available online at http://www.aaanet.org/edtf/final/preface.htm.

Canada Tri-Council Working Group on Ethics
  1996   Code of Conduct for Research Involving Humans Ottawa: Minister of Supply and Services.

Carneiro da Cunha, Manuela
  1989   Letter to the editor. Anthropology Newsletter 30:3.

Carvalho, Dr. Fernando Sergio Viana Martins
  2001   Report of the Medical Team of the Federal University of Rio de Janeiro on Accusations Contained in Patrick Tierney's Darkness in El Dorado. (Tr. Catherine Howard).

Cassell, Joan, and Sue-Ellen Jacobs, eds.
  1987   Handbook on Ethical Issues in Anthropology. Special Publication no. 23.
          Washington, DC: American Anthropological Association.
Cetina, Karin Knorr
  1999   Epistemic Cultures: How the Sciences Make Knowledge. Cambridge:
          Harvard University Press.
Chagnon, Napoleon
  1968   Yanomamö: The Fierce People. First Edition. New York: Holt, Rinehart and
          Winston.
  1974   Studying the Yanomamö. New York: Holt, Rinehart and Winston.
  1977   Yanomamö: The Fierce People. Second Edition. New York: Holt, Rinehart
          and Winston.
  1983   Yanomamö: The Fierce People. Third Edition. New York: Holt, Rinehart
          and Winston.
  1988   Life Histories, Blood Revenge, and Warfare in a Tribal Population. Science
          239:985–92.
  1989a   On Yanomamö Violence: A Reply to Albert. Current Anthropology 31:49–
          53.
  1989b   Letter to the Editor. Anthropology Newsletter, January, 3, 24.
  1992a   Yanomamö. Fourth Edition. Fort Worth: Harcourt Brace College
          Publishers.
  1992b   Yanomamö: Last Days of Eden. New York: Harcourt Brace Jovanovich.
  1993a   Covering Up the Yanomami Massacre. New York Times, October 23, Op-Ed
          Section: 21.
  1993b   Killed by Kindness? Times Literary Supplement, December 24,
          Commentary: 11.
  1996   Review of Yanomami Warfare. American Anthropologist 98(3):670–72.
  1997   Yanomamö. Fifth Edition. Fort Worth: Harcourt Brace College Publishers.
Chagnon, Napoleon, et al.
  n.d.   Napoleon Chagnon Responds to Darkness in El Dorado. Electronic
          document, http://www.anth.ucsb.edu/chagnon.html.
Chiñas, B.
  1992   The Isthmus Zapotec. New York: Harcourt Brace Jovanovich.
Clifford, James
  1983   Power and Dialogue in Ethnography: Marcel Griaule's Initiation. In
          Observers Observed, George Stocking, ed. Pp.121–56. Madison: University
          of Wisconsin Press.
Coimbra Jr., C. E. A., and R. V. Santos
  1996   Ética e pesquisa biomédica em sociedades indígenas no Brasil. Cadernos de
          Saúde Publica 12(3):417–22.
Comision Pro Yanomami (CPY)/Médecins Sans Frontières (MSF-Holland)
  1998   Expedicion a la región del área Yanomami Venezolana en carácter emergen-
          cial. Informe final. October 1997–May 1998. Unpublished manuscript.
Cristaldo, Janer
  1994a   Massacre ou "panelocídio"? Folha de São Paulo, May.
  1994b   Os bastidores do Inablefe. Folha de São Paulo, April.
Cronk, L., N. Chagnon, and W. Irons
  2000   Adaptation and Human Behavior: An Anthropological Perspective. New
          York: Aldine de Gruyter.

Cunningham, H.
　1998　Colonial Encounters in Postcolonial Contexts: Patenting Indigenous DNA and the Human Genome Diversity Project. Critique of Anthropology 18:205–33.
Curran, Jeanne, and Susan Takata
　2000　Research among the Yanomami. American Anthropological Association. Electronic document, http://www.scudh.edu/dearhabermas/yanomami02.htm.
Davis, S.
　1976　The Yanomamö: Ethnographic Image and Anthropological Responsibilities. In The Geological Imperative: Anthropology and Development in the Amazon Basin of South America. P. 123. Cambridge, MA.: Anthropology Resource Center.
Durkheim, Emile
　1933/　The Division of Labor in Society. New York: Free Press.
　1893
Early, John D., and John F. Peters
　1990　The Population Dynamics of the Mucajai Yanomama. San Diego: Academic Press.
　2000　The Xilixana Yanomami of the Amazon: History, Social Structure, and Population Dynamics. Gainesville: University Press of Florida.
Eguillor Garcia, M. I.
　1984　Yopo, Shamanes Y Hekura. Caracas, Venezuela: Libreria Editorial Salesiana.
El Nacional
　2000a　La prohibicion de investigar rige para todas las zonas indigenas, November 24, http://members.aol.com/anavanax/darkness_in_el_dorado/documents/0428.htm.
　2000b　Por denuncias de Tierney prohibieron investigaciones en zonas indigenas, November 26, http://members.aol.com/anavanax/darkness_in_el_dorado/documents/0431.htm.
Ember, Carol, and Melvin Ember
　1996　Cultural Anthropology. Eighth Edition. Upper Saddle River, NJ: Prentice-Hall.
Evans, Patsy
　1998　Who We Are and What We Want: AAA Polls Membership. Anthropology Newsletter 39(2):1, 6–7.
Evans-Pritchard, E. E.
　1940　The Nuer: A Description of the Modes of Livelihood and Political Institutions of a Nilotic People. Oxford: Clarendon Press.
Fabian, Johannes
　1983　Time and the Other: How Anthropology Makes Its Object. New York: Columbia University Press.
Fackelman, K.
　1998　Tuberculosis Outbreak: An Ancient Killer Strikes a New Population. Science News 153(5) (January 31):73–75.
Farage, N.
　1999.　Communication to the Roundtable "Use of Animals in Scientific Experiments." Araraquara: FCL-UNESP (October).

Ferguson, R. B.
    1989   Do Yanomamö Killers Have More Kids? American Ethnologist 16:564–65.
    1995   Yanomami Warfare: A Political History. Santa Fe: School of American
            Research Press.
    2001   Materialist, Cultural and Biological Theories on Why Yanomami Make War.
            Anthropological Theory 1(1):99–116.
Fluehr-Lobban, Carolyn, ed.
    1991   Ethics and the Profession of Anthropology: Dialogue for a New Era.
            Philadelphia: University of Pennsylvania Press.
Folha de São Paolo
    1997   June 1:5–15.
Fontenay, E. de
    2000   Pourquoi les animaux n'auraient-ils pas droit B un droit des animaux? Le
            Débat 109:138–55.
Fortes, M., and E. E. Evans-Pritchard, eds.
    1940   African Political Systems. New York: Oxford University Press.
Foster, M. W., A. J. Eisenbraun, and T. H. Carter
    1997   Communal Discourse as a Supplement to Informed Consent for Genetic
            Research. Nature Genetics 17 (November):277–79.
Friedlaender, J., ed.
    1996   Genes, People, and Property: Furor Erupts over Genetic Research on
            Indigenous Peoples. Cultural Survival Quarterly 20(2).
Furtado Filho, C.
    2001   Memo no. 019/CGAE/20001 to the General Coordination of Studies and
            Research. Brasília: FUNAI (Social Communication Department).
Galison, Peter
    1997   Image & Logic: A Material Culture of Microphysics. Chicago: University of
            Chicago Press.
Geertz, Clifford
    2001   Life among the Anthros. New York Review of Books, February 8:18–22.
Gonçalves, Marco Antônio
    2001   Senado cria CPI para investigar demarcaçno de terras indígenas na
            Amazônia. Electronic document, http://www.socioambiental.org/website/
            notícias/índios/20012903, accessed July 18, 2001.
Good, Kenneth
    1991   Into the Heart: One Man's Pursuit of Love and Knowledge among the
            Yanomama. New York: Simon and Schuster.
Greely, H. T.
    1998   Genomics Research and Human Subjects. Science 282 (5389):265.
Gregor, Thomas, and Daniel Gross
    2002   Anthropology and the Search for the Enemy Within. Chronicle of Higher
            Education Review, July 26, B11.
Gregory, Juno
    2000   Macho Anthropology. Salon, September 28, http://members.aol.com/
            nymiiiiiii/darkness_in_el_dorado/documents/0041.htm.
Grinker, Roy Richard
    2000   In the Arms of Africa: The Life of Colin M. Turnbull. New York: St.
            Martin's Press.

Habermas, Jürgen
1989   The Structural Transformation of the Public Sphere. Cambridge, MA: MIT
        Press.
Hames, R.
1991   Wildlife Conservation in Tribal Societies. *In* Biodiversity: Culture,
        Conservation, and Ecodevelopment, M. Oldfield and J. Alcorn, eds.
        Pp. 172–202. Boulder, CO: Westview Press.
2001a   Exposure of an Exposé. Current Anthropology 42(2):271–73.
2001b   Human Behavioral Ecology. *In* International Encyclopedia of the Social and
        Behavioral Sciences. Pp. 6946–51. New York: Elsevier.
2002   My Resignation Letter. Electronic document, http://members.aol.com/
        anavanax/darkness_in_el_dorado/documents/0514.htm.
Hammond, E.
2000   Phase II for Human Genome Research: Human Genetic Diversity Enters
        the Commercial Mainstream. Electronic document, http://www.etcgroup
        .org/documents/com_phase2.pdf.
Harry, D.
1995   Patenting of Life and Its Implications for Indigenous People. IPR-Info 7
        (January).
Haviland, William
2002.   Cultural Anthropology. Tenth Edition. New York: Harcourt College
        Publishers.
Headland, Tom
n.d.   When Did the Measles Epidemic Begin among the Yanomami?
        Electronic document, http://www.sil.org/sil/roster/headland-t/measles1
        .htm#measles1.
Hemming, John
1978   Red Gold and the Conquest of the Brazilian Indians. Cambridge, MA:
        Harvard University Press.
Hereniko, Vilsoni
2000   Indigenous Knowledge and Academic Imperialism. *In* Remembrance
        of Pacific Pasts. Robert Borofsky, ed. Pp. 78–91. Honolulu: University
        of Hawaii Press.
Hill, Jane
2000   Getting Out the Real Story. Anthropology News, November 5.
Hitchcock, R.
1996   Botswana's Decision to Relocate People of the Central Kalahari Game
        Reserve: Consensus or Genocide? Indigenous Affairs 3:44–77.
Holy, Ladislav
1987   Introduction. Descriptions, Generalization and Comparison: Two
        Paradigms. *In* Comparative Anthropology, L. Holy, ed. Pp. 1–21. Oxford:
        Basil Blackwell.
Human Genome Diversity Project (HGDP)
n.d.   Human Diversity Project. South America Chapter. Unpublished
        manuscript.
Humboldt, A. V.
1967/   De Orinoco al Amazonas. Barcelona, Spain: Editorial Labor.
1851

Hume, Douglas
  n.d.   *Darkness in El Dorado* Information: The Anthropological Niche of Douglas
        W. Hume. Electronic document, http://members.aol.com/archaeodog/
        darkness_in_el_dorado/index.htm.

Hurtado A. M.
  1990   Letter to the Editor. Anthropology Newsletter 31(3).

Hurtado, Magdalena, Kim Hill, Hillard Kaplan, and Jane Lancaster
  2001   Disease among Indigenous South Americans. Anthropology News 42:5, 6.

Hymes, Dell
  1969   The Use of Anthropology: Critical, Political, Personal. *In* Reinventing
        Anthropology, Dell Hymes, ed. Pp.3–79. New York: Random House.

Irons, W.
  1979   Cultural and Biological Success. *In* Evolutionary Biology and Human Social
        Behavior: An Anthropological Perspective, N. Chagnon and W. Irons, eds.
        Pp. 257–72. North Scituate, MA: Duxbury Press.

Kame'eleihiwa, Lilikal
  1994   Review. Pacific Studies 17(2):111–18.

Keesing, Felix
  1958   Cultural Anthropology: The Science of Custom. New York: Rinehart.

Kessing, Roger
  1976   Cultural Anthropology: A Contemporary Perspective. New York: Holt,
        Rinehart and Winston.

Kidd, J. R., F. L. Black, K. M. Weiss, I. Balazs, and K. K. Kidd
  1991   Studies of Three Amerindian Populations Using Nuclear DNA
        Polymorphisms. Human Biology 63(6):775–94.

Koch-Grünberg, T.
  1990/   De Roraima al Orinoco. Vol. I. Caracas, Venezuela: Ediciones del Banco
  1917   Central de Venezuela.

Kottak, Conrad
  1997   Anthropology: The Exploration of Human Diversity. Seventh Edition. New
        York: McGraw-Hill.

Kroeber, Alfred
  1948   Anthropology. New York: Harcourt, Brace and World.

Kuper, Adam, and Jessica Kuper, eds.
  1985   The Social Science Encyclopedia. Boston: Routlege and Kegan Paul.

Lamphere, Louise
  2001   From the President. Anthropology News 42(4):59.

Lee, R.
  1979   The !Kung San: Men, Women, and Work in a Foraging Society. Cambridge:
        Cambridge University Press.

Leo, John
  1975   Beastly or Manly? Time magazine, May 10.

Lévi-Strauss, Claude
  1994   Anthropology, Race, and Politics: A Conversation with Didier Eribon.
        In Assessing Cultural Anthropology, Robert Borofsky, ed. Pp. 420–26.
        New York: McGraw-Hill.

Lewin, Roger
  1993   Genes from a Disappearing World. New Scientist, May 29:25–29.

Lewontin, Richard
   2000   It Ain't Necessarily So: The Dream of the Human Genome and Other
           Illusions. New York: New York Review Books.
Lindee, S.
   2000a   Review of Neel Field Notes. September 21, 2000. Electronic document,
           http://members.aol.com/nymıııııı/darkness_in_el_dorado/documents/
           0021.htm.
   2000b   Neel's Field Trip in 1968. Paper presented at the Annual Meeting of the
           American Anthropological Association, November 16.
   2001a   A Tangled Web in More Ways than One. Pennsylvania Gazette January/
           February 2001, http://www.upenn.edu/gazette/0101/0101gaz9.html.
   2001b   Review in Perspectives on Tierney's Darkness in El Dorado: CA Forum on
           Anthropology in Public. Current Anthropology 42(2):272–74.
Lizot, J.
   1970   Compte rendu de mission chez les Indiens Yanomami. l'Homme
           (2):116–21.
   1976   The Yanomami in the Face of Ethnocide. Copenhagen: IWGIA.
   1977   Population, Resources, et Guerre chez les Yanomami. Libre 2:111–45.
   1985   Tales of the Yanomami: Daily Life in the Venezuelan Forest. New York:
           Cambridge University Press.
   1989   Sobre la guerra: Una respuesta a N. A. Chagnon (Science, 1988). La Iglesia
           en Amazonas, April:23–34.
Lobo, Dr. Maria Stella, Dr. Karis Maria Pinho Rodrigues, Dr. Diana Maul de Carvalho,
   and Dr. Fernando Sergio Viana Martins
   2000   Report of the Medical Team of the Federal University of Rio de Janeiro
           on Accusations Contained in Patrick Tierney's Darkness in El Dorado.
           Tr. Catherine Howard. Electronic document, http://www.tamu.edu/
           anthropology/UFRJ-Final.html.
Marcos A.
   2000   Povos Indígenas e a Conquista da Cidadania no Campo da Saúde, In Povos
           Indígenas no Brasil, 1996/2000. Carlos Alberto Ricardo, ed. Pp. 139–42.
           São Paulo: Instituto Socioambiental.
Marcus, George, and Michael Fischer
   1986   Anthropology as Cultural Critique. Chicago: University of Chicago Press.
Mariz Maia, L.
   2000   Haximu: Foi genocidio! CCPY, Pro-Yanomami Documents. English version,
           http://www.proyanomami.org.br/frame1/Ingles/massacreHX1.htm.
Mauss, M.
   1991/   Essai sur le don. In Sociologie et anthropologie. Paris: PUF. Translated
   1925   by W. D. Halls as The Gift: The Form and Reason for Exchange in Archaic
           Societies. (New York: Norton, 1990).
McFeely, Eliza
   2001   Zuni and the American Imagination. New York: Hill and Wang.
Meek, James
   2000   Professor Denies Causing Measles Epidemic. The Guardian, October 4,
           http://members.aol.com/lithicat/darkness_in_el_dorado/documents/0128
           .htm.

Miller, D. W.

2000a   Anthropologists Debate a Controversial Book and Their Own Research Ethics. Chronicle of Higher Education, December 1:A22.

2000b   Scholars Fear That Alleged Misdeeds by Amazon Anthropologists Will Taint Entire Discipline. Chronicle of Higher Education, September 20, http://chronicle.com/prm/daily/2000/09/2000092001n.htm.

2001   Anthropologists Criticize Release of Preliminary Report on Controversy Over Research on the Yanomami. Chronicle of Higher Education, December 3, http://chronicle.com/prm/daily/2001/12/2001120303n.htm.

Milliken, W., and B. Albert, with G. Goodwin Gomez

1999   Yanomami: A Forest People. Kew, England: Royal Botanical Garden.

Monaghan, Peter

1994   Bitter Warfare in Anthropology. Chronicle of Higher Education, October 26:A10–11, 18–19.

Moreno, J. D.

2000   Undue Risk: Secret State Experiments on Humans. New York: W. H. Freeman.

Nader, Laura

1969   Up the Anthropologist—Perspectives Gained from Studying Up. In Reinventing Anthropology, Dell Hymes, ed. Pp. 284–311. New York: Random House.

1994   Comparative Consciousness. In Assessing Cultural Anthropology, Robert Borofsky, ed. Pp. 84–94. New York: McGraw-Hill.

Nanda, Serena, and Richard Warms

2002   Cultural Anthropology. Seventh Edition. Belmont, CA: Wadsworth/Thomson Learning.

National Academy of Sciences

2000   A Statement from Academy President Bruce Albert Regarding Darkness in El Dorado: Setting the Record Straight Regarding Darkness in El Dorado, November 9. Electronic document, http://www4.nationalacademies .org/nas/nashome.nsf/b57ef1bf2404952b852566ddoo671bfd/ 57065f16ff25837185256992oo52d283?OpenDocument.

National Commission for the Protection of Human Subjects of Biomedical and Behavioral Research

1979   The Belmont Report: Ethical Principles and Guidelines for the Protection of Human Subjects of Research. Electronic document, http://ohrp.osophs .dhhs.gov/humansubjects/guidance/belmont.htm.

Neel, James V.

1970   Lessons from a Primitive People. Science 170:815–22.

1980   On Being Headman. Perspectives in Biology and Medicine 23(Winter): 277–94.

1994   Physician to the Gene Pool: Genetic Lessons and Other Stories. New York. John Wiley.

Neel, J. V., W. R. Centerwall, and N. A. Chagnon

1970   Notes on the Effects of Measles and Measles Vaccine in a Virgin Soil Population. American Journal of Epidemiology 91(4):418–29.

New Scientist

2000   They Need Your DNA. But People Who Give a Blood Sample Have a Right to Know What It Is Used For (editorial), September 30.

Nuñez, Marielba.
  2000   Por denuncias de Tierney prohibieron investigaciones en zonas indígenas
          El Nacional, November 26. Electronic document, http://members.aol.com/
          anavanax/darkness_in_el_dorado/documents/0431.htm.
Oliveira, D. de
  1977   Memo no. 202/COAMA/77C14/6/77 to the President of FUNAI. Brasília:
          FUNAI (Amazonia Coordination).
Oliven, R. G.
  2000   Statement of the Brazilian Anthropological Association to Be Read at
          the Panel "Ethical Issues in Field Research among the Yanomami" at
          the Annual Meeting of the American Anthropological Association, San
          Francisco, November 16. Electronic document, http://members.aol.com/
          anavanax/darkness_in_el_dorado/documents/0256.htm.
Paul, Diane, and John Beatty
  n.d.   James Neel, Darkness in El Dorado and Eugenics: The Missing Context.
          Electronic document, http://members.aol.com/lithicat/darkness_in_el_
          dorado/documents/0186.htm.
Peters, John F.
  1998   Life among the Yanomami: The Story of Change among the Xilixana on the
          Mucajai River in Brazil. Orchard Park, NY: Broadview Press.
Putnam, Robert
  1993   Making Democracy Work. Princeton, NJ: Princeton University Press.
  2000   Bowling Alone. New York: Simon and Schuster.
Rabben, L.
  1998   Unnatural Selection: The Yanomami, the Kayapó, and the Onslaught of
          Civilization. Seattle: University of Washington Press.
Ramos, A. R.
  1998   Indigenism: Ethnic Politics in Brazil. Madison: University of Wisconsin
          Press.
  2000   The Commodification of the Indian. Anthropology series 281. Department
          of Anthropology, University of Brasília.
  2001   CA Commentary. Current Anthropology 42(2):274–76.
Rawls, John
  2001   Justice as Fairness: A Restatement. Edited by Erin Kelly. Cambridge, MA:
          Harvard University Press.
  1971   A Theory of Justice. Cambridge, MA: Harvard University Press.
Regush, Nicholas
  2000   Who Should Investigate: Looking at Conflict of Interest in Biomedicine,
          Part Two. ABC News Online, October 5, http://members.aol.com/
          nym11111111/darkness_in_el_dorado/documents/0070.htm.
Reiss, S.
  1990   The Last Days of Eden: The Yanomami Indians Will Have to Adapt to the
          20th Century or Die. Newsweek, December 3:48–50.
Ribeiro, D.
  1967   Indigenous Cultures and Languages of Brazil. In Indians of Brazil in
          the 20th century, Janice Hopper, ed. Pp. 77–165. Publication no. 2.
          Washington, DC: Institute for Cultural Research Studies.

Ricardo, Carlos Alberto, ed.
  2000   Povos Indígenas no Brasil, 1996–2000. São Paulo: Instituto
         Socioambiental.
Ridley, Matt
  1999   Genome: The Autobiography of a Species in 23 Chapters. New York:
         HarperCollins.
Ritchie, M.
  1996   Spirit of the Rainforest: A Yanomamö Shaman's Story. Chicago: Island
         Lake Press.
Roosevelt, Margot
  2000   Yanomami: What Have We Done to Them? Time Magazine, October
         2:77–78.
Saffirio, G., and R. Hames
  1983   The Forest and the Highway. In Working Papers on South American
         Indians #6 and Cultural Survival Occasional Paper #11 (joint publication),
         K. Kensinger and J. Clay, eds. Pp. 1–52. Cambridge, MA: Cultural Survival.
Sahlins, Marshall
  1994   Goodbye to Tristes Tropes: Ethnography in the Context of Modern World
         History. In Assessing Cultural Anthropology, Robert Borofsky, ed. Pp. 377–
         94. New York: McGraw-Hill.
  2000   Review of Darkness in El Dorado. Washington Post, December 10, 2001.
Salamone, Frank, ed.
  1996   Who Speaks for the Yanomami. Studies in Third World Societies (#57).
         Williamsburg, VA: Anthropology Department, College of William and
         Mary.
  1997   The Yanomami and Their Interpreters: Fierce People or Fierce Interpreters.
         Lanham, MD: University Press of America.
Salopek, Paul
  1997a Basically, We Are All the Same. Controversial Genetic Quest Is Unlocking
         Secrets of the Human Rainbow. Chicago Tribune, April 27.
  1997b Genes Offer Sampling of Hope and Fear. Cures Possible, but Groups Worry
         about Exploitation. Chicago Tribune, April 28.
Salzano, F. M.
  2000   James V. Neel and Latin America, or How Scientific Collaboration Should
         Be Conducted. Genetic and Molecular Biology 23(3):557–61.
Santos, R V.
  2002   Indigenous Peoples, Post-Colonial Contexts, and Genetic/Genomic
         Research in the Late 20th Century: A View from Amazonia (1960–2000).
         Critique of Anthropology 22(1):81–104.
Santos, R. V., and C. Coimbra Jr.
  1996   Sangue, bioética e populaçtes indígenas. Parabólicas 20. São Paulo:
         Instituto Socioambiental.
Scheper-Hughes, Nancy
  1995   The Primacy of the Ethical. Current Anthropology 36:399–440.
Secoy, F.
  1953   Changing Military Patterns on the Great Plains. Monograph No. 21. Seattle:
         American Ethnological Society.

Segerstrale, Ullica
    2000   Defenders of the Truth: The Battle of Science in the Sociobiology Debate
            and Beyond. New York: Oxford University Press.
Shapin, Steven
    1994   A Social History of Truth: Civility and Science in Seventeenth-Century
            England. Chicago: University of Chicago Press.
Shapiro, J.
    1976   Beastly or Manly? Letter to Editor. Time Magazine, May 31.
Smiljanic Borges, M. I.
    1999   O Corpo cósmico: O Xamanismo entre os Yanomae do Alto Toototobi.
            Doctoral dissertation, University of Brasília.
Smith, Geri
    2000   Atrocities in the Amazon? Business Week, December 18:21–24.
Smith, E., M. Borgerhoff Mulder, and K. Hill
    2001   Controversies in the Evolutionary Social Sciences: A Guide to the
            Perplexed. Trends in Ecology and Evolution 16:128–35.
Smith E., and B. Winterhalder, eds.
    1992   Evolutionary Ecology and Human Behavior. New York: Aldine de Gruyter.
Sontag, Susan
    1966   The Anthropologist as Hero. In Against Interpretation and Other Essays.
            Pp. 69–81. New York: Doubleday.
Souza, A. O. de, et al.
    1997   An Epidemic of Tuberculosis with a High Rate of Tuberculin Energy
            among a Population Previously Unexposed to Tuberculosis, the Yanomami
            Indians of the Brazilian Amazon. Proceedings of the National Academy of
            Sciences 94 (November 25):13227–32.
Spindler, George, and Louise Spindler
    1983   About the Third Edition. In Yanomamö: The Fierce People. Napoleon
            Chagnon. Third Edition. Pp. vi–viii. New York: Holt, Rinehart and
            Winston.
Sponsel, Leslie
    1998   Yanomami: An Arena of Conflict and Aggression in the Amazon.
            Aggressive Behavior 24:97–122.
Sponsel, Leslie, and Terence Turner
    2002   Charges of Wrongdoing by Anthropologists. Counterpoint. Chronicle of
            Higher Education Review, August 9.
Srikameswaran, Anita
    2000   Pittsburgh Author's Charges Stir Up Anthropologists. Controversy of
            Epidemic Proportions. Pittsburgh Post-Gazette, November 15, http://www
            .post-gazette.com/magazine/20001115tierney2.asp.
Survival International
    2001   Statement Regarding the Current Allegations That Scientists and
            Journalists Devastated the Yanomami. January 17. Electronic document,
            http://members.aol.com/nym11111111/darkness_in_el_dorado/documents/
            0297.htm.
Taylor, K.
    1974   Sanuma Fauna, Prohibitions and Classification. Monograph 18. Caracas,
            Venezuela: Fundación La Salle de Cienciais Naturales.

Thomas, E. M.
    1958   The Harmless People. New York: Vintage Books.
Thomas, William, ed.
    1956   Current Anthropology: A Supplement to Anthropology Today. Chicago:
            University of Chicago Press.
Tierney, Patrick
    1989   The Highest Altar: The Story of Human Sacrifice.
    2000   Darkness in El Dorado: How Scientists and Journalists Devastated the
            Amazon. New York: Norton.
Time Magazine
    1995   The Evolution of Despair, August 28.
    2001   Cover, March 19.
Todorov, T.
    1989   Nous et les autres. La réflexion française sur la diversité humaine. Paris:
            Editions du Seuil.
Trask, Haunani-Kay
    1991   Natives and Anthropologists: The Colonial Struggle. Contemporary Pacific,
            Spring:159–77.
Turnbull, Colin
    1987   The Mountain People. New York: Touchstone (Simon and Schuster).
Turner, Terence
    1994   The Yanomami, Truth and Consequences. Anthropology Newsletter
            35:46, 48.
    1997   Human Rights, Human Difference, and Anthropology's Contribuition to
            an Emancipatory Cultural Politics. Journal of Anthropological Research
            53:273–91.
    2000a   Letter to Dr. Katz, September 28. Electronic document, http://www.anth
            .ucsb.edu/discus/html/messages/62/63.html.
    2000b   The Turner-Sponsel Memo, November 13. Electronic document, http://
            www.umich.edu/~idpah/SEP/sep_ts.html.
    2001a   Turner on Turner on Turner, Point by Point by Point. Comment on the
            Working Papers of the American Anthropological Association's El Dorado
            Task Force. Electronic document, http://members.aol.com/lithicat/
            darkness_in_el_dorado/documents/0152.htm.
    2001b   The Yanomami and the Ethics of Anthropological Practice. Unpublished
            manuscript, Cornell University.
    2002   The Yanomami and the Ethics of Anthropological Practice. Electronic
            document, http://members.aol.com/anavanax/darkness_in_el_dorado/
            documents/0497.htm.
Turner, Terence, and John Stevens
    2000   Imminent Anthropological Scandal. Darkness in El Dorado Information. The
            Anthropological Niche of Douglas W. Hume. Electronic document, http://
            members.aol.com/archaeodog/darkness_in_el_dorado/statements.htm.
    2001   Annotated Index of Selected Documents and Correspondence from the
            Collection of James V. Neel's Papers in the Archive of the American
            Philosophical Society. Electronic document, http://www.umich.edu/
            ~idpah/SEP/sep_tn.html.

Turner, Terence, and Leslie Sponsel.
    2000   Imminent Antrhopological Scandal. Electronic document, http://members
            .aol.com/nymIIIIIIII/darkness_in_el_dorado/documents/0055.htm.
Turner, T., and C. Nagengast, eds.
    1997   Special Issue on Human Rights. Journal of Anthropological Research 53(3).
Turner, Trudy, and Jeffrey Nelson
    2001   Turner Point by Point. In El Dorado Task Force Final Report. Electronic
            document, http://www.aaanet.org/edtf/final/vol_two.pdf. Pp. 107–23.
UNESCO
    2000   La propriété intellectuelle dans le domaine du génome humain. Paris
            (December).
Urihi Saúde Yanomami
    2000   Quem são os Yanomami. Kahiki Totihi 1.
Valero, H.
    1984   Yo Soy Napëyoma. Caracas, Venezuela: Editorial Texto.
Vergano, Dan
    2000   Darkness Shadows Pursuit of Anthropology. USA Today, October 2.
            Available online, http://members.aol.com/nymIIIIIIII/darkness_in_
            el_dorado/documents/0203.htm.
Weber, M.
    1958/   Politics as a Vocation. In From Max Weber: Essays in Sociology, H. H.
    1919   Gerth and C. Wright Mills, trans. and eds. Pp. 77–128. New York: Oxford
            University Press.
Weiss, K. M.
    1976   Demographic Theory and Anthropological Inference. Annual Review of
            Anthropology 5:351–81.
Weiss, K., et al.
    1994   Optimizing Utilization of DNA from Rare or Archival Anthropological
            Samples. Human Biology 66(5):796–804.
Wilbert, J., and K. Simoneau, eds.
    1990   Folk Literature of the Yanomami Indians. Los Angeles: UCLA Latin
            American Center Publications.
Wilford, John Noble
    2000   Book Leads Anthropologists to Look Inward. New York Times, November
            18, http://query.nytimes.com/search/article-page .html?res=9D07E2DE103
            BF93BA25752C1A9669C8B63.
Wilford, John Noble, and Simon Romero
    2000   Book Seeks to Indict Anthropologists Who Studied Brazil Indians. New
            York Times, September 28, http://members.aol.com/nymIIIIIIII/darkness_
            in_el_dorado/documents/0042.htm.
Wong, K.
    2001   Fighting the Darkness in El Dorado. Scientific American, March 2001:26–
            28, http://www.sciam.com/2001/0301issue/0301profile.html.
World Medical Association
    2000   Declaration of Helsinki: Ethical Principles for Medical Research Involving
            Human Subjects. Electronic document, http://ohsr.od.nih.gov/guidelines/
            helsinki.html.

INDEX

Compositor: BookMatters, Berkeley
Indexer: Leonard Rosenbaum
Text: 9.5/12 Scala
Display: Bauer Bodoni and Scala Sans
Printer and binder: Edwards Brothers, Inc.